Experiments in Public Management Research

Interest in experimental research in public management is on the rise, yet the field still lacks a broad understanding of its role in producing substantive findings and theoretical advances. Written by a team of leading international researchers, this book sets out the advantages of experiments in public management and showcases their rapidly developing contribution to research and practice. This book offers a comprehensive overview of the relationship between experiments and public management theory and the benefits for examining causal effects. It will appeal to researchers and graduate-level students in public administration, public management, government, politics, and policy studies.

The key topics addressed are: the distinct logic of experimental methods in the laboratory, in the field, and in survey experiments; how leading researchers are using different kinds of experiments to build knowledge about theory and practice across many areas of public management; and the research agendas for experimental work in public management.

OLIVER JAMES, PHD, is Professor of political science at the University of Exeter. His research is widely published with recent work focusing on: citizen and users' responses to public service performance (and performance information), political and managerial leadership change and organisational performance, and the comparative politics of government structural reform (an Open Research Area project of the United Kingdom, France, Germany, and the Netherlands). He serves on the board of the Public Management Research Association and is a member of the Evidence in Governance and Politics network focused on experimental research. He is director of the Master in Public Administration programme at Exeter and has acted as a consultant to bodies including the World Bank, OECD, UK Treasury, and UK National Audit Office.

SEBASTIAN R. JILKE, PHD, is an Assistant Professor in the School of Public Affairs and Administration at Rutgers University-Newark, where he co-directs the Center for Experimental and Behavioral Public Administration. He has published articles in journals such as the *Journal of Public Administration Research and Theory, European Journal of Political Research, Public Administration Review,* and *Regulation & Governance.* He is currently co-chairing the EGPA Permanent Study Group on "Behavioral Public Administration." His interests include citizen–state interactions and equality in service provision, and his recent work examines how citizens and public officials respond to market-type mechanisms in public service delivery.

GREGG G. VAN RYZIN, PHD, is Professor in the School of Public Affairs and Administration at Rutgers University-Newark, where he directs the PhD program and co-directs the Center for Experimental and Behavioral Public Administration. He has interests in both survey research and experimental methods and conducts empirical studies on a range of topics, including citizen satisfaction with urban services, coproduction, performance measurement, nonprofit organisations, housing and neighbourhood issues, and comparative public opinion about government policy and institutions. Prof. Van Ryzin is widely published in scholarly journals in public administration, policy analysis, and urban affairs and is author (with Dahlia K. Remler) of *Research Methods in Practice* (2011/2014).

Experiments in Public Management Research

Challenges and Contributions

Edited by

OLIVER JAMES
University of Exeter

SEBASTIAN R. JILKE
Rutgers University, New Jersey

GREGG G. VAN RYZIN
Rutgers University, New Jersey

CAMBRIDGE
UNIVERSITY PRESS

CAMBRIDGE
UNIVERSITY PRESS

University Printing House, Cambridge CB2 8BS, United Kingdom

One Liberty Plaza, 20th Floor, New York, NY 10006, USA

477 Williamstown Road, Port Melbourne, VIC 3207, Australia

4843/24, 2nd Floor, Ansari Road, Daryaganj, Delhi – 110002, India

79 Anson Road, #06–04/06, Singapore 079906

Cambridge University Press is part of the University of Cambridge.

It furthers the University's mission by disseminating knowledge in the pursuit of education, learning, and research at the highest international levels of excellence.

www.cambridge.org
Information on this title: www.cambridge.org/9781107162051
DOI: 10.1017/9781316676912

First published 2017

Printed in the United Kingdom by Clays, St Ives plc

A catalogue record for this publication is available from the British Library.

ISBN 978-1-107-16205-1 Hardback
ISBN 978-1-316-61423-5 Paperback

Contents

Figures

Tables

Contributors

Lotte Bøgh Andersen – Professor
Department of Political Science
Aarhus University

Simon Calmar Andersen – Professor
Department of Political Science
Aarhus University

Nicola Belle – Assistant Professor
Policy Analysis and Public Management
Bocconi University

Anne Bøllingtoft – Associate Professor
Department of Management
Aarhus University

Robin Bouwman – PhD Student
Department of Public Administration
Institute for Management Research
Radboud University Nijmegen

Louise Ladegaard Bro – PhD Student
Department of Political Science
Aarhus University

Paola Cantarelli – PhD Candidate
Public and Nonprofit Management
School of Economics, Political and Policy Sciences
University of Texas at Dallas

Kendall D. Funk – PhD Candidate
Department of Political Science
Texas A&M University

Stephan Grimmelikhuijsen– Assistant Professor
Utrecht University School of Governance
Utrecht University

Morten Jakobsen – Associate Professor
Department of Political Science
Aarhus University

Oliver James – Professor
Department of Politics
University of Exeter

Sebastian Jilke – Assistant Professor
School of Public Affairs and Administration (SPAA)
Rutgers University-Newark

Peter John – Professor
Department of Political Science
University College London

Mirae Kim – Assistant Professor
Harry S Truman School of Public Affairs
University of Missouri

Alexander Kroll – Assistant Professor
Steven J. Green School of International and Public Affairs
Florida International University

Jacob Ladenburg – Professor (mso)
The Danish Institute for Local and Regional Government Research

M. Jin Lee – Research Fellow
Laboratory for Public Management and Policy,
Department of Public Policy
City University of Hong Kong

Huafang Li – PhD Candidate
School of Public Affairs and Administration
Rutgers University

Dyana Mason – Assistant Professor
Department of Planning, Public Policy & Management
University of Oregon

Kenneth J. Meier – Distinguished Professor of Political Science
Charles H. Gregory Chair in Liberal Arts
Department of Political Science
Texas A&M University

Jue Young Mok – PhD Student
Martin School of Public Policy and Administration
University of Kentucky

Alice Moseley – Lecturer
Department of Politics
University of Exeter

Donald P. Moynihan – Epstein Professor of Public Affairs
Robert M. La Follette School of Public Affairs
University of Wisconsin – Madison

Poul A. Nielsen – Assistant Professor
Department of Political Science and Public Management
University of Southern Denmark

Asmus Leth Olsen – Associate Professor
Department of Political Science
University of Copenhagen

Sanjay K. Pandey – Shapiro Professor of Public Policy and Public Administration
Trachtenberg School of Public Policy and Public Administration
The George Washington University

Sheela Pandey – Assistant Professor
School of Business Administration
Pennsylvania State University at Harrisburg

Christine Prokop – Research Assistant
Department of Political Science/Political System of Germany
University of Oldenburg

Norma M. Riccucci – Distinguished Professor
School of Public Affairs and Administration
Rutgers University, Newark

Scott E. Robinson – Professor
Bellmon Chair of Public Service, Department of Political Science
University of Oklahoma

Søren Serritzlew – Professor
Department of Political Science
Aarhus University

Susumu Shikano – Professor
Department of Politics and Public Administration
University of Konstanz

Michael F. Stoffel – Postdoctoral Researcher
Department of Politics and Public Administration
University of Konstanz

James W. Stoutenborough – Assistant Professor
Department of Political Science
Idaho State University

Markus Tepe – Professor
Department of Social Science/Political System of Germany
University of Oldenburg

Mette Kjærgaard Thomsen – Assistant Professor
Department of Political Science
Aarhus University

Lars Tummers – Associate Professor
Utrecht University School of Governance
Utrecht University

Gregg G. Van Ryzin – Professor
School of Public Affairs and Administration
Rutgers University

Steven Van de Walle – Professor
Public Governance Institute
KU Leuven

Arnold Vedlitz – Professor
Institute for Science, Technology and Public Policy
The Bush School of Government and Public Service
Texas A&M University

Richard M. Walker – Professor
Laboratory for Public Management and Policy,
Department of Public Policy
City University of Hong Kong

Ulrike Weske – PhD Student
Utrecht University School of Governance
Utrecht University

Preface and Acknowledgements

The genesis of this project is in the editors' shared interest in experiments and their collaborative research on substantive topics in public management using these methods. In the course of these activities we came to appreciate the benefits of a book to help set out the role of experimental public management in producing substantive empirical findings, advancing knowledge about theories, and informing policy and practice. This book examines the distinct logic of experimental research, especially for estimating causal effects, and shows how leading researchers are using different kinds of experiment to build knowledge about theory and practice across many areas of public management. A goal of this book is to help develop an agenda for experimental work that recognises both the strengths and limitations of the method for research on public management. This content is intended to be of interest both to those using experiments and to the broader community in public management interested in the contribution of experiments and how they relate to other, more established methods.

We identified a group of researchers currently using experimental methods in innovative ways across a range of topic areas in public management and were delighted when all those approached agreed to be involved. We thank them very much for participating and helping to make this project a reality. The use of the method is expanding rapidly, and we have not sought to include all experimental work but instead hope to show the breadth of the contribution. We are particularly pleased to draw on insights from the disciplines of psychology, political science, and economics and to discuss several different types of experimental method, notably laboratory experiments, survey experiments, and field experiments. However, this book is not only about the considerable opportunities for more use of experiments; it also actively engages with critiques of their use. In this way, it considers both their strengths and limitations and the implications of these characteristics for designing and deploying experiments appropriately.

The overall framework of this book and specific chapters were developed through a two-year process, including presenting ideas and draft chapters at international conferences and workshops. Many people provided valuable comments in this process. We are especially grateful to the Public Management Research Association for permission to run workshops at its 2015 (Minnesota) and 2016 (Aarhus) Public Management Research Conferences. In addition, the ideas were discussed at panels we ran in recent International Research Society for Public Management conferences (2015 in Birmingham, UK, and 2016 in Hong Kong). We are also grateful for the support of our universities, including the Center for Experimental and Behavioral Public Administration at Rutgers University, and grateful to the UK Economic and Social Research Council for supporting public management research using experiments at the University of Exeter. The European Union also funded some of the editors' collaborative research on which this book draws, including as part of the project Coordinating for Cohesion in the Public Sector of the Future (COCOPS) funded under the European Commission's 7th Framework Programme.

PART I

Context

1 | Introduction: Experiments in Public Management Research

OLIVER JAMES, SEBASTIAN JILKE,
AND GREGG G. VAN RYZIN

Introduction

There is an emerging experimental approach to public management research that is reflected in a substantial increase in published studies using this method. Experimental studies are becoming more common across a broad range of topic areas in public management and, relatedly, public organisations and public services.[1] This trend is, in part, a response to increasing recognition of the limitations of non-experimental, so-called observational, methods, including the analysis of surveys or administrative data. In many contexts observational methods risk providing ambiguous or even misleading evidence about causal relationships. In contrast, experiments of the kind we focus on in this book involve active interventions (sometimes termed *treatments*) by researchers, with randomly assigned treatment conditions to experimental subjects, accompanied by outcome measures, in order to produce more valid evidence about cause and effect.[2]

This book develops an approach to experimentation that recognises the distinctive set of issues about their use in public management as a discipline and area of professional practice.[3] In pursuit of this goal, this book takes stock of the current emerging interest in public

---

[1] We treat public management as synonymous with public administration whilst acknowledging that the term *public administration* is sometimes used to emphasise the role of democratic processes and constitutional procedures whereas the term *public management* is sometimes used to emphasise managerial structures and behaviour, often seen as generic across public and private sectors (Hood 2005). This book considers experiments and both sets of topic areas.

[2] Broader definitions of experiments do not require random assignment of the intervention and/or require only some form of exogenous treatment (rather than additionally requiring this intervention to be implemented by researchers). For a discussion, see Shadish, Cook, and Campbell (2002).

[3] We acknowledge that there is long-running debate about public management as a distinct discipline, although there has been increasing consensus in recent

3

management experiments and associated debates about their proper role. It seeks to show how experimental methods can be most suitably advanced in a way that reflects the distinctive topic areas, interest in theories, research practices, and ambitions of public management as a discipline. In particular, public management aspires to be a design science, informing policy making and the practice of public management, and evidence from experimentation is especially useful in this regard. However, the practices and institutions of public management need to be modified in order to take advantage of the opportunities offered by experimentation and this book sets out some reforms in support of this agenda.

Public management researchers develop and assess theory using different methods and present and discuss findings to build cumulative knowledge about public management topic areas. Looking at experiments in related disciplines is especially instructive because of public management's interdisciplinary characteristics, drawing as it does on management, political science, law, psychology, economics, and sociology. Some of the contemporary interest in experiments has been triggered by the use of the method in several of these disciplines. For example, books have been written about experiments as an increasing trend in political science (Morton and Williams 2010; Druckman et al. 2011) and economics (Frechette and Schotter 2015; Friedman 2010; Guala 2005). There has also been increased use of experiments in generic management research, although, despite calls for more, there are still relatively few experimental studies (Colquitt 2008). In contrast, the experimental method is long established in psychology (Field and Hole 2003) and the health sciences (Friedman, Furberg, and DeMets 2010; Matthews 2006). Insights from these disciplines are helpful, but can leave public management scholars wondering about how best to apply experiments to the issues of most direct interest to them. It is a good time for public management to consider the challenges and opportunities presented by the use of experimental methods.

Interest in the experimental approach to public management comes not only from the practice of current social sciences more generally, it has deep roots within our own discipline. Some form of experimentation has

decades about the need for use of systematic methods to gather evidence in order to generate cumulative knowledge(for an overview, see Wright 2015).

been part of the practice of public management and administration research from the beginning of academic study in this area. As Meier and Funk discuss in Chapter 3 on the 'classical roots' of public administration, Frederick W. Taylor's scientific management studies at the turn of the twentieth century were experimental, in the sense of intervening or manipulating various working conditions in order to measure their effects on productivity, although they predated the modern use of random assignment. The use of experiments is especially relevant to public management because of its ambitions to produce useable knowledge to inform policy making and the practice of public management. Herbert Simon (1946) advocated an experimental approach to administration as a design science, a term Simon himself coined to describe a science aimed at finding institutional, policy, and management design solutions to practical, real-world problems. Experiments make this contribution through producing reliable estimates of the causal effects of public management policy and practices. The relationship between experimental researchers and policy makers is often by necessity a close one, especially where experiments are undertaken in naturalistic 'field' contexts. Such field experiments typically require active collaboration to be able to make the interventions necessary for the experiment.

Despite the clear reference to experimentation in its classical roots, and its relevance for informing policy and practice, the history of public management has shown only limited use of experimental methods. In Chapter 2, Li and Van Ryzin's systematic review of the literature shows that only one or two experimental studies have been published on an annual basis for much of the past few decades in the 20 leading public management journals. However, in more recent years, the number of published experimental studies in these journals increased rapidly (see also Anderson and Edwards 2014; Bouwman and Grimmelikhuijsen 2016; Margetts 2011). Much of the work from this recent flourishing of experimental studies is represented in the pages of this volume. At the same time, calls for experimental work in public management have become more frequent (Anderson and Edwards 2015; Blom-Hansen, Morton, and Serritzlew 2015; Bozeman and Scott 1992; Brewer and Brewer 2011; Jilke, Van de Walle, and Kim 2016; Margetts 2011; Perry 2012). Experimental methods now appear more prominently in textbooks in the field than has been the case historically, for example in Van Thiel (2014), McNabb (2015), and Remler and Van Ryzin (2015). Furthermore, the strengths and limitations of experiments are currently the subject of much active debate (Baekgaard et al. 2015; Jilke et al. 2016; Walker, James, and Brewer 2017).

By highlighting the contributions and prospects of experimental methods in public management research, and by emphasising their advantages for probing causal effects, this book might risk conveying the message that experiments are a generally preferred or superior approach in contrast to all other methods. This is not our position, and different methods, including experimental methods, have their strengths and weaknesses for different types of research (see also Haverland and Yanow 2012). Indeed, the chapters in Part IV discuss the main limitations of using experiments in public management research. Moreover, public management research addresses a remarkably wide range of issues and problems – including normative and public value issues, historical traditions, legal foundations, and organisational culture – that require a diverse range of methods to fully understand and explain. Observational methods of both quantitative and qualitative character are often required, including using historical methods or case studies. Sometimes description rather than identifying cause and effect relations is the main focus of research, whether this is done by traditional methods or by complex correlations between multiple variables in the analysis of so-called big data. The increased use of experiments does not rule out these forms of analysis when best suited to the research question. We do, however, maintain that experiments are currently under-utilised and have much potential to add to the set of methods employed to investigate key issues in public management.

We advocate an approach to the use of experiments that views them as an important additional research method. However, there are several methods that are often described using the term *experiment*, as set out in Table 1.1. The experiments that we primarily focus on in this book, and whose design and analysis are discussed more fully in Chapter 4, have three main elements. First, an intervention/treatment on experimental units/participants that is undertaken by the researcher. Second, random allocation of the treatment to a group receiving it and a 'control' group not receiving it (or the use of multiple different treatment, or placebo groups). Third, the measurement of outcomes and comparison across the different groups. We particularly focus on elaborating the use of three different types of experiment, those conducted in the laboratory, field experiments

Table 1.1: *Methods containing the term experiment (those in bold are the main focus of this book)*

	Intervention by researcher and comparison with control or across interventions	Random allocation of intervention	Outcome measures	Naturalistic domain
Laboratory experiment	Yes	Yes	Yes	No
Field experiment	Yes	Yes	Yes	Yes
Survey experiment	Yes	Yes	Yes	No
Natural experiment*	No	Yes	Yes	Yes
Quasi-experiment**	No	No	Yes	Yes

Notes: * A strict definition requires random allocation but conducted by someone other than researchers, for example a public lottery (Gerber and Green 2012). An alternative definition allows allocation to be equivalent to random (Shadish, Cook, and Campbell 2002; Dunning 2012).
** Sometimes the comparison is between policies implemented or not in different places in a process argued to entail near random allocation, but typically not, with some authors emphasising research focused on policy interventions that could potentially be manipulated (Shadish et al. 2002).

conducted in more naturalistic domains, and experiments with treatments embedded in surveys.

A distinction is often made between the experimental method and non-experimental, observational methods. However, increasingly, similarities between aspects of experiments and a variety of related types of method are recognised. Table 1.1 sets out the relationship between the three main types of experiment in this book and so-called natural and quasi-experiments. There is a degree of inconsistency in the use of these latter two terms in the literature, but they are closely related to experiments.

Natural experiments are usually considered as not involving an intervention by researchers but where an event can be considered to be allocated at random. Some authors (Gerber and Green 2012: 15) insist on a strict definition of natural experiments, such that the process has to be exactly random but not conducted by researchers themselves, for example when the US government conducted the Vietnam draft lottery. Others use the term to describe a naturally occurring contrast between a treatment and comparison condition which allows a comparison but does not necessarily involve random allocation (Shadish, Cook, and Campbell 2002: 12–17). These latter authors also stress the non-manipulability of the cause of a naturally occurring 'experiment', for example an earthquake creates a shock that can be used to contrast areas that are affected with those that are unaffected. This form of natural experiment does not involve researchers intervening in the world to make something happen, but instead the research design takes advantage of events that occur in ways argued to closely resemble randomisation.

Quasi-experiments involve near random processes, although not random assignment by researchers or policy makers, that cause some units under investigation to receive a treatment but not others. For example, the narrow winners or losers of an election are sometimes considered separated as if random, although whether this is equivalent to random allocation is often debated. Shadish, Cook, and Campbell (2002) discuss the historical use of quasi-experiments and stress that the interest is often in causes that potentially could be manipulated to inform policy making. They also emphasise that, whilst quasi-experiments lack true randomisation, researchers often have considerable control over how they define comparison groups and measure outcomes.

We do not include extensive discussion of natural or quasi-experimental methods, or studies that utilise them, in this book because of the variety of approaches. The methods raise distinctive issues of their own (for a more in depth discussion, Dunning 2012; Gerber and Green 2012; Shadish et al. 2002). However, the methods are referred to at several points in this book, including in Meier and Funk's chapter on classical roots (Chapter 3) and John's chapter on the transformative potential of experiments in public management (Chapter 23). These discussions show that methods often use some but not all elements of the logic of an experiment. A solid foundation in experimental methods is useful for considering the strength of such quasi-experimental designs and evidence, especially as an emerging literature on modern causal inference treats the randomised experiment as a benchmark to assess and interpret non-experimental, observational research more generally (Angrist and Pischke 2014; Imbens and Rubin 2015; Morgan and Winship 2014; Pearl 2000). In this way, experimental methods can play a role in public management research, even when they are not themselves directly used, by alerting researchers and reviewers to issues involved in trying to draw valid conclusions about causes and effects from different research designs.

In the rest of this introduction we develop the rationale for using experiments in public management research. First, we set out the important contribution of experiments for assessing public management theory and contributing to theory development across a wide range of topics. Second, we describe how experiments can enhance public management's role as a design science providing guidance to policy makers about policies, management practices, and programmes. Third, we discuss implications for the conduct of the discipline and its institutions. The concluding section provides an overview of the structure of this book.

1.1 The Contribution to Public Management Theory

Public management researchers are interested in many different types of questions. These include normative questions about values and ethical conduct (Dobel 2005) or questions of due process and legality (Drewry 2003). However, much research in public management is focused on empirical questions about causal effects (Remler and Van

Ryzin 2015). Typical examples include: Does a management training programme improve managerial performance? What is the effect of a system of performance-pay on public employees' work performance? Such research questions about causal effects are very well suited to be answered by experiments that, if properly implemented, can produce evidence with strong internal validity in the sense of convincing inferences about the causal relationship from the manipulated cause to the measured effect (Shadish et al. 2002: 38). Indeed, the experimental turn in public management research in part reflects growing unease about the internal validity of evidence about causality from observational studies, on which public management traditionally has been heavily reliant. As discussed in Chapter 4 on causal inference and the design and analysis of experiments, observational studies use data that is not generated from researchers' interventions in experiments with randomisation, but instead use data from measurement or observation of existing phenomena. This data is often incorporated in large-N quantitative analysis, especially using regression, or qualitative case study analysis, to generate empirical knowledge and assess theory. But such studies often have difficulty in isolating or identifying causal effects because of the complex patterns of influence among observed and unobserved variables at work in causal relationships in the social and political world.

Experiments can assist with these difficulties in establishing causal effects to evaluate the empirical implications of a potentially broad and diverse set of public management theories. Public management theories that can be assessed by experimentation have a broad range of objects, for example they can focus on individuals or organisations. At the organisational level of analysis, characteristics of organisational structures, management routines, or less formal practices of working can be varied, for example systems of training or for rewarding public employees. Many theories about individual-level perceptions, beliefs, attitudes, and behaviour, such as the multitude of theories informed by psychology or behavioural economics, can be assessed in experiments with public managers, service users, or citizens as participants (Grimmelikhuijsen et al. 2017; Tummers et al. 2016). Indeed, many of the contemporary experiments in public management directly use or are informed by individual-level psychological theories, for example in a recent journal special issue (Jilke et al. 2016). There are, however, many sources of theory to which experimental methods can be applied and this current association should not discourage a much broader focus of investigation.

Many of the requirements that theories have to meet in order to make them suitable for evaluation using experiments are consistent with the typical concerns of public management researchers, such as the requirement that theories have clear empirical implications. However, the need to think about experimental design *ex ante* is particularly valuable in focusing researchers' attention on such issues before the research is conducted. The experimental approach helps clarify the causal mechanisms being subject to empirical investigation because researchers need to know what they should be manipulating and how this should be achieved. The mechanisms can help give clear expectations about the direction of effects caused by an intervention and their magnitude. Theories in public management can be formally stated with axioms that allow the development of expectations using logical rules, as is often the case in experimental economics and is discussed at more length in Chapter 19. However, depending on the context and so long as expectations about effects are clear, verbally expressed theories about causal relations are often sufficient and experimentation is not necessarily linked to strong formalism.

Theories have domains for their applicability which set the contexts where particular effects of causes are expected. The need for public management theories to be more explicit about context is increasingly noted (O'Toole and Meier 2015). Discussions in experimental research often refer not only to the internal validity of a study relating to inference about the causal effect within the experiment, but also to the external validity of experimental findings to populations of interest beyond the immediate sample. The findings may apply to a particular sample, more broadly to a population where the sample came from, for example public managers in a given sector in one country, or may apply to still broader populations. Cross-national or cross-contextual replication experiments may help to increase the external validity of experimental evidence, as Chapter 21 discusses, and can help test and refine theories of the institutional or cultural boundary conditions of expected findings (but see also Jilke et al. 2016).

Experiments differ in the domains in which they are conducted. A major distinction is between laboratory experiments and those that are conducted in naturalistic contexts, often called *field experiments*. Field experiments, as discussed in Chapter 5, seek to produce relevant findings on several dimensions, including the subject pool being that of the population of interest, having authentic treatments and outcome measures, and a naturalistic environment for the experiment. Survey experiments, as discussed in Chapter 6, embed treatments in surveys and often take large samples from a broader population in order that the findings can be generalised more broadly (Mutz 2011). Laboratory experiments are discussed in Chapter 7. It is sometimes suggested that laboratory experiments have more internal validity than field experiments because of the greater difficulty of control in the field, but that field experiments have more external validity because of their more naturalistic settings. However, the issue is more complex. Without internal validity the issue of external validity has limited meaning because there are no valid causal effects to apply beyond the experiment. In addition, some laboratory experiments focus on basic processes (for example, risk aversion in human decision-making) that have very broad relevance and strong external validity to most people in most situations. In contrast, some field experiments may focus on very specific local issues and settings (for example, willingness to pay taxes for a particular local public service) and so have low external validity to other policy issues or contexts.

There are limitations to the use of the experimental method to examine the empirical implications of theory, and not all theories are equally well suited to experimentation. Theories that concern macro-level causation, for example structural theories about the operation of entire economies or societies, present particular difficulties for the design of experiments. This kind of theory relates to units that are difficult to disaggregate into groups that might be allocated to receive different interventions, and the experimental interventions are potentially very demanding in scale or scope. However, even in the case of macro-theory there is potential for developing smaller-scale experimentation using more limited interventions that examine the 'micro-foundations' of macro-level theories (Jilke 2015). As chapters in Part III of this book show, experiments can be used to assess a wide variety of theories.

1.2 Public Management as a Design Science

An important role of experiments is to produce knowledge for public management as a *design science*, resulting in useable knowledge to inform policy makers by estimating the effects of policies and programmes. This ambition of the discipline is long-standing and has recently been restated for the contemporary context (Perry 2012; Raadschelders 2011). In general terms, public policy and management involves attempting to intervene in the world in pursuit of goals. This focus makes experimental research using intervention to make things happen particularly appropriate and provides a common interest with practitioners. Chapter 5 on field experiments points out the extensive use of randomised controlled trials to generate evidence to inform practice in health sciences and in social and economic policy (Bloom 2006; Levitt and List 2009). Development economics has made much use of experimental studies to assess the effectiveness of development interventions (Banerjee and Duflo 2009). Policy interventions based on behavioural theories, such as so-called nudge theories that seek to alter choice architecture (Thaler and Sunstein 2008), often use experimental evaluations. The Behavioural Insights Team in the United Kingdom and the Social and Behavioral Sciences Team in the United States are examples of the contemporary policy interest in experimentation.

In the development of useable knowledge to inform policy and practice, just as in the assessment of theory, experiments are complementary to other methods. The field of medicine, another design science, provides an analogy. Take for example the salt hypothesis, the idea that dietary sodium intake can raise blood pressure and thus the risk of heart attacks or strokes. The evidence for this hypothesis comes in part from large-scale epidemiological studies, using survey research methods, showing an association between dietary consumption of salty foods and hypertension. Further evidence comes from vital statistics (administrative data) comparing the causes of death in different countries, some with diets higher in sodium than others. Added to the picture are laboratory experiments, involving mice or another animal model, that probe the causal mechanism of salt's influence on cardiovascular processes at the anatomical and biochemical levels. Clinical trials in which people suffering from hypertension are randomly assigned to an intervention, such as a low-sodium diet, provide still more evidence. Even with all this, some doubts have been raised about the validity of the salt hypothesis (Freedman and Petitti 2001). Such is the nature of evidence in much of the health sciences, largely because the causal mechanisms and clinical solutions are complex and often uncertain. The same is true in many ways in public management research, and thus the need for cumulative evidence about important questions is similar. Yet we also need to bear in mind the strengths and limitations that come with each research method.

1.3 The Institutions and Conduct of the Discipline

Experiments have implications for the discipline in the sense of how public management is organised through institutions to facilitate research and its characteristic modes of working. Experiments offer benefits by making research more transparent and replicable by other researchers. Whilst the transparency agenda is a general movement across the natural and social sciences the practice of experimentation is consistent with it. Experimentation typically involves specification of interventions and description of practices, and lends itself to pre-registration of designs, including hypotheses about causal effects. Experimental researchers specify their designs in advance and because they tend to focus on just one or two key independent variables manipulated by the researcher, experiments reduce the risk of researchers engaging in fishing for statistically significant results. In addition, the transparent description of interventions increases the possibility to replicate studies using the same or similar methods. However, poor practice is possible in experimentation as in any other method, including going beyond planned analysis to search for interactions between treatment variables and other factors in hopes of a significant finding of some kind to report.

The practice of experimentation raises issues of the appropriate way for researchers to conduct their studies. Serious irregularities in the practice of experimentation are possible, for example as discovered by Broockman and colleagues (2015). Ethics are an important consideration in any kind of study, experimental or otherwise. Principles of voluntary participation, informed consent, protection of privacy, and minimisation of risk apply to surveys, qualitative interviews, and even the use of administrative data. But experimental research raises unique ethical concerns, in part because of its key features of intervening in conditions in order to test human responses. Therefore, experiments have implications for the skills required by researchers and consequently for training and the structuring of professional associations. In the American Political Science Association, for example, there is a separate experimental section with an associated journal, the *Journal of Experimental Political Science*. Whilst we think that there is more need for specialist research training in public administration and management, and more consideration of the requirements of handling experimental research and publishing its findings, we are not in favour of a separation of experiments from other parts of public management research. A core rationale of this volume is the valuable complementarities between experimental and other methods and how this can facilitate the accumulation of knowledge about public management topics.

1.4 The Structure of this Book

This book is structured in four parts. Part I sets the context of the rise of experimental research in public management. This trend is documented in the leading journals of the discipline. The classical roots of experimentation in the field are also reviewed. Part II then sets out the methodological issues presented by experiments, looking first at general issues of the approach to causation and the design and analysis of experiments, then at different types of experiments, especially field experiments, survey experiments, and laboratory experiments.

Part III shows how experiments are adding to knowledge of important public management topics across a broad range of subject areas. Some examples illustrate, but do not exhaust, the areas discussed in these chapters. Experiments have been conducted with different kinds of units or participants, including organisations, services, and individual public managers, politicians, citizens, and services users. The experimental interventions relate to changes in the presentation of information, oversight regimes, management practices, tasks, training routines, service provision, materials for service users, and structures for cooperation between actors. The outcomes considered include individuals' motivations, perceptions, attitudes, and behaviour, including the performance of organisations, employees' work motivation, citizens and users' perceptions of performance, satisfaction, coproduction, and user choice and voice behaviour. Further outcomes are those for organisations, services, and beneficiaries of public programmes and services. The experiments discussed are in many different countries, are at multiple levels of government, and relate to many different kinds of organisation. Each chapter in Part III sets out the contribution of experiments to the topic area and their relationship with non-experimental research, concluding with an agenda for future research.

Part IV draws out themes from the discussion of experimental work in public management and examines challenges and opportunities. Possible risks of adopting an experimental approach for the kind of questions addressed by public management are considered, for example whether it would lead to the neglect of important topics that are less amenable to experimentation. The need to develop cooperative working relationships with public organisations in order to undertake experimental work in the field is outlined. Finally, the conclusion returns to the issues set up in this introduction to set out an agenda for public management experiments. This agenda uses experiments as complementary to other methods to assess the empirical implications of theory and to inform its development, and uses experiments to help public management better achieve its ambitions as a design science. We conclude with suggestions for how experimental research can be reported by researchers and set out how the institutions and practices of public management need to change in order to deliver more of the potential benefits from using experimental methods.

References

Anderson, D. M. and Edwards, B. C. 2015. 'Unfulfilled promise: laboratory experiments in public management research'. *Public Management Review* 17(10): 1518–42.

Angrist, J. and Pischke, J.-S. 2014. *Mastering Metrics: The Path from Cause to Effect*. Princeton, NJ: Princeton University Press.

Baekgaard, M., Baethge, C., Blom-Hansen, J., Dunlop, C. A., Esteve, M., Jakobsen, M., Kisida, B., Marvel, J., Moseley, A., Serritzlew, S., and Stewart, P., 2015. 'Conducting experiments in public management research: a practical guide'. *International Public Management Journal*, 18(2): 323–42.

Banerjee, A. and Duflo, E. 2009. 'The experimental approach to development economics'. *Annual Review of Economics*, 1, 151–78.

Blom-Hansen, J., Morton, R., and Serritzlew, S., 2015. 'Experiments in public management research'. *International Public Management Journal*, 18(2): 151–70.

Bloom, H. S., ed. 2006. *Learning More from Social Experiments*. New York: Russell Sage.

Broockman, D., Kalla, J., and Aronow, P. 2015. 'Irregularities in LaCour (2014): A36–A38'. https://people.stanford.edu/dbroock/sites/default/files/b roockman_kalla_aronow_lg_irregularities.pdf (last accessed 23 Feb 2016).

Bouwman, R. and Grimmelikhuijsen, S. 2016. 'Experimental public administration from 1992 to 2014: a systematic literature review and ways forward'. *International Journal of Public Sector Management*, 29(2): 110–31.

Bozeman, B. and Scott, P. 1992. 'Laboratory experiments in public policy and management'. *Journal of Public Administration Research and Theory*, 2(3): 293–313.

Brewer, G. A. and Brewer, G. A. Jr. 2011. 'Parsing public/private differences in work motivation and performance: an experimental study'. *Journal of Public Administration Research and Theory*, 21(s3): i347–62.

Cartwright, N. and Hardie, J. 2012. *Evidence-Based Policy: A Practical Guide to Doing It Better*. Oxford: Oxford University Press.

Charness, G. and Kuhn, P., 2011. 'Lab labor: what can labor economists learn from the lab?' *Handbook of Labor Economics*, 4, 229–330.

Colquitt, J. A. 2008. 'From the editors publishing laboratory research in AMJ: a question of when, not if'. *Academy of Management Journal*, 51(4): 616–20.

Dobel, J. P. 2005 Public management as ethics, in Ferlie, E., Lynn, L., and Pollitt, C. (eds.) *The Oxford Handbook of Public Management*. Oxford: Oxford University Press, 156–81.

Drewry, G. 2003. Introduction: law and administration, in Peters, B. G. and Pierre, J. (eds.) *Handbook of Public Administration*. London: Sage, 257–9.

Druckman, J. N., Green, D. P., Kuklinski, J. H., and Lupia, A. eds. 2011. *Cambridge Handbook of Experimental Political Science*. Cambridge: Cambridge University Press.

Dunning, T., 2012. *Natural Experiments in the Social Sciences: A Design-Based Approach*. Cambridge: Cambridge University Press.

Ferlie, E., Lynn, L. E., and Pollitt, C. 2005. Afterword, in Ferlie, E., Lynn, L., and Pollitt, C. (eds.) *The Oxford Handbook of Public Management*. Oxford: Oxford University Press, 720–9.

Field, A. and Hole, G. 2002. *How to Design and Report Experiments*. London: Sage.

Frechette, G. R. and Schotter, A. 2015. *Handbook of Experimental Economic Methodology*. Oxford: Oxford University Press.

Freedman, D. A. and Petitti, D. B. 2001. 'Salt and blood pressure: conventional wisdom reconsidered'. *Evaluation Review*, 25(3): 267–87.

Friedman, D. 2010. *Experimental Methods: A Primer for Economics*. Princeton, NJ: Princeton University Press.

Friedman, L. M., Furberg, C. D., and DeMets, D. L. 2010. *Fundamentals of Clinical Trials* (4th Edition). London: Springer.

Gerber, A. S. and Green, D. P. 2012. *Field Experiments: Design, Analysis and Interpretation*. New York: Norton.

Gill, J. and Meier, K. J. 2000. 'Public administration research and practice: a methodological manifesto'. *Journal of Public Administration Research and Theory*, 10(1): 157–99.

Grimmelikhuijsen, S., Jilke, S., Leth Olsen, A., and Tummers, L. 2017. 'Behavioral public administration: combining insights from public administration and psychology'. *Public Administration Review*, 77(1): 45–56.

Guala, F. 2005. *The Methodology of Experimental Economics*. Cambridge: Cambridge University Press.

Harrison, G. W. and List, J. A. 2004. 'Field experiments'. *Journal of Economic Literature*, 42(4): 1009–55.

Haverland, M. and Yanow, D. 2012. 'A hitchhiker's guide to the public administration research universe: surviving conversations on methodologies and methods'. *Public Administration Review*, 72(3): 401–8.

Hood, C. 2005. Public management: the word, the movement, the science, in Ferlie, E., Lynn, L., and Pollitt, C. (eds.). *The Oxford Handbook of Public Management*. Oxford: Oxford University Press, 7–26.

Imbens, G. and Rubin, D. 2015. *Causal Inference for Statistics, Social and Biomedical Sciences: An Introduction*. Cambridge: Cambridge University Press.

Jakobsen, M. and Jensen, R. 2015. 'Common method bias in public management studies'. *International Public Management Journal*, 18(1): 3–30.

Jilke, S. 2015. *Essays on the Microfoundations of Competition and Choice in Public Service Delivery*. PhD dissertation. Rotterdam: Erasmus University Rotterdam.

Jilke, S., Van de Walle, S., and Kim, S. 2016. 'Generating usable knowledge through an experimental approach to public administration'. *Public Administration Review*, 76(1): 69–72.

Jilke, S., Petrovsky, N., Meuleman, B., and James, O. 2016. 'Measurement equivalence in replications of experiments: when and why it matters and guidance on how to determine equivalence'. *Public Management Review* (ahead-of-print).

Levitt, S. D. and List, J. A. 2009. 'Field experiments in economics: the past, the present, and the future'. *European Economic Review*, 53(1): 1–18.

Lynn, Laurence E. 1996. *Public Management as Art, Science, and Profession*. London: Chatham House Publishers.

Margetts, Helen Z. 2011. 'Experiments for public management research'. *Public Management Review*, 13(2): 189–208.

Matthews, J. N. S. 2006. *Introduction to Randomized Controlled Clinical Trials* (2nd Edition). Boca Raton, FL: Chapman & Hall.

McNabb, D. E. 2015. *Research Methods in Public Administration and Nonprofit Management*. Routledge.

Morgan, S. L. and Winship, C. 2014. *Counterfactuals and Causal Inference*. Cambridge: Cambridge University Press.

Morton, R. B. and Williams, K. C. 2010. *Experimental Political Science: From Nature to the Lab*. Cambridge: Cambridge University Press.

Mutz, D. 2011. *Population-Based Survey Experiments*. Princeton, NJ: Princeton University Press.

O'Toole, L. J. and Meier, K. J. 2015. 'Public management, context, and performance: in quest of a more general theory'. *Journal of Public Administration Research and Theory*, 25 (1): 237–56.

Pearl, J. 2000. *Causality: Models, Reasoning, and Inference*. Cambridge: Cambridge University Press.

Perry, J. L. 2012. 'How can we improve our science to generate more usable knowledge for public professionals?' *Public Administration Review*, 72(4): 479–82.

Peters, B. G. and Pierre, J., eds. 2003. *Handbook of Public Administration*. London: Sage.

Raadschelders, J. C. 2011. 'The future of the study of public administration: embedding research object and methodology in epistemology and ontology'. *Public Administration Review*, 71(6): 916–24.

Remler, D. K. and Van Ryzin, G. G. 2015. *Research Methods in Practice: Strategies for Description and Causation* (2nd Edition). London: Sage.

Shadish, W. R., Cook, T. D., and Campbell, D. T. 2002. *Experimental and Quasi-experimental Designs for Generalized Causal Inference*. Boston: Houghton Mifflin.

Simon, H. A. 1946. 'The proverbs of administration'. *Public Administration Review*, 6(1): 53–67.

Sunstein, C. R. 2014. *Why Nudge?: The Politics of Libertarian Paternalism*. New Haven, CT: Yale University Press.

Thaler, R. H. and Sunstein, C. R. 2008. *Nudge: Improving Decisions about Health, Wealth, and Happiness*. New Haven, CT: Yale University Press.

Tummers, L., Olsen. A. L., Jilke, S., and Grimmelikhuijsen, S. 2016. 'Introduction to the virtual issue on behavioral public administration'. *Journal of Public Administration Research and Theory*, (2016): 1–3.

Van Thiel, S. 2014. *Research Methods in Public Administration and Public Management: An Introduction*. Routledge.

Walker, R, James, O. and Brewer, G. A. 2017. 'Replication, experiments and knowledge in public management research'. *Public Management Review*, 19(10).

Wright, B. 2015. 'The science of public administration: problems, presumptions, progress, and possibilities'. *Public Administration Review*, 75(6): 795–805.

2 | A Systematic Review of Experimental Studies in Public Management Journals

HUAFANG LI AND GREGG G. VAN RYZIN

Introduction

Before the 1990s, there was very little public management research that employed experimental methods, despite some evidence of early experimentation in the classical roots of public management as discussed in Chapter 3. Margetts (2011), in her review of public management studies using experimental methods, found only a scattering of experiments since 1960 in leading journals at that time (including *Journal of Public Administration Research and Theory*, *Public Administration Review*, *Public Administration*, and *Public Management Review*). In an early statement of the case for experiments, Bozeman argued that perhaps the lack of an experimental tradition was 'because public policy management researchers are more interested in the problem than in problem-solving techniques' (1992, pp. 440–1). But the situation has begun to change in more recent years, as this chapter documents, with a marked increase in experimental studies in the top public management journals. In this chapter, we take a systematic look at these trends and the characteristics of experimental studies published in top public management journals, focusing on the period 1990–2015.

How We Did Our Systematic Review

The studies in our systematic review come from the top 20 journals in Google Scholar's category of *public policy and administration* and are listed in Table 2.1. Using Google Scholar's category provides a wider range of journals than previous reviews (Anderson and Edwards 2014; Bouwman and Grimmelikhuijsen 2016; Margetts 2011) and avoids relying on personal judgment, although a few of the journals in the Google Scholar category are more public policy journals than public management journals. The Google Scholar ranking we use is based on

Table 2.1: *Top 20 journals in public policy and administration*

Ranking	Publication	h5-index	h5-median
1	Journal of Public Administration Research & Theory (JPART)	42	57
2	Public Administration Review (PAR)	35	53
3	Public Administration (PA)	29	46
4	Policy Studies Journal (PSJ)	27	42
5	Governance	24	35
6	Science and Public Policy (SPP)	24	33
7	The American Review of Public Administration (ARPA)	23	30
8	International Review of Administrative Sciences (IRAS)	22	31
9	Social Policy & Administration (SPA)	22	27
10	Public Management Review (PMR)	20	26
11	Administration & Society (AS)	20	25
12	Review of Policy Research (RPR)	19	25
13	International Public Management Journal (IPMJ)	18	26
14	Publius: The Journal of Federalism (Publius)	18	24
15	International Journal of Public Administration (IJPA)	17	25
16	International Journal of Public Sector Management (IJPSM)	17	23
17	Policy & Politics (P&P)	16	22
18	Policy Studies (PS)	16	22
19	Australian Journal of Public Administration (AJPA)	15	25
20	Public Money & Management (PMM)	15	23

*Journal ranking is based on the 2015 value of the h5-index. Source: https://scholar
.google.com/citations?view_op=top_venues&hl=en&vq=soc_publicpolicyadministra
tion (accessed Feb. 20, 2016)

the h5-index, which is the h-index for the most recent five-year period, where h is the highest number such that h articles have at least h citations. The h-index is designed to provide a score that avoids over-weighting a journal with just a few highly cited articles, or one with a great many articles with just a few citations (because the journal simply publishes more articles than other journals). In other words, journals do better in the h5-index ranking when they publish more highly cited articles.

To locate experimental studies in these 20 journals, we visited the official website of each journal and searched the journal using the key word 'experiment' in both article titles and abstracts from January 1957 to January 2016. The search method used here is more inclusive than the search method used by Margetts (2011), which searched only in titles of articles in four journals from 1960 to 2009. Anderson and Edwards (2014) discuss experimental studies in the same four journals from 2010 to the middle of 2014. And another recent review of experimental studies from 1992 to 2014 was based on the Institute for Scientific Information (ISI)–ranked public administration journals (Bouwman and Grimmelikhuijsen 2016). Our review in this chapter differs from and builds on these previous reviews by including experimental studies over a longer timeframe and by using Google Scholar. Experimental studies appearing in January 2016 are also included for most of our content analyses, in part because of a *Public Administration Review* symposium that included a dozen new articles all using experimental methods (Jilke, Van de Walle and Kim 2016). (We only exclude January 2016 articles from our analysis of trends over time, since we have only a month's and not a year's worth of article for 2016.) Since we rely on the online database of each journal, and not all the journals have uploaded full achieves online, this chapter may underestimate the actual amount of experimental studies in the field in some of the earlier years. As shown in Table 2.1, we do not find any experimental studies published in the 20 top journals before 1990.

In total, using these criteria and search terms, we found 72 experimental studies published in the top 20 journals through January 2016. Articles that have 'experiment' in the title, but use 'experiment' to refer to something new or untried rather than experimental research per se, are excluded. Importantly, we also searched the abstracts and added articles using experimental methods even when 'experiment' was not in the title. We believe this approach captures more of the actual, true number of experimental studies published to date. Note that we allowed both natural and quasi experiments to be counted when researchers labelled their studies as experiments, although we recognise that these studies vary a great deal in the degree to which they actually do resemble a fully randomised experiment. However, we did not venture to make such judgments, but rather erred on the side of including them in our tally and analysis of published studies in the field.

Trends and Characteristics of Experiments in Public Management Journals

As Figure 2.1 shows, using these criteria, there has been a significant increase in the number of experimental studies published each year in the top 20 journals, especially in the most recent years. In 2012, for example, there were just five experimental studies. The number of published experimental studies per year almost doubled between 2012 and 2013, and by 2015 was running at more than three times the level of publications compared to 2012.

Eleven leading journals published a total of 72 experimental studies over the 25-year period (including January 2016). Interestingly, only 3 out of 20 top journals have published 10 or more experimental studies during the period: *JPART* (25), *PAR* (17) and *IPMJ* (10). In fact, the experimental studies published in just these three journals account for more than 70 per cent (see Figure 2.2) of the total published experimental studies in all of the top 20 journals. One explanation for this

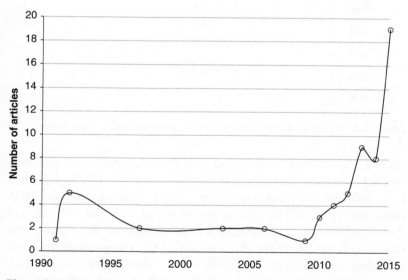

Figure 2.1: Trend in published experiments in the 20 top public policy and administration journals, 1990–2015

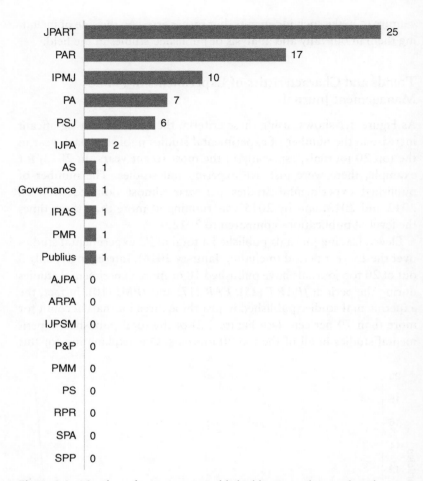

Figure 2.2: Number of experiments published by journal, in rank order

pattern is that *JPART, PAR* and *IPMJ* have all published symposia focused on experimental studies. For instance, IPMJ published a symposium on experiments in public management in 2015 (Baekaard et al. 2015), and as mentioned already the first issue of *PAR* published in 2016 included a large symposium on experimental studies (Jilke et al. 2016). Almost half of the top journals have not published any experimental studies (9 of the 20; see Figure 2.2). To provide a point of reference, the *American Economic Review*, one of the leading journals in economics, has already published 286 papers using experimental methods from January 1990 until January 2016 (based on our own calculations).

Returning to our review of experimental studies in public management journals, it is interesting to look at where these studies come from – that is, which countries are most active in conducting and publishing experiments in the field. For simplicity, we include only the corresponding author of each article, which of course is not a complete representation of authorship and nationalities, but provides at least a basic indication. As Figure 2.3 shows, the United States (33) is the largest contributor, followed by Denmark (11), the United Kingdom (11) and the Netherlands (7). That the United States tops the list is perhaps not too surprising, given the sheer size of the country's population; impressively, Denmark is tied for second, yet with

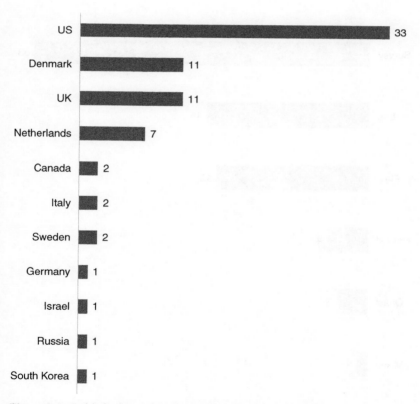

Figure 2.3: Published experiments by country (of first author)

a much smaller population. The United Kingdom and the Netherlands are also clearly hubs of this emerging experimental turn in public management research. But because of the publication lag, we believe this representation of countries is likely to grow in geographic extent and frequency of publication in the years ahead.

Another important characteristic to examine is the setting of the experiment, meaning whether the experiment is conducted in the field, as part of a survey, or in the laboratory. Each of these settings is discussed more fully in Chapters 5, 6, and 7, respectively. Where studies included more than one method, we classified them by their predominant method. We include natural and quasi experiments in our systematic review, as mentioned earlier, although there have only been a few such studies published in the public management journals. As Figure 2.4 shows, survey experiments are by far the most popular

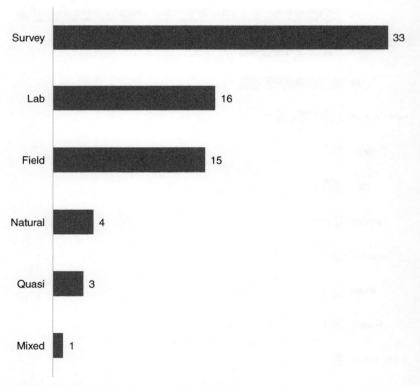

Figure 2.4: Setting and type of experiments

setting or type of experiment in public management research, accounting for nearly half of all published experiments in the field. This no doubt reflects in part the convenience and low cost of online surveys these days, and indeed nearly all of the survey experiments in our review were done as online surveys. Moreover, most online survey software includes features for randomisation that greatly facilitate the design and implementation of survey experiments, which has encouraged this approach. Laboratory and field experiments are somewhat distant seconds in frequency, as Figure 2.4 demonstrates. As Chapter 7 discusses, laboratory experiments are particularly useful in advancing public management research about managerial decision making or strategic behaviour (see also Anderson and Edwards 2014; Bozeman 1992; Bozeman and Scott 1992). And as Chapter 5 discusses, field experiments have many advantages with respect to the realism of the interventions and the contexts, which often involves actual public managers, workers or citizens in real-life situations (see for example Bellé 2014, 2015; James 2011b; James and Moseley 2014). Some of the important advantages of field experiments for working with public organisations to improve practice are also discussed by Peter John in Chapter 23. Finally, as indicated earlier, we found relatively few natural and quasi experiments in our review, which is somewhat surprising in a way, given that public management is an applied field in which the regular ebb and flow of policy and management reforms would seem to provide good opportunities for such studies.

Another key characteristic of experiments that we analysed was the type of study participants. As Figure 2.5 shows, ordinary citizens are by far the most frequent participants in public management experiments. This parallels the finding for survey experiments as the most popular setting, as surveys often sample or recruit from general populations (Kim and Kim 2016; Riccucci et al. 2014; Riccucci et al. 2016; Van De Walle and Van Ryzin 2011) Indeed, among the 33 survey experiments we found (Figure 2.4), fully 25 use citizens as participants. The next most common participants are students, who of course are widely used as volunteers for experiments across the social sciences. In our review, all 16 laboratory experiments use students as participants (see Esteve et al. 2016; Knott, Miller and Verkuilen 2003; Landsbergen, Bozeman and Bretschneider 1992; Landsbergen et al. 1997). Experiments in public management journals tend to use managers, workers or other professionals, but not as frequently as might be expected. We found some

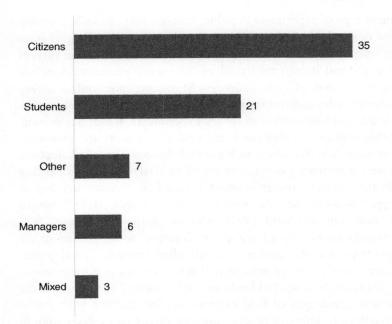

Figure 2.5: Types of participants

laboratory experiments that used professionals, such as social workers (Scott 1997), budget officers (Thurmaier 1992) and public managers (Landsbergen et al. 1992). Several of the field experiments we reviewed also involve administrators and other professionals (see Avellaneda 2013; Bækgaard 2011; Chalkley et al. 2010; Nutt 2006). Participants in natural and quasi experiments vary. The natural experiments reviewed in this study involved dentists (Chalkley et al. 2010), hospital staff (Fenn et al. 2010), citizens (Greenwald et al. 2003) and politicians and administrators (Bækgaard 2011). And for the three quasi experiments, they involved citizens (Bhatti et al. 2015), local government inspectors (Dunlop et al. 2015) and students (Yakovlev et al. 2015).

Of course, an important feature of any study is the substantive theory or question addressed by the research. We attempted to examine these substantive issues using a fairly basic and straightforward coding scheme, the results of which appear in Figure 2.6. It turned out to be rather difficult to classify each study into just one substantive area. A study can investigate multiple policy areas, such as health care and city aid (Lawrence et al. 2013), or environmental policy and communications (Lachapelle et al.

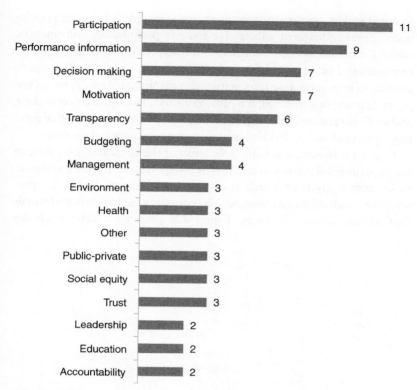

Figure 2.6: Main topics of research

2014). In addition, the same author(s) may use different experimental methods in various studies. For example, De Fine Licht uses a survey experiment to study the impacts of transparency on citizens' trust in public spending (De Fine Licht 2014) and also uses a laboratory experiment to investigate how transparency influences legitimacy (De Fine Licht et al. 2014). Grimmelikhuijsen and colleagues also employ multiple experimental methods to investigate how transparency influences trust in government (Grimmelikhuijsen 2012; Grimmelikhuijsen and Klijn 2015; Grimmelikhuijsen and Meijer 2014; Grimmelikhuijsen et al. 2013). Experiments can be used to explore some uncommon topics such as game payoffs (Knott et al. 2003) and ethical sensitivity (Wittmer 1992). What is interesting to note in Figure 2.6 is how many experiments deal with aspects of citizen participation, which includes related topics like volunteering and coproduction. This no doubt reflects the large emphasis, as noted earlier, on survey experiments using samples of general populations. Another frequent substantive issue is performance information, which includes how such information is interpreted and judged by both managers and citizens. Performance information use lends itself to experimentation in part because information can manipulated easily, for example by framing or presenting it in different ways. Finally, decision making and motivation were fairly frequent topics as well. Interestingly, all of these top topics deal with individual behaviours or psychological processes.

To get a different, less subjective sense of the substantive content of the experimental studies in our review, we performed a more systematic content analysis of words in the studies' abstracts. Figure 2.7 presents the resulting word cloud, which represents the frequency of words that appear across abstracts. Figure 2.8 presents a related cluster

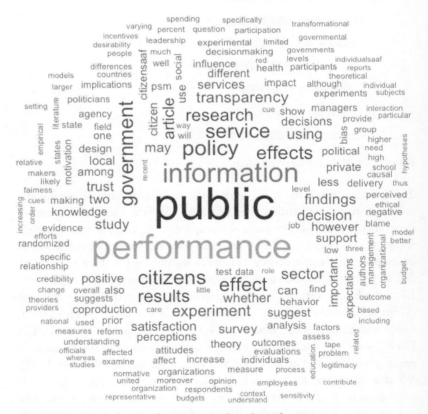

Figure 2.7: Word clouds of experimental studies' abstracts

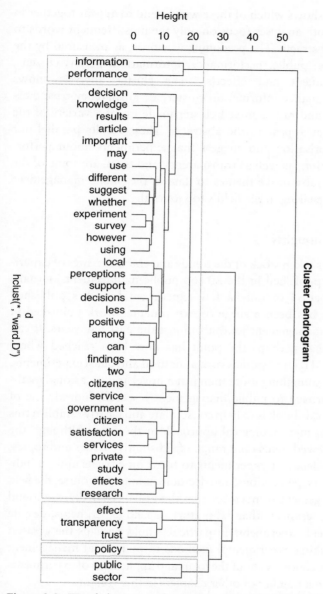

Figure 2.8: Word clustering of experimental studies' abstracts

analysis, which shows which of these words tend to appear together in the abstracts. Both analyses focus on only the most frequent words to appear in the abstracts. The predominant words, as measured by the word cloud, are: public, performance, information, policy, citizens, service, government and effect(s). The cluster analysis shows a distinct performance-information cluster, a transparency-trust cluster and a large and rather mixed cluster made up of a variety of the other words that appear in the abstracts. These results parallel our previous categorisation and suggest that experiments about performance information, as well as transparency and trust, are some of the most common substantive themes to date in the public management experiments appearing in the field's top journals.

Concluding Thoughts

This chapter has taken stock of the trends and characteristics of experimental studies published in the 20 top public management journals. After a long period of only a few experimental studies published annually, there has been a surge of experimental work published in the top public management journals in just the past few years. It can even be said that perhaps the point has now been reached where experiments, and related studies such as natural and quasi experiments, now constitute something more than just a novel and occasional methodological approach to public management research. Indeed, one of the key aims of this book is to help consolidate and clearly establish this newly emergent methodological approach in the field. Although the studies we reviewed focus on a range of substantive issues and topics, we found a tendency of experiments to focus on citizens and on individual behaviours, perceptions, and decision making. Of course, the field of public management is much broader than this. Relatedly, we found more survey experiments than laboratory or field experiments, despite the fact that field experiments in particular hold perhaps the greatest promise for linking experimental methods to policy and management practices. These concerns about the focus and application of experiments are addressed in a number of other chapters in this volume.

There are certain limitations to this systematic review, however, that should be noted. To begin with, this study does not include some important public policy and administration journals, such as *the Journal of Policy Analysis and Management* and *Nonprofit and*

Voluntary Sector Quarterly, because of how Google Scholar classifies these journals. It also does not include public management research that appears in the journals of other disciplines, such as organisational behaviour, applied psychology or political science. Because of this, our count and content analysis of experimental studies in public management journals under-represent the complete body of experimental work that has been done in the field of public administration and management. Importantly, the experimental turn in public management is only just getting started and thus our review captures only the first large wave, as it were. We know of a great many working papers in circulation, papers under review, dissertations being written and research projects under way around the world that will contribute substantially not only to the number, but also the variety of experimental studies to be published in the near future. But our review at least sheds some early light on the methodological features and substantive issues represented by this newly emerging experimental public management literature. The chapters in this volume provide a flavour of some of the best of this new work.

References

Anderson, D. M. and Edwards, B. C. 2015. 'Unfulfilled promise: laboratory experiments in public management research', *Public Management Review*, 17(10), pp. 1–25.

Avellaneda, C. N. 2013. 'Mayoral decision-making: issue salience, decision context, and choice constraint? An experimental study with 120 Latin American mayors', *Journal of Public Administration Research and Theory*, 23(3), pp. 631–61.

Bækgaard, M. 2011. 'The impact of formal organizational structure on politico-administrative interaction: evidence from a natural experiment', *Public Administration*, 89(3), pp. 1063–80.

Bellé, N. 2014. 'Leading to make a difference: a field experiment on the performance effects of transformational leadership, perceived social impact, and public service motivation', *Journal of Public Administration Research & Theory*, 24(1), pp. 109–36.

Bellé, N. 2015. 'Performance-related pay and the crowding out of motivation in the public sector: a randomized field experiment', *Public Administration Review*, 75(2), pp. 230–41.

Bhatti, Y., Gørtz, M. and Pedersen, L. H. 2015. 'The causal effect of profound organizational change when job insecurity is low – a quasi-experiment analyzing municipal mergers', *Journal of Public Administration Research and Theory*, 25(4), pp. 1185–1220.

Bouwman, R. and Grimmelikhuijsen, S. G. 2016. 'Experimental public administration from 1992 to 2014: a systematic literature review and ways forward', *International Journal of Public Sector Management*, 29(2), pp. 110–31.

Bozeman, B. 1992. 'Experimental design in public policy and management research: introduction', *Journal of Public Administration Research and Theory*, 2(4), pp. 440–2.

Bozeman, B. and Scott, P. 1992. 'Laboratory experiments in public policy and management', *Journal of Public Administration Research and Theory*, 2(3), pp. 293–313.

Chalkley, M. et al. 2010. 'Incentives for dentists in public service: evidence from a natural experiment', *Journal of Public Administration Research and Theory*, 20(s2), pp. i207–i223.

Dunlop, C. A., Kamkhaji, J. C. and Radaelli, C. M. 2015. 'Regulators and reform: a quasi-experimental assessment of the effects of training inspectors', *International Public Management Journal*, 18(2), pp. 304–22.

Esteve, M., Urbig, D., Van Witteloostuijn, A., and Boyne, G. 2016. 'Prosocial behavior and public service motivation', *Public Administration Review*, 76(1), pp. 177–87.

Fenn, P. et al., 2010. 'Enterprise liability, risk pooling, and diagnostic care', *Journal of Public Administration Research and Theory*, 20(s2), pp. i225–i242.

De Fine Licht, J. 2014. 'Policy area as a potential moderator of transparency effects: an experiment', *Public Administration Review*, 74(3), pp. 361–71.

De Fine Licht, J. et al. 2014. 'When does transparency generate legitimacy? Experimenting on a context-bound relationship', *Governance*, 27(1), pp. 111–34.

Greenwald, H. P. et al. 2003. 'Polling and policy analysis as resources for advocacy', *Journal of Public Administration Research and Theory*, 13(2), pp. 177–91.

Grimmelikhuijsen, S. 2012. 'Linking transparency, knowledge and citizen trust in government: an experiment', *International Review of Administrative Sciences*, 78(1), pp. 50–73.

Grimmelikhuijsen, S. et al. 2013. 'The effect of transparency on trust in government: a cross-national comparative experiment', *Public Administration Review*, 73(4), pp. 575–86.

Grimmelikhuijsen, S. G. and Klijn, A. 2015. 'The effects of judicial transparency on public trust: evidence from a field experiment', *Public Administration*, 93(4), pp. 995–1011.

Grimmelikhuijsen, S. G. and Meijer, A. J. 2014. 'Effects of transparency on the perceived trustworthiness of a government organization: evidence from an online experiment', *Journal of Public Administration Research and Theory*, 24(1), pp. 137–57.

James, O. 2011a. 'Managing citizens' expectations of public service performance: evidence from observation and experimentation in local government', *Public Administration*, 89(4), pp. 1419–35.

James, O. 2011b. 'Performance measures and democracy: information effects on citizens in field and laboratory experiments', *Journal of Public Administration Research and Theory*, 21(3), pp. 399–418.

James, O. and Moseley, A. 2014. 'Does performance information about public services affect citizens' perception, satisfaction, and voice behaviour? Field experiments with absolute and relative performance information', *Public Administration*, 92(2), pp. 493–511.

Jilke, S., Van de Walle, S. and Kim, S. 2016. 'Generating usable knowledge through an experimental approach to public administration', *Public Administration Review*, 76(1), pp. 69–72.

Kim, S. H. and Kim, S. 2016. 'National culture and social desirability bias in measuring public service motivation', *Administration & Society*, 48(4), pp. 444–76.

Knott, J. H., Miller, G. J. and Verkuilen, J. 2003. 'Adaptive incrementalism and complexity: experiments with two-person cooperative signaling games', *Journal of Public Administration Research and Theory*, 13(3), pp. 341–65.

Lachapelle, E., Montpetit, É. and Gauvin, J. 2014. 'Public perceptions of expert credibility on policy issues: the role of expert framing and political worldviews', *Policy Studies Journal*, 42(4), pp. 674–97.

Landsbergen, D. et al. 1997. 'Decision quality, confidence, and commitment with expert systems: an experimental study', *Journal of Public Administration Research and Theory*, 7(1), pp. 131–58.

Landsbergen, D., Bozeman, B. and Bretschneider, S. 1992. '"Internal rationality" and the effects of perceived decision difficulty: results of a public management decisionmaking experiment', *Journal of Public Administration Research and Theory*, 2(3), pp. 247–64.

Lawrence, E., Stoker, R. and Wolman, H. 2013. 'The effects of beneficiary targeting on public support for social policies', *Policy Studies Journal*, 41(2), pp. 199–216.

Margetts, H. Z. 2011. 'Experiments for public management research', *Public Management Review*, 13(2), pp. 189–208.

Nutt, P. C. 2006. 'Comparing public and private sector decision-making practices', *Journal of Public Administration Research and Theory*, 16(2), pp. 289–318.

Riccucci, N. M., Van Ryzin, G. G. and Lavena, C. F. 2014. 'Representative bureaucracy in policing: does it increase perceived legitimacy?' *Journal of Public Administration Research and Theory*, 24(3), pp. 537–51.

Riccucci, N. M., Van Ryzin, G. G. and Li, H. 2016. 'Representative bureaucracy and the willingness to coproduce: an experimental study', *Public Administration Review*, 76(1), pp. 121–30.

Scott, P. G. 1997. 'Assessing determinants of bureaucratic discretion: an experiment in street-level decision making', *Journal of Public Administration Research and Theory*, 7(1), pp. 35–58.

Thurmaier, K. 1992. 'Budgetary decisionmaking in central budget bureaus: an experiment', *Journal of Public Administration Research and Theory*, 2(4), pp. 463–87.

Van De Walle, S. and Van Ryzin, G. G. 2011. 'The order of questions in a survey on citizen satisfaction with public services: lessons from a split-ballot experiment', *Public Administration*, 89(4), pp. 1436–50.

Wittmer, D. 1992. 'Ethical sensitivity and managerial decisionmaking: an experiment', *Journal of Public Administration Research and Theory*, 2(4), pp. 443–62.

Yakovlev, A. et al. 2015. 'The impacts of different regulatory regimes on the effectiveness of public procurement', *International Journal of Public Administration*, 38(11), pp. 796–814.

3 Experiments and the Classical Roots of Public Administration: Comments on the Potential Utility of Experiments for Contemporary Public Management

KENNETH J. MEIER AND KENDALL D. FUNK

Public management represents a science of the artificial, a design science that is concerned as much with how things might be as how they actually are (Simon 1969). The practice of public administration and management involves individuals confronted with real-world problems that need to be fixed. Although there have always been approaches to problem solving in public administration (Fayole 1949; Weber 1946) that relied on theories, logical deduction, or cumulative hunches, such approaches have always had skeptics (Simon 1946). The skeptics often charge that public administration problems are too varied to apply a 'one size fits all' nostrum, that more formal theories of public administration are too detached from actual problems to be of real use, or that the complexity of public problems is such that figuring out in advance what causes what is just not possible. The use of experiments either in the field or in the laboratory is a reasonable response to the concerns raised about the validity and applicability of public administration research, and a strong renaissance in experimental work in public administration and management is currently under way.

This chapter seeks to set the current experimental movement within the context of classical public administration with three objectives in mind. First, through an examination of early work, this chapter demonstrates that public administration has always accepted experimental work as a central and legitimate approach to public management research. The absence of a large body of experimental work in public administration for much of the twentieth century, as a result, is highly ironic. Second, current experimental work has been greatly influenced by developments in the scientific design of experiments and its focus on randomization, control groups, precise measurement, and the examination of the psychological micro-theory behind behavioral actions. Early work might even be more accurately characterized as quasi-experiments rather than true, randomized experiments. Third, the initial quasi-experimental work of early public administration is used to provide some suggestions of fruitful areas for current empirical work.

Taylor, Hawthorne, and Simon

The origins of the systematic study of management are linked to the early efficiency experts' studies and the publication of Taylor's (1911) *Principles of Scientific Management*. Taylor's book is one of those public administration classics that everyone cites but few actually go back and read for themselves (instead relying on brief summaries in basic texts). Taylor describes at least six different experiments done under this approach to scientific management: the pig iron handler, the machine shop and fatigue, the optimal size shovel, bricklaying, bicycle ball inspection, and metal cutting. The optimal size shovel experiment illustrates Taylor's (1911: 31–3) basic approach. The objective was to determine what size shovel would permit workers to load the most material in a day given the varying weight and other characteristics of the material shoveled. Too light a shovel load would mean underproduction for a day's work; too heavy a load would prematurely tire the worker and also result in lower production. In essence this is an optimization problem with a single peaked production curve. A group of highly productive shovelers was selected, and the shovelers were given different size shovels and had their performance tracked. Taylor concluded that the optimal size shovel should carry a load of 21 pounds, and thus management should provide different sized shovels for different tasks.

The shovel experiment illustrates a set of basic principles in regard to Taylor's empirical work. First, because these are optimization experiments, they are not done with a randomly selected set of workers. The studies sampled off the high production tail of the curve among workers who already showed that they were strongly motivated by monetary incentives; in this way the subjects are akin to white rats in laboratory experiments that are bred to have specific traits. This selection bias meant that the workers involved not only were predisposed to seek greater economic incentives, but also accepted management instruction without question. As Taylor (1911: 72) notes, 'the pig-iron handler is not an extraordinary man difficult to find, he is merely a man more or less of the type of the ox, heavy both mentally and physically.'[1]

Second, the incentives used are always individual incentives, not group incentives; piece rate production was integral to the micro-theory behind scientific management. Taylor (1911: 37–8) gleefully tells a story about how a Pittsburgh competitor offered a 53 percent wage premium to his workers from a company that relied on team production rather than individual production and how he encouraged the workers to take the offered jobs, but assured them they could always come back to Bethlehem Steel. Anticipating some of the findings of the Hawthorne experiments, Taylor reports that the workers did return when they found that lack of effort by other team members limited their payoffs.

Third, the Taylor experiments generally do not involve a control group. The design of the experiments is essentially a before-after comparison, or what Shadish, Cook, and Campbell (2002) term a one-group pretest-posttest quasi-experiment, where results are compared to some established prior set of results. Favorable results call for greater experimentation (such as larger shovels), and unfavorable results indicate a need to rethink the variable under consideration. The exception to this generalization is Taylor's bicycle ball experiment, where workers were given previously inspected balls (without being told that they were such) to measure the ideal length of work time and the length of breaks. Even in this experiment, however, there was substantial selection bias and workplace manipulation before the start of the experiment (see footnote 1).

Fourth, the paternalism of Taylor clearly comes through in his discussion of why scientific management was good for the workers, even those workers who were discharged from the company. This paternalism was even allowed to compromise Taylor's basic belief in monetary incentives, which he limited to 60 percent more than the prevailing

---

[1] An excellent illustration of the human side of Taylor (1911: 45) is the bicycle ball experiments. 'It became necessary to exclude all girls who lacked a low "personal coefficient." And unfortunately this involved laying off many of the most intelligent, hardest working and most trustworthy girls merely because they did not possess the quality of quick perception followed by quick action.'

wage. 'When, on the other hand, they receive much more than a 60 per cent increase in wages, many of them will work irregularly and tend to become more or less shiftless, extravagant, and dissipated. Our experiments showed, in other words, that it does not do for most men to get rich too fast' (1911: 37).

Despite the limitations of Taylor's experimental method, the results appeared to have external validity – in the context for which they were designed. The experiments worked for workers where individual production could be closely monitored and if those workers were motivated by economic incentives. They were not designed for interrelated tasks where individuals had to rely on the prior work of other individuals or where the workers operated in teams. The bicycle ball experiments in fact were designed to limit the interaction of the workers with each other. The experiments also relied on a credible commitment on the part of management – meaning that management would not reduce wages once production rose so that workers would have to work harder for the same amount of money. That lack of credible commitment on the part of management in other cases led to some of the most serious abuses of scientific management and even generated congressional hearings on scientific management and its misuses (Fischer and Sirianni 1994: 179).

The context dependence of the Taylor experiments also limited their ability to contribute to general theories of management or human behavior. The absence of control groups, the insistence on selection bias in terms of workers, the problems with before-after designs (Campbell and Stanley 1963; Shadish et al. 2002), and the restricted range of incentives considered illustrate how far we have come in designing valid experimental work.

The experiments conducted in the Hawthorne Works plant of Western Electric are well integrated into the literature and lore of public administration and management (Roethlisberger and Dickson 1939), although focus has generally been on only one of the several experiments conducted over a five-year period. The famed lighting experiment varied the degree of illumination and measured the changes in worker productivity. As illumination increased, so too did production. The study then decreased the illumination and productivity continued to rise until the lighting was reduced to levels that clearly limited vision. The conclusion later scholars drew from the study was that, by demonstrating a concern for the workers and including them in the discussion of study objectives, the experiments actually motivated the employees to increase their production. This finding and subsequent work generated a wealth of management literature that focused on the human relations aspects of management (McGregor 1960). A more recent analysis of the archival data from the lighting experiment, however, calls into question the basic findings and argues that the timing of the changes (on a Monday after a day of rest) could not be ruled out as a determinant of the overall results (Levitt and List 2011).

Equally important for the development of management theory, but not given as much attention in the applied literature, is the bank wiring room experiment. In that study, efforts to experimentally manipulate production with pay incentives failed; in fact, production dropped with increased incentives. Observation revealed that the working group adopted norms of a 'fair day's work' and limited its production to that amount because workers feared that responding to the incentives would encourage management to reduce their pay rate and thus generate more work for the same salary. Informal group norms created pressure on 'rate busters' to conform to the group's predetermined effort levels.

Numerous other experiments conducted at the Western Electric Hawthorne plant focused on rest periods, monotony, supervisors' relations with workers, and nonmonetary incentives (see the full discussion in Roethlisberger and Dickson 1939). Although these experiments greatly influenced the study of organizational behavior and contributed to contemporary management theory, they should again be characterized more as quasi-experiments than true, randomized experiments. All the efforts were essentially optimization attempts similar to Taylor's work. And because they lacked control groups, the basic problems of before-after designs remain threats to the internal validity of the research.

Herbert Simon's *Administrative Behavior* (1947) is one of the seminal works in behavioral research in public administration and management. Simon's challenge of economic man and rational decision making, substituting the concept of satisficing in decisions, was an effort to describe how individuals actually made decisions. The logic of satisficing is based on a status quo that for whatever reason is not acceptable. Unlike a synoptically rational man, 'administrative man' compares a few similar alternatives, selects one of the alternatives based on limited analysis, and then monitors the results. If the situation improves to the point where it is satisfactory, the manager stops the process. If the situation does not improve, an additional iteration is undertaken until a satisfactory outcome is attained. In its basic logic, satisficing is in effect a quasi-experimental approach. The manager designs an 'experiment' to determine if outcomes improve compared to a baseline, evaluates the experiment, and then makes a managerial decision. Such an experiment could be an actual experiment, designed with full control groups and randomization, or it might just be trial and error based on the experience of the manager.

Simon clearly prefers experiments, and sets out the logic of experiments, but he positively cites only Frederick Taylor's work, the Hawthorne experiments, and some World War I work in Great Britain (Simon 1947: 43). He notes, 'In the field of public administration, almost the sole example of such experimentation is the series of studies that have been conducted in the public welfare field to determine the proper caseloads for social workers' (p. 43). Included in the footnote to this sentence is a citation to Simon's own work in California (Simon et al. 1941). Simon oversaw a field experiment on the size of caseloads for intake workers and 'carrier' workers (who determined actual eligibility and benefits). Intake workers were randomly assigned cases, but with different work-loads of 50, 75, 100, and 125 cases. Carrier workers were randomly assigned cases (including randomization from the intake assign-ments) of 8, 12, and 16 cases per week. Notable in the design was the use of two district offices that were as different as possible to determine how generalizable the results were. The experiment showed the best results for the smallest caseload for intake workers and null results for the carrier workers. Given that one set of the experimental conditions matched the existing work standards, the study incorporated a control group.

The limited number of experiments in public administration that Simon could cite in *Administrative Behavior* was not augmented in subsequent editions of the book. Experiments in public administration were so rare, in fact, that Robert Presthus (1965) in *Behavioral Approaches to Public Administration* did not cite a single experiment in his discussion of behavioral methods. Simon himself conducted many future experiments, but these were focused on economics and decision making rather than field experiments in public administration and management.

The Contemporary Era

It is ironic that the field of public administration and management lacked experimental studies for such a long period of time given the prevalence of (quasi-) experiments in the classical works. A virtual issue on experiments in the *Journal of Public Administration Research and Theory* in 2014 included all the prior published experimental work in the journal, which numbered fewer than 20 articles over 24 years. Other public administration journals exhibit similar trends (see Chapter 2 of this volume). As demonstrated throughout this volume, however, interest in experimental research in public administration and management has increased tremendously in recent years. We highlight some of these studies to show how recent research has used innovative experimental methods and designs to study some of the same basic problems that were featured in the early studies of management.

The recent renaissance in experiments has been broad based, including survey and field experiments with citizens, experiments with public officials, natural and quasi-experiments, laboratory experiments, or some combination thereof. This spike in experimental research is largely due to an increase in studies using survey experiments with citizens. These studies have examined a diverse range of topics, such as how citizens attribute blame in situations of delegation and contracting (James et al. 2016), the effect of information cues on citizens' perceptions of local government (James 2011b), how performance information affects expectations about public services (James 2011a), and how representative bureaucracy affects perceptions of the police force (Riccucci, Van Ryzin, and Lavena 2014) and the willingness to coproduce (Riccucci, Van Ryzin, and Li 2015).

Although less common than survey experiments, the number of public administration studies using field experiments is increasing as well. These studies are especially noteworthy since they create more realistic scenarios by manipulating actual outcomes in the world, as opposed to most survey experiments that instead ask participants to put themselves in hypothetical situations. Recent field experiments have examined issues such as how text message notifications affect the collection of delinquent fines in the United States (Haynes et al. 2013), if a television series that exposes citizens to the judicial process can increase citizens' trust in the judicial system in the Netherlands (Grimmelikhuijsen and Klinj 2015), whether government initiatives can increase citizen coproduction in Denmark schools (Jakobsen 2013), and how various performance-related pay schemes affect the task performance of nurses in Italy (Bellé 2015). Although these are only a few of the field experiments that have been published in recent years, they demonstrate the creativity that scholars have used to design and implement experiments in the field relevant to interesting questions in public administration and management.

In addition to experiments with citizens, a handful of studies have used experiments with public officials to address questions of interest in public management. In a survey experiment with Latin American mayors, Avellaneda (2013) examines how issue salience, context, and external constraints affect mayors' decisions to delegate spending authority. Bellé and Cantarelli (2015) examine how financial incentives influence job effort using a survey experiment with civil servants in the Italian central government. Jakobsen and Andersen (2013) use a field experiment with public employees in Denmark to study the effect of organizational support on work motivation. Though survey and field experiments with public officials have been rare to date, we expect the number of these studies to increase tremendously due to initiatives like the Leadership and Performance (LEAP) project at Aarhus University and growing interest on the part of public administration and management scholars around the globe (see Andersen et al., Chapter 9, this volume).

Another peculiarity of contemporary public administration and management research is the lack of laboratory experiments. While other social sciences, such as political science, psychology, and economics, are dominated by laboratory experiments, few laboratory studies have been published in public administration journals. This shortage has led scholars to call for an increase in laboratory research, citing the potential benefits of these types of experiments, particularly the ability to manipulate variables that are difficult or impossible to manipulate in the real world and the increased control over the research environment (Anderson and Edwards 2015; Bozeman and Scott 1992). Like much of the experimental research in other disciplines, many of the laboratory experiments that have been conducted in public administration use undergraduate university students as participants (Anderson and Stritch 2016; Clerkin, Paynter, and Taylor 2009; Grimmelikhuijsen et al. 2013). Other studies make use of the greater diversity in background and career experiences offered by graduate students (James 2011b; Landsbergen et al. 1992; Moynihan 2013). Laboratory studies using participants outside of the university, however, are virtually nonexistent in public administration and management (see Landsbergen et al. 1992 for an exception).

To some readers, these studies may seem far different from the classical (quasi-) experimental management studies that we discussed earlier. A more nuanced look at recent experimental scholarship, however, reveals that public management scholars have returned to experiments as a way to study the same basic problems of management, efficiency, performance, and work motivation that were of chief concern in management studies of the early twentieth century. There is no doubt that contemporary research has greatly improved theory development, research methods, and experimental designs since the time of the classical works, but there is still much room for progress and improvement. Later in this chapter, we provide some guidance for future experimental studies in public administration and management and highlight opportunities for natural and quasi-experimental research using real-world processes and outcomes.

Implications of the Classical Works for Contemporary Public Administration: Guidance and Opportunities for Future Work

One of the most remarkable aspects of the early management experiments by Taylor, Hawthorne, and Simon was their realism and external validity. These studies were highly applicable to real-world settings precisely because the experimental environment largely mirrored the actual settings in which managers and their employees operated. Though perhaps lacking in internal validity and methodological rigor by today's standards, these classical studies had great experimental realism, mundane realism, and potential for external validity.[2] The early management studies used real managers and real workers to study real problems in the real environments in which they work. As methodologically primitive as these studies may have been, we believe that such simple study designs allowed for more ready experimentation with real work settings and processes and thus constitute

---

[2] It is unclear whether these studies are actually externally valid since internal validity is a prerequisite for external validity. That is, researchers must first ensure that a causal effect has been demonstrated before the study's findings could be generalized to subjects outside of the original experiment.

a strength that should be replicated in current and future public management studies. There are several ways in which researchers can improve the external validity, internal validity, and realism of their experimental research.

First, researchers should give substantial consideration to the design of their experiments and measurements of the theoretical concepts. Experimentalists should avoid self-reported measures that are likely to elicit socially desirable responses, such as self-reported assessments of participants' efforts, performance, or work motivation. Simply asking a participant 'How much effort do you put into your job?' is unlikely to be correlated with actual effort and more likely to be correlated with individual self-confidence or desire to meet some ideal standard of effort. Better measures of these concepts would involve objective measures, such as performance assessments based on the completion of a task, or multiple subjective measures that are less likely to provoke socially desirable answers, such as a series of indirect survey questions that could be used independently or as part of an index. Experimental studies should avoid asking participants to role-play positions with which they have no prior experience (e.g., asking undergraduate students to make decisions as if they were public managers). Role-playing and hypothetical scenarios are appropriate in some contexts; however, researchers should be cautious about asking the participants of an experiment to act within a world that is unfamiliar to them.

Another way that experimentalists can improve the internal and external validity of their studies is to increase the realism of the experimental environment. Field experiments and experiments with public officials are a great way to do so. These designs create more realism by bringing the experimental procedures closer to the actual setting in which participants operate and limiting the role-playing component of many laboratory and survey experiments. Researchers should also strive to increase the experimental realism and mundane realism of their experimental designs. Experimental realism is the extent to which participants accept the experimental treatments as real. For example, if a researcher is studying how external constraints affect decision making, the experimental treatment needs to actually cause participants to feel constrained. Mundane realism is the extent to which the experimental context reflects the everyday activities of participants. For example, asking public managers to draft a mock budget or create an agenda for a meeting has greater mundane realism than having them list the priorities of their organization, which is something they are unlikely to do on a regular basis.

Public administration research would also benefit by adopting the best practices in other disciplines, particularly the use of multiple experiments within a single study (as is common practice in psychology), the combination of laboratory and field experiments, or experimental and observational studies (e.g., James 2011b), and other multi-method approaches that combine the best of experimental and natural variation data. One practice that deserves more attention in public administration experiments is the use of manipulation checks to ensure that participants actually receive the intended treatment. Manipulation checks can be crucial for internal validity and should be used *when possible* for experimental research designs. Researchers should ask themselves 'How would I know if the treatment was (not) received?' and then design an indicator that can measure whether participants received the treatment as intended.[3]

Finally, there are a number of opportunities of which public administration and management scholars have yet to take advantage. Graduate students, especially those with previous work experience in the public sector, provide not only convenience samples, but also useful participants for examining the decision making and behaviors of public managers. While we hesitate to recommend that public administration scholars increase their use of university students in experiments, we do think that making more use of certain graduate students (e.g., in public administration, management, business administration, social work, education policy, human resources management, leadership, public health) will increase the potential utility of experimental work in public administration. Using mid-career students is an exceptionally promising strategy.

Researchers should also be quick to exploit data from natural experiments or quasi-experiments. From time to time, governments will design public policies and institutions using experimental methods, such as

---

[3] Though manipulation checks are useful for checking internal validity, researchers should assess whether manipulation checks are appropriate for their study. In some cases, such as experimental studies wherein the treatment is an unconscious prime or cue that operates below awareness, a manipulation check might change the natural behavior of the participant by alerting them to the treatment condition. In other cases, subjects may not be accessible for a manipulation check (e.g., did the citizen actually see the message?).

randomization or the use of treatment and control groups, or a significant policy change will create a before-after, quasi-experimental design. In some contexts, academic researchers have been instrumental in designing these policy experiments (e.g., LEAP project in Denmark, see Chapter 9; King et al. 2007). A few natural experiments are worth discussion here, some of which researchers have used, while others remain underutilized. In several developing countries, a lack of resources and uncertainty about the effects of new policies led policy makers to use experimental methods in the design of these public policies. A prime example is the creation of Mexico's conditional cash transfer program, Oportunidades (formerly Progresa), which provides cash transfers to needy families contingent on the families attending regular health checkups and their children attending school. The program was implemented randomly at the village level in seven Mexican states (De La O 2013). A number of countries, including Colombia, Nicaragua, Indonesia, and the Philippines, have followed Mexico's lead by implementing cash transfer programs in a randomized fashion.

A second policy experiment worth mentioning is the random auditing of municipalities in Brazil. In 2003, the Brazilian federal government, through the auspices of the Comptroller General (Controladoria-Geral da União), started randomly selecting municipalities to be audited in order to monitor municipal spending of federal transfers. The reports of these audits are made available to the public, and some have been coded to measure mismanagement and corruption at the municipal level (Brollo et al. 2013; Ferraz and Finan 2008, 2011). The final policy experiment we highlight is the implementation of random gender quotas in India and Lesotho. Both countries randomly assigned gender quotas for leadership positions at the village level, and India also randomized quotas for scheduled castes and ethnic minority groups (see Beaman et al. 2009 on India; Clayton 2015 on Lesotho). These are just a few of the randomized policy experiments that have been implemented around the globe. We suggest that researchers who are interested in using the data generated through government experiments explore the policy evaluations conducted by affiliates of the Abdul Latif Jameel Poverty Action Lab (J-PAL, www.povertyactionlab.org), which include both randomized and nonrandomized policy studies from across the globe.

In addition to natural experiments, there are a number of quasi-experiments in naturalistic settings that public administration researchers should exploit. Though quasi-experiments may not meet the 'gold standard' set by true randomization, they combine important aspects of both experimental and natural variation studies, which is useful for the accumulation of scientific knowledge. Some scholars have already made use of quasi-experiments, such as the implementation of decentralization reforms in Bolivia (Faguet 2012), adoption of various tax schemes in Russia (Baccini, Li, and Mirkina 2014), and municipal structural reform in Denmark (Blom-Hansen, Houlberg, and Serritzlew 2014). Quasi-experiments may be more difficult to spot than natural randomized experiments, but they are likely to be more abundant since most policy makers and public managers are unlikely to be trained in experimental methods and there are political costs to relinquishing control over a particular area, which is required for true randomized experimentation.

Cross-national experiments or quasi-experiments can take advantage of differences in the public management context (O'Toole and Meier 2015) across countries to control for factors that one cannot control for within a country by randomization. An experiment in the United States that attempted to control for the degree of professionalization among local public managers, such as school superintendents, would be hampered by the limited variation within the United States compared to the level of variation cross-nationally. Paired experiments or quasi-experiments that consider such factors as the level of corruption, relationships between politicians and bureaucrats, or levels of environmental munificence could provide leverage on the importance of these contextual variables in influencing experimental results.

In substantive terms, experiments are clearly an excellent way to study decision making as illustrated in psychology, economics, and political science. In addition to the areas noted earlier in this chapter, experiments could go a long way to building a knowledge based on how public managers make decisions. Much of the performance management literature (see Moynihan 2008) assumes that performance drives public sector decisions; yet, despite theoretical work on the topic (Cyert and March 1963; Meier, Favero, and Zhu 2015), this area is virtually unexplored. Similarly, we do not know how public managers trade off different objectives such as equity or efficiency or any of the numerous goals that public organizations have. Management reform and managerial change seeks to instill creative decision making and risk taking, but we have no studies of when managers decide to take risks versus rely on bureaucratic processes to buffer change.

A second substantive area with great potential for the use of experiments is the management of nonprofit organizations, as discussed in Chapter 20. We know that nonprofits attract different personnel than public or private organizations. These values that individuals bring with them to their sector of choice seem ripe for experimental studies to compare decision making across types of organizations. Small nonprofits frequently operate on tight budgets and rely on government or other grants to deliver services. Experiments focused on program performance or individual decision making might be more feasible given the relatively smaller incentives involved. The United Way or other funding organization, for example, might experiment with nonprofits in terms of effort to increase governing board diversity.

Conclusions: Limitations and Advantages of Experimental Research

Although experiments offer a great deal of potential to public management scholarship, they are similar to all other methods. They entail limitations as well as advantages. First, experiments generally require a trade-off between control over the experimental condition and the ability to generalize to the practical situations of public management. The relative distribution of experiments that are survey based or involve citizens rather than using public managers reflects this difficulty. Second, as many authors in this volume note, there are ethical questions that experiments must address because the research is relatively more reactive. Political scientists have frequently done field experiments to increase voter turnout, and at times have relied on misleading information to do so (Willis 2014). Much as medicine faces the question of whether it is ethical to deny a control group a medicine that is effective, at some point public management scholars will need to address similar ethical questions. Third, at least judging by the existing work in political science, there is often a tendency to eschew theory when designing experiments and opt for clever experiments that do not link to important questions. The use of experiments has the advantage of allowing the researcher to focus on the micro-theory behind human behavior and link this behavior to broader theories of public administration and public management. Using experiments in this manner requires greater effort and care, but also holds the potential for a greater scholarly and practical impact.

Fourth, a set of issues centers on the idea that real-world settings will impose political or other limits on the experimental process. A survey of work in this volume, especially in terms of field experiments, shows that they are clearly more frequent in some countries than others. Government support for research using experiments is clearly stronger in Europe, for example, than in the United States. This difference in support is then coupled with the bureaucratic and cumbersome process that US institutions of higher education use to regulate research. The institutional review board process in the United States is widely criticized for using a medical model to evaluate and limit research that poses little harm to research participants.

An additional practical issue is the recognition that experimental participants do not come to the experiments as blank slates. They have preconceived notions and personal experiences that could well interact with the experimental conditions. Public managers also read the scholarly literature and might well respond based on their knowledge of the literature or on social desirability concerns. Such concerns are not unique to experimental research, and in fact, may be a more significant problem in survey research, but at the same time they need to be recognized. Because such preexisting conditions cannot be controlled, replication of experiments in different contexts becomes very important for generalization.[4]

A final concern that is not specific to experiments is publication bias (Easterbrook et al. 1991; Rosenthal 1979), the well-documented finding that positive results are more likely to be published than negative or null results. Experiments have an advantage over other forms of research that could be exploited in this regard. Separate from the findings, the technical quality of experiments is easier to judge than

---

[4] Of particular concern are convenience samples where individuals agree to participate in panels used for Internet surveys. Individuals who frequently participate in experiments for monetary gain (even modest amounts) are likely to hold much different values and interests than citizens in general or public managers. The low cost of such samples needs to be weighed against the potential selection bias and experimental bias. Such samples might have their best value as corroboration of experiments done with other subject pools.

other data-based research. Design issues are relatively clear; the use of control groups, the clear specification of the experimental condition, and the nature of the statistical analysis make assessing an experiment separate from its findings more straightforward. It is clearly possible to create a review process for experiments that meets high academic standards that could certify the technical quality of experiments generating null results. A permanent publication forum for such studies would be of great value in terms of making future experimental work more efficient, but also in terms of systematic reviews or meta-analyses of published research.

This chapter has situated the current uptick in experimental research in public administration within the classical management literature. While the classical studies were surely flawed and perhaps even unethical, these studies provide a number of lessons for contemporary experimental public administration and management research. Chiefly, scholars should attempt to mimic the experimental and mundane realism present in the classical works, and aim for greater external validity. The current scholarship has made significant progress since the time of the early studies, but there is still much room for improvement.

References

Anderson, D. M. and B. C. Edwards 2015. 'Unfulfilled promise: laboratory experiments in public management research', *Public Management Review* 17(10): 1518–42.

Anderson, D. M. and J. M. Stritch 2016. 'Goal clarity, task significance, and performance: evidence from a laboratory experiment', *Journal of Public Administration Research and Theory* 26(2): 211–25.

Avellaneda, C. N. 2013. 'Mayoral decision-making: issue salience, decision context, and choice constraint? An experimental study with 120 Latin American mayors', *Journal of Public Administration Research and Theory* 23(3): 631–61.

Baccini, L., Q. Li, and I. Mirkina 2014. 'Corporate tax cuts and foreign direct investment', *Journal of Policy Analysis and Management* 33(4): 977–1006.

Beaman, L. A., R. Chattopadhyay, E. Duflo, R. Pande, and P. Topalova 2009. 'Powerful women: does exposure reduce bias?' *Quarterly Journal of Economics* 124(4): 1497–1540.

Bellé, N. 2015. 'Performance-related pay and the crowding out of motivation in the public sector: a randomized field experiment', *Public Administration Review* 75(2): 230–41.

Bellé, N. and P. Cantarelli 2015. 'Monetary incentives, motivation, and job effort in the public sector: an experimental study with Italian government executives', *Review of Public Personnel Administration* 35(2): 99–123.

Blom-Hansen, J., K. Houlberg, and S. Serritzlew 2014. 'Size, democracy, and the economic costs of running the political system', *American Journal of Political Science* 58(4): 790–803.

Bozeman, B. and P. Scott 1992. 'Laboratory experiments in public policy and management', *Journal of Public Administration Research and Theory* 2(3): 293–313.

Brollo, F., T. Nannicini, R. Perotti, and G. Tabellini 2013. 'The political resource curse', *American Economic Review* 103(5): 1759–96.

Campbell, D. T. and J. C. Stanley 1963. *Experimental and Quasi-experimental Designs for Research*. Washington, DC: American Educational Research Association.

Clayton, A. 2015. 'Women's political engagement under quota-mandated female representation: evidence from a randomized policy experiment', *Comparative Political Studies* 48(3): 333–69.

Clerkin, R. M., S. R. Paynter, and J. K. Taylor 2009. 'Public service motivation in undergraduate giving and volunteering decisions', *American Review of Public Administration* 39(6): 675–98.

Cyert, R. M. and J. G. March 1963. *A Behavioral Theory of the Firm*. Englewood Cliffs, NJ: Prentice-Hall.

De La O, A. L. 2013. 'Do conditional cash transfers affect electoral behavior? Evidence from a randomized experiment in Mexico', *American Journal of Political Science* 57(1): 1–14.

Easterbrook, P. J., R. Gopalan, J. A. Berlin, and D. R. Matthews 1991. 'Publication bias in clinical research', *The Lancet* 337(8746): 867–72.

Faguet, J.-P. 2012. *Decentralization and Popular Democracy: Governance from Below in Bolivia*. Ann Arbor: University of Michigan Press.

Fayol, H. 1949. *General and Industrial Management*. London: Pitman.

Ferraz, C. and F. Finan 2008. 'Exposing corrupt politicians: the effects of Brazil's publicly released audits on electoral outcomes', *The Quarterly Journal of Economics* 123(2): 703–45.

Ferraz, C. and F. Finan 2011. 'Electoral accountability and corruption: evidence from the audits of local governments', *American Economic Review* 101: 1274–1311.

Fischer, F. and C. Sirianni, eds. 1994. *Critical Studies in Organization and Bureaucracy*. Philadelphia, PA: Temple University Press.

Grimmelikhuijsen, S. and A. Klinj 2015. 'The effects of judicial transparency on public trust: evidence from a field experiment', *Public Administration* 93(4): 995–1011.

Grimmelikhuijsen, S., G. Porumbescu, B. Hong, and T. Im 2013. 'The effect of transparency on trust in government: a cross-national comparative experiment', *Public Administration Review* 73(4): 575–86.

Haynes, L. C., D. P. Green, R. Gallagher, P. John, and D. J. Torgerson 2013. 'Collection of delinquent fines: an adaptive randomized trial to assess the effectiveness of alternative text messages', *Journal of Policy Analysis and Management* 32(4): 718–30.

Jakobsen, M. 2013. 'Can government initiatives increase citizen coproduction? Results of a randomized field experiment', *Journal of Public Administration Research and Theory* 23(1): 27–54.

Jakobsen, M. and S. C. Andersen 2013. 'Intensifying social exchange relationships in public organizations: evidence from a randomized field experiment', *Journal of Policy Analysis and Management* 32(1): 60–82.

James, O. 2011a. 'Managing citizens' expectations of public service performance: evidence from observation and experimentation in local government', *Public Administration* 89(4): 1419–35.

James, O. 2011b. 'Performance measures and democracy: information effects on citizens in field and laboratory experiments', *Journal of Public Administration Research and Theory* 21(3): 399–418.

James, O., S. Jilke, C. Petersen, and S. Van de Walle 2016. 'Citizens' blame of politicians for public service failure: experimental evidence about blame reduction through delegation and contracting', *Public Administration Review* 76(1): 83–93.

King, G. et al. 2007. 'A "politically robust" experimental design for public policy evaluation, with application to the Mexican universal health insurance program', *Journal of Policy Analysis and Management* 26(3): 479–506.

Landsbergen, D., B. Bozeman, and S. Bretschneider 1992. '"Internal rationality" and the effects of perceived decision difficulty: results of a public management decisionmaking experiment', *Journal of Public Administration Research and Theory* 2(3): 247–64.

Levitt, S. D., and J. A. List 2011. 'Was there really a Hawthorne effect at the Hawthorne plant? An analysis of the original illumination experiments', *American Economic Journal: Applied Economics* 3(1): 224–38.

McGregor, D. 1960. *The Human Side of Enterprise.* New York: McGraw-Hill.

Meier, K. J., N. Favero, and L. Zhu. 2015. 'Performance gaps and managerial decisions: a Bayesian decision theory of managerial action', *Journal of Public Administration Research and Theory* 25(4): 1221–46.

Moynihan, D. P. 2008. *The Dynamics of Performance Management.* Washington, DC: Georgetown University Press.

Moynihan, D. P. 2013. 'Does public service motivation lead to budget maximization? Evidence from an experiment', *International Public Management Journal* 16(2): 179–96.

O'Toole, L. J. Jr. and K. J. Meier 2015. 'Public management, context, and performance: in quest of a more general theory', *Journal of Public Administration Research and Theory* 25(1): 237–56.

Presthus, R. V. 1965. *Behavioral Approaches to Public Administration*. Tuscaloosa: University of Alabama Press.

Riccucci, N. M., G. G. Van Ryzin, and C. F. Lavena 2014. 'Representative bureaucracy in policing: does it increase perceived legitimacy?' *Journal of Public Administration Research and Theory* 24(3): 537–51.

Riccucci, N. M., G. G. Van Ryzin, and H. Li 2015. 'Representative bureaucracy and the willingness to coproduce: an experimental study', *Public Administration Review* 76(1): 121–30.

Roethlisberger, F. J. and W. J. Dickson 1939. *Management and the Worker*. Cambridge, MA: Harvard University Press.

Rosenthal, R. 1979. 'The file drawer problem and tolerance for null results', *Psychological Bulletin* 86(3): 638–41.

Shadish, W. R., Cook, T. D., and Campbell, D. T. 2002. *Experimental and Quasi-experimental Designs for Generalized Causal Inference*. Boston, MA: Houghton Mifflin Harcourt.

Simon, H. A. 1946. 'The proverbs of administration', *Public Administration Review* 6(1): 53–67.

Simon, H. A. 1947. *Administrative Behavior*. New York: The Free Press.

Simon, H. A. 1969. *The Sciences of the Artificial*. Cambridge, MA: MIT Press.

Simon, H. A., W. R. Divine, E. M. Cooper, and M. Chernin 1941. *Determining Work Loads for Professional Staff in a Public Welfare Agency*. Berkeley: Bureau of Public Administration: University of California.

Taylor, F. W. 1911. *The Principles of Scientific Management*. New York: Harper and Brothers.

Weber, M. 1946. *From Max Weber: Essays in Sociology*. H. H. Gerth and C. Wright Mills, trans. New York: Oxford University Press.

Willis, D. 2014. 'Professors' research stirs political outrage in Montana', *New York Times* (October 28, 2014), www.nytimes.com/2014/10/29/upshot/professors-research-project-stirs-political-outrage-in-montana.html?_r=0, accessed November 28, 2015.

PART II

Methods

4 | Causal Inference and the Design and Analysis of Experiments

OLIVER JAMES, SEBASTIAN JILKE, AND
GREGG G. VAN RYZIN

Introduction

This chapter introduces key concepts in causal inference, with a focus
on the design and analysis of experiments. It is principally aimed at
readers who do not have formal training or extensive experience in
experimentation but who want to get the most out of the chapters in
this volume, critically interpret experimental studies and their findings,
or understand how experimental methods relate to more conventional,
non-experimental methods of public management research. This chapter also serves as a starting place for those interested in designing and
carrying out their own experiments and should also be of interest to
those reviewing experiments for publication or commissioning experimental research, for example, to inform policy or practice.

This chapter begins with a discussion of what counts as a research
method producing valid findings about causation and uses this perspective to review conventional, non-experimental, observational methods.
Research using observation of correlations to establish causation has
limitations as a method, including the 'research as regression' approach
that has come to dominate public management research. Next, this
chapter sets out the fundamental concepts, logic, and advantages of
experimentation. It discusses how experiments involve researchers
intervening in the world by giving treatments to people or other experimental units. In the experiments that form the focus of this book,
treatments are randomly assigned to experimental units placed in groups
on the basis of treatment received (e.g., a treatment or control group).
Researchers then compare the outcomes between these groups, typically
to estimate average treatment effect.

This chapter then introduces the counterfactual approach to causation
and the potential outcomes framework, which helps further demonstrate
the benefits of experimental as opposed to non-experimental methods.

Having set out the general approach of experimentation, the main designs of experiment are introduced, including the use of multiple treatments and different timings of the measurement of outcomes. Next, the analysis of data from experiments is discussed. This chapter moves on to examine potential problems with the implementation of experiments that can threaten the validity of findings. It concludes by noting the importance of carrying out a series of experiments in support of research on a topic area and introduces field, survey, and laboratory experiments as types of experiment that are covered in subsequent chapters.

4.1 Causation, Observational Studies, and the Limits of Research as Regression

Scholars use many different methods to address research questions in contemporary public management. Indeed, the pluralism of methods is one of the discipline's strengths. Researchers have a strong interest in empirical questions about the existence and nature of phenomena and events. These questions are investigated through data gathered by careful scientific measurement. For example, researchers measure the performance of public organisations on different dimensions or the characteristics of individual public managers, such as their training or experience. Researchers are also sometimes interested in describing what phenomena or events are correlated with each other, and consider correlation for its own sake. For example, there may be a positive correlation between the level of training of managers in an organisation, their managerial performance, and the performance of the organisation overall. However, much of the time, researchers are further interested in whether such correlations reflect causal relationships between phenomena or events.

Although the pattern of causal relations can be complicated, researchers are often interested in whether changes in one variable (the independent variable, or X) produce subsequent changes in another variable (the dependent variable, or Y) and the size of these effects. Researchers develop and refine theory about the causal relationship, and test their empirical implications using data. For example, researchers might want to assess the effect of increasing managers' training on their individual managerial performance, before going on to consider the effects for organisational performance. To do so, they must separate out the stages in the causal chain. At the first stage, they need to consider the effect of training an individual manager has on his or her managerial performance. They must consider the possibility that the effect runs in the opposite direction (from managerial performance to training). They must separate out the effect of training from other causes of managerial performance (perhaps high-performing mangers choose to undertake more training or are selected to receive it). Because public management is a design science, the knowledge about causes can then be used for such things as making recommendations to policy makers about training programmes or to inform refinements to training methods which are then subject to further investigation. The interest in causal questions means that the methods researchers use should provide valid evidence about cause and effect. Campbell and colleagues described this issue as one of *internal validity*, in the sense of valid evidence that gets as close as possible to the truth about the existence of causal relations. Often, as in the case of many experiments, the interest is not only in the particular instance of the causal relation, but in its more general relevance. The findings of a method are said to have *external validity* if the causal relation can be generalised to other circumstances of interest, for example at different times or across different settings or across people of interest (Campbell and Stanley 1966; Guala 2005: 141–60; Shadish, Cook, and Campbell 2002).

The issues involved in causation discussed previously can be illustrated graphically. Figure 4.1 represents a hypothesised causal relationship in data consisting of an independent variable X having an effect on a dependent variable Y. Researchers are typically interested in whether X causes Y, the size of the effect of X on Y, and how the effect of X on Y compares to other causes of Y. There are other causal questions of possible interest, such as identifying a causal structure of mediation (as is often done in path analysis or SEM modelling) or moderation (interaction) effects. However, a basic issue remains how to establish whether X causes Y and the size of the effect. To establish causation, it is necessary that variation in the dependent variable Y has

Figure 4.1: Independent variable X as a cause of dependent variable Y

been produced by changes in the independent variable X. Although X could be one of many causes of Y, researchers often focus on one independent variable at a time and aim to establish the size of its independent effect on Y.

The typical research designs in management research rely on non-experimental methods. Studies using non-experimental methods are described by experimentalists as *observational studies* because researchers observe the social or political world rather than intervening to manipulate the variables thought to bring about effects. A range of methods are used in observational research, including case studies and other qualitative techniques. However, quantitative methods have gained ground in public management research in recent decades (Groeneveld et al. 2014). Quantitative data can come from new measurements by researchers themselves (e.g., surveys of managers asking them about what training they have done) or from the use of existing data, such as existing surveys or administrative data (such as records of training events and performance data). In an observational study, researchers passively observe the relationships between variables rather than trying to influence them although, usually inadvertently, measurement itself can sometimes influence behaviour. A range of statistical techniques are then adopted to estimate the effect of X on Y using the gathered data. For example, multiple regression analysis applied to observational data estimates a coefficient for the effect of X on Y, whilst controlling for other variables thought to affect Y that may be confounded with X. Whilst theory is sometimes taken as a guide for presuming X is cause and Y is effect, at some point theoretical propositions need to be examined in the light of empirical evidence. However, the difficulties that multiple regression methods using observational data often have in estimating causal effects are increasingly recognised across the social sciences (Angrist and Pischke 2010, 2014; Gerber and Green 2012; LaLonde 1986).

The example of whether a training programme for public managers (independent variable X, measured using a dummy variable with the values X = 1 trained, X = 0 not trained) improves their managerial performance (dependent variable Y, say a continuous measure of performance) illustrates these difficulties. Theory might suggest that training improves performance with an empirical implication that trained managers will have higher performance, other things being equal. To test this hypothesis and estimate the size of the effect, researchers conducting an observational study might gather survey data from a sample of public managers or from administrative data to see if they have undertaken a training programme and relate this to a measure of managerial performance. Using regression, researchers then regress Y (managerial performance) on X (trained or not) to estimate the size of the coefficient and conduct a test for a statistically significant relationship (often against the null hypothesis of no effect), with a set of control variables held constant.

In the example, however, the regression results by themselves cannot reveal if training leads to higher managerial performance. So-called omitted variable bias in the estimate of X occurs when there is a failure to include potential control variables that are correlated both with the X variable of interest (in this case, training) and the outcome variable Y (in this case, performance). This problem is very commonly found in public management research, including research on training programmes. Well-performing managers may be more inclined to take up training, so that in reality Y is causing X (Y → X). Another possibility is that more motivated managers may be more inclined to get training, so that motivation is a common cause of both X and Y. If, say, both motivation and participation in training are correlated positively with performance, failing to include motivation in the analysis leads to an upward bias in the estimated effect of training. Alternatively, the causation may flow in both ways at the same time (X←—→Y), for example, if high-performing managers may select training and yet training indeed enhances performance, a situation referred to as *simultaneity bias*. Conventional regression cannot handle reverse causation, and important common-cause variables correlated with both Y and X (such as motivation) sometimes go unmeasured, leading to omitted variable bias with their effects misattributed to the X variable (Remler and Van Ryzin 2015).

The surveys often used in observational public management research make the difficulties of using regression even more salient. Common source bias (e.g., Podaskoff et al. 2003) arising from both X (the cause) and Y (the effect) being measured by the same survey or source has been noted as particularly problematic, including studies focused on organisational performance. For example, if the same survey is used to measure perceptions of performance and administrative practices, then correlated errors (including from general attitudes towards an organization or even styles of responding to questionnaires) may produce correlations between variable that do not reflect causal relations, but rather a common method effect or factor (Favero and Bullock 2015; Jakobsen and Jensen 2015; Meier and O'Toole 2013). Because these sources of bias are difficult to observe and control for, they often produce bias in causal estimates reported in public management research.

Several more sophisticated regression and related techniques have been developed over recent decades to tackle the difficulties of establishing causal relations. For example, structural equation modelling (SEM) has sometimes been used to impose a causal order on relationships between variables. However, it is often difficult to justify empirically the causal structure imposed. The straight arrows and precise coefficients of the graphical SEM path model can risk a misleadingly strong interpretation as being more causal than the evidence allows. The timing at which measures are made can sometimes help address causation in regression-based modelling. In the example of management training, if measures of managerial performance are gathered both before and after the training, then this helps suggest that the training may have played a role. Relatedly, regression models to analyse panel data of repeated observations on the same cases (e.g., managers or organisations at different points in time) make use of information contained in such data. Temporal precedence can help establish that changes in X come before changes in Y and can be coupled with considering unit fixed effects to remove time-invariant unobserved features of units (e.g., managers) that affect Y. These factors would otherwise contribute to omitted variable bias. Whilst such models are useful for public management (e.g., they would help address the issue of differences between managers' ability that affect their performance), they have limitations, notably in not removing time-varying unobserved heterogeneity (e.g., fluctuations in managers' motivations to do their job over time).

The cautious use of appropriate regression methods remains useful in many contexts. Undertaking sensitivity analysis to see how the coefficient of an independent variable of interest is influenced by changing the controls included in a regression model can give some indication of whether findings are robust to whether particular variables are added or dropped from the model. However, researchers need always to bear in mind the possibility of omitted variable bias arising from controls they cannot include. Experiments offer a valuable alternative to relying on the analysis of observational data. As later sections of this chapter also show, the experimental method sheds light on how observational methods that are closely related to experiments, sometimes termed *natural experiments* or *quasi-experimental methods*, are useful for studying causal effects.

4.2 Experiments: Causation through Intervention

Experimental research, in contrast to observation based studies, use controlled interventions in the world. Observational studies involve researchers '*watching things happen*' and observing the outcomes of causal processes. In contrast, researchers in an experimental study intervene in the world in order to try to '*make things happen*' (Remler and Van Ryzin 2015). Figure 4.2 illustrates this logic of intervention, where I symbolises the experimental intervention or manipulation of the independent variable X, which is thought to have a causal effect on the dependent variable Y. With the management training programme, for example, the programme is an intervention aimed at providing an opportunity for managers to learn new knowledge and skills. Sometimes the intervention (I) and the independent variable X are one and the same thing, such as when the intervention is merely brief exposure to some basic image or information (and X is perceiving the image or information). But thinking about an intervention (I) on X, with the intervention separable from X, as in Figure 4.2, has some utility. In the example of the management training programme, not all managers assigned to the programme will necessarily end up attending or completing the training. So intervening to offer training (I) and being trained (X) are not the same. Some experiments use a manipulation check to see if the intended treatment has been fully applied in a way that affects the level of X.

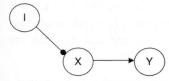

Figure 4.2: Experimental intervention on independent variable X that is a cause of dependent variable Y

Typical social science experiments not only involve an intervention or treatment, but also the random allocation of experimental units to receive treatment. In a simple two group experiment, units may be allocated either to a group of units that get the treatment or to a separate control group of units that do not. We will address the role of treatment and control groups and random allocation shortly. But it is important to note that using separate treatment and control groups contrasts with a great deal of science, both historically and even nowadays, that happens by scientists simply measuring some feature of interest, intervening in the world by manipulating a causal factor, and then observing the result by measuring the feature again to detect change. For example, in natural science, the chemist adds one element or compound to another, then notes the reaction. This kind of basic before-after study is fundamental to much work in these sciences – and indeed to much early scientific management research, as Chapter 3 discussed. However, in many contexts, before-after change does not provide sufficient evidence to draw conclusions about causal effects. Researchers often do not know what would have happened had they not intervened in a group – the *counterfactual* – especially where human behaviour or institutions are involved.[1] For example, in the case of management training, managers may change in lots of ways during a period of training (as typically training programmes take some time) and these changes, for example in motivation, ongoing work experience, or in other aspects of the organisation itself, may be confounded with the direct effect of the training.

There is a further difference between much experimentation in natural science and experiments in social contexts, including public management. In best operating natural science experiments, the units being experimented on are in effect identical, such as being composed of particular elements in a chemistry experiment. In laboratory settings, scientists can take care with these units to make sure that they are not contaminated by the presence of other elements or compounds. However, in the social world, the units that are allocated to experimental groups are not identical; they differ in lots of subtle ways that are difficult to remove or even measure. This means that the units are

---

[1] We extend the discussion of the counterfactual way of thinking about causation, and its application to experimental methods in the following section but set out the intuition here.

not fully interchangeable between being put in treatment or control groups. In the example of public managers, people have differences of personality, motivation, ability, skills, or experience.[2]

Random allocation of an experimental unit to treatment or control groups is undertaken to help address these issues. A simple form of random allocation assigns treatments such that every unit has the same probability of being treated or not, such as by the flip of a coin. In a two-group experiment about management training, with $D = 1$ treatment (training) and $D = 0$ control (no training) groups, random allocation makes the groups *statistically equivalent*. This means that the groups are the same as each other prior to getting the treatment, apart from variation that occurs by chance.[3] Public managers that are allocated to treatment are a random subset of the broader set of public managers. The essential elements of the basic two-group experimental approach are summarised in Figure 4.3. First, units (e.g., managers) are randomly assigned to a treatment and to control groups, which by definition are at least

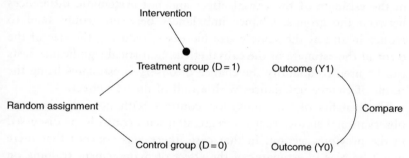

Figure 4.3: Experiment with a treatment and control group

---

[2] This is one reason why experiments with individuals typically describe them as experimental subjects or participants rather than units. For the exposition of experimental methods, using the term *units* is easiest because experiments can be about not only individuals, but also places, organizations, or other kinds of units.

[3] Random allocation of units within a sample to treatment or control groups is separate from random sampling to obtain the sample from a population. Random sampling from a population is used to make inferences about a general population based on having taken a random sample from it. Random allocation of treatment in an experiment can be carried out on a sample that has been taken at random from a general population or can be performed on samples obtained in other ways, such as a convenience sample.

statistically equivalent. Next, an intervention is applied to units (e.g., managers) in the treatment group. The intuition of the need for a control group is that it helps establish the counterfactual: what would have happened to those in the treatment group, absent the intervention. The final element is measurement of the outcome of interest and comparison between the treatment and control groups.

In the example of the training programme, the random allocation of the programme implies that treatment allocation bears no systematic relationship with public managers' observed or unobserved attributes. Application of this procedure rules out, for example, more able or motivated managers disproportionately selecting themselves, or perhaps being selected by their superiors, into the programme. Random allocation removes the risk of bias in estimates of the causal effect of treatment arising from these and other factors. By chance in the allocation process, however, there could still be differences in the characteristics of those who are allocated to the treatment and control groups in ways that affect the outcome. However, the chance imbalances can be considered random error in the estimate of the causal effect and not systematic differences between the groups. Chance imbalances between groups tend to reduce in size as the sample size increases, reducing the size of the error of the estimate of the causal effect. Statistical significance tests can be used to quantify the chance of observed estimates being the result of chance imbalances with a null of no true effect.

The benefits of randomisation contrast with non-experimental, observational studies that use regression with controls, as discussed in the previous section. In that case, there was concern that there might be bias in estimates of the effect of management training on managerial performance, including from more able or motivated managers who have higher managerial performance selecting in to do the training and only inadequate controls for these factors. Matching methods are sometimes used in observational studies to estimate causal effects using observational data, for example, by setting up treated and control groups with similar covariate distributions (Stuart 2010). However, choosing well-matched groups is difficult when many variables need to be balanced simultaneously. Moreover, it is difficult to anticipate and thus match on all of the observable and unobservable factors that could influence the allocation of treatment or outcomes.

4.3 Counterfactuals and the Potential Outcomes Framework

The logic of causal inference and benefits of the use of experiments as a method can be considered more formally within the counterfactual approach to thinking about causation. This approach to causation focuses attention on states of affairs in different possible worlds and allows the formulation of precise counterfactual research questions about these states (Holland 1986; Morgan and Winship 2015; Rubin 1974). The question of does X cause Y, and if so how large is the effect, is restated as the question: if individuals with a certain value of X had instead had a different value of X, how much would their value for Y have changed? In this framework, individuals have *potential outcomes* on Y for each value of X, even though in reality at a specific point in time and space they are exposed to only one value of X. The potential outcomes not then realised for individuals are thus *counterfactuals*.

In the counterfactual approach, the key idea is to think of all individuals of interest as having potential outcomes for Y under the different states of the world that are denoted by different values of the causal variable X. For a binary case of two distinct states of the world, individuals' potential outcomes would be Y^1 in one state of having the causal factor X present or Y^0 in the other state of not having X present (as shown in the columns in Table 4.1).

Turning to the actual state of the world, individuals cannot be exposed to both distinct states of the world (causal factor X present and X absent) at the same time. Using the language of experimentation, the actual exposure to the state of the world where X is present is referred to as being exposed to the treatment, labelled D in Table 4.1. In the example of an experiment about the effects of management training, the treatment is a management training programme. Treatment takes the values of D = 1 if individuals are actually exposed

Table 4.1: *Potential outcomes and differing actual exposure to treatment: implications for what researchers can see*

	Potential outcome Y^1	Potential outcome Y^0
Exposure to treatment (D = 1)	*Y is seen by researchers*	*Counterfactual (Y not seen)*
Control (Non-exposure to treatment) (D = 0)	*Counterfactual (Y not seen)*	*Y is seen by researchers*

to treatment, and D = 0 if they are not exposed. For example, assuming effective treatment, being exposed to management training (D = 1) makes the individual trained (which we can write as X = 1). Someone not exposed to the treatment (D = 0), not being exposed to the training programme (D = 0), makes an individual untrained (X =0).

Focusing on Table 4.1, all public managers have potential outcomes for their managerial performance when they are in the casual state of having had a management training programme/being trained (Y^1) or not having had a management training program/not trained (Y^0). However, Table 4.1 also shows how these potential outcomes relate to whether individuals are actually treated (i.e., trained X = 1 when D = 1), or actually are not treated (i.e., not trained X = 0 when D = 0). Table 4.1 shows the difficulty for empirical researchers to work out the causal effect from what they are able to see.

The *individual-level causal effect* is the individual's potential outcome in that state minus his or her potential outcome in the other state, calculated as $Y_i^1 - Y_i^0$ for an individual *i*.[4] The fundamental problem of causal inference is that researchers see the potential outcome of the state in which the causal factor is present only for those individuals who are actually exposed to the treatment (this can be expressed as seeing Y_i^1 if $D_i = 1$). In the training programme example, this means they see the outcome of managerial performance for the causal state of being trained only for public managers who are actually trained. Similarly, researchers see the potential outcome of not having the causal factor present only for those individuals who are actually not exposed to the treatment (expressed as Y_i^0 if $D_i = 0$). Researchers only see the potential outcome causal state for the treatment people are actually exposed to, and this idea can be expressed as:

$$Y_i = D_i Y_i^1 + (1 - D_i) Y_i^0$$

Thus, when an individual's $D_i = 1$, then Y_i^0 is unobserved; and when an individual's $D_i = 0$, then Y_i^1 is unobserved, as shown in Table 4.1. Because researchers cannot observe all potential outcomes – in other words, because individuals cannot be in a treated and not treated state at the same time – individual-level causal effects cannot be calculated from the data. For every individual, one portion of the information

---

[4] Alternative ways of considering individual-level causal effects are also possible, such as the ratio of the potential outcomes.

needed for the calculation is always missing; these missing data points are the counterfactuals (Holland 1986; Morgan and Winship 2015).

The problem of missing data is also a difficulty for attempting to calculate the Average Treatment Effect (ATE) of the causal factor. The ATE is the amount the outcome would change on average, if every subject were to go from being untreated to being treated (e.g., if every public manager were to go from being untrained to being trained under the programme). Whilst individuals may have different treatment effects, the ATE is the average of the individual-level effects and is calculated as the sum of the individual treatment effects (i.e., the difference between their two potential outcomes) divided by the number of subjects. Restating this definition:

$$ATE = \frac{1}{N} \sum_{i=1}^{N} (Y_i^1 - Y_i^0).$$

Because of the fundamental problem of causal inference, as we have seen, estimating the ATE with this formula is not possible using data from every individual in both states because researchers do not observe both treated and untreated potential outcomes at the same time for any particular individual.

Experiments with random allocation of units, for example to a treatment group or control group, provide a way to address the problem. Random allocation of units makes the two groups statistically equivalent before treatment is applied. For example, public managers that are allocated to treatment in this way are a random subset of the broader set of public managers. This allocation method makes the expected potential outcome among treated public managers the same as the expected potential outcome for the overall set of public managers. The data from the treatment group can be used to inform researchers about the potential outcome of those in the control group if they had instead been exposed to the treatment. The same logic of random allocation applies to those who are not treated but are in the control group. The control group outcome values can be used to estimate the potential outcomes of those in the treatment group if instead they had been in the control group. This design allows the average treatment effect to be estimated as a parameter using a *difference in means estimator* from the data simply by subtracting the mean of the outcome for the control group from the mean of the outcome for the treatment group.[5] We address issues about the analysis of data from more complex experiments in later sections.

4.4 Variations in the Design of Experiments

Experiments often involve more complex designs than the simple random allocation of units to treatment or control groups. There are many possibilities, but this section focuses on some commonly used variants: using different timing for measuring outcomes (including before as well as after treatment), different levels or dosages of a treatment, testing multiple treatments (or factors) and their interaction, and different forms of randomisation. An extensive literature on experimental designs for the social sciences covers these and other variants in more detail (e.g., Brown and Melamed 1990; Gerber and Green 2012; Kirk 2012; Shadish, Cook, and Campbell 2002).

Many experiments involve only a *posttest* – a measurement of the outcome after the intervention. For example, often in studies of perception or judgment, such as work on the framing of government performance metrics (see Chapter 12 on citizens' use of performance information), there is often only a final judgment after exposure to the performance report (which is framed in different ways). This approach can be necessary in order to avoid priming or in other ways affecting experimental participants' response to the treatment. In other experiments, it makes sense to capture a baseline or pretest measurement of the outcome, before the intervention, as well as a posttest. This approach allows estimation of changes within individuals and reduces error in estimates from baseline heterogeneity. For example, James and Van Ryzin's (2017) study of motivated reasoning about how citizens judge the performance of the Affordable Care Act (Obamacare), in response to being shown performance indicators, used measures of perceptions of the programme's performance both before and after exposure to the information. Change in perceptions was measured for each participant and these were compared across different treatment groups. When the experimenter is interested in longer-term effects, the posttest itself can be repeated, for example, to assess decline

---

[5] Using expectations notation (with E[.] denoting the operator from probability theory because the outcomes are considered to be random variables), the $ATE = E[Y_i^1] - E[Y_i^0]$.

Table 4.2: *Measurement designs (where X is the treatment and O an observation of the outcome)*

	Posttest only	Pre-post	Multiple posttests	Time series
Treatment:	X O	O X O	X O ... O	O O O X O O O
Control:	O	O O	O ... O	O O O O O O

in the effect of a treatment over time. It is possible to compare a *time-series* of observations before and after the treatment, which, for example, may be facilitated by there being regular administrative data about a public organisation. Table 4.2 summarizes these various measurement designs.

Experiments can also involve multiple treatment groups, sometimes to assess the effect of variation in the intensity or dosage of a treatment, so-called *dose-response design*. An example is a study in Van Ryzin and Riccucci's chapter in this volume (Chapter 14) on representative bureaucracy; they report an experiment in which the number female (versus male) names in a description of an agency was varied: no of female names (0%), half female names (50%), all female names (100%). Indeed, their results show a monotonically increasing willingness to cooperate, on the part of women in the study, as the names become increasingly female. Multiple treatment groups can also be used to compare the outcomes of several treatments, which may be important for examining the empirical expectations of theory. For example, as discussed in Chapter 17 in this volume on responses to public service performance, a study by James and colleagues (2016) used four treatments to examine citizens' blame of politicians for a hypothetical failing public service under different information cues about the structure of service delivery. The four treatments enabled cues about delegated delivery to public mangers and contracted out service delivery to a private firm to be compared both with a no information cue and one where politicians explicitly noted their role in managing delivery. The study found that delegation to public managers, but not contracting out, reduced blame compared to the cue in which politicians were involved in management.

Experiments can test two or more distinct treatments, or factors, at once, along with their interaction, which may itself be of interest.

Table 4.3: *Factorial design (2 × 2)*

	Treatment (Factor) A	
Treatment (Factor) B	Group 1: Control	Group 2: A only
	Group 3: B only	Group 4: Both A and B

The most basic version of this type of *factorial design* is the 2 × 2 factorial experiment with four treatment groups, as shown in Table 4.3. For example, Chapter 17 on citizen and users' responses to service failure describes an experiment conducted by Jilke, Van Ryzin, and Van de Walle (2015). They studied the effects of service failure within public service markets by manipulating two factors at once: service failure (versus no failure), and the number of alternative service providers available (few versus many). Their parameter of interest was the interaction between both factors, asking whether people who experience a severe service failure and are simultaneously exposed to many alternative public service providers become less likely to switch away from their current service provider. They found that increasing provider choice reduced individuals' likelihood of switching away from a failing provider by about 10 percentage points.

Another dimension of variation in experimentation is in the form of randomisation, which can go beyond simple random allocation. In *block random allocation* the people or experimental units are split into sub-groups (blocks) and the random allocation is used within each block, creating in a sense a set of mini-experiments, one within each block. This method may be used to reduce variability in the sample, for example, to avoid the risk of people with particularly high or low values on a variable by chance disproportionately ending up in one group. It also makes sure that certain subgroups participate in the experiment and are available for analysis by ensuring enough of certain subgroups are in treatment and control groups to enable statistical analysis. Returning to the public management training example, blocks might be defined on the basis of the length of time the managers had worked for the organisation prior to the experiment being conducted. This might be done to enable subgroup analysis of the effect of training for new, established, and long-serving managers.

Cluster randomisation involves treatments being given to groups or clusters rather than individuals, for example, classrooms randomized to a new curriculum rather than individual students. Sometimes this method is required because individuals cannot be separately allocated to treatments, for example, students in a school or individuals in a household. In the case of the management training programme, the training might be provided at different sites of a public organisation for groups of managers at each site rather than separately to individual managers. In such an experiment, the sites (clusters), not the individuals, would be randomly allocated, and thus all of the individuals in each site would receive the same treatment. But a note of caution: the success of cluster randomisation in terms of achieving statistical equivalence is influenced by the number of clusters. If an experiment with only a small number of clusters is involved, the treatment and control groups can end up with large differences that make estimating causal effects with precision difficult.

4.5 The Analysis of Data from Experiments

One of the strengths of an experiment and a key to its probative force – especially compared to studies that rely on complex statistical analysis with debatable assumptions, or case studies where the research process can be difficult to ascertain – is the relative simplicity and transparency of the method, data, and analysis. This relative simplicity is especially found when a well-designed experiment is successfully implemented because the research design rather than ex-post statistical analysis has done most of the work in helping researchers estimate causal effects. Experimental estimates, for example of the average treatment effect, are uncertain because of the chance imbalances between groups arising from the random allocation of experimental units to these groups. However, random allocation of treatments enables statistical techniques to be used to test hypotheses, for example, comparing a treatment effect with a null of no effect, or to identify a range of values within which the treatment effect falls at a particular confidence level.

The use of statistical techniques requires that researchers pay attention to the statistical power of the tests used. Power is the probability of detecting an effect, given that there is an effect of a given magnitude.

In a statistical test run on data from an experiment, power often refers to the probability that the experimenter will reject the null hypothesis of no treatment effect when the alternative hypothesis (e.g., about a positive average treatment effect) is true. In an experiment with treatment and control groups, in a situation where there is a true treatment effect of a given magnitude, the power is the probability of finding a difference of this magnitude between the two groups. For example, power of 0.9 means that, if a difference of a given magnitude exists and the experiment is conducted many times, 90 per cent of the experiments run would find a statistically significant difference between the treatment and control groups; 10 per cent of the experiments run would not, even though there really is a true effect. Experiments need to have sufficient power to detect an effect when it is there and this is influenced, in part, by sample size. Deciding sample size requires knowledge of the magnitude of the expected effect size and choice of a desired level of power (most recommendations for power fall between 0.8 and 0.9). The initial estimate of the expected effect size can sometimes be derived from the findings of prior studies on the topic that can act as a guide.

However, researchers must also consider other factors affecting statistical power, especially the implications of experimental design, for example, of using cluster or block randomisation (Gerber and Green 2012: 51–93; Murphy et al. 2014).

Experimental results should generally report means and standard deviations of all experimental groups on the outcome variable prior to any additional analysis. Usually, a next step is to give an estimate of an effect size with associated confidence interval. A simple comparison of means between groups, with associated tests of significance, can often provide sufficient evidence to test a hypothesis from a theory. A basic two-sample procedure (such as a t-test for independent means, or z-test or chi-square for proportions) may well be sufficient. Results can be presented graphically, demonstrating the magnitude of the difference with a bar or line graph, and confidence intervals used to represent statistical variability.

Reporting effect sizes from experiments with confidence intervals is particularly important so that findings can be incorporated in reviews of evidence on particular topic areas. In addition, researchers often want to generalize findings from an experimental sample to a broader population. For example, a large random sample from a well-defined population with full compliance with treatment makes an estimate based on simple comparisons of means or proportions an appropriate estimate for broader populations. More generally, it is always important to think about how characteristics of the sample used in an experiment relate to those of the population to which some kind of inference is being made.

In cases where the experiment is more complicated in design, including block or cluster randomisation, or the implementation of the experiment was problematic, more sophisticated methods may be required. This is especially an issue in the case of field experiments, in which compliance with the treatment, attrition, or other difficulties of implementation are more likely to occur than in the laboratory. Gerber and Green (2012) pay particular attention to discussing some of the statistical methods that can be used when data from experiments reflect more complex designs or problems of implementation.

The use of regression can be appropriate for analysing data from experiments (e.g., using a dummy independent variable coded for treatment and control). However, the use of control variables, typically referred to as *covariates* in the experimental tradition, can be unnecessary and can even mislead. One justification sometimes given for the use of control variables is covariate imbalance reflected in statistically significant differences between treatment and control group on background characteristics or other factors. A reason for this (and an imbalance that is statistically significant and substantively very large may give a hint of this possibility) could be that the random assignment procedure failed to be implemented properly, which renders the study more like a quasi-experiment rather than a true randomised experiment. In that case, control variables (covariates) might be used, for example, to try and model selection into treatment to try and address potential selection bias. Of course, the better solution is to get the randomisation right to begin with. The other reason for covariate imbalance is the fact that, even with proper random assignment (and assuming a standard 0.05 significance level), about 1 in 20 covariates will turn out to be statistically different just by chance. With random assignment, in other words, some covariate imbalance is to be expected. But should you adjust for these chance differences? Statistician David Freedman (2008) argues that covariate adjustment is not justified in the analysis of randomised experiments, and simpler methods are to be preferred. One argument for the use of covariates is statistical precision: using covariates can reduce standard errors and thereby enhance statistical power. But much depends on how strongly the covariates are related to the outcome or dependent variable; if the relationship is weak, not much is to be gained from controlling for that variable. On the other hand, a strong relationship with the independent variable makes statistical adjustment for a covariate open to biasing the results (by attributing some of the treatment effect to the covariate imbalance). Freedman's preference for unadjusted estimates also helps transparency and avoids the dangers of specification search (Lin 2013), which in some cases could even make the statistical significance of a treatment effect dependent on the inclusion of otherwise arbitrary covariates. Our suggestion is that simpler analysis should always be done – and reported – before covariate adjustment, which should only be used with a clear justification and awareness of limitations.

In a factorial design, such as the kind of 2 × 2 factorial experiment shown in Table 4.3, the analysis of the *interaction effect* is often one of the aims of the study. Researchers ask: what are the *main effects* of each treatment (factor) – and, moreover, is there an interaction – (a larger, or smaller effect) – when the two factors are combined? The traditional approach for a quantitative outcome is two-way *analysis of variance* (ANOVA). Having their statistical training based in regression, however, many public management researchers remain unfamiliar with this approach. ANOVA tests the statistical significance of the two *main effects*, along with the significance of the *interaction effect*. In Table 4.3, the main effects would be the comparison of column means (for Factor A) or the row means (for Factor B). ANOVA does not produce coefficients (the outputs are sums of squares and F statistics), so it is often accompanied by descriptive statistics, such as a graph or table of the actual group means.

Factorial experiments can be analysed with multiple regression instead of ANOVA, using dummy variables (coded 0 or 1) for each factor and an interaction of the two. But there can be a problem with this dummy-variable regression approach: the resulting regression coefficients of the treatment variables within interaction models are *simple effects*, not main effects, and the results will not match the ANOVA unless they are properly coded. Public management researchers should be aware of the general problem, however, and use dummy variable regression with understanding and not just out of habit. Using descriptive statistics and either ANOVA or contrast-coded treatment dummies may be a better option in many cases. Wendorf (2004) provides a more comprehensive discussion and illustrations of these coding issues in regression and their relationship to ANOVA.

Whilst the focus on an experimental investigation is often on average treatment effects, researchers are sometimes interested in variation in treatment effects. Such *heterogeneous treatment effects* can be found with variation by subgroups. Indeed, theory would often lead researchers to expect some people to react more or less to a treatment than others. The average treatment effect for a subgroup is often called a *conditional average treatment effect*. The variation across subgroups can be analysed in several ways. One approach is simply to subset the data and analyse the relevant groups separately. Another approach, which can sometimes have more statistical power, is to estimate interaction effects between the treatment and a dummy variable for the subgroup of interest. The interaction effects show the differences between the conditional average treatment effects of subgroups. For example, with gender as a subgroup, analysis has a 2 (treatment/control) × 2 (male/female) structure. Like a factorial experiment, the data can be analysed using ANOVA, or regression with dummy variables. Of course, there may be more than two categories for some subgroups or even continuous variables of interest (such as age). There are many possibilities, but a key issue is that subgroup analyses or interactions should be specified in advance, if possible, or at least be limited by plausible theory to just a few important subgroups. One should certainly not search for significance in the data by testing all possible subgroups or interactions, then report on what passes the usual 0.05 threshold of statistical significance as being an important difference in treatment effect. This would risk becoming just an exercise in capitalizing on chance, rather than uncovering substantive causal relationships.

This problem of multiple comparisons can also occur if one collects multiple outcome measures (such as 20 different measures of performance). Assuming a 0.05 significance level, indeed, it is likely one measure of performance will exhibit statistical significance just by chance. Gerber and Green (2012: 300) suggest using the *Bonferroni correction* to address the multiple comparisons problem. This approach divides the respective *p-value* through the number of significance tests that are conducted. However, this adjustment has been criticized as too conservative and, therefore, alternative forms of adjustments have been proposed, such as the Holm correction (Holm

1979) or the Benjamini-Hochberg correction (Benjamini and Hochberg 1995). Yet this does not remedy the threat of fishing and underreporting of all measures that have been collected/tested. Therefore, a well-specified *pre-analysis plan* may help greatly to deal with the multiple testing problem by outlining the measures to be collected, the number of comparisons to be conducted and how analysts plan to adjust *p-values*. This transparency helps boost the credibility of the results.

4.6 Dealing with Violations of Experimental Designs

We focus here on some of the main ways in which the key assumptions of experimental designs can be violated in their implementation, which has implications for how data from experiments should be analysed. One assumption is that the randomisation of treatment is implemented. In the case of simple random allocation, the treatment allocation needs to be independent of participants' potential outcomes, a condition that is satisfied if a random procedure, such as the flip of a coin, is used and the allocation is not compromised by those implementing treatment. For example, those training public managers should stick to the random allocation and not choose to whom the training is delivered on some other basis, for example, using their own assessment of managers who might particularly benefit. Two further assumptions are that, first, potential outcomes must respond solely to having a clear treatment, not to the allocation process or any by-products. For example, a public manager being allocated to training should not trigger some kind of compensatory help for public managers allocated to the control, perhaps to try and make up for not being given the full training. Second, the potential outcomes of a particular experimental unit need to remain stable regardless of which other units happen to be treated (also called the *stable unit treatment value assumption*). So, for example, the outcomes for a public manager treated or not treated by training should not be affected by the treatment or control status of other managers in the organisation. However, in practice the potential outcomes of a unit may be affected not only by its own allocation to treatment, but by the treatments that other units receive. For example, there could be communication effects, such as where managers undertaking treatment talk with those who are supposedly in the control group, thereby sharing some of the relevant knowledge or skills. Gerber and

Green (2012: 253–87) discuss at greater length such issues of 'interference' between experimental units and some ways of addressing this issue.

We now turn to some issues that can arise in the implementation of experiments that have important implications for data analysis. Severe problems of implementation can even mean that the experiment fails to deliver much useable data at all, and thus considering the potential for these problems in the design stage can help researchers take steps to avoid them. Differences in type of experiment according to laboratory, more naturalistic field settings, or intervention embedded in a survey can affect the degree of risk, especially insofar as they reduce researchers' control over implementation. Issues characteristic of particular domains are discussed in later chapters, but this section sets out some of the key problems as they apply in general within experimentation.

Attrition

The difference between the means of treatment and control group can only be used as an unbiased estimator of the average treatment effect if researchers have data on outcomes for all the experimental units that were allocated to treatment or control, unless data is missing at random. *Attrition* refers to people or units dropping out of the experiment, so that outcome data is missing. When systematically related to potential outcomes, attrition can mean that those left in a group are no longer a random sample of the original units subject to the experiment. If so, the comparison of group means may not be an unbiased estimator of the average treatment effect. There are many reasons why outcome measures may be missing. In the example of training public managers, if those who were treated with the training programme left the organisation before their managerial performance could be assessed, then the treated managers whose outcome measures are used in the calculation of the mean outcome may not reflect the original set of managers. The direction of any bias is uncertain and dependent on context. For example, it might be that more able managers in the treatment group get job offers and drop out of the study, which might lead to downward bias in the estimate of the treatment effect of training on managerial performance. If missing observations are independent of potential outcomes, on the other hand, then comparing group means will still produce unbiased estimates. Attrition can be a particular problem for field experiments, as discussed in Chapter 5, because it can be more difficult to gather outcome data in the field than in the laboratory (Gerber and Green 2012: 211–47). Methods to address attrition are also discussed in the more general literature on missing data (Graham 2012).

Treatment Non-compliance

The term *compliance* is used to denote whether the assigned treatment was taken up or fully received by an experimental unit. With full compliance, all those in the treatment group get the treatment and no unit in the control group receives the treatment. On this basis, non-compliance can involve those in the treatment group not getting the treatment, so-called failure to treat, or those in the control group getting the treatment, or both of these situations.

Looking first at failure to treat, it can be that the treatment does not reach or get taken up by all of the intended targets in the treatment group. Whilst compliance or non-compliance is often analysed in binary terms, it is important to note that it is sometimes a matter of judgement if a treatment is partially applied, for example, if a public manager attended some but not all of a training programme. One measure of interest in the case of non-compliance is the average *intent to treat effect* (ITT) on the potential outcome Y, which measures the average effect of experimental allocation on outcomes. This is the effect of allocation regardless of the actual treatment units receive. In an experiment with full compliance, the allocated treatment is the same as the treatment the participants in the experiments get and the ITT is the same as the average treatment effect. The ITT measure is useful for public management research because, as a design science, researchers are often interested in whether attempting a policy has an effect, regardless of whether non-compliance occurred. For example, management training might be offered to managers, after all, a public organisation can typically only offer training to managers, not force them fully to complete it. The interest maybe in the treatment effect of the offer to train regardless of whether people completed the training.

Often researchers will not be satisfied with the ITT, however, because they want to know the average treatment effect of the treatment as fully implemented, for example, the effect of managers actually completing the training programme. The *complier average causal effect* (CACE), which is also sometimes referred to as the *local average treatment effect* (LATE), is the average treatment effect for the subset of participants in the experiment who comply with the treatment when allocated to it. Provided some assumptions are satisfied, including that no one in the control gets the treatment, the CACE can be estimated by taking the average intent to treat effect and dividing it by the proportion of participants who are treated in the event that they are allocated to the treatment group. The ITT and the CACE converge as experiments move toward full compliance. There is a more extensive discussion of non-compliance, including the case of when participants in the control group also get the treatment, in Gerber and Green (2012: 131–209).

An illustrative example of issues around the compliance with experimental treatments in public management can be found in a recent study by Grimmelikhuijsen and Klijn (2015). They studied the effect of judicial transparency on citizens' trust, in which the treatment was a phone call encouraging participants to watch a Dutch television series about the courts. The treatment group got the encouragement and, compared to the control group, more watched the series – but not all. Moreover, some of those in the control watched the series anyway, despite not being encouraged to do so. This is not an unusual issue in research in field contexts. In public health studies of exercise or diet, the treatment group is encouraged to be active or to eat healthy food – but not all comply, and some in the controls are active or healthy eaters on their own. How the analysis of causal effects is undertaken depends on what researchers want to know in such situations.

The ITT analysis is relatively straightforward: simply compare the treatment and control groups, as randomly assigned, for example, by comparing means for those who got the telephone encouragement to watch and those who did not. In other words, analyse the data as you would any other experiment – regardless of how much compliance there was with the actual treatment. This gives the effect of the encouragement (the ITT) as such. But of course, knowing the causal effect of the treatment itself matters too – How much did actually watching the televisions series change people's trust of the courts? – which is the CACE (or LATE). There is both a simple and a more sophisticated way of doing this kind of analysis, as alluded to earlier. The simple way assumes that, since the control group mirrors the treatment, an equal proportion of those in the control would similarly have not complied with the treatment, say one half. If the ITT effect is, say, 20 points, then we divide this effect by 0.5 to get an effect $- 20 / 0.5 = 40$. We got a 20-point boost when only half the treatment group complied, so we would get a 40-point boost if they had all complied. This approach obviously comes with the strong assumption that an equal proportion of people in control and treatment condition did not comply, and we would need to know its exact overall proportion as well. The more sophisticated and also arguably more robust approach is to use an instrumental variable (IV) regression analysis, with intention-to-treat (randomly assigned) as the instrument for the treatment itself as taken up (see Gerber and Green 2012 for more on IV regression of experiments). This is what Grimmelikhuijsen and Klijn (2015) did: they used the random assignment to receive encouragement to predict the likelihood of someone watching the television series, then used the predicted likelihood of watching the series to estimate its causal effect on trust. Their results showed that the TV programme did have positive effects on trust, especially among those with only a modest level of prior knowledge of the judiciary.

4.7 Conclusions: Developing Experiments for Public Management Research

It is important that experimental treatments are validly linked to the public management theoretical constructs to be tested with a clear logic of translation from concept to intervention. Experiments are of particular benefit where interventions are possible, and it is important to acknowledge the limitations of the method where experimental manipulation is not possible. However, interventions can be undertaken in many topic areas of interest to public management researchers. Sometimes theories may entail several elements thought to have causal effects and a series of experiments can tease out the effects of different elements on outcomes of interest. For example, in the management training programme, there are several causal elements that help improve managerial performance: the specific materials used in the training, modes of interacting with participants, the form of participation of the managers, and the skills and experiences of trainers. These factors are potentially separable such that researchers might reflect on initial results and think about how different aspects of the training programme have effects. A series of experiments might vary different aspects of the training (e.g., assessing different combinations of training materials and modes of interacting with participants). Experiments can examine mediating effects where the presence of an additional factor is necessary to complete a causal relationship between X and Y. In this case, varying X causes variations in the mediating factor, which in turn causes changes in Y. In management training, it is highly likely that such an intervention acts on skills and knowledge, which in turn affect managerial performance. Experiments can examine moderating effects that can promote or inhibit the action of X on Y. For example, the training programme may be expected to be more effective for managers with higher levels of motivation than those with lower levels. Whilst motivation itself might be difficult to manipulate experimentally, some form of incentives or social recognition of effort might be suitable interventions to consider forms of moderation.

However, sometimes in contrast to the use of experiments to inform theory, public management researchers may be interested more narrowly in 'what works', particularly when responding to requests for assistance from public organisations. When interest focuses on evaluating the effects of a particular policy or practice, it may sometimes be sufficient to assess the programme as it is, rather than seeking to dismantle it into constituent elements that theory suggests are important. In this mode of working, the experimental method can be used randomly to allocate the programme, for example, the whole package of training in an existing programme, as a treatment to individuals. Outcomes can then be compared with those found for individuals in a control condition.

Whilst experiments share fundamental features in addressing questions about causal effects, it is common to distinguish field, survey, and laboratory experimental types. These types are not fully distinct from each other; instead, they reflect particular approaches to experimentation. Chapter 5 describes field experiments that try to combine the internal validity of randomised experimental treatment with external validity to real-world contexts. Field experiments typically use participants directly relevant to researchers' interests (as opposed to generic student subjects), authentic rather than abstract treatments, and real contexts and outcomes, with participants not always knowing that they are in an experiment. A field experiment could randomly allocate a realistic programme of training to public managers in one group of public organisations, but not another group, and use measures of managerial performance of direct contextual relevance to that type of organisation. Chapter 6 discusses survey experiments that involve randomization of question wording, text, images or other information in a survey instrument that is administered to a sample, often representing a larger population. Studying the effects of a training programme on managers would be difficult in a survey experiment. It might be possible, however, to present a treatment group of survey respondents (say, a sample of managers) with some basic management training materials, in the form of a short reading or perhaps even a short training video, embedded in an online survey, and then ask them to make a set of hypothetical management decisions. Chapter 7 examines laboratory experiments where they are carried out in specialist facilities, enabling strong control over treatments administered and the environment in which they are given. These features facilitate careful measurement of behavioural and even physiological responses. Students or other convenience samples are typically used and the experimental tasks are often artificial. Continuing with the example of a management training programme, this might be tested in a laboratory by giving public managers (or students acting as public managers) specific training materials or a training video in a laboratory and then asking them to make a set of hypothetical management decisions. As the subsequent methodological chapters discuss, and as the substantive contributions in Part III illustrate, public management research can take advantage of these different types of experiment to exploit their strengths, and evidence from experiments can be integrated with findings from observational research.

References

Angrist, J. D. and Pischke, J. S. 2010. 'The credibility revolution in empirical economics: how better research design is taking the con out of econometrics', *Journal of Economic Perspectives*, 24(2): 3–30.

Angrist, J. D. and Pischke, J. S. 2014. *Mastering 'Metrics: The Path from Cause to Effect*. Princeton, NJ: Princeton University Press.

Benjamini, Y. and Hochberg, Y. 1995. 'Controlling the false discovery rate: a practical and powerful approach to multiple testing', *Journal of the Royal Statistical Society. Series B (Methodological)*, 289–300.

Brown, S. R. and Melamed, L. E. 1990. *Experimental Design and Analysis*. (Quantitative Applications in the Social Sciences, No. 74). London: Sage Publications.

Campbell, D. T. and Stanley, J. C. 1966. *Experimental and Quasi-experimental Designs for Research*. Chicago: Rand-McNally.

Favero, N. and Bullock, J. 2015. 'How (not) to solve the problem: an evaluation of scholarly responses to common source bias', *Journal of Public Administration Research and Theory*, 25(1): 285–308.

Freedman, D. 2008. 'On regression adjustment to experimental data', *Advances in Applied Mathematics*, 40(2): 180–93.

Gerber, A. S. and Green, D. P. 2012. *Field Experiments: Design, Analysis and Interpretation*. New York: W.W. Norton and Company.

Graham, J. W. 2012. *Missing Data: Analysis and Design*. New York: Springer.

Grimmelikhuijsen, S. and Klijn, A. 2015. 'The effects of judicial transparency on public trust: evidence from a field experiment', *Public Administration*, 93: 995–1011. doi: 10.1111/padm.12149.

Groeneveld, S., Tummers, L., Bronkhorst, B., Ashikali, T., and Van Thiel, S. 2014. 'Quantitative methods in public administration: their use and development through time', *International Public Management Journal*, 18(1): 61–86.

Guala, F. 2005. *The Methodology of Experimental Economics*, Cambridge, Cambridge University Press.

Holland, P. W. 1986. 'Statistics and causal inference'. *Journal of the American Statistical Association*, 81(396): 945–60.

Holm, S. 1979. 'A simple sequentially rejective multiple test procedure', *Scandinavian Journal of Statistics*, 6(2): 65–70.

Jakobsen, M. and Jensen, R. 2015. 'Common method bias in public management studies', *International Public Management Journal*, 18(1): 3–30.

James, O., Jilke, S., Petersen, C., and Van de Walle, S. 2016. 'Citizens' blame of politicians for public service failure: experimental evidence about blame reduction through delegation and contracting', *Public Administration Review*, 76(1): 83–93.

James, O. and Van Ryzin, G. 2015. 'Motivated reasoning about public performance: an experimental study of how citizens judge Obamacare', Paper presented to PMRA 2015 Annual Conference, University of Minnesota, Minneapolis, MN.

Jilke, S., Van Ryzin, G., and Van de Walle, A. 2015. 'Responses to decline in marketized public services: an experimental evaluation of choice-overload', *Journal of Public Administration Research and Theory*, doi: 10.1093/jopart/muv021.

Kirk, R. E. 2012. *Experimental Design: Procedures for the Behavioral Sciences: Procedures for the Behavioral Sciences*. London: Sage Publications.

LaLonde, R. J. 1986. 'Evaluating the econometric evaluations of training programs with experimental data', *The American Economic Review*, 76(4): 604–20.

Lin, W. 2013. 'Agnostic notes on regression adjustments to experimental data: Reexamining Freedman's critique', *The Annals of Applied Statistics*, 7(1): 295–318.

Meier, K. J. and O'Toole L. J. 2013. 'Subjective organizational performance and measurement error: common source bias and spurious relationships', *Journal of Public Administration Research and Theory*, 23(2): 429–56.

Morgan, S. L. and Winship, C. 2015. *Counterfactuals and Causal Inference*. 2nd Edition. Cambridge: Cambridge University Press.

Murphy, K. R., Myors, B., and Wolach, A., 2014. *Statistical Power Analysis: A Simple and General Model for Traditional and Modern Hypothesis Tests*. New York: Routledge.

Remler, D. K. and Van Ryzin, G. G. 2015. *Research Methods in Practice: Strategies for Description and Causation*. London: Sage Publications.

Rubin, D. B. 1974. 'Estimating causal effects of treatment s in randomized and non-randomized studies', *Journal of Educational Psychology*, 66, 688–701.

Shadish, W. R., Cook, T. D., and Campbell, D. T. 2002. *Experimental and Quasi-experimental Designs for Generalized Causal Inference*. Boston: Houghton Mifflin Company.

Stuart, E. A. 2010. 'Matching methods for causal inference: a review and a look forward', *Statistical Science: A Review Journal of the Institute of Mathematical Statistics*, 25(1): 1–21.

Wendorf, C. A. 2004. 'Primer on multiple regression coding: common forms and the additional case of repeated contrasts', *Understanding Statistics*, 3(1): 47–57.

5 | Field Experiments in Public Management

OLIVER JAMES, PETER JOHN AND ALICE
MOSELEY

Introduction

Field experiments, consistent with the definition of experiments developed in Chapter 4, entail the random allocation of experimental participants to different treatment conditions (e.g. treatment or control) and the measurement and comparison of outcomes. However, their 'field' component entails that the experiment is undertaken with substantial use of relevant participants, authentic treatments, a naturally occurring setting and real-world outcomes. In this way, field experiments are typically contrasted with conventional laboratory experiments that typically have a more artificial domain on these dimensions. The combination of field features and the benefits of experimentation using randomisation gives field experiments a distinctive contribution to public management research. They aspire to both internal validity of identifying causal relations within a given experimental setting and external validity of the findings to domains where the causal relations are of interest.

Field experiments can make control over treatment interventions and contextual conditions more difficult than in conventional laboratory experiments. However, an alternative of using laboratory experiments in isolation can be of limited interest to researchers unless there is a claim that the relevance of the study is very general (e.g. as being about human cognition), which is a strong claim to make for most public management research topics. In other words, seeking control in the laboratory can take researchers away from features present in their actual domain of interest, which is rarely the laboratory for its own sake. Despite the use of naturalistic, real-world domains, field experiments still contrast markedly with non-experimental observational studies where there is fully naturally occurring data and researchers do not attempt to intervene through randomly allocated treatment conditions.

The first section of this chapter defines different types of field experiment in contrast to other experimental and non-experimental methods. The term historically comes from agricultural experiments that were literally carried out in fields growing crops. This section clarifies the sometimes inconsistent use of the terminology in the literature and, in setting out the main types of field experiment, pays particular attention to the ways they differ from conventional laboratory experiments (that are discussed separately in Chapter 7). The section goes on to discuss the implications of 'field' domains for the external validity of findings and the relationship between field experiments and randomised controlled trials (RCTs), a method that has been extensively used in medicine and in the evaluation of social and economic policies. Field experiments assess theory in realistic settings such as actual public organisations and real public services, creating knowledge about theory that is also useful for public management as a design science informing practical policies and management practices.

The second section sets out the contribution that field experiments are making to understanding substantive topics in public management. Even when compared to other kinds of experiment, there are relatively few such studies in public management. However, there is an emerging movement towards more use of the method in public management, and a substantial part of this work is included in other chapters of this book. The third section addresses the challenges of using field experiments, including difficulties in implementing experimental designs in the field, working with governmental and other organisations, and distinctive ethical issues. This section suggests ways to overcome these barriers and learn from experience in related areas, especially from the use of RCTs. The fourth section concludes that field experiments should be complementary to other kinds of experimental and non-experimental method, and can make a major contribution to a broad set of topics in public management research.

5.1 Types of Field Experiment

Field experiments are often defined in contrast to conventional laboratory experiments, with the term 'field' drawing attention to the naturalistic, real-world setting of such experiments. The term 'field' reflects the historical influence of agricultural research in the development of the method which was originally used to study growing crops in fields.

Different areas of fields were allocated at random to treatment or control conditions thought to affect agricultural productivity. R. A. Fisher's article 'The Arrangement of Field Experiments' drew on his work as statistician for Rothamsted Agricultural Research Centre, and the methods were popularised by Fisher's article and subsequent book (Fisher 1926, 1935). Whilst field experiments can allocate units subject to treatment or control without random allocation (List and Metcalfe 2014), we take the use of randomisation as integral to the definition of a field experiment, consistent with Fisher's advocacy of random allocation of treatments (Gerber and Green 2012).

The 'field' aspect of an experiment denotes its naturalistic domain defined on several dimensions usually contrasted with a conventional laboratory domain. Using a distinction between internal and external validity of findings, field experiments are argued to be particularly useful not only for *internal validity*, defined as identifying a causal relation within a given experimental setting, but also for *external validity* defined as generalising from a given experiment to some other situation of interest (see Chapter 4). Some experimental research may be about finding things out about topics that apply only in the laboratory, or alternatively may be about issues that are generic and unaffected by the laboratory context, perhaps including near-universal human cognitive processes. However, external validity in the sense of relevance to domains that are not exactly like the conventional laboratory is usually something that is a central concern in public management research. The concern comes because of researchers' typical focus, to take some examples, on public managers or politicians, organisations, citizens and users and their interactions and consequent outcomes. Laboratory experiments may have external validity to these domains, but the concern to be relevant makes field experiments especially important to public management.

Rather than a simple binary distinction between field and conventional laboratory experiments, multiple dimensions help define different kinds of field experiment that vary in certain respects from each other (Gerber and Green 2012; Harrison and List 2004: 1012). These dimensions have implications for the domain to which findings from experiments refer. Harrison and List identified six main factors to determine the field context of an experiment: the nature of the subject pool (especially contrasting the participation of students – which they took as the typical conventional laboratory subject pool, with the participation of non-students), the nature of the information that the subjects bring to the task, the nature of the commodity, the nature of the task or trading rules applied, the nature of the stakes and the environment in which the subjects operate. They also noted that the presence of any one of these factors by itself typically should not automatically qualify an experiment for description as a field experiment and they are often used in combination (2004: 1011–13). Harrison and List's approach was developed for experimental economics and includes factors specifically related to market exchange (e.g. it focuses on the nature of the commodity or trading rules). It is similar to the discussion of four key dimensions defining field experiments adopted by Gerber and Green (2012: 11), who have a similar focus on the field as non-laboratory experiments. These dimensions also correspond closely to those raised by researchers advocating more use of the field approach within social psychology (Salovey and Williams-Piehota 2004). Consequently, in this discussion, we integrate the Harrison and List dimensions with those of Gerber and Green and emphasise issues of most relevance to public management. The four dimensions that we examine are:

– the nature of subjects who participate in the experiment
– the authenticity of treatments used in the experimental intervention
– the context of the experiment
– the outcomes of interest to researchers that are potentially affected by the treatments

If these four dimensions are simplified to dichotomies, this defines 16 types of experiment. However, in practice, different dimensions are typically combined in more limited ways, and the literature on field experiments suggests that some combinations tend to be particularly important in affecting the relevance of experimental findings to researchers' interests. On that basis, types of field experiment formed by combinations on two dimensions, simplified to dichotomies, are in Table 5.1. First, the subjects who participate in the experiment (generic student or non-student) and, second, the nature of the experimental intervention/treatment (abstract or authentic). The terms for the types of experiment are used by Harrison and List (2004) with the exception of the 'generic participants framed field experiment' which we draw attention to as a type. Each type can be split into further types

Table 5.1: *Types of field experiment defined by subjects participating in the experiment and the nature of the experimental treatment*

	Generic (typically student) experimental participant	Specific type of experimental participant
Abstract treatment	Conventional laboratory experiment	Artefactual field experiment
Authentic treatment	Generic participants framed field experiment	Framed field experiment (or natural field experiment where, additionally, the context entails subjects being unaware they are in an experiment)

on the other two dimensions. Context of the experiment is whether the context is a laboratory (a special research facility) or a more naturalistic environment where the activity normally occurs. Type of outcome measured refers to whether the outcomes of the experiment are measured using authentic or more abstract measures. We discuss each of these dimensions, and their implications for use of the method in public management, in turn.

Participants in the Experiment

Conventional laboratory experiments use student samples which, if the interest is in findings applying more generally beyond students, assumes that this group is suitable to the domain of interest. Sometimes this approach may be sound, such as in researching fundamental psychological cognitive processes that are supposed to apply to humans generally. However, students are often used because of their relative ease of availability to researchers or because it is the usual procedure, as has been the case in psychology over several decades and in the more recent development of experimental economics. In psychology, sometimes students are compelled to participate for credit on their courses, making their relationship a particular form of participation related to their position in a university.

The evidence about the extent to which the participation of students compared to other groups affects experimental findings is limited. Recent work has questioned some of the criticisms of using student samples (Druckman and Kam 2011). However, in the sort of settings of interest to public management researchers, the issue merits close attention. Students are likely poor equivalents to professional politicians or public managers with experience of working in these roles, although students on professional courses or with work experience may be more suitable. In experiments about citizens and service users, whilst students themselves can sometimes have both these characteristics, they typically differ from more general populations. Students tend to be disproportionately young and well educated, and there can be further self-selection of particular types of students who volunteer to participate in experiments. Students in most experiments to date typically come from Western, educated, industrialised, rich and democratic (described using the acronym 'WEIRD') societies (Henrich, Heine and Norenzayan 2010). In experimental economics, Harrison and List (2004: 1012) argue that many subjects that are the target of research differ from students on a range of variables likely to affect outcomes, including not just on obvious sociodemographic measures, but by bringing relevant information from their previous work or other experiences to the experiment which affect how they respond to interventions. Reading across this issue to public management, it is particularly salient, for example in research focused on professional public managers who often have specific training or years of work experience, or regular users of public services who may have built up long-standing patterns of interacting with service providers.

To avoid relying on the student participants of conventional laboratory experiments, non-standard subject pools (i.e. non-students) can be used, with the participants chosen according to the interests of the researcher. Harrison and List (2004) describe abstract laboratory experiments that use these subject pools as 'artefactual field experiments' (see Table 5.1). They give the example of an artefactual field experiment analysing discount rates used to value future costs and benefits by repeating a conventional lab experiment that used students with a sample of ordinary people (Harrison, Lau and Williams 2002). They used a form of laboratory experiment in the field in which people from a general population of citizens were invited to participate in the experiment. In seeking broad subject pools, researchers can use random samples taken from general populations if they seek findings about these groups. The recent interest in population-based survey experiments shows how methods from the field can blend with other kinds of experiments, notably survey experiments as discussed in Chapter 6 (see also Mutz 2011). The increased availability of samples gathered through the Internet allows the greater use of survey experiments to access samples from these populations, and crowd-sourced Internet labour markets offer an opportunity not only to recruit convenience samples, but to target specific groups. In some areas of research, the differences between findings from students and the target group of interest are likely to be important.

Authenticity of Treatment

Sometimes an experimental manipulation of interest to researchers cannot be studied effectively in the laboratory because the treatment cannot be made authentic, in the sense of being close enough to resemble the phenomenon of interest. In this case, abstract, simplified or general interventions do not capture the causal factor that researchers seek to assess. A more authentic, naturalistic and typically richer intervention is sometimes required (this dimension is summarised as a distinction between abstract and authentic treatments in Table 5.1). Elements of this authenticity include factors noted by Harrison and List (2004), who define artefactual field experiments (which, like framed field experiments, have participants who are those of interest to the researcher, typically not students) but also have a realistic commodity, task or information of the kind used by real-world subjects.

Public management research questions often require close attention to be paid to authenticity of treatment. For example an authentic treatment may require public service users to experience a service of interest, or public managers to deliver a service using different routines, which would not be adequately captured by a simplified, abstract form of treatment. The context of actual tasks may be especially influential on participants developing specific heuristics or ways of approaching tasks that cannot be replicated by abstracting from that real-world task. The nature of the stakes can also affect field responses, with consequences for payoffs often differing greatly between a laboratory (perhaps a few dollars of income in an incentivised experiment) and the field (e.g. the use of an important public service).

Context of the Experiment

The context within which participants experience an experimental intervention can influence how they receive the treatment and respond to it. In principle, the dimension of context creates further variegation within each of the types in Table 5.1. Often the focus of inquiry will require findings to be relevant to the context of real public organisations or services rather than the artificial context of the laboratory. The context of the laboratory is usually not one that is familiar to participants from their previous experience, unless they have previously participated in laboratory studies (which itself might make them unattractive to researchers if this alters their reaction to interventions and the focus of research is on general populations' reactions). The laboratory context helps control differences in subjects' experiences or interpretation of the experimental setup and treatment, reducing the risk of distortion of treatment and measurement of results. However, this context at the same time means that the treatment and its effects may have only a very specific relevance to that particular laboratory context.

In field experiments, interventions often fit into subjects' everyday life experiences and measures of attitudes, behaviour or other consequences are of real-world significance. Laboratory experimenters often actively consider whether the use of classrooms encourages role-playing behaviour, and this consideration is one reason for experimental economists' use of salient monetary rewards to motivate participants. However, without the specification of contexts of interest in a laboratory experiment, participants might adopt some referent gained through their broader day-to-day experience to make sense of the tasks in the laboratory, but this may not be known to the researcher and may limit or create uncertainty about the external validity of findings.

As part of the context, the non-obtrusive nature of many field experiments means that subjects are not aware they are participating in an experiment (Gerber and Green 2012: 10). The unobtrusiveness of the treatment is often afforded particular importance in giving relevance to experimental findings. They seem most related to the natural world without the presence of the researchers possibly interfering with its operation, which might make findings the creation of the research process such that they might not be present more generally. Harrison and List (2004) describe framed field experiments (that use natural treatments with participants who are the real-world group of interest) where subjects are not aware they are in an experiment as 'natural field experiments', as noted in Table 5.1. In laboratory experiments subjects are in a more 'artificial' environment in which they are aware of being monitored, with potentially strong effects of the way in which instructions are framed. Levitt and List (2009) argue that this especially risks more prosocial behaviours and experimenter Hawthorne effects, including attempting to please the experimenter.

The 'generic participants framed field experiment' in Table 5.1 is the same as a framed or natural field experiment but with generic, typically student, participants, not the domain-specific participants that Harrison and List (2004) emphasise in defining the framed or natural experiment types. Harrison and List do not themselves discuss the generic participants framed field type, but this type is relevant to public management insofar as generic processes, for example general cognitive psychology processes, are in play in experiments using authentic domains. For example, experiments with citizens who are given real numerical performance information about public services to inform their judgements (discussed in Chapter 12) entail generic human mental reception and processing of information. The information being given to the students makes the experiment 'field' in the sense that the treatment is authentic in using real information that is part of actual governments' performance reporting regimes, rather than giving participants abstract numbers to process. On this basis, the use of students is suitable because they share at least the fundamentals of mental processing with citizens more generally. However, researchers may need to consider differences in treatment effects between those with different education levels, age or other characteristics if differences in processing is suspected.

Outcomes Affected by Experimental Treatments

The measured outcome is a further dimension that cuts across each of the types of field experiment summarised in Table 5.1. Field experiments share the feature that the outcome is typically something that is found in a real-world public organisation or service. However, experiments vary on this dimension with some having outcomes more towards the abstract end of the spectrum whilst others are strongly authentic, for example adopting measures of performance used by public organisations themselves. Decisions about outcome measures' authenticity are often related to the same considerations that researchers use to decide on the degree of abstraction in the treatment imposed in the experiment. The broad range of outcomes used in field experiments means that a variety of measurement instruments are employed. When these instruments include surveys of participants this gives the experiment a similarity to survey experiments discussed in Chapter 6, although field experiments always emphasise dimensions of the field domain. Field experiments sometimes make use of measures of behaviour that come from monitoring by researchers. For example, in the context of public services, outcomes of interest may include users' political voice to managers or politicians or their participation in co-production of services. Field experiments about changes to practices or structures in public organisations may use outcome measures of performance as already gathered by the organisation itself, for example the level of use of a service or its cost, or gathered by other bodies to which the organisation is accountable. These measures contrast with the more abstract outcomes gathered by researchers in conventional laboratory experiments, for example the level of cooperation by participants in a public goods game in a typical economics experiment.

Field Experiments and Randomised Controlled Trials

The use of relevant participants and authentic treatments, outcomes and settings gives many field experiments strong similarities to randomised controlled trials (RCTs). Whilst some economists do not include a requirement for randomisation to describe something as a field experiment (List and Metcalfe 2014), in this chapter we take randomisation as an integral part of field experimentation. RCTs have long been used in medical research and include trials of the effects of drugs and changes in medical practices, as well as studies of the effects of behavioural modifications for patients or citizens to improve their health, for example through information campaigns or education programmes. Clearly, social and institutional interventions usually have stronger relevance to the interests of public management researchers than pharmacological trials.

Social policy experimentation extended the domain of the RCT approach and was influenced particularly by the work of Donald Campbell and colleagues (Shadish, Cook and Campbell 2002). As discussed at more length in Chapter 23, RCTs have been applied to policy evaluations across a broad range of public activity, including that of social, educational, criminal justice, employment and welfare programmes (Levitt and List 2009; Orr 1999; Riccio and Bloom 2002). Similarly, in the private sector, many companies regularly use random allocation of practices to assess their effectiveness, especially in experiments that undertake incremental changes in product lines or advertising strategies to assess the outcomes of levels of sales or costs (Manzi 2012).

In RCTs participants are often allocated to receive the standard service or 'usual care', whilst those in the treatment group receive the enhanced treatment that is the subject of investigation for potential adoption. For example, smoking cessation RCTs have involved those in the treatment group being allocated an information-based treatment combining elements of self-administered cognitive behavioural therapy, whilst the control group received a standard information pack about the dangers of smoking. In this way, the term 'trial' in RCT draws attention to the aim of evaluating a policy intervention or programme subject to testing. Whilst the typical interest of policy makers in an RCT is to compare a new policy relative to the existing one, the term 'field experiment', in contrast, does not imply a direct application to a particular policy or programme on trial (although field experiments can be applied in this way). Field experiments can have a more pure social science rationale, in the sense of primarily testing the empirical implications of theories or assessing the effects of practices that might only in another time or place be combined in an actual policy or programme.

Related to RCTs, natural experiments are a method where there is random allocation of interventions, but it is done by someone other than the researcher, such as a government or another organisation. We follow Green and Gerber (2012: 15–16) in considering that, so long as the researcher can be confident that the allocation is truly random, this form of natural experiment can be analysed as if it was a researcher-designed field experiment. However, as discussed in Chapter 4, we do not consider methods that are sometimes called natural experiments but that utilise 'as if' randomisation as being best described as natural experiments. Studies that use 'as if' randomisation allocation methods where observations either side of a cut-point, such as an arbitrary geographical boundary or eligibility for a policy program, are better described as quasi-experimental and not natural experiments, despite the term 'natural experiment' sometimes being used to describe these types of study (see Dunning 2012).

5.2 The Emerging Contribution of Public Management Field Experiments

Despite the relatively scarce use of field experimentation in public management research, there is evidence of growing use of the method. Some illustrative examples show their specific contribution to research topics that are discussed more extensively in later chapters in this book. One branch is field experimentation about the motivation and behaviour of bureaucrats. For example, Belle (2015) extended findings about the effects of monetary incentives and transparency of reward on performance from student subject pools to groups of more direct interest to public management by studying public service professionals (nurses in his study) in real service contexts (assembling of surgical kits). These experiments are discussed at more length in Chapter 8.

Field experiments on the boundaries of public management and political science research have been conducted on citizens' interactions with public services and organisations. For example, the implications of performance information about public services for citizens and service users have been addressed as discussed in Chapter 12. Published performance information about the relative performance of different local governments has been found to influence citizens' perceptions of service performance and their satisfaction with services (James 2011). These experiments cross-checked findings across different subject pools by using both a conventional laboratory experiment subject pool of students and a field domain subject pool of general citizens in a locality. The use of the laboratory with the student subject pool enabled strong control over participants' engagement with the information. The findings from the field and the laboratory were similar, giving confidence that the information treatment caused the effect of changes in perceptions and satisfaction and that the findings have relevance to citizens in general, not just students. Field experiments have addressed whether this information has effects on behaviour, showing that providing information about poor performance does not always trigger voice about service performance when citizens are given an opportunity to do so (James and Moseley 2014). As discussed in Chapter 17, the experimental agenda is now to discover under what circumstances citizens do and do not voice in response to poor performance.

Field experiments have been applied to other areas of citizen–state interactions, notably to examine citizen co-production of services (Jakobsen 2013; Jakobsen and Andersen 2013). These field experiments share some research questions with field experiments on prosocial behaviour more broadly (Arceneaux and Butler 2015; John et al. 2011; Moseley et al. 2015; Moseley and Stoker 2015). The findings about successful ways to stimulate user coproduction with public organisations, such as Jakobsen's (2013) experiment showing that government initiatives to provide citizens with knowledge and materials to facilitate their contribution increases levels of coproduction, provide important insights into more general processes and outcomes in the specific field context of public services. Experiments about citizen involvement in the delivery of public services are discussed at greater length in Chapter 15.

5.3 Challenges and Opportunities of Using Field Experiments

There is a developing literature discussing some of the difficulties of designing and implementing field experiments (Bækgaard 2015; Cotterill and Richardson 2010; John 2016). The field context can put at risk the internal validity of findings both by making control over a variable that is manipulated by the experimenter more difficult and by increasing the difficulty of controlling other background conditions. Without internal validity the issue of external validity does not arise because there are no reliable findings to have some situation potentially to be relevant to. A challenge is that problems can arise that are specific to particular topics or even experiments. Learning by doing a set of related experiments is often an important way for researchers to develop appropriate techniques. However, some more general issues can be identified and this section discusses how the most important common challenges can be addressed.

Field Experiments and Public Management Theory

Field experiments have been criticised in related disciplines for making insufficient contribution to assessing and developing theory. In economics, a recent systematic review showed that 68 per cent of field experiments conducted between 1975 and 2010 were 'descriptive', in the sense of not evaluating hypotheses drawn explicitly from a formal model, which was higher than for laboratory economics experiments (Card, DellaVigna and Malmendier 2011). There are too few field experiments in public management to justify a quantitative analysis of this sort, but field experiments to date have tended not to test hypotheses deduced from formal theory. However, their contribution to theory is broader than this observation might appear to suggest. The empirical implications of theory are not always about testing formally derived hypotheses, especially outside the discipline of experimental economics where formal theory is very dominant, and field experiments can evaluate the empirical implications of non-formal theory. When findings are not consistent with expectations from theory, field experimental evidence can stimulate reflection on current theory and the development of new theory for subsequent empirical evaluation.

Some types of theory and associated research questions can be difficult to address with field experiments. Very broad theories of macro-structures and, relatedly, theories that require interventions consisting of complete step changes in whole systems are difficult to examine using field experiments. For example, theory about high-level, general, institutional features of a country such as the effects on bureaucracy of having a separation of powers versus a parliamentary regime, is difficult to assess using experimentation. A substantial institutional treatment would be needed in an experiment to assess such effects, and there would be difficulty in getting sufficient units, as well as obvious practical problems of implementation.

Much public management theory is related to less macro-scale institutions than whole country systems, relating instead to management practices, policies and programmes. Experimental treatments can consist of reasonably scaled variations from the status quo on these variables. However, even here, researchers cannot always persuade policy makers to undertake the necessary experiments. For example, those in positions of authority in public organisations who commission or facilitate research may not support it if they fear findings might be critical of them or their favoured programmes. Sometimes researchers can work to create analogues, even running their own, perhaps small-scale, public services or public organisations.

Field experiments have been used to study questions that can reasonably be described as 'big' in the sense of important for key theories or about major issues of institutional design or management practice.

Researchers have designed interventions that examine the effects of institutional structures of major importance to theory at sub-unit or local level where there can be more opportunity than at the national level. The experiments with citizens' responses to performance information discussed earlier make use of local service contexts but are of broader relevance for the democratic control of public services. Other examples of big questions addressed by field experiments include work by Beath and colleagues (2013), who randomised 500 villages in Afghanistan where one experimental group required women's participation in elite decisions as a condition of the aid being delivered and the other did not. The experiment was able to examine the effect of institutions requiring participation of women on outcomes, which would potentially have relevance to the level of the nation-state, and found increases in mobility and income generation. Another field experiment giving major insights into accountability in the public sector is Olken's (2007) research into factors affecting corruption in Indonesia which also has broader relevance to understanding how government audit can reduce levels of malpractice.

Defining and Delivering the Treatment

Being clear about the treatment as the intervention carried out by researchers and maintaining treatment integrity during the experiment can be more difficult in field contexts than in the laboratory. The practice of medical RCTs offers insights. In setting up different experimental groups to assess effects, RCTs often administer placebos such as a non-treatment pill to those in the control condition, so change due to the treatment can be attributed to the 'active ingredient' or specific content of the true treatment rather than simply to patients having something done to them, which can itself cause changes, including improvements (known as a placebo effect). Such studies often have both an untreated control group who get nothing at all, and a placebo control group who get the apparent treatment. This practice implies that public management researchers should be careful to define their experiments to focus on specific interventions. They should consider use of experimental groups receiving conditions similar to the treatment of interest that vary only in the absence of the feature that is being specifically investigated by the research. For example, if researchers are interested in identifying the effects of a particular mode of delivering public services (e.g. electronic versus face to face) that theory says should affect outcomes for users, then they should be careful that participants should all receive a similar service such that the difference between experimental groups is focused on the mode of delivery rather than having other differences. If the field intervention includes many different aspects, it is difficult to isolate the effect of variation of mode by itself and difficult to consider the implications for theory.

Public management field experiments sometimes use a placebo-like method as in a medical or healthcare RCT, even where a full placebo is not strictly possible. For example, the control group may be given something to do that has similarities with the treatment group in terms of undertaking a task of approximate length and amount of cognitive processing required, but one which differs from the treatment because it does not contain the 'active ingredient' the effect of which is being tested. An example of this method comes from a study of citizens' proclivity to voice to a local public service provider following receipt of performance information about the relative (to other similar providers) and absolute performance of that service (James and Moseley 2014). Those in the treatment groups received particular forms of performance information and were invited to take part in a consultation, whilst those in the control group were given information about the service (to expose them to a placebo of some information but not the specific treatment form of performance information), before also being invited to take part in the consultation. In a further example, in an experiment investigating whether offering to provide social recognition could encourage people to come forward to sit on a council committee (Arceneaux and Butler 2015), the treatment group received a message about the committee, an offer of publicity on a local city website for those who took part and an invitation to participate. Those in the control group received a simple message about the committee and an invitation to come forward, but without the offer of social recognition.

Ensuring that the treatment is delivered in the way it is intended can be more difficult in the field than in the laboratory where researchers have more direct control over its delivery. Where treatments are delivered in person, such as a training programme or message communicated to a citizen by a public official, it is easy for the treatment to become distorted as those administering the intervention may interpret its contents differently. For this reason, it is important that treatments are standardised to make them less open to interpretation. The use of clear protocols, scripts and training for people administering treatments is therefore important for interventions delivered face to face or even by telephone. Related to this issue is that of treatment dosage and ensuring that an appropriate 'dose' of the intervention is delivered to have an effect consistent with that suggested by theory. For example, if the dose implemented is much less than that suggested by theory, then a consequent failure to detect an effect is the result of a poor experiment rather than providing information about whether the theory is correct.

Ensuring Randomisation of Treatment Allocation

In the field it is often more difficult than in the laboratory to ensure effective implementation of randomisation. Verifying randomisation can be difficult if public authorities cooperating in implementing experiments cannot pass identifying information onto the researchers. For example, it is more difficult to assign a random number sequence to achieve randomisation than if the process was fully under the control of a research team. Usually, this can be overcome by the public authority assigning dummy identification numbers to individuals and passing these numbers to the research team – or ideally independent statisticians – who then generate the treatment and control group assignments. The public authority must then correctly assign the treatment allocations to the correct individuals.

Bias can creep into the randomisation process if those assigning the random numbers subvert the randomisation process, perhaps with the best of intentions for doing so in terms of trying to assist beneficiaries of a programme. It is important that those assigning people to the different groups are 'blind' to treatment group allocation. In practice for a case where there was one treatment and one control group of equal size this would involve the person assigning half of the participants to one group and half to the other, without knowing which is the treatment and which is the control group. Several other practical steps can be taken to maintain the integrity of the randomisation process. These include setting clear guidance for those involved in implementing a field experiment, having a formal written contract that outlines the process of randomisation, conducting test randomisations as well as diagnostics of the randomisation, ensuring that once random assignment takes place participants remain in their correct groups, and informing those in the public body of the reasons why ensuring integrity of the randomisation process is so important.

Maintaining Compliance with the Treatment

It is typically more difficult to ensure that the treatment and control groups differ only in whether the treatment is administered to them in the field than in the laboratory. Sometimes those in the treatment group will not comply with the treatment allocated to them, for example public managers on a training programme may not attend. Alternatively, sometimes those in a control group may get the treatment, for example if public managers in the non-treatment group talk with colleagues in the treatment group to obtain the training materials and related skills and knowledge. These issues are sometimes presented in combination as the so-called problems of one-sided non-compliance (where some in the treatment group do not take the treatment) and two sided non-compliance (where not only do some in the treatment group not take the treatment, but also some in the control group take the treatment) (Gerber and Green 2012: 131–209).

In laboratory contexts, experimental participants can even be physically screened off to help keep treatment and control groups separated. In the field domain, separation can be more difficult to achieve. The challenge is substantial where experimental participants are in the same organisation or network, which is often the case for bureaucrats and related professionals. The risk of participants exchanging information about interventions received, or sharing intervention materials, requires consideration. Even in studies involving citizens it can be hard to avoid contamination occurring where neighbours or service users may have contact with one another and exchange information about interventions they have been exposed to, for example letters they have received from researchers or communications from their service provider. Sometimes treatments may have to be allocated to clusters of participants, for example groups of service users who use the service at the same time, if they cannot be allocated at the individual level.

Attrition in Field Experiments

Attrition, involving outcome data being missing for participants who were randomised to treatment, tends to be greater in the field compared to the laboratory. In the laboratory, the participants are physically present and the researcher can usually ensure that outcome measures are implemented. In the field context, participants may refuse to cooperate, not filling in surveys or not being available for other measures. Refusal to cooperate may occur because public organisations are reluctant to report some outcomes, especially if they perceive the outcome as not reflecting well on them.

If researchers exclude participants who have missing outcomes from their analysis, this risks biasing their estimates of causal effects if participants being missing is systematically related to the participants' potential outcomes. Gerber and Green (2012: 211–47) discuss different forms of attrition and how they can sometimes be addressed in analysis of data from field experiments. However, the best solution is for researchers to design and implement experiments with outcome measures that minimise attrition in the first place.

Ethical Challenges of Field Experimentation

Ethical issues for field experiments can in many cases be more complex than similar laboratory studies because their naturalistic context involves a broader set of social actors and processes and less control than in the laboratory, although these features vary with type of field experiment. As well as the obvious issue of what the intervention is about and what effects (with associated risks of harm) might occur, a major ethical challenge with field experiments is the question of informed consent of participants in the experiment. This issue involves how much information to give to participants about the experiment they are involved in and the purpose of research and possible outcomes for them and others. The extent to which participants need to be fully informed about all the reasons for conducting an experiment matters particularly in cases where if they were fully informed it would undermine the experimental design. Participants being completely unaware they are part of a trial or experiment is part of the definition of an unobtrusive, natural field experiment. Awareness of the experiment may change behaviour and therefore undermine the validity of the research findings to contexts beyond the experiment. If the goal is to observe people in their natural environment, not telling people they are in an experiment, or even a research project more generally, may be the only way to observe behaviour (McClendon 2012).

It is fairly common practice in policy and public management field experiments, and in other disciplines such as psychology and sociology, to limit information provision to participants. However, depending on the treatment and risk of harm it could be unethical to conduct an unobtrusive field experiment, as has been discussed in the context of RCTs (Colson et al. 2015; Rousu et al. 2015). A few critics argue that anything but full information is hard to defend, but most researchers defend unobtrusive methods provided that there is review of the issues, that risk of harm is limited or absent and that societal need for the research is great enough. If the interventions being delivered are 'ordinary', that is something that might typically happen in any case in the course of public organisations or managers performing their roles, fewer specific ethical concerns about experimentation are likely to arise than if a novel, high-risk of harm treatment were to be proposed (Bonetti 1998; Rousu et al. 2015).

Public management field experiments that do not need to be fully unobtrusive could strike a balance on the issue of informed consent by ensuring that participants are aware that a research study is being conducted but without detailed information about the design or interventions being tested to avoid compromising validity. Another approach, as discussed by McClendon (2012) is to debrief participants after the experiment has been completed. However, this approach is easier in the laboratory than in many field contexts where participants can be difficult to contact after the experiment. Sometimes telling participants, such as public officials, that they have unknowingly been part of an experiment may still be detrimental and cause negative emotions such as feelings of betrayal or anger. McClendon (2012) notes that, in research involving public officials, negative perceptions of a research project may detrimentally affect future proclivity to engage in, fund and be supportive of such research.

Deception involves researchers or other collaborators in an experiment making active use of false information and practices intended to mislead participants. Whilst there are differing views on what constitutes deception, a consensus has emerged that intentional provision of misinformation is deception and that withholding information about research hypotheses or the range of experimental manipulations is not deception (Colson et al. 2015; Hertwig and Ortmann 2008). For example, deception in a study testing citizen responsiveness to different types of framing of public service performance information might involve realistic frames using false information about the levels of service performance, in order to be able to test theory. This raises the ethical issue of potentially leaving participants with enduring false perceptions of public services, organisations, managers or politicians which would typically be difficult to justify. An alternative is to use hypothetical scenarios designed in ways to be as similar as possible to real situations.

Experimental economists are typically very concerned to avoid deception, not only because of ethical concerns, but because they fear that researchers will lose control over their interventions and related instructions to participants because the participants will not know if the instructions are true or not. Deception can risk a loss of clarity and control in the field although economists' hope that, by not deceiving, experimenters will gain a reputation for telling the truth is less relevant where subject pools are unlikely to be involved in multiple experiments. In contrast, student panels often repeatedly participate in laboratory studies.

Field experiments can involve withholding a potentially beneficial treatment from the control group. Practitioners or public managers are often particularly concerned about this ethical issue, feeling it is unfair to treat some participants and not others. One way to address this concern is to establish a 'wait list control', or a 'staged implementation of the treatment', where the control group receives the treatment after the experiment is over (Gerber and Green 2012: 276–81). Until an approach is properly evaluated, it is unknown as to whether the treatment itself is actually effective; it may even cause harm. On this basis, it can be unethical to implement or roll out a new programme or practice without a proper randomised controlled trial which assesses both positive and potentially also negative effects.

Institutions can assist researchers in the process of ethical review and enhance the legitimacy of funding and carrying out field experiments by providing an input beyond that of the researchers directly involved in the experiment. Ethical review boards in universities can help examine issues for particular experiments and programmes of research. In cases where review boards are less familiar with experimental than observational work, researchers need to engage in dialogue with them. These structures mean that research is subject to more ethical scrutiny than most public policy programmes where formal ethical review is not typically part of the authorisation process within the bureaucracy or broader political system. In some policy fields, such as development and health services research, the use of experiments has been a spur to the strengthening of procedures for ethical scrutiny within the bureaucracy, with peer review of ethics now part of the design stage of RCTs in many contexts.

5.4 Conclusions: Prospects for Field Experiments as a Complement to Other Methods

Field experiments stand between the conventional laboratory and the full naturalism of non-experimental, observational methods. This position makes them especially relevant to public management research. In contrast to much research in psychology or economics where researchers tend to be interested in theory that is very broad in scope and often abstract or formal, which often suits conventional laboratory methods, public management theory is typically more closely focused on real-world domains. The theories take their public contexts to heart, including management in particular political systems, public organisations and public services. Field experiments are set up to build these domains in to the experimental design. The relevance of field experiments is further enhanced because the findings from naturalistic domains help public management, as a design science, inform policy makers and public management practice.

Despite the many benefits, field experiments are best used in research programmes alongside or in combination with other kinds of experimental and non-experimental methods. In contrast to many research programmes in psychology or experimental economics that rely on having numerous experiments on an ongoing basis, major field experiments in public management may be difficult to set up such that they occur only in limited jurisdictions for limited time periods. In some circumstances the specific field domain of an experiment might limit external validity to other domains, hampering the transfer of insights to other contexts and making generalisation of results difficult. Researchers should be cautious about the possibility of general equilibrium effects which might not be detected from a single experiment if they only occur when scaling up an intervention from participants to a broader population or extending it to a longer time period. For example, in an experiment giving training and improving the qualifications of some groups of public managers, it could be that career advancement or additional personal income from this intervention diminishes as an increasing proportion of the pool of available managers has the same qualifications. The selection of the specific site for a field experiment can also matter, with sites potentially having different effects even for experiments with identical interventions. Where site selection for trials is biased, for example with trials disproportionately located in areas where management quality is high and this is reflected in openness to collaboration with researchers, then effect sizes can be misleading for broader populations even after replications of the same intervention. For example, the same intervention might be better run by a high-quality management area giving greater improvement in outcomes compared to areas with average management quality, overestimating the effects for the broader population of interest (Allcott 2015).

Recent reviews have noted a correspondence of laboratory and field results in several areas where findings have been compared, suggesting that the field increases confidence in findings and external validity when used together with laboratory studies (Coppock and Green 2015). However, if unexpected behaviours arise when loosening control in the field, this could indicate that some important features of public management have been neglected in the laboratory and experiments in this context could subsequently be redesigned. Drawing on field findings, researchers can conduct laboratory experiments with parameter values estimated from the field data, so as to study laboratory behaviour in a 'field relevant' domain (Harrison and List 2004: 1013).

Field experiments are sometimes criticised for being black box analysis, telling researchers that an intervention has an effect which may also help policy makers know that a programme works, but providing little information on why an intervention has an effect. A series of field experiments varying different aspects of the intervention according to mechanisms suggested by theory can assist in fine-tuning understanding of the potent elements that bring about an effect. However, it can also be valuable to combine field and laboratory experiments, with the latter giving insights into perceptions, attitudes and behaviour that may be more difficult to detect in the field.

When research moves beyond laboratory experiments, field experiments act as a bridge to a broad range of natural, quasi-experimental and observational methods. For example, observational research using panel data that covers a sufficient time period and set of jurisdictions can help confirm the broader relevance of more isolated field or laboratory experiments. Developing the example of performance information outlined earlier, studies using panel data have established that poor performance of local government services can trigger voting against incumbent politicians (Boyne et al. 2009). Experiments have helped establish the role of published performance information as part of this process and showed public organisations that regimes of public reporting of performance can be effective (see Chapter 12). When used as part of methodologically pluralistic research programmes, field experimentation can inform both theory and practice and lead us to wish for, and indeed expect, that public management field experiments will grow in number and ambition in the years to come.

References

Allcott, H. 2015. 'Site selection bias in program evaluation', *Quarterly Journal of Economics* 130(3): 1117–65.

Anderson, D. M. and Edwards, B. C. 2014. 'Unfulfilled promise: laboratory experiments in public management research', *Public Management Review* doi: 10.1080/14719037.2014.943272.

Arceneaux, K. and Butler, D. M. 2015. 'How not to increase participation in local government: the advantages of experiments when testing policy interventions', *Public Administration Review* Early view.

Avellaneda, C. N. 2013. 'Mayoral decision-making: issue salience, decision context, and choice constraint? An experimental study with 120 Latin American mayors', *Journal of Public Administration Research and Theory* 23: 631–61.

Bækgaard, M. Baethge, C. Blom-Hansen, J., Dunlop, C., Esteve, M., Jakobsen, M., Kisida, B., Marvel, J., Moseley, A., Serritzlew, S., Stewart, P., Kjaergaard Thomsen, M. and Wolf, P. 2015. 'Conducting experiments in public management research: a practical guide', *International Public Management Journal* 18(2): 323–42.

Banerjee, A. V. and Duflo, E. 2014. 'The experimental approach to development economics', in *Field Experiments and Their Critics: Essays on the Uses and Abuses of Experimentation in the Social Sciences*, edited by Dawn Langan Teele, 78–114. New Haven, CT: Yale University Press.

Barnow, B. S. 2010. 'Setting up social experiments: the good, the bad, and the ugly', *Zeitschrift für Arbeitsmarkt Forschung* 43: 91–105.

Barrett, C. B. and Carter, M. R. 2014. 'Retreat from radical skepticism: rebalancing theory, observational data, and randomization in development economics', in *Field Experiments and Their Critics: Essays on the Uses and Abuses of Experimentation in the Social Sciences*, edited by Dawn Langan Teele, 58–77. New Haven, CT: Yale University Press.

Beath, A., Fontina, C. and Enikolopov, R. 2013. 'Empowering women through development aid: evidence from a field experiment in Afghanistan', *American Political Science Review* 107: 540–57.

Belle, N. 2015. 'Performance-related pay and the crowding out of motivation in the public sector: a randomized field experiment', *Public Administration Review* 75 (2): 230–41.

Bonetti, S. 1998. 'Experimental economics and deception', *Journal of Economic Psychology* 19: 377–95.

Boyne, G. A., James, O., John, P. and Petrovsky, N. 2009. 'Democracy and government performance: holding incumbents accountable in English local governments', *Journal of Politics* 71(4): 1273–84.

Bozeman, B and Scott, P. 1992. 'Laboratory experiments in public management and management', *Journal of Public Administration Research and Theory* 2(4): 293–313.

Brewer, G. A. and Brewer, G. A., Jr. 2011. 'Parsing public/private differences in work motivation and performance: an experimental study', *Journal of Public Administration Research and Theory* 21(suppl 3): i347–62.

Butler, D. M. 2010. 'Monitoring bureaucratic compliance: using field experiments to improve governance', *Public Sector Digest* 2010 (winter): 41–4.

Butler, D. M. and Brockman, D. E. 2011. 'Do politicians racially discriminate against constituents? A field experiment on state legislators', *American Journal of Political Science* 55: 463–77.

Card, D., DellaVigna, S. and Malmendier, U. 2011. 'The role of theory in field experiments', *Journal of Economic Perspectives* 25(3): 39–62.

Colson, G. Corrigan, J. R., Grebitus, G., Loureiro, M. L. and Rousu, M. C. 2015. 'Which deceptive practices, if any, should be allowed in experimental economics research? Results from surveys of applied experimental economists and students', *American Journal of Agricultural Economics*, Early View 1–12. doi: 10.1093/ajae/aav067.

Coppock, A. and Green, D. P. 2015. 'Assessing the correspondence between experimental results obtained in the lab and field: a review of recent social science research', *Political Science Research and Methods* 3: 113–31.

Cotterill, S. and Richardson, R. 2010. 'Expanding the use of experiments on civic behavior: experiments with local governments as research partners', *The Annals of the American Academy of Political and Social Science* 628: 148–64.

Druckman, J. N. and Kam, C. D. 2011. 'Students as experimental participants: a defense of the "narrow database"', in *Handbook of Experimental Political Science*, edited by James Druckman, Donald P. Green, James H. Kuklinski and Arthur Lupia, 41–57. New York: Cambridge University Press.

Duflo, E., Glennerster, R. and Kremer, M. 2006. *Using Randomization in Development Economics Research: A Toolkit*. Cambridge, National Bureau of Economic Research.

Dunning, T. 2012. *Natural Experiments in the Social Sciences*. New York: Cambridge University Press.

Falk, A. and Heckman, J. J. 2009. 'Lab experiments are a major source of knowledge in the social sciences', *Science* 326(5952): 535–8.

Fisher, R. A. 1926. 'The arrangement of field experiments', *Journal of the Ministry of Agriculture of Great Britain* 33: 503–13.

Fisher, R. A. 1935. *Design of Experiments*. Edinburgh: Oliver and Boyd.

Gerber, A. S. and Green, D. P. 2012. *Field Experiments: Design, Analysis and Interpretation*. New York: Norton.

Green, D. P. and Thorley, D. 2014. 'Field experimentation and the study of law and policy', *Annual Review of Law and Social Science* 10: 53–72.

Guala, F. 2005. *The Methodology of Experimental Economics*. Cambridge: Cambridge University Press.

Harrison, G., Lau, M. and Williams, M. 2002. 'Estimating individual discount rates in Denmark: a field experiment', *American Economic Review* 92(5): 1606–17.

Harrison, G. W. and List, J. A. 2004. 'Field experiments', *Journal of Economic Literature* 42(4): 1009–55.

Henrich, J., Heine, S. J. and Norenzayan, A. 2010. 'Beyond WEIRD: towards a broadbased behavioural science', *Behavioral and Brain Sciences* 33(2–3): 111–35.

Hertwig, R. and Ortmann, R. 2008. 'Deception in experiments: revisiting the arguments in its defense', *Ethics and Behavior* 18 (1): 59–82.

Hess, D. R., Hanmer, M. J. and Nickerson, D. M. 2015. 'Encouraging local bureaucratic compliance with federal civil rights laws: field experiments with agencies implementing the national voter registration act', unpublished paper. www.douglasrhess.com/uploads/4/3/7/8/43789 009/hess_hanmer_nickerson_may_2015_nvra_compliance.pdf. Accessed 8 August 2015.

Jakobsen, M. 2013. 'Can government initiatives increase citizen coproduction? Results of a randomized field experiment', *Journal of Public Administration Research and Theory* 23(1): 27–54.

Jakobsen, M. and Andersen, S. 2013. 'Coproduction and equity in public service delivery', *Public Administration Review* 73(5): 704–13.

James, O. 2011. 'Performance measures and democracy: information effects on citizens in field and laboratory experiments', *Journal of Public Administration Research and Theory* 21: 399–418.

James, O. and Moseley, A. 2014. 'Does performance information about public services affect citizens' perceptions, satisfaction, and voice behaviour? Field experiments with absolute and relative performance information'. *Public Administration* 92(2): 493–511.

John, P. (2016) *Experimentation in Political Science and Public Policy The Challenge and Promise of Field Trials*. London: Routledge.

John, P., Cotterill, S., Moseley, A., Richardson, L., Smith, G., Stoker, G. and Wales, C. 2011. *Nudge, Nudge, Think, Think: Experimenting with Ways to Change Civic Behaviour*. London: Bloomsbury Academic.

Levitt, S. D. and List, J. A. 2009. 'Field experiments in economics: the past, the present, and the future', *European Economic Review* 53: 1–18.

List, J. 2011. 'Why economists should conduct field experiments and 14 tips for pulling one off', *Journal of Economic Perspectives* 25(3): 3–16.

List, J. and Metcalfe, R. 2014. 'Field experiments in the developed world: an introduction', *Oxford Review of Economic Policy* 30(4): 585–96.

Manzi, J. 2012. *Uncontrolled: The Surprising Payoff of Trial-and-Error for Business, Politics, and Society*. New York: Basic Books.

Margetts, H. Z. 2011. 'Experiments for public management research', *Public Management Review* 13(2): 189–208.

McClendon, G. H. 2012. 'Ethics of using public officials as field experiment subjects', *Newsletter of the APSA Experimental Section* 3: 13–20.

Medical Research Council 1948. 'Streptomycin treatment of pulmonary tuberculosis', *British Medical Journal* 2(4582): 769–82.

Moher, D., Hopewell, S., Schulz, K. F., Montori, V., Gøtzsche, P. C., Devereaux, P. J., Elbourne, D., Egger, M., Altman, D. G. 2010. 'CONSORT 2010 explanation and elaboration: updated guidelines for reporting parallel group randomized trials', *British Medical Journal* 340: c869.

Moseley, A., James, O., John, P. Richardson, L. Ryan, M. and Stoker, G. 2015. 'Can approaches shown to increase monetary donations to charity also increase voluntary donations of time? Evidence from field experiments using social information', Unpublished working paper.

Moseley, A. and Stoker, G. 2015. 'Putting public policy defaults to the test: the case of organ donor registration', *International Public Management Journal* 18(2): 246–64.

Mutz, D. C. 2011. *Population-Based Survey Experiments*. Princeton, NJ: Princeton University Press.

Olken, B. 2007. 'Monitoring corruption: evidence from a field experiment in Indonesia', *Journal of Political Economy* 115: 200–49.

Orr, L. L. 1999. *Social Experiments: Evaluating Public Programs with Experimental Methods*. Thousand Oaks, CA: Sage.

Pawson, R. and Tilley, N. 1997. *Realistic Evaluation*. London: Sage.

Riccio, J. and Bloom, H. S. 2002. 'Extending the reach of randomized social experiments: new directions in evaluations of American welfare-to-work and employment initiatives', *Journal of the Royal Statistical Society: Series A* (Statistics in Society) 165: 13–30.

Rothwell, P. M. 2015. 'External validity of randomized controlled trials: to whom do the results of this trial apply?' *The Lancet* 365: 82–93.

Rousu, M. C., Colson, G., Corrigan, J. R., Grebitus, C. and Loureiro, M. L. 2015. 'Deception in experiments: towards guidelines on use in applied economics research', *Applied Economic Perspectives and Psychology* 37(3): 524–36.

Salovey, P. and Williams-Piehota, P. 2004. 'Field experiments in social psychology message framing and the promotion of health protective behaviors', *American Behavioral Scientist* 47(5): 488–505.

Salsburg, D. 2001. *The Lady Tasting Tea: How Statistics Revolutionized Science in the Twentieth Century.* New York WH Freeman.

Shadish, William R., Thomas D. Cook, T. D., and Donald T. Campbell 2002. Experimental and Quasi-Experimental Designs for Generalized Causal Inference. Boston: Houghton Mifflin Company.

Shafir, E. (ed.) 2013. *The Behavioral Foundations of Public Policy.* Princeton, NJ: Princeton University Press.

Sherman, L. W. and Rogan, D. P. 1995. 'Deterrent effects of police raids on crack houses: a randomized, controlled experiment', *Justice Quarterly* 12: 755–81.

Sherman, L., Rogan, D., Edwards, T., Whipple, R., Shreve, D., Witcher, D., Trimble, W., The Street Narcotics Unit, Velke, R., Blumberg, M., Beatty, A. and Bridgeforth, C. 1995. 'Deterrent effects of police raids on crack houses: a randomized, controlled experiment', *Justice Quarterly* 12: 755–81.

Sherman, L. W. and Weisburd, D. 1995. 'General deterrent effects of police patrol in crime hot spots: a randomized, controlled trial', *Justice Quarterly* 12(4): 635–48.

Soloman, P., Cavanaugh, M. M. and Draine, J. 2009. *Randomized Controlled Trials: Design and Implementation for Community Based Psychosocial Interventions.* Oxford: Oxford University Press.

Teele, D. L. 2015. 'Reflections on the ethics of field experiments', in *Field Experiments and Their Critics: Essays on the Uses and Abuses of Experimentation in the Social Sciences*, edited by Dawn Langan Teele, 115–40. New Haven, CT: Yale University Press.

Torgerson, D. J. and Torgerson, C. J. 2008. *Designing Randomized Trials in Health, Education and the Social Sciences.* Basingstoke: Palgrave.

Vivalt, E. 2015. 'Heterogeneous treatment effects in impact evaluation', *American Economic Review: Papers & Proceedings* 105: 467–70.

Worthy, B., John, P. and Vannoni, M. 2015. 'Information requests and local accountability: an experimental analysis of local parish responses to an informational campaign', Unpublished paper.

Yates, F. 1964. 'Sir Ronald Fisher and the design of experiments', *Biometrics* 20: 307–21.

6 | Survey Experiments for Public Management Research

SEBASTIAN JILKE AND GREGG G. VAN RYZIN

Introduction

Over the past decades, public management and administration research has generated a vast body of knowledge using survey research. Some even argue that surveys have become the modus operandi for much contemporary public management scholarship (Groeneveld et al. 2015). Indeed, a large share of published empirical evidence about public management and administration comes from surveys about such topics as work motivations (Steijn 2008; van Loon 2016), experiences with red tape (Brewer and Walker 2010; Kaufmann and Feeney 2012), strategic management practices (Andrews, Boyne and Walker 2006) or citizen satisfaction with and trust of government (Van de Walle, Roosbroek and Bouckaert 2008; Van Ryzin 2007). While the sheer number of studies using data from surveys of public managers or citizens has increased, so has the methodological advancement of survey research more generally. Most recently, public management scholars have started using surveys collected in multiple countries (Bullock, Stritch and Rainey 2015; Jilke 2015) and at different points in time (Kjeldsen and Jacobsen 2013; Vogel and Kroll 2016), and have complemented these undertakings with elaborations on survey measurement (Jilke, Meuleman and Van de Walle 2015; Meier and O'Toole 2013). The aim of these efforts is to increase the empirical credibility of survey research.

Yet critiques have increasingly pointed to the limitations of conventional survey research to draw firm causal conclusions (e.g., Perry 2012). Problems of selection bias, spurious correlations, omitted variables or reverse causation constitute serious challenges (see Chapter 4 for more discussion of these issues). And indeed, the potentially endogenous nature of a great deal of public administration and management survey research has clear drawbacks. As Chapter 1 in this volume

117

notes, this has led public management researchers to turn increasingly toward experimental studies, including so-called *survey experiments*. Survey experiments involve randomisation of question wording, text, images or other information in a survey instrument that is administered to a sample, often representing a larger population. Survey experiments can be used to study a large variety of research questions, both substantive and methodological. When conducted on large, representative samples, they combine the internal validity provided by randomised experiments with the external validity provided by survey sampling. Indeed, as Chapter 2 documents, survey experiments have been the most common type of experimental research published in the top 20 public policy and administration journals. This chapter provides an introduction to the use of survey experiments within the social sciences, with a focus on their application to public management research.

History of Survey Experiments

The first appearance of survey experiments dates back to the late 1930s when survey researchers began using so-called split-ballot experiments to test the effects of varying question wording and question order. The term 'split ballot' refers to the fact that researchers produced two similar versions of a questionnaire (paper instruments back then) that differed in terms of the wording or order of questions. One version of the ballot was randomly administrated to half the respondents, the other version to the other half, so that any differences in the results obtained could be solely attributed to manipulations of question wording or order. But because they had to be administrated in print, which was clumsy and somewhat difficult to do properly, most of these early studies manipulated only a limited number of rather basic elements in the questionnaire.

Split-ballot experiments have a long yet often neglected history in public opinion research. Bishop and Smith (1991) report from a series of split-ballot studies that were conducted by Gallup (one of the first survey research firms) from 1938 onward. These early Gallup experiments had their heyday between 1938 and 1949 (see also Cantril 1944, or Payne 1951). In the first 50 years of split-ballot experimentation, Bishop and Smith identify more than 3,000 individual split-ballot surveys, which have been conducted within 332 different polls (for a meta-analysis of these experiments, see Bishop and Smith 2001).

Indeed, most of these split-ballots were done for practical reasons: pollsters simply wanted to find out which wording or question order worked 'best'. Applied public opinion researchers realised soon that simple changes in survey question wording and ordering can have profound effects on the results obtained. In other words, people's opinions or attitudes could be easily altered by how a question was asked. This contributed to a realisation that citizens had less stable and enduring attitudes and beliefs than previously assumed (Sniderman 2011). Besides public opinion firms such as Gallup, or the West German Allensbach Institut fuer Demoskopie, which under the leadership of Elisabeth Noelle-Neumann extensively experimented with split-ballots (see Noelle-Neumann 1970), public opinion researchers started using split-ballots for more substantive research purposes such as studying attitudes toward press freedoms, racial integration or welfare spending. The resulting body of evidence that survey respondents can be strongly influenced by the context, order and wording of survey questions led researchers to develop a psychology of survey response (e.g., Tourangeau, Rips and Rasinski 2000). Indeed, the study of the cognitive aspects of survey methodology (CASM) has now become a major area of investigation in the field of public opinion and survey research.

With the introduction in the 1980s of computer-assisted telephone interviewing (CATI) in telephone surveys, which had by then become the dominant mode of survey data collection, the feasibility and complexity of split-ballot designs increased. With CATI, complex variations of wording and order could be programmed into the system, while telephone interviewers would see only the one version of the questionnaire on a screen as they interviewed respondents. This permitted researchers to expand the number of experimentally varied factors in a questionnaire and to move beyond testing only methodological aspects of a survey, leading to a steep increase in survey experiments from the 1990s onward. For example, Sniderman (2011) reports about his efforts in 1994 to launch the Multi-Investigator Project, funded by the National Science Foundation of the United States, which eventually led to the establishment of the Time-Sharing Experiments for the Social Sciences (TESS). Sniderman's idea was to administer one CATI survey in which multiple researchers could each implement their own small survey experiment; thus, they '[...] *would do thirteen studies for the price of one*' (105). The Multi-Investigator

Project was a great success and led to a wide range of important publications in the field of public opinion research. But more importantly, it laid the foundations for a great share of modern survey experiments.

What Are the Distinct Features of a Survey Experiment?

For public management researchers, survey experiments are particularly attractive because they can be administered to a large population at a comparatively low cost by, for example, including them in an existing data collection effort. Survey experiments allow researchers to move beyond the limited scope of narrow and stylised research questions that are typically examined using volunteers in a laboratory (usually university students), by studying causal research questions among a much larger, more diverse and often more representative sample. In this way, survey experiments combine the internal validity of experiments with the external validity of survey research, which, as mentioned, is one of the key advantages of such studies. The defining feature of a survey experiment is that the treatment (or intervention) and outcome measure are both administered to respondents in the context of a survey instrument. They may be embedded in a larger survey, possibly including other survey experiments, or other unrelated survey items. But it could also be through a survey instrument whose only purpose is the one experiment it entails. Survey experiments can be included in a single survey, or in a series of surveys administered to the same individuals over time (sometimes referred to as a panel survey). Second, a survey experiment entails randomisation of one or more features of the questionnaire. This may include question wording or ordering, but also textual alterations in the description of a scenario, images or other types of information. However, it does not involve an intervention implemented outside of the questionnaire, such as a policy change in a community. In other words, if a survey is used only to measure the outcomes, and the treatment is administered separately in a social, organisational or laboratory setting, it is not a survey experiment. Third, survey experiments are often used to make inferences about a larger population. This is done, for example, by administrating them to random probability samples. Yet various survey experiments exist that do not meet this criterion, for example, survey experiments administered to a voluntary subject pool or a convenience sample. For this reason, Mutz (2011) makes the distinction of a *population-based survey experiment*, which refers to a survey experiment based on a probability sample representing a population.

While a survey experiment administrated to a large probability sample, representative of a specific population, allows generalising treatment effects, we would argue that whether survey experiments have to fulfil this third criterion depends on the purpose of the study and the availability of prior theoretical knowledge about the manipulation. In a similar vein, Gaines and Kuklinski (2011) argue that if treatment effects ought to be homogenous, it would not matter to whom we may distribute the treatment and whether our sample is representative of any larger population in a strict sense. But if we suspect treatment effects to be heterogeneous – varying by demographic or other characteristics – then the representativeness (or at least sufficient variation on these characteristics) of the sample becomes more of a concern. At the very least, we would then need to have variation in the sample on those particular characteristics that interact with treatment effects. Of course, it is often difficult to identify the relevant characteristics in advance, which would depend on prior research or theory.[1] In addition, we would note that a large share of treatment effects in the social sciences are likely to be heterogeneous.

But hybrid forms of survey experiments also exist. For example, a survey experiment may be administrated to subjects within an experimental laboratory, or within the field (see also Chapters 7 and 5 in this book, respectively), and in doing so may be combined with behavioural, or more unobtrusive outcome measures. We may call these hybrid forms of survey experiments *survey-in-the-field* and *survey-in-the-lab* experiments, acknowledging that it is not necessary to have pure forms of experimental types. One example of a survey-in-the-lab experiment is a recent study by Tummers and colleagues (2015) in which the authors test the effects of red tape on respondents' satisfaction with a hypothetical passport application process. The experiment was conducted within a classroom setting at two Dutch universities, where versions of two questionnaires (low versus high red tape) were randomly allocated to students. The study found that a more burdensome passport

---

[1] Gaines and Kuklinski (2011) provide guidance on how to effectively 'control' for such heterogeneous treatment effects, but see also Green and Kern's (2012) discussion about how to reduce scholars' discretion in the choice of heterogeneous subgroups.

application procedure decreased subjects' satisfaction levels substantially. The procedure of the experiment mirrored that of a conventional survey experiment, but differed by its location, allowing investigators to more closely control the data-gathering process. An example of a survey-in-the-field experiment comes from James and Moseley's (2014) study on citizen responses to the performance of local public services that randomly allocated different forms of performance information in a questionnaire to respondents within a naturalistic setting, the town centres of two UK cities. Respondents were recruited on the go and administered a questionnaire that contained different types of real information about local governments' recycling service performance. The experiment's main difference to a conventional field experiment was that subjects were aware that they were part of a research project, although not an experiment, and that the means for both delivering the treatment and collecting outcome measures was a questionnaire. In addition to the outcome measures contained in the survey, the experiment used an unobtrusive outcome measure of collective voice by giving participants the opportunity to participate in a public consultation about the service.

Different Kinds of Survey Experiments

While the basic thrust of a survey experiment involves a survey instrument with randomisation of some aspect of the questionnaire, how survey experiments are actually designed can vary substantially. They may include classical split-ballots, list-experiments, factorial vignette surveys or conjoint experiments, economic or social games or other designs. These types of survey experiments can be roughly differentiated by their primary purposes. While split ballots and list experiments mainly aim to study methodological issues, factorial vignette and conjoint experiments are predominantly used to study substantive questions. We introduce these different kinds of survey experiments later, as well as present recent applications of the techniques in public administration and management research, or related disciplines.

Split-Ballot Experiments

As noted already, split-ballot experiments are used mostly to probe methodological or measurement issues. For example, they often aim to investigate the effects of systematically altering question wording or ordering. In its most simple form, two questionnaires are randomly allocated to respondents, including manipulating one aspect of the questionnaire. For example, Presser and Schuman (1980) conducted a series of split ballots to examine the effects of explicitly offering a middle category in scales of survey questions about citizen attitudes. They independently examined the inclusion of a middle category across five different domains: marijuana use, the Vietnam War, partisanship, federal government control and divorce. In all of these split ballots, respondents were randomly allocated to a version of the questionnaire with, or without, a middle category. Across all experiments, the explicit mentioning of a middle category increased its usage substantially. However, it did not affect the items' univariate distribution, exemplifying that those choosing the middle category come from both ends of the scale.

But there exist also applications with a more substantive flavour. For example, a more recent split ballot experiment by Van de Walle and Van Ryzin (2011) tests whether concrete versus specific evaluations of public services are less likely to be influenced by individuals' predispositions toward government. Therefore, they conducted a question-order experiment among a large online sample of US citizens. In the first version of the questionnaire, they asked three general questions about satisfaction with public services, followed by 11 rating questions of specific services. In the second version of the questionnaire, the specific rating questions were asked first, followed by the more general satisfaction questions. Respondents were randomly allocated to one of the two versions of the questionnaire. The study found that some of the items of the second version of the questionnaire displayed slightly higher, statistically significant performance ratings (about 3 per cent), but also that general satisfaction items seem to prime more general predispositions toward government in the assessment of specific public services. These results suggest that question order is not just a minor methodological consideration, but can lead to substantive differences in citizens' evaluations of public services.

While more complex forms of split-ballot experiments also exist, the basic notion of altering methodological-procedural aspects in the survey instrument remains the technique's primary purpose. Indeed, modern survey administration techniques have given way to design more complex split ballots, which, at times, resemble the design of related types of survey experiments, such as factorial designs, or list experiments. Therefore, it has to be acknowledged that boundaries between split-ballot experiments and related techniques seem not always very clear.

List Experiments

Another form of survey experimentation that is predominantly concerned with methodological aspects is the so-called list experiment or item-count technique. The technique aims to reduce respondents' dishonest or evasive answering behaviours, such as reporting about subjects that are sensitive or socially undesirable (see, e.g., Chaudhuri and Christofides 2007; Droitcur et al. 1991; Glynn 2013; Miller 1984; but also Gossen 2014). In a list experiment, like with the split-ballot approach, two versions of a list question are randomly allocated to respondents. One version of the list contains the sensitive item; the other version of the list does not. Respondents are then asked to report how many items apply to them (without having to actually name or endorse any one item). Then averages in responses between both versions are compared to tease out the net proportion of respondents who would agree with the sensitive item.

A classic example comes from Kulinskis, Cobb and Gilens (1997), who studied the prevalence of racial prejudice in the United States. To do so, they designed a simple list experiment by asking: '*Now I am going to read you three [four] things that sometimes make people angry or upset. After I read all three [four], just tell me HOW MANY of them upset you. I don't want to know which ones, just HOW MANY.*' The first version of the questionnaire serves as a control group (also called the baseline group). It includes a list of the following three non-sensitive items:

(1) The federal government increasing the tax on gasoline;
(2) Professional athletes getting million-dollar contracts;
(3) Large corporations polluting the environment.

The second version of the question (i.e., the treatment group) just adds one sensitive item that is thought to be subject to some form of response bias (in this example, social desirability bias).

(4) A black family moving in next door.

These two versions were randomly allocated to 275 respondents from the South, and 886 respondents from other regions of the United States. Kuklinski and colleagues then estimated the proportion angered by a black family moving in next door, using a simple difference-in-means estimator (see also Blair and Imai [2012] for recent advances in analysing list experiments). The difference between list groups was 42 per cent in the South, meaning that 42 per cent expressed anger at the idea of a black family moving in next door. There were no significant differences between list groups in the other regions of the United States. This finding clearly indicated stark differences in racial prejudice in the South that were not captured with conventional public opinion surveys at the time, presumably because of social desirability bias in answering more direct questions about race.

Further possible areas of application of list experiments include studying sensitive topics such as political support, voting behaviour, charitable giving, support for extremist views, and corruption. Yet despite its broad range of possible applications, very few list experiments have been conducted to date in the field of public administration and management research. One example is Kim and Kim's (2013) recent study of social desirability bias when measuring public service motivation (PSM), which was conducted across four different country settings: Japan, Korea, the Netherlands and the United States. They studied respondents' propensity to over-report on two aspects of public service motivation, their attraction to public service and self-sacrifice, as well as their levels of job satisfaction. Thus the list experiment involved three different types of sensitive items:

(1) Meaningful public service is very important to me.
(2) I am willing to risk personal loss to help society.
(3) I like my job better than the average worker does.

This resulted in three experimental treatment groups that were compared with the control group, which contained none of the sensitive items, but only three non-sensitive statements. Their study finds clear evidence for socially desirable responding for all three items, indicating that conventional survey measures of PSM and the item on job satisfaction are likely to be subject to over-reporting. Put simply, fewer people are actually as motivated by public service and as satisfied with their work than we might assume from only examining traditional survey questions on these topics.

Factorial (Vignette) Survey Experiments

Factorial experiments, or vignette studies as they are sometimes called, have a long history in sociology, but remain relatively underutilised in public management research, despite much potential. Introduced by sociologist Peter Rossi (Rossi and Nock 1982) and further developed by Guillermina Jasso (2006), factorial surveys provide a way to study the components of positive beliefs and normative judgments (such as fair wages, just punishments and appropriate welfare support). In a factorial survey experiment, an object of judgment, or vignette, is constructed with various features. Participants are then presented with a set of vignettes and asked to rate or respond to each of them. In this way, vignettes have the advantage of testing the causal effects of various features or elements on judgment in a relatively unobtrusive manner. As a result, they are often well suited for investigating sensitive or socially undesirable attitudes that may be hard to study with more direct questioning.

For example, in a study of just punishment by Miller, Rossi and Simpson (1991), the vignettes involved randomised characteristics of a crime and its punishment, including the criminal (gender, race, occupation), the crime (violent, nonviolent, etc.), the victim (family, friend, stranger, etc.) and the punishment (number of years in prison). Respondents were shown up to 50 vignettes, and after each vignette were asked to rate the fairness of punishment on a scale from 'much too low' to 'much too high'. Each deck of 50 vignettes was randomly selected from the universe of thousands of possible combinations. Each feature of the vignette is a randomised factor, orthogonal (uncorrelated) with other features of the vignette. As a result, the causal effect of each factor on the final judgment can be estimated.

It should be pointed out that factorial surveys are almost always within-subjects experiments, meaning each participant rates multiple objects or vignettes, often many vignettes, as in the crime and punishment study just discussed. As a consequence, experimental variation within subjects (and not just between) can be examined. In some studies, participants rate each and every possible vignette, which can number in the hundreds. However, fatigue and other methodological effects can set in when too many vignettes are presented in one sitting. As a result, researchers often create decks or sets of vignettes, rather than presenting all of them. In either case, the within-subjects design of factorial surveys implies a much larger sample than in traditional survey experiments. If, say, 100 participants rate 20 vignettes each, the researcher has essentially 2,000 observations to work with. Of course, these observations are clustered by respondent, so appropriate methods must be used (such as clustered standard errors or multilevel modelling). Still, the enhanced statistical power of factorial survey experiments remains one of their key advantages.

One of the few examples of a factorial survey in public management research comes from a study by Weibel, Rost and Osterloh (2010) in which they use experimental vignettes to probe responses to pay for performance incentives using a sample of executive MBA students. Specifically, the researchers varied 10 factors in their vignettes having to do with job design, work climate and external incentives. Respondents were then asked to estimate their likely extra work effort in hours. The findings are a bit complex, but suggest that pay for performance has positive effects on effort but also crowds out intrinsic motivation, especially among those with relatively high levels of intrinsic motivation to begin with. It is quite possible that factorial surveys like this can be used in many other areas of public management research. For example, they could be used to study features of public sector jobs that attract interest in working for government; they could be used to probe aspects of public service delivery arrangements that inspire confidence on the part of citizens; or they could be used to study elements of government performance reporting that influence public managers' judgments of effectiveness. Indeed, in public management research, many of the topics of interest involve complex social or organisational objects about which people need to make decisions. Thus, we would expect to see more use of factorial survey experiments in the field in the coming years.

There are, however, many considerations in the design and analysis of factorial survey experiments that complicate their ready use. For example, there is a trade-off between the complexity (and thus realism) of vignettes and the need to limit the number of vignettes to a reasonable amount. In addition, there are complexities involved when creating and assigning decks or subsets of vignettes to avoid confounding. Another issue concerns the analysis of vignettes, which, as mentioned, must take into account the clustering of observations by participant, and would benefit from employing analytical techniques that can effectively separate between- and within-subjects variation (e.g., multilevel modelling). These issues are discussed in a specialist literature (e.g., Auspurg and Hinz 2015; Jasso 2006).

Conjoint Experiments

The conjoint experiment is another form of survey experimentation. Coming originally from the field of mathematical psychology, it has become a prime technique within marketing research (e.g., Green, Krieger and Wind 2001; Green and Rao 1971; Raghavarao, Wiley and Chitturi 2010), but also received some attention within political science very recently (e.g., Hainmueller, Hangartner and Yamamoto 2014; Hainmueller, Hopkins and Yamamoto 2014; Hansen, Olsen and Bech 2015). The primary purpose of conjoint experiments is to study so-called multidimensional choices, such as whether to purchase a certain product, elect a politician, support the naturalisation of an immigrant or help others. Conventional survey experiments in public management typically focus on one experimental factor at a time (see Bouwman and Grimmelikhuijsen 2016). That could be the price of a product, a candidate's political affiliation or an immigrant's level of education. When analysing complex multidimensional decision-making processes, however, this might be problematic because despite identifying the causal effect of a single manipulation, it might not be possible to identify its distinct components. Take for example whether respondents would be more likely to support a political candidate with high income. Without at the same time independently randomising education – which is arguably correlated with income – scholars will not be able to separate these two components from each other (a problem referred to as *composite treatment effect*); the two components would likely mask each other. Therefore, within a conjoint specification, all theoretically important decision-making components and their attributes are fully randomised and thus made statistically independent.

The conjoint design typically features a set of pairs (e.g., two politicians, or two products) and their attributes, which are mostly presented within a table, and subsequently asks subjects which one they would choose. An alternative would be to give each of the two a rating, or a combination of both choosing and rating (see Hainmueller, Hangartner and Yamamoto 2014). Conjoint experiments usually involve multiple pairs that are presented to respondents, thus a within-subjects design, so that each subject is confronted with a number of different choices to make. A respondent, for example, may choose between two politicians each time in three consecutive pairs, with each pair profile independently randomising the politicians' characteristics. Due to its rather complex design, it is typically embedded within an online survey so as to more effectively implement the complex randomisation procedures. For the technicalities of design, implementation and analysis procedures of conjoint experiments, see, for example, Hainmueller, Hopkins and Yamamoto (2014).

Conjoint experiments are able to include a large number of different attributes of multidimensional choices, thereby not only examining their net effects (i.e., decomposing treatment effects), but also more closely resembling real-world decision-making processes. Indeed, a recent comparison of conjoint experiments with a behavioural benchmark in the field of immigrant naturalisation in Switzerland revealed that the result of the paired conjoint was within two percentages of the effects of real naturalisation decisions (Hainmueller, Hopkins and Yamamoto 2014). In this experiment, authors independently randomised immigrant's gender, origin, age, years since arrival, education, integration status and German language proficiency (28 attributes in total, resulting in 9,216 distinct combinations) among a representative sample of Swiss citizens, and asked them to choose which they would vote for to be naturalised. The study compared the results of the conjoint experiment (and other types of design) with the real naturalisation decisions that have been made within Swiss cantons (i.e., subnational units) by their citizens.

Another example comes from public management and administration research. Jilke and Tummers (2016) looked at US teachers' potential tendency to favour certain types of students over others. They designed a paired conjoint experiment in which they randomly varied students' gender, race, work effort and academic achievement (11 attributes in total, resulting in 54 distinct combinations). Presenting three sets of pairs of student profiles with each pair profile independently varying these attributes, they asked teachers to indicate which of the two students they would help if they would have only a limited amount of time available, and could devote it to one student only. Results showed that while gender did not matter, teachers were more likely to help students who make an effort and those who are not performing well academically, as well as racial minorities. This study shows that these attributes serve as cues of deservingness that can influence how teachers respond to students.

Internet Panels and Crowd-Sourcing

One of the reasons for the rise of survey experiments not only in public management research, but across the social sciences has to do with new technologies of survey sampling and participant recruitment. Indeed, an entire industry has arisen in the past decade or so around the potential of Internet panels (also known as online access panels) to recruit large numbers of potential survey respondents. YouGov, Ipsos MORI, Lightspeed GMI, GfK Knowledge Networks and even Google (Consumer Surveys) are just a few of the many companies that have recruited online panels with millions of potential survey respondents from around the world. Coupled with the power and features of online survey software, these large online panels provide unprecedented opportunities for researchers to conduct experiments on large samples of diverse respondents representing national and even international populations. Although often not probability samples, these online panels nevertheless have distinct advantages over the traditional experimental subject pools composed of university students, which are much more homogeneous and less representative of real citizens, voters or workers. A number of studies in public management journals have used Internet panels, and indeed the ease and potential of the method may well be a key reason why survey experiments and studies of citizens are among the most popular types of experiments in the field thus far, as discussed in Chapter 2. But there are some concerns about Internet panels having to do with the motivations and quality of respondents, for example, concerns about semiprofessional survey respondents who speed through surveys to earn incentives or even automated 'bots' that respond in place of real people (e.g., Goodman, Cryder and Cheema 2013; Suri and Watts 2011). Despite these drawbacks, Internet panels have undeniable advantages and are rapidly becoming the dominant method of survey data collection in both commercial and academic research.

Another source of survey participants has gained traction rapidly in recent years, especially for more academic studies, and that is online labour markets, of which Amazon's Mechanical Turk (MTurk) is by far the best known example. MTurk is described by Amazon as a marketplace for work that requires human intelligence. Businesses use MTurk for temporary intelligence tasks, such as coding or identifying information in texts or images. Researchers, however, use MTurk to recruit participants, essentially presenting their survey or experiment as a human intelligence task. MTurk workers get paid for each task they complete, often only small amounts (sometimes less than a US dollar per task). This allows researchers to vary the incentives for different studies, depending on length and difficulty, as well as structuring the payments as an economic incentive that can become part of the experiment itself (as in the case of economic games). More generally, MTurk provides a way to recruit many hundreds of participants for a survey experiment rapidly and with relatively little expense. A methodological literature is developing on the characteristics and quality of MTurk samples (e.g., Bohannon 2011; Christenson and Glick 2012; Huff and Tingley 2015; Paolacci and Chandler 2014). Experiments using MTurk have started to appear already in public management research (e.g., Christensen and Stritch 2016; Jilke, Van Ryzin and Van de Walle 2015; Marvel 2015), and we would expect to see many more in the years ahead.

Conclusions and Prospects for Public Management Research

Survey experiments have emerged as a major method in public management research, and indeed across the social sciences, due in large part to rapid advances in computer-assisted telephone interviewing, web survey software and an abundance of participants recruited by online panels and crowd-sourcing platforms like MTurk. And survey experiments have evolved over the years from relatively basic split-ballot studies, focused on narrow measurement issues, to multifactor experiments of substantive issues that make use of complex randomisation, multimedia elements and even interactive games. As discussed earlier, survey experiments often combine the external validity of representative survey sampling with the internal validity of rigorous experimental designs. Indeed, the growing use and expanding potential of survey experiments guarantees that this method will play a major role in experimental public management research for some time to come. However, there are some challenges and concerns about the field's reliance on survey experiments.

As we have seen, and as several of the chapters within this book demonstrate, survey experiments have been the most common type of experimental study in public management research to date, particularly survey experiments involving citizens. One issue for the field to consider is how to expand the potential of survey experiments to other populations of interest, especially public managers and frontline workers, as well as politicians and related actors, such as nonprofit managers. Surveying these specialised populations can be a challenge, as they are not necessarily well represented in online panels of the general population or in crowd-sourcing platforms like MTurk. Some commercial Internet panels allow targeting by profession, which would enable public management researchers to sample government workers only, rather than the general public. Another option is for the field to develop its own specialised Internet panels of public sector worker or managers, recruiting from professional associations and networks. The Public Service Research Panel, housed at Rutgers University's Center for Experimental and Behavioral Public Administration in the United States, is an example of an effort along these lines (see PSRPanel.org). Of course, some public officials can also be sampled and contacted directly, as in the study of performance information and blame avoidance by Nielsen and Bækgaard (2015) involving several hundred Danish city counsellors. Another possibility would be to partner with professional associations to get access to their members, as Jilke and Tummers (2016) did in their conjoint experiment involving US teachers.

Although survey experiments claim to combine internal and external validity, they often involve artificial or hypothetical treatments, such as vignettes, or stylised outcomes, such as behavioural intentions rather than real behaviours. For example, a survey experiment might present photos of street cleanliness and then ask people to rate their satisfaction with government performance, as Van Ryzin (2013) did. However, this approach raises the question of how far this means of presentation resembles how people actually experience street cleanliness and make real satisfaction judgments about actual public services in their daily lives. Sampling is only one aspect of external validity, in other words, while the generalisability of the experimental treatments and procedures to their real-world counterparts (also referred to as *mundane realism*) is another important aspect. Survey experiments do well on the first count, but often less well on the second. Thus, public management researchers should look for ways to make survey experiments more realistic, for example, by using real rather than fictitious information about government. Still, typical survey experiments have limitations in this regard, and thus an important role remains for other methods, notably field experiments with behavioural outcomes, to test real-world interventions.

A related problem of survey experiments concerns the durability of treatment effects. In many survey experiments, whether treatment effects last over time, and under what conditions, is seldom examined. For example, if the display of performance information would only temporarily alter subjects' perceptions or attitudes but vanish along the way when it comes to being transformed into actual behaviour, then the real-world relevance of such effects may be questioned. However, as Mutz (2011) points out, often the assumption in survey experiments is that the short-term treatment (such as exposure to government performance information) is repeated or ongoing in the real world, and thus even short-term effects in the context of a survey can have practical implications if they suggest a cumulative or sustained causal process operating in the social or political world. In either case, public management researchers should examine ways to assess the durability of treatment effects within the survey experiments they conduct, or at least to address these issues more explicitly. Indeed, longitudinal surveys are well suited to assess the timespan of treatment effects but are underutilised in public management research.

The use of survey experiments administered through online platforms has increased the feasibility of their use but comes with some loss of control. Researchers using online platforms cannot be sure whether study participants actually read or comprehend all experimental materials, or just rush through the questionnaire. Therefore, survey experimenters are well advised to include checks to make sure that these *survey satisficers* do not reduce the statistical power and reliability of their data. One of the options for doing so is to include so-called *instructional manipulation checks* (Oppenheimer, Meyvis and Davidenko 2009) in the survey – preferably before experimental treatments are allocated to participants. These are small questions that can be used to filter out subjects who rush through the questionnaire. However, researchers clearly need to report whenever and why participants are screened out.

As we have discussed in this chapter, survey experiments have become one of the most popular modes of experimentation in public management research. And there exist a great variety of designs to choose from, such as split ballots, list experiments, factorial designs or conjoint experiments. Some of these designs have been discussed in this chapter, but many other types exist as well (for an overview, see Mutz 2011). But while survey experiments hold great potential to advance our knowledge about substantive and methodological issues in public management research, we also need to acknowledge their limitations. A research agenda that combines different types of experiments such as laboratory, field and survey experiments – together with findings from nonexperimental quantitative and qualitative methods – will, in our opinion, provide the best approach to building a credible evidence base. Therefore, replicating and extending findings from survey experiments across various methods is particularly important for the continued success of an experimental public management.

References

Auspurg, K. and Hinz, T. 2014. *Factorial Survey Experiments*. Thousand Oaks, CA: Sage Publications.

Andrews, R., Boyne, G. and Walker, R. 2006. 'Strategy content and organizational performance: an empirical analysis', *Public Administration Review*, 66(1): 52–63.

Bishop, G. and Smith, A. 2001. 'Response-order effects and the early Gallup split-ballots', *Public Opinion Quarterly*, 65(4): 479–505.

Bishop, G. and Smith, A. 1991. 'Gallup split ballot experiments', *The Public Perspective*, July/August: 25–7.

Blair, G. and Imai, K. 2012. 'Statistical analysis of list experiments', *Political Analysis*, 20: 47–77.

Bohannon, J. 2011. 'Social science for pennies', *Science*, 334(6054): 307.

Bouwman, R. and Grimmelikhuijsen, S. 2016. 'Experimental public administration from 1992 to 2014: a systematic literature and ways forward', *International Journal of Public Sector Management*, 29(2).

Brewer, G. and Walker, R. 2010. 'The impact of red tape on governmental performance: an empirical analysis', *Journal of Public Administration Research and Theory*, 20(1): 233–57.

Bullock, J., Stritch, J. and Rainey, H. 2015. 'International comparison of public and private employees' work motives, attitudes, and perceived rewards', *Public Administration Review*, 75(3): 489–97.

Cantril, H. 1944. *Gauging Public Opinion*. Princeton, NJ: Princeton University Press.

Chaudhuri, A. and Christofides, T. 2007. 'Item count technique in estimating the proportion of people with a sensitive feature', *Journal of Statistical Planning and Inference*, 137(2): 589–93.

Christenson, D. P. and Glick, D. M. 2012. 'Crowdsourcing panel studies and real-time experiments in MTurk', *The Political Methodologist*, 20(2): 27–32.

Christensen, R. and Stritch, J. 2016. 'Prosocial Dr. Jekyll, meet Deviant Mr. Hyde: exploring the confluence of other-oriented public values and self-centered narcissism'. Paper presented at The Public Values Consortium Workshop, Arizona State University.

Droitcour, J., Caspar, R., Hubbard, M., Parsley, T., Visscher, W. and Ezzati, T. 1991. 'The item count technique as a method of indirect questioning: a review of its development and a case study application', in *Measurement Errors in Surveys*, eds. P. Briemer, R. Groves, L. Lyberg, N. Mathiowetz and S. Sudman, 185–210. New York: John Wiley & Sons.

Gaines, B. and Kuklinski, J. 2011. 'Treatment effects', in *Cambridge Handbook of Experimental Political Science*, eds. J. Druckman, D. Green, J. Kuklinski and A. Lupia. Cambridge: Cambridge University Press.

Gaines, B., Kuklinski, J. and Quirk, P. 2007. 'The logic of the survey experiment reexamined', *Political Analysis*, 15: 1–20.

Glynn, A. 2013. 'What can we learn with statistical truth serum? Design and analysis of the list experiment', *Public Opinion Quarterly*, 77: 159–72.

Goodman, J., Cryder, C. and Amar, C. 2013. 'Data collection in a flat world: the strengths and weaknesses of mechanical Turk samples', *Journal of Behavioral Decision Making*, 26(3): 213–24.

Gossen, S. 2014. Social Desirability in Survey Research: Can the List Experiment Provide the Truth? PhD Dissertation. Phillips-University Marburg.

Green, D. and Holger, K. 2012. 'Modeling heterogeneous treatment effects in survey experiments with Bayesian additive regression trees'. *Public Opinion Quarterly*, 76(3): 491–511.

Green, P., Krieger, A. and Wind, Y. 2001. 'Thirsty years of conjoint analysis: reflections and prospects', in *Marketing Research Modelling: Progress and Prospects*, eds. Y. Wind and P. Green, 117–39. New York: Springer.

Green, P. and Rao, V. 1971. 'Conjoint measurement for quantifying judgemental data', *Journal of Marketing Research*, 8: 355–63.

Groeneveld, S., Tummers, L., Bronkhorst, B., Ashikali, T. and Van Thiel, S. 2015. 'Quantitative methods in public administration: their use and development through time', *International Public Management Journal*, 18(1): 61–86.

Hainmueller, J., Hangartner, D. and Yamamoto, T. 2015. 'Validating vignette and conjoint survey experiments against real-world behavior', *Proceedings of the National Academy of Sciences*, 112(8): 2395–2400.

Hainmueller, J., Hopkins, D. and Yamamoto, T. 2014. 'Causal inference in conjoint analysis: understanding multidimensional choices via stated preference experiments', *Political Analysis*, 22: 1–30.

Hansen, K., Olsen, A. and Bech, M. 2015. 'Cross-national yardstick comparisons: a choice experiment on a forgotten voter heuristic', *Political Behavior*, 37(4): 767–89.

Huff, C. and Tingley, D. 2015. '"Who are these people?" Evaluating the demographic characteristics and political preferences of MTurk survey respondents', *Research & Politics*, 2(3): 2053168015604648.

James, O. and Moseley, A. 2014. 'Does performance information about public services affect citizens' perceptions, satisfaction, and voice behaviour? Field experiments with absolute and relative performance information', *Public Administration*, 92(2): 493–511.

Jasso, G. 2006. 'Factorial survey methods for studying beliefs and judgments', *Sociological Methods & Research*, 34(3): 334–423.

Jilke, S. 2015. 'Choice and equality: are vulnerable citizens worse off after liberalization reforms?' *Public Administration*, 93(1): 68–85.

Jilke, S., Meuleman, B. and Van de Walle, S. 2015. 'We need to compare, but how? Measurement equivalence in comparative public administration', *Public Administration Review*, 75(1): 36–48.

Jilke, S. and Tummers, L. 2016. 'Cues of deservingness and street-level decision making: evidence from a conjoint experiment among US teachers'. Paper presented at IRSPM 2016 in Hong Kong.

Jilke, S., Van Ryzin, G. and Van de Walle, S. 2015. 'Responses to decline in marketized public services: an experimental evaluation of choice-overload', *Journal of Public Administration Research and Theory*, online first.

Kaufmann, W. and Feeney, M. K. 2012. 'Objective formalization, perceived formalization and perceived red tape', *Public Management Review*, 14(8): 1195–1214.

Kim, S. H. and Kim, S. 2013. 'National culture and social desirability bias in measuring public service motivation', *Administration & Society*, online first.

Kjeldsen, A. M. and Botcher Jacobsen, C. 2013. 'Public service motivation and employment sector: attraction or socialization?' *Journal of Public Administration Research and Theory*, 23(4): 899–926.

Kuklinski, J., Cobb, M. and Gilens, M. 1997. 'Racial attitudes and the "new South"', *Journal of Politics*, 59(2): 323–49.

Marvel, J. 2015. 'Unconscious bias in citizen's evaluations of public sector performance', *Journal of Public Administration Research and Theory*, online first.

Meier, K. and O'Toole, L. 2013. 'Subjective organizational performance and measurement error: common source bias and spurious relationships', *Journal of Public Administration Research and Theory* 23(2): 429–56.

Nielsen, P. and Bækgaard, M. 'Performance information, blame avoidance, and politicians' attitudes to spending and reform: evidence from an experiment', *Journal of Public Administration Research and Theory* 25(2): 545–69.

Miller, J. 1984. A New Survey Technique for Studying Deviant Behavior. PhD dissertation. George Washington University.

Miller, J. L., Rossi, P. H., Simpson, J. E. and Simpson, J. O. N. E. 1991. 'Felony punishments : a factorial survey of perceived justice in criminal sentencing', *Criminal Sentencing*, 82(2).

Mutz, D., 2011. *Population-Based Survey Experiments*. Princeton, NJ: Princeton University Press.

Noelle-Neumann, E. 1970. 'Wanted: rules for wording structured questionnaires', *Public Opinion Quarterly*, 34(2): 191–201.

Oppenheimer, D., Meyvis, T. and Davidenko, N. 2009. 'Instructional manipulation checks: detecting satisficing to increase statistical power', *Journal of Experimental Social Psychology*, 45: 867–72.

Paolacci, G. and Chandler, J. 2014. 'Inside the Turk: understanding mechanical Turk as a participant pool', *Current Directions in Psychological Science*, 23(3): 184–8.

Payne, S. 1951. *The Art of Asking Questions*. Princeton, NJ: Princeton University Press.

Presser, S. and Schuman, H. 1980. 'The measurement of a middle position in attitude surveys', *Public Opinion Quarterly*, 44(1): 70–85.

Raghavarai, D., Wiley, J. and Chitturi, P. 2010. *Choice-Based Conjoint Analysis: Models and Design*. Boca Raton, FL: CRC Press.

Rossi, P. H. and Nock, S. L. 1982. *Measuring Social Judgments: The Factorial Survey Approach*. London: Sage Publications.

Sniderman, P. M. 2011. 'The logic and design of the survey experiment: an autobiography of a methodological innovation', in *Cambridge Handbook of Experimental Political Science*, eds. J. Druckman, D. Green, J. Kuklinski and A. Lupia. Cambridge: Cambridge University Press.

Steijn, B. 2008. 'Person-environment fit and public service motivation', *International Public Management Journal*, 11(1): 13–27.

Suri, S. and Watts, S. 2011. 'Cooperation and contagion in web-based, networked public goods experiments', *PLoS ONE*, 6(3): e16836.

Tourangeau, R., Rips, L., and Rasinski, K. 2000. *The Psychology of Survey Response*. Cambridge: Cambridge University Press.

Tummers, L., Weske, U., Bouwman, R. and Grimmelikhuijsen, S. 2016. 'The impact of red tape on citizen satisfaction: an experimental study', *International Public Management Journal*, 19(3): 320–41.

Van Loon, N. M. 2016. 'Is public service motivation related to overall and dimensional work-unit performance as indicated by supervisors?' *International Public Management Journal*, 19(1): 78–110.

Van Ryzin, G. 2007. 'Pieces of a puzzle: linking government performance, citizen satisfaction, and trust', *Public Performance & Management, Review*, 30(4): 521–35.

Van Ryzin, G. 2013. 'An experimental test of the expectancy-disconfirmation theory of citizen satisfaction', *Journal of Policy Analysis and Management* 32(3): 567–614.

Van de Walle, S., Van Roosbroek, S. and Bouckaert, G. 2008. 'Trust in the public sector: is there any evidence for a long-term decline?', *International Review of Administrative Sciences*, 74(1): 47–64.

Van de Walle, S., and Van Ryzin, G. 2011. The order of questions in a survey on citizen satisfaction with public services: lessons from a split-ballot experiment', *Public Administration*, 89(4): 1436–50.

Vogel, D. and Kroll, A. 2016. 'The stability and change of PSM-related values across time: testing theoretical expectations against panel data', *International Public Management Journal*, 19(1): 53–77.

Walker, R., Andrews, R., Boyne, G., Meier, K. and O'Toole, L. 2010. 'Wakeup call: strategic management, network alarms, and performance', *Public Administration Review*, 70(5): 731–41.

Weibel, A., Rost, K. and Osterloh, M. 2010. 'Pay for performance in the public sector – benefits and (hidden) costs', *Journal of Public Administration Research and Theory*, 20(2): 387–412.

7 | Laboratory Experiments: Their Potential for Public Management Research

MARKUS TEPE AND CHRISTINE PROKOP

Introduction

The controlled environment of a laboratory experiment enables researchers to have a great deal of control over exogenous and endogenous variables and thereby provides ideal conditions to identify causal relationships (e.g., Iyengar 2011; Levitt and List 2007; Roth 1995; Wilde 1981). Even though the identification of causal relationships drives the accumulation of scientific knowledge, laboratory experiments are only seldom utilised in public administration research. Despite early calls for more experimental research in the fields of public administration and public management (e.g., Bozeman and Scott 1992), the use of laboratory research designs has only recently attracted broader scholarly interest (see Anderson and Edwards 2014; Baekgaard et al. 2015; and Margetts 2011 for review). Between 1990 and 2010, only 17 experiments were published in leading public administration and management journals. This number has increased to 22 over the past four years (Anderson and Edwards 2014: 5).[1] Yet despite the potential benefits of laboratory experiments, the majority of experimental studies in public administration and management are either survey experiments (e.g., Van De Walle and Van Ryzin 2011) or field experiments (e.g., Grimmelikhuijsen and Klijn 2015).

In order to encourage public management researchers to realise the potential and consider the use of laboratory experiments in their own work, this chapter starts with a brief introduction to the methodological foundation of laboratory research by focusing on the key differences

This work was supported by the Fritz Thyssen Foundation (FTF). The FTF is not responsible for any of the findings reported here.
[1] The investigated journals are: *Public Administration Review, Public Management Review, Journal of Public Administration Research and Theory*, and *Public Administration* (Margetts 2011: 194).

between psychological and economic experiments (Dickson 2011: 58). After outlining the basic practical steps in conducting laboratory experiments, this chapter concludes with a discussion of laboratory designs that have been published in public administration and management journals and lays out a research agenda on how laboratory experiments may improve the methodological toolbox available to public administration research.

Methodological Foundations

Internal and External Validity

Scholars in public administration tend to prefer externally valid data obtained through representative samples (e.g., survey data) over internally valid data produced in the laboratory (Anderson and Edwards 2014: 10). The strength of laboratory experiments, their high degree of internal validity, is a matter of research design and experimental control. As explained more fully in Chapter 4, internal validity refers to the question of how confidently an effect can be traced back to a cause. External validity, on the other hand, refers to the issue of whether a causal relationship can be generalised to variations in persons, settings, treatments, and outcomes (Shadish et al. 2002: 21).

On the continuum of experimental and quasi-experimental designs, the principal advantage of laboratory experiments is a strong manipulation control that enables researchers to isolate and test the causal effect of certain variables (Iyengar 2011: 77). The controlled variation of the independent variable (treatment), and a random assignment of participants to treatments, enables researchers to attribute differences in subjects' behaviour to the differences in treatments. In a well-designed laboratory experiment, simple statistical tests can be sufficient to explore the treatment effect, as the laboratory environment provides strong preconditions to exclude a large set of environmental influences (Morton and Williams 2010: 17).[2] Survey data, in contrast, can only provide indirect evidence on self-reported exposure to a causal variable (Iyengar 2011: 76). Depending on their disciplinary tradition and methodological foundation, psychologists and economists have

---

[2] Depending on the experimental design (e.g., group matching, repeated interactions), the statistical analysis can become more demanding (see Woon 2012).

developed different experimental styles and conventions to address the internal and external validity of laboratory data.

Presentation of the Experimental Task

The internal validity of experimental data may be threatened by the so-called experimental demand. Experimental demand occurs if cues in the experimental setting and procedures convey to subjects what is expected of them (Iyengar 2011: 77). In this case, subjects respond to subtle clues rather than the experimental manipulation itself (Iyengar 2011: 77). To minimise such demand effects, economic experiments tend to be carried out in a highly stylised environment. Economic experiments avoid the usage of normatively charged words (e.g., bureaucrat, politician, fairness), since such words are expected to evoke emotional reactions that undermine internal validity (Dickson 2011: 59). Thus, in economic experiments, the experimental setting is explained to subjects using neutral terminology with a minimum of moral or emotional connotations (Dickson 2011: 59). It is self-evident that many research questions of interest to scholars in psychology cannot be posed in stylised scenarios. Psychological laboratory experiments therefore tend to draw on contextually rich settings (Dickson 2011: 59). The instructions and experimental procedures provide subjects with a plausible but probably false description of a real-world situation so that subjects are presumed to mimic their real-world behaviour in the laboratory (Iyengar 2011: 77). The use of normative language in the contextually rich descriptions of decision scenarios is a way to make subjects feel and behave as-if they are in a real-world situation.

Student Sample

Conducting experiments with university students is a common practice in laboratory research in both psychology and economics. University students are, compared to other target groups, easy to recruit and typically require only moderate monetary incentives (Baekgaard et al. 2015: 326), which makes them a convenient sample. Due to the multiple specifics of student samples (e.g., age, income, level of education), the use of such samples has been criticised as producing externally invalid data (e.g., Dobbins et al. 1988; Levitt and List 2007).

This critique draws on a narrow concept of external validity that focuses on the generalisability of findings across subject pools. Druckman and Kam (2011) suggest a nuanced view on how to address the issues involved with the use of student samples for laboratory experiments. Drawing on Anderson and Bushman (1997: 21), they point out that external validity refers more generally to whether a conceptually equivalent relationship can be detected across samples, times, places, and operationalisations (Druckman and Kam 2011: 43). Depending on the purpose of the experimental study (e.g., testing a theory vs. searching for facts), achieving generalisability across samples might be of lesser interest (see Roth 1995). This applies in particular to experiments that aim to explore the empirical validity of game-theoretical models. According to Pott (1991: 906), such an experiment 'should be judged by the lessons it teaches about the theory and not by its similarity with what nature might have happened to have created'. Taking a similar position, Lucas (2003: 240 f.) points out that when an experiment is designed to test theoretical principles, it would be misleading to focus only on whether the sample allows for generalisation to a larger population (Anderson and Edwards 2014: 10).

In order to evaluate the external validity of a single study, Druckman and Kam (2011: 44) suggest distinguishing between experimental realism, which emphasises the question of whether an experimental 'situation is involving to the subjects, if they are forced to take it seriously, [and] if it has an impact on them' (Aronson et al. 1985: 485), and mundane realism, which refers to the question of whether the 'events occurring in the research setting are likely to occur in the normal course of subjects' lives' (Aronson et al. 1985: 485). If the goal of a laboratory experiment is to generalise a theory, experimental realism is more important than mundane realisms and there is nothing inherent to student subjects that would reduce experimental realism (Druckman and Kam 2011: 53). On the contrary, Druckman and Kam (2011: 51) presume that in this instance, the use of students, who are accustomed to following instructions and are in need of money, even enhances experimental realism (Druckman and Kam 2011: 51). The use of student samples only creates a problem if the treatment effect is moderated and the moderating variable varies between students and nonstudent samples (Druckman and Kam 2011: 51). In this case, Druckman and Kam (2011: 51) advise researchers to model the interaction and to use samples of students and nonstudents to discover the moderating dynamics.

Monetary Incentives

Monetary incentives are an important ingredient in most laboratory experiments, although such incentives play different roles depending on disciplinary tradition. Most psychological experiments tend not to offer inducements that are conditional on subjects' actions (Dickson 2011: 58) since the relevant quantiles of interest cannot be monetised in a reasonable way (Dickson 2011: 62). Subjects are usually paid fixed amounts or given academic credit points simply for participating in the study. Here, the incentives have the function of merely recruiting participants and compensating them for the time spent on completing the laboratory task.

Compared to psychological experiments, which are interested in the direct inquiry into subjects' preferences (e.g., effect of negative images on attitudes and behavior), economic experiments seek to control for subjects' preferences by manipulating them exogenously (Dickson 2011: 62). In behavioural economics, monetary rewards are an integral part of the laboratory task itself. Subjects receive cash payments that depend on their own choices and, in the case of a game-theoretic experiment, the choices of others (Dickson 2011: 61). Monetary incentives are used to control for subjects' preferences and as a means to elicit social preferences (Dickson 2011: 63).

The principle of using monetary incentives is derived from Smith's induced value theory (1976, 1982). According to this theory, the researcher induces preferences by choosing an appropriate compensation of subjects. This compensation scheme has to meet three essential conditions: First, higher rewards must be preferred over lower rewards without satiation (*nonsatiation*), meaning that there is a monotone increase in utility from compensation (Smith 1982: 931). Unlike monetary rewards paid in cash, other payment methods, like sweets or chocolate cake (Brennan and Charbonneau 2009), are potentially prone to a declining utility function among most subjects. Second, rewards must not depend solely on the actions of the subjects, but on a combination of strategies, meaning that rewards must be indirectly associated with the actions of other subjects (*salience*). Third, changes in the subjects' utility functions from the experiment must be based predominantly on the reward medium used, while other influences (e.g., priming through labelling) are negligible (Smith 1982: 934). Monetary rewards fulfil these conditions, and, in addition, most people are used to the concept of getting paid for effort, and monetary rewards are therefore easily implemented (see also Hertwig and Ortmann 2001: 390).

Anonymity and Deception

Anonymity and deception are two other important issues in laboratory experiments. Anonymity is not only important for subjects' recruitment and treatment assignment (Baekgaard et al. 2015: 327), but also to make sure that no subject feels compelled to adhere to any form of social punishment in the aftermath of the experimental session (e.g., for behaving selfishly). To achieve anonymity, subjects are randomly drawn from a subject pool and randomly assigned to the different experimental treatments (Baekgaard et al. 2015: 326). Furthermore, in the case of economic experiments, privacy screens on either side of the participants' computer monitors are recommended to make sure that the subjects cannot see the entries of the other subjects. In more general research ethics, it is important to ensure the privacy and confidentiality of information obtained from participants in an experiment.

Deception is another important and often controversial issue that has been widely debated in economics, psychology, and other social sciences. Following the broad definition of Sell (2008: 213), deception is any 'intentional misrepresentation of the study to the participants'. Cook and Yamagishi (2008: 215) give certain examples of what deception could include; it can 'involve providing limited information about the true purpose of the research, omitting information in the instructions to subjects not deemed central to the study but important to the research effort, or giving a "cover story" for the study that does not reveal the actual topic of study'. What is, of course, not covered by this definition is providing incomplete information about the full purpose of the study or its hypotheses (Sell 2008: 213). Since this particular information could alter the participants' behaviour (experimental demand), it is self-evident that researchers need to withhold it (see Bozeman and Scott 1992: 304; Kruglanski 1975).

In psychological experiments, deception is frequently used to test various hypotheses. For example, in social psychology confederates – actors who play a role in a contrived social setting – are often used in the laboratory as part of the experimental manipulation. Stanley Milgram's (1974) studies of obedience to authority are perhaps the best-known example, in which the participant and a confederate were allegedly randomly assigned to be teacher and learner. The confederate always became the learner, of course, and the participant always became the teacher, who was instructed to ask questions and administer electric shocks as punishment for wrong answers. The real aim of the experiment was to test how willing the participant was to follow the experimenter's instructions and administer increasingly strong electrical shocks to the confederate learner, who acted as if he were suffering increasing pain. Although providing fascinating insights on the extent to which ordinary people would harm others rather than disobey an authority figure, these studies were widely criticised for their use of deception and the resulting psychological trauma to participants. Nonetheless, the use of confederates and other forms of deception is a widely used tool in actual psychological experiments.

Economists, however, strictly oppose deception because of their interest in exploring rational decision making, and their concern with deception is that it may potentially contaminate the subject pool (Anderson and Edwards 2014: 6). Laboratory experiments in behavioural economics are often designed to test the empirical validity of a formal or game-theoretic model. The mathematical solution of the formal model, which serves as the benchmark for the experimental results, assumes common knowledge. Common knowledge means that subjects have all the relevant information to make a rational choice. With the use of deception, the experimental data would be invalid to test the empirical validity of the formal model.

Types of Laboratory Experiments

The purpose of laboratory experiments can be broadly classified into designs that focus on testing the predictions of a formal model, and designs that focus on the measurement of empirical facts. 'Model testing' laboratory experiments aim to identify the effect of a certain model parameter by manipulating that parameter. In this case, a well-defined formal model (e.g., derived from principal agent theory) is translated into an experimental vehicle to test the empirical validity of its game-theoretical solution. 'Model testing' laboratory experiments enable researchers to test a formal model with alternative parametrisations when this is impossible in the natural environment (Webster and Sell 2014: 33 f.). The outcome of such a laboratory experiment can be directly connected to the causal effect of altering a parameter of the formal model (Webster and Sell 2014: 33).

However, 'model testing' laboratory experiments impose high demands on the researcher's theoretical reasoning, in the sense that they require the researcher to formulate and solve a formal model analytically (Morton 1999). As Chapter 19 on formal modelling discusses, while in the beginning formal modelling of bureaucratic behaviour was guided by mainly economic research questions, like Niskanen (1971) for example, only a few scholars, like Weingast and Moran (1983), McCubbins and colleagues (1987), or Shepsle (1992), applied formal modelling to address topics in public administration and management. Nowadays, there is a large and growing field of literature on formal models of bureaucracy that researchers can build on when they are interested in the analysis of issues such as accountability, transparency, delegation, expertise, or oversight, as Chapter 19 discusses in more detail.

Formal models grounded in rational choice theory start from the assumption that agents are equipped with instrumental rationality and are self-interested. If such agents are placed in a well-defined decision situation in which the decision of one agent affects the well-being of another and vice versa (interdependence), formal models enable the researcher to analytically explore how altering a model parameter affects the outcome. Game theory provides the methodological toolset to solve such formal models (see, e.g., Morrow [1994] and McCarty and Meirowitz [2014] for introductory textbooks). The analytical solution of the formal model provides the benchmark of how subjects are predicted to behave in a given interdependent decision situation under the presumption of common knowledge and instrumental rationality. Once the parameter setting of the formal model is implemented in a laboratory experiment, this theoretically driven prediction will be compared to the actual behaviour of subjects. Usually, the game-theoretical analysis of a formal model will explore how parameter changes alter the predicted outcome (*comparative statics*). Rather than comparing the predicted and laboratory outcomes for a single parameter setting, researchers conduct multiple laboratory sessions in which they change the value of the theoretically interesting model parameter step by step, while keeping all other parameters constant. In doing so, laboratory experiments provide a powerful tool to explore the empirical validity of formal models of bureaucracy.

'Measurement' experiments, in contrast, focus on evaluating social preferences. Public administration and management research is often interested in the subjects' social preferences such as work satisfaction, interpersonal trust, work effort, fairness, or risk appetite. Observational studies rely on large-scale surveys in which these constructs are measured on a single or multi-item scale. Survey responses, however, have no consequence for the respondent; in a strictly rational choice sense, these stated preferences are 'cheap talk' and may deviate fundamentally from the respondents' true preference or actual behaviour. Several studies comparing stated preferences with preferences revealed in a laboratory experiment show that self-reported attitudinal measures of social preferences reported in surveys are weakly correlated with behavioural measures of social preferences obtained via incentivised laboratory experiments (e.g., Glaeser et al. 2000; Wilson and Eckel 2011).

Besides the 'cheap talk' argument, it is well known from survey research that, particularly in cases where items touch on social topics, responses can be biased through social desirability in one direction or another (Maccoby and Maccoby 1954). Kim and Kim (2014), for example, detected the social desirability bias in surveys on Public Service Motivation (PSM). Laboratory experiments with monetary incentives played under the condition of anonymity certainly do not provide a panacea against social desirability bias, but they are expected to provide a better environment to keep such biases to a minimum.

While, in some cases, it might be sufficient to aim for an improved measurement of social preferences, the full potential of 'measurement' experiments unfolds when they are conducted on different subject pools. A motive behind the variation of the target population can be to determine the external validity of previous laboratory results (Morton and Williams 2010: 347). Scholars in public management research, however, often work with the assumption that the public sector attracts a certain motivational type of agent (e.g., Delfgaauw and Dur 2010; Luechinger et al. 2010). In this case, conducting a measurement experiment, for example, measuring altruism on students of public administration compared to students of other disciplines can be used to explore an argument derived from public management theory.

The label 'measurement' laboratory experiment is to some extent misleading since 'measurement' experiments also tend to rely on some simple formal games. The dictator game has become a popular experimental vehicle to measure altruism; the ultimatum game is frequently used to measure fairness, and the trust game evaluates trust and trustworthiness (e.g., Ostrom and Walker 2005). These games, just to name a few, come with an analytical solution, yet the focus of 'measurement' experiments lies on using them as a vehicle to measure social preferences. Moreover, 'model testing' and 'measurement' experiments do not exclude each other. On the contrary, researchers might want to explore whether a treatment effect (e.g., higher punishment fees increase compliance) is conditional on the subject pool (e.g., students of public administration compared to students from other disciplines). Laboratory experiments provide a methodologically reliable tool to evaluate such conditional relationships.

Laboratory Experiments in Practice

Recruitment and Subject Pool Management

Subjects are typically recruited voluntarily and registered in a database from which they are randomly invited to participate in an experimental session. The invitations are usually distributed via e-mail and subjects choose an experimental session that suits their schedule. The recruitment systems Online Recruitment System for Economic Experiments (ORSEE)[3] by Greiner (2015) and the Hamburg Registration and Organisation Online Tool (Hroot)[4] by Bock and colleagues (2012) are software tools that allow researchers to schedule experimental sessions and manage the subject pool. Over the course of the registration process, subjects are informed about the conditions of participation (e.g., monetary incentives, no deception, anonymity). Subject management systems are important not only to randomly assign subjects to experimental sessions (Greiner 2015: 115), but also to keep track of participants in order to avoid subjects participating in the same experiment more than once. The aim of ORSEE and Hroot, both of which are free of charge, is to simplify the organisation of laboratory experiments

---

[3] www.orsee.org/web/ (accessed February 08, 2016)
[4] www.wiso.uni-hamburg.de/forschung/forschungslabor/experimentallabor/aktu elle-projekte/hroot/ (accessed February 08, 2016)

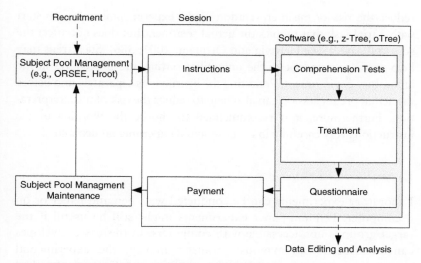

Figure 7.1: Process of accomplishing a laboratory session

Note: Online Recruitment System for Economic Experiments (ORSEE), Hamburg Registration and Organisation Online Tool (Hroot), Zurich Toolbox for Readymade Economic Experiments (z-Tree), Open-Source Platform for Laboratory, Online and Field Experiments (oTree)

and thereby reduce its personnel costs. More importantly, however, these tools increase the quality and transparency of the recruitment and assignment process (Greiner 2015: 115).

Instructions

The instructions (either computerised or by pen and paper) must state clearly how the experiment will proceed. They have to provide all necessary information on the subjects' resources and options, the structure of social interaction and how the subjects' payoff is affected by their own decisions and the decisions of the other subjects. Due to the common knowledge assumption, it is absolutely crucial that the instructions are easy to understand and that they cover every aspect of the experiment required for deriving a rational solution.

To evaluate whether all subjects have fully understood the experimental procedure, their options, and the consequences of their choices for their monetary payment, the experiment may proceed with a comprehension test (Baekgaard et al. 2015: 327). Another option to reduce the risk of misinterpretation of the experimental task is to start with a trial task that mimics the actual treatment but does not affect the subjects' payoff (see Hertwig and Ortmann 2001: 386). Such trials may help participants adapt to the unfamiliar setting and procedures in the laboratory environment. Pretesting the instructions separately and before the actual pretest session can also help to reduce the risk of misinterpretation. Furthermore, it is recommended to choose the wording of the instructions very carefully in order to avoid experimental demand.

Experimental Software

Laboratory experiments can be conducted with pen and paper or on a computer. Pen-and-paper experiments might still be useful if the target group is not accessible with computers. In this case, envelopes can be used to anonymously transfer money, the experimental currency, and information between participants. The use of linked computers, referred to as computer pools, makes conducting game-theoretical experiments much easier, however. The computers must be set up to be connected with each other (LAN or WLAN) and equipped with appropriate experimental software.

The experiments can be conducted either in a campus computer lab or on a mobile laboratory. Mobile laboratories consist of a set of notebooks and can therefore be moved wherever the subjects of interest are located (Morton and Williams 2010: 296). This approach enables researchers to reach subject pools who are otherwise difficult to access, but who possess particular backgrounds of interest, such as government employees or recipients of specific public services (Harrison and List 2004: 1014; Morton and Williams 2010: 296). Using the unique mobility potential of the laboratory equipment, these laboratory-in-the-field experiments can further mitigate the homogeneity bias that plagues student samples and thereby improve the external validity of experimental results, as discussed in Chapter 5 on field experiments.

There are various software packages to program and conduct laboratory experiments.[5] Among economists, and increasingly other social scientists, the Zurich Toolbox for Readymade Economic Experiments (z-Tree) is used very frequently. The software package, developed by Fischbacher (2007), is free of charge, comes with

---

[5] See Baekgaard et al. (2015: 329) for a list of experimental software.

a detailed documentation and supporting tutorial, and is therefore easily accessible for social scientists with moderate experience in computer programming (www.ztree.uzh.ch). z-Tree software for developing and conducting economic experiments provides a server-client (ztree) to conduct the experiment and as many user-clients as needed (zleafs) for the participants. The experimental data are stored in spreadsheets that are easily convertible for statistical software packages.

Z-Tree is limited in the sense that it requires the installation of software on the subjects' devices. The Open-Source Platform for Laboratory, Online and Field Experiments (oTree) developed by Chen et al. (2015) provides a promising extension of the set of experimental software available to researchers as it can run on any device that has a web browser (www.otree.org). However, the use of oTree requires advanced programming skills in Python.

Experimental Design Issues

Building on the general overview of experimental design and analysis in Chapter 4, this section discusses some specific issues for laboratory experiments, where simplicity is certainly the best guideline. Common design mistakes are, to list a few examples, either to forget to include a baseline or reference treatment, or to overload the design by having too many independent variables (treatments). Note, by using a factorial design, an increase in independent variables (treatment parameters) corresponds to an exponential increase in laboratory sessions. Depending on the size of the accessible subject pool, however, the number of laboratory sessions may be limited.

A related question is whether a single subject should be confronted with more than one treatment condition ('within-subjects' design) during a laboratory session, or whether each subject is exposed to only one treatment condition ('between-subjects' design). Another important design question concerns the repetition of treatments vs. one-shot interactions. While in some cases a game needs to be played repeatedly in order to observe subjects' strategy, repetition also creates learning effects that can bias results (Hertwig and Ortmann 2001: 387).

With repeated interactions, the experimenter also has to decide on the matching protocol (e.g., 'partner' vs. 'stranger' matching). Another design aspect concerns the role of order effects (e.g., when the subjects are informed about their payoff). Answering these design questions is in many cases not a matter of right or wrong, but a matter of the focus of the experimental vehicle. There is a growing number of textbooks on how to conduct laboratory experiments in social sciences that discuss experimental design issues in detailed length (e.g., Druckman et al. 2011; Kittel, Luhan, and Morton 2012; Morton and Williams 2010; Webster and Sell 2014).

Questionnaire and Payment

The experimental treatment is followed by a standardised questionnaire collecting subjects' standard socioeconomic information (e.g., age, gender, field of study). Depending on the research question and the analytical focus of the experiment, it can be useful to collect additional information that records some self-reported attitudes related to the topic of the experimental treatment. These items can later be used within the robustness analysis or to explore differences between stated and revealed preferences. If the questionnaire contains items that are of substantive theoretical interest, one might pay particular attention to the issue of whether the experimental task itself may influence these self-reported attitudes. Under these circumstances it might be advisable to alter the order of events and begin the experimental session with the standardised questionnaire followed by the treatment.

After the treatment and after all subjects have finished the questionnaire, they will privately receive their payoff in cash. The payoff consists of two components: First, the show-up fee, which is paid to each subject regardless of the performance in the experiment. Second, the larger part of the payoff is the money earned over the course of the experiment. Depending on the type of experiment, it can be convenient to let subjects play using an experimental currency (e.g., tokens). These tokens are translated into cash at the end of the experiment using an exchange rate explained in the instructions.

Another design question concerns the actual scale of monetary incentives. Using an appropriate scale of monetary incentives is not only important to motivate subjects to participate in a certain experimental treatment, but also to maintain a willing subject pool (Dickson 2011: 63). Morton and Williams's (2010) exploration of payment policies in experimental economics laboratories suggest that subjects' payments are between 50 and 100 per cent above the minimum wage for the time spent in the laboratory. They find that the fit between subjects' behaviour and the game's theoretically predicted behaviour increases with stronger monetary incentives. For the case of Germany, it has become common practice in behavioural experiments with student subject pools that the show-up fee amounts to about five to eight euros and the average hourly payoff should not be less than the hourly wage of a student assistant (e.g., 10 to 15 euros).

Depending on the structure of the game (e.g., ultimatum bargaining vs. public goods game), subjects' actual payment can deviate substantially from the average payment. Before ordering cash money the experimenter should therefore calculate the expected sum of payoffs. Experimental designs that allow subjects to lose money need to define a procedure of how to deal with bankruptcy (e.g., bankrupt subjects continue the game, but will only receive the show-up fee). Another design-related question in experiments that run over more than a single period is how to determine the actual payoff (sum of profits over all periods, the average profit or the profit from a randomly selected period). The very last step of an experimental session is to update the subject pool management system to keep track of who participated in the laboratory session.

Public Management Experiments

Among those studies in public administration and management that rely on an experimental research design, laboratory experiments are still an exception (see Anderson and Edwards 2015: 24 f.). The following section will therefore exemplify some of the laboratory experiments that have been published in public administration and management journals against the criteria and styles of psychological and economic experiments discussed previously.

Examples of Psychology-Style Experiments

The studies by Nutt (2006), Brewer and Brewer (2011), and to a lesser extent James (2011) represent examples of laboratory studies in public administration and management that adhere to the methodological principles of psychological experiments. Nutt (2006) draws on the manipulation of contextually rich decision scenarios to compare the

Table 7.1: Laboratory experiment published in public administration and management

Author(s) and date	Journal	Topic	Style	Sample	Monetary incentives	Deception
Nutt (2006)	JPART	Decision making in the public and private sectors	Contextually rich (scenarios)	Senior managers (from the private and public sectors)	No	No
James (2011)	JPART	Perception of and satisfaction with local government performance	Contextually rich (information cues)	Local residents (and students)	No	Yes
Brewer and Brewer (2011)	JPART	Vigilance and sector affiliation	Contextually rich	Students	No (but course credits)	Yes
Esteve et al. (2015)	IPMJ	PSM and collaboration in prisoners dilemma	Stylised	Students	Yes	No
Esteve et al. (2016)	PAR	PSM and willingness to contribute in the public good game	Stylised	Students	Yes	No
Tepe (2016)	PMR	PSM and behavior in the trust game	Stylised	Students (from three subject pools)	Yes	No
Smith (2016)	PAR	Mission matching and performance in a real-effort task	Stylised/Contextually rich	Students	Yes	No

Note: Journal of Public Administration Research and Theory (JPART), Public Management Review (PMR), International Public Management Journal (IPMJ), Public Administration Review (PAR); also see Anderson and Edwards (2015: 24).

decision-making practices among 103 private sector and 134 public sector mid-level managers. Participants were asked to review different budget requests and to indicate their likelihood of approving such a request. The budget requests were presented to subjects as contextually rich scenarios and these scenarios were manipulated according to the amount of analytical support and budgeting approaches. Their findings suggest that public sector managers were less likely to support budget decisions backed by analysis, and more likely to support those that are derived from bargaining with agency people. Nutt (2006) is an example of the use of scenarios in laboratory experiments (also see De Fine Licht 2014; Grimmelikhuijsen et al. 2013).[6]

James (2011) estimated the effect of information cues about the relatively good performance of services provided by a local government on experimental subjects' perceived performance and satisfaction with those services. The design used an experiment with 100 student participants, who were not paid for participation, conducted in a controlled class-setting to explore the robustness of findings from a field experiment with an identical treatment that was delivered to general citizens. The treatments (no information about performance or information about performance) were randomly allocated to participants (50 in each group), who were not aware of the other treatment condition. All participants were then surveyed about their perceptions of performance and satisfaction with services, with the information cue about performance raising perceptions of performance and satisfaction. A related experiment with information cues about relatively bad performance had opposite effects (James 2011: 403–9).

Brewer and Brewer (2011) utilise a psychomotor vigilance task to measure subjects' vigilance and test whether vigilance changes when performing the task in a government-funded research project compared to a research project that is funded privately. In the psychomotor vigilance task subjects' goal is to press the space bar on a computer keyboard

---

[6] In the study by Grimmelikhuijsen et al. (2013), subjects were randomly exposed to different government web sites to explore the effect of transparency on subjects' trust in government. This experiment was carried out with 381 students from the Netherlands and 279 in South Korea in order to explore cultural variation on the treatment effect. De Fine Licht (2014) used a similar scenario-based-approach to explore the effect of transparency on legitimacy beliefs. In this study, the stimulus was presented to subjects in the form of fictional newspaper articles. The experiment was conducted with a total of 1,032 subjects from an electronic panel of Swedish citizens.

any time a visually displayed time-counter begins. This counter is time locked and after participants press the space bar, the counter stops and participants can gauge how quickly they have responded. At the very beginning of the psychomotor vigilance task, subjects read that the research they were about to take part in was being funded by either a 'government agency' or a 'business firm'. The experiment was conducted with undergraduate students who got partial credit toward a research appreciation requirement. Their findings suggest that subjects are significantly faster, more accurate, and more vigilant when their work is announced to be funded by a government agency rather than a private business firm (Brewer and Brewer 2011: i347). This study is not only an example of how deception is used in psychological experiments, but also an example of how to use psychological measurement techniques (e.g., vigilance) for a research question in public administration and management. There are plenty more psychological measurement vehicles that may be applied to public administration and management related issues.[7]

Examples of Economics-Style Experiments

The studies by Esteve and colleagues (2015, 2016) are examples of using standard game-theoretic measurement vehicles to compare subjects' behaviour and self-reported attitudes obtained through a post-experimental survey. Specifically, Esteve and colleagues (2016) utilise a modified version of the public goods game to measure subjects' willingness to cooperate and compare this behavioural measure with subjects' self-reported PSM. In the public goods game, subjects decide how to allocate an initial endowment between two options: contributing to a public good that will benefit all members of the group (with a known multiplier), or keeping the money for their own individual benefit. Subjects' PSM was collected with paper and pencil. The experimental data obtained from 263 students indicate that the willingness to contribute is positively associated with self-reported PSM.

In a related study, Esteve and colleagues (2015) explore the effect of PSM on student subjects' collaborative behaviour in three different

---

[7] Other examples of laboratory experiments in public administration and management that adhere to the principles of psychological experiments are, for example, Scott (1997) and Knott et al. (2003).

prisoner's dilemma games. In the prisoner's dilemma two randomly matched subjects can choose to either 'cooperate' or 'defect'. If both subjects cooperate, they both receive the reward A. If both subjects defect, they both receive the reward B, with A > B. If one subject cooperates and the other defects, the cooperating subject receives the reward C and the defecting subjects receives reward D, with D > C. If D > A > C > B, the rational solution for both players is not to cooperate even though both could be better off cooperating. The experiment was conducted with 320 students who were incentivised by payoffs between 10 and 490 euros. However, among the 320 subjects only 12 were randomly selected to receive the amount based on their behaviour and the behaviour of the other player. The experimental findings suggest that PSM affects collaboration when the individual decides to cooperate.

Tepe (2016) also utilises a standard game-theoretic vehicle to measure subjects' behaviour but compares subjects' behaviour between different student subject pools. Specifically, the study utilises the trust game proposed by Berg and colleagues (1995). In this game, subjects are matched anonymously and randomly sorted into groups of two. One subject is endowed with a certain amount of money (trustor). The trustor can keep the entire sum or can send a part of the money to the second subject, the trustee. Both individuals know that any amount sent will be tripled in value and that the receiving subject has the option of sending back a part of the tripled sum of money. In sending money, the trustor is demonstrating trust; in returning money, the second subject, the trustee, is demonstrating trustworthiness. The trust game was conducted on three different student subject pools, namely students of public administration, economy, and law, in order to explore the role of self-selection into different fields of study for the level of trust and trustworthiness. The experimental data suggest that public administration students in a sample of 208 subjects were more trusting and trustworthy than those in the two reference groups. This study also provides an example of how to explore public/private sector differences with the help of a mobile laboratory to reach different subject pools.[8]

---

[8] Another example of a subject-pool experiment in public administration is the study by Alatas et al. (2009). They conducted a corruption experiment with 147 Indonesian public servants and 180 Indonesian students. Their results suggest that the Indonesian public servant subjects have a significantly lower tolerance of corruption than the Indonesian students.

Smith (2016) presents another economic-style experimental design. Rather than using a game-theoretical measurement vehicle, Smith (2016) utilises a real-effort task to explore the motivational effect of mission matching on subjects' effort. The experiment was conducted with 117 university students and a minimum payment of 20 US dollars. To measure effort, the study utilises the 'slider task' programmed by Gill and Prowse (2015), conducted with the software z-Tree (Fischbacher 2007). In this task, subjects were shown 48 sliders on a computer screen (Smith 2016: 15). Each slider, ranging from 0 to 100, was initially set to the value of 0, and the task was to move as many sliders to the value of 50 as possible within a given time limit (Smith 2016: 15). The subjects' performance in the task then results in a donation to one of two diametrically opposed advocacy organisations: the National Rifle Association or the Brady Campaign to Prevent Gun Violence (Smith 2016: 15). In the post-experimental survey, subjects were asked how much they agreed with the goals of the organisations they performed the task for in order to measure mission matching. The experimental results indicate that matched subjects exert more effort than mismatched subjects (Smith 2016: 1).

Even though there is a rich and flourishing literature on formal models in public administration (e.g., Gailmard and Patty 2012), to the knowledge of the authors there is no study published in a leading journal on public administration and management that uses laboratory experiments to test the predictions derived from an explicit formal model. An example of such a model-testing laboratory experiment is presented in Chapter 19 on formal models.

Concluding Remarks

This chapter provided a brief introduction to the methodological corner-stones of laboratory research, and described the different conventions and research styles that apply to laboratory experiments in psychology and economics. These styles come with different strengths and weaknesses, depending on the type of research question explored. The review of laboratory designs published in the field of public management shows that scholars have employed both styles of laboratory experiments. Compared to public management, both disciplines – psychology and economics – have a long tradition of using laboratory experiments. On these grounds, there is no need for public management to develop a methodological foundation for laboratory research on its own. On the contrary, depending on the specific nature of the research question, scholars in public management should decide which experimental style is more suitable to address their research question. Once this decision has been made, efforts should be made to fully apply to the conventions and research styles of either laboratory experiments in psychology or economics.

Two more suggestions on how to proceed with laboratory experiments in public management can be drawn from the review of existing laboratory studies. First, the setup, conventions, and measurement techniques in psychological experiments provide optimal conditions to explore cognitive evaluation and decision processes. Here, laboratory experiments might be used to explore how heuristics are developed, and how they are applied in the private and public sectors, or more generally, how scenarios and information cues affect the subjects' decision mode (affectional mode vs. analytical mode). Second, current laboratory research in public management that partially or fully adheres to the conventions of economic experiments focuses on exploring the nexus between behaviour in the laboratory and self-reported attitudes (in particular PSM), usually collected through a post-experimental survey. The full potential of laboratory experiments conducted in the style of economic experiments, however, lies in creating and manipulating institutional environments that reflect certain features of public organisations (e.g., delegation, hierarchy). The design of institutional environments and manipulation of certain institutional features within requires a well-defined theoretical framework. Such a framework can be found, for example, in the literature on formal models of bureaucracy (e.g., Gailmard and Patty 2012). Many of these models, some of which are now considered modern classics in political economy (e.g., Niskanen 1971), have not yet been examined experimentally.

Even though laboratory experiments currently fill only a limited niche in public administration research to date, there are good reasons to be optimistic about their growing usage in the near future. Compared to observational methods, laboratory experiments had been considered to be resource intense since running a laboratory for behavioural experiments requires trained staff, technology, and space (Iyengar 2011: 74). These costs, however, have gradually declined over recent decades primarily due to technological progress. First, almost every university offers their students computer pools either for their personal use or for teaching. With some easily implementable reconstructions (e.g., privacy screens between workplaces), these campus computer pools can also be used to conduct laboratory experiments. Second, software packages to program and conduct laboratory experiments such as z-Tree and oTree and subject pool management tools such as ORSEE and Hroot can be easily installed and are free to use for scientific purpose. Even though programming skills are rare among students of public management, the widespread use of statistical software, which is compulsory in most curricula, provides students with a basic understanding of how to program computational routines. Software packages such as z-Tree come with a detailed tutorial[9] and support material,[10] which helps interested researchers to learn to program an experiment by themselves. In addition, professional associations, such as the European Consortium for Political Research (ECPR), regularly offer summer and winter school courses on designing and implementing laboratory experiments.

Finally, it is important to point out that any attempt to strengthen the use of laboratory experimentation in public management research has to start with strengthening the role of micro-level decision theory. Thus, in order to get more students interested in laboratory experiments of this kind, it appears crucial to put more emphasis on psychological, social, and economic decision theories in the curriculum of public administration and management programmes.

References

Alatas, V., L. Cameron, A. Chaudhuri, N. Erkal, and L. Gangadharan 2009. 'Subject pool effects in a corruption experiment: a comparison of Indonesian public servants and Indonesian students', *Experimental Economics* 12 (1): 113–32.

Anderson, C. A. and B. J. Bushman 1997. 'External validity of "trivial" experiments: the case of laboratory aggression', *Review of General Psychology* 1 (1): 19–41.

Anderson, D. M. and B. C. Edwards 2015. 'Unfulfilled promise: laboratory experiments in public administration research', *Public Management Review* 17 (10): 1–25.

---

[9] z-Tree 3.5. Tutorial and Reference Manual www.ztree.uzh.ch/static/doc/man ual.pdf (accessed February 08, 2016)

[10] Sample treatments can be found on the z-Tree website www.iew.uzh.ch/ztree/ index.php (accessed February 08, 2016)

Aronson, E., M. B. Brewer, and M. J. Carlsmith 1985. 'Experimentation in social psychology', in G. Lindzey and E. Aronson (eds.) *Handbook of Social Psychology*, Vol. 2. New York: Random House, pp. 441–86.

Baekgaard, M., C. Baethge, J. Blom-Hansen, C. Dunlop, M. Esteve, M. J., B. Kisida, et al. 2015. 'Conducting experiments in public management research: a practical guide', *International Public Management Journal* 18 (2): 323–42.

Berg, J., J. Dickhaut, and K. McCabe 1995. 'Trust, reciprocity, and social history', *Games and Economic Behavior* 10 (1): 122–42.

Bock, O., A. Nicklisch, and I. Baetge 2012. 'Hroot: Hamburg registration and organization online tool', *WiSo-HH Working Paper Series*, no. 1.

Bozeman, B. and P. Scott 1992. 'Laboratory experiments in public policy and management', *Journal of Public Administration Research and Theory* 2 (3): 293–313.

Brennan, M. and J. Charbonneau 2009. 'Improving mail survey response rate using chocolate and replacement questionnaires', *Public Opinion Quarterly* 73 (2): 368–78.

Brewer, G. A. and G. A. Brewer Jr. 2011. 'Parsing public/private differences in work motivation and performance: an experimental study', *Journal of Public Administration Research and Theory* 21 (suppl 3): i347–62.

Chen, D., M. Schonger, and C. Wickens 2015. 'oTree – an open-source platform for laboratory, online, and field experiments – otree.pdf', www.otree.org/oTree.pdf (accessed November 29).

Cook, K. S. and T. Yamagishi 2008. 'A defense of deception on scientific grounds', *Social Psychology Quarterly* 21 (3): 215–21.

De Fine Licht, J. 2014. 'Policy area as a potential moderator of transparency effects: an experiment', *Public Administration Review* 74 (3): 361–71.

Delfgaauw, J. and R. Dur 2010. 'Managerial talent, motivation, and self-selection into public management', *Journal of Public Economics* 94 (9): 654–60.

Dickson, E. S. 2011. 'Economics vs. psychology experiments: stylization, incentives, and deception', in Druckman, Green, Kuklinski, and Lupia (eds.), pp. 58–70.

Dobbins, G. H., I. M. Lane, and D. D. Steiner 1988. 'A note on the role of laboratory methodologies in applied behavioral research: don't throw out the baby with the bath water', *Journal of Organizational Behavior* 9 (3): 281–6.

Druckman, J. N., D. P. Green, J. H. Kuklinski, and A. Lupia 2011. *Cambridge Handbook of Experimental Political Science*. Cambridge: Cambridge University Press.

Druckman, J. N. and C. D. Kam 2011. 'Students as experimental participants: a defense of the narrow data base', in Druckman, Green, Kuklinski, and Lupia (eds.), pp. 41–57.

Druckman, J. N. and T. J. Leeper 2012. 'Learning more from political communication experiments: pretreatment and its effects', *American Journal of Political Science* 56 (4): 875–96.

Esteve, M., D. Urbig, A. van Witteloostuijn, and G. Boyne 2016. 'Prosocial behavior and public service motivation', *Public Administration Review* 76 (1): 177–87.

Esteve, M., A. van Witteloostuijn, and G. Boyne 2015. 'The effects of public service motivation on collaborative behavior: evidence from three experimental games', *International Public Management Journal* 18 (2): 171–89.

Fischbacher, U. 2007. 'Z-Tree: Zurich toolbox for ready-made economic experiments', *Experimental Economics* 10 (2): 171–8.

Gailmard, S. and J. W. Patty 2012. 'Formal models of bureaucracy', *Annual Review of Political Science*, 15: 353–77.

Gill, D. and V. Prowse 2015. A Novel Computerized Real Effort Task Based on Sliders. (http://users.ox.ac.uk/~nuff0229/GillProwseSliders.pdf).

Glaeser, E. L., D. I. Laibson, J. A. Scheinkman, and C. L. Soutter 2000. 'Measuring trust', *The Quarterly Journal of Economics* 115 (3): 811–46.

Greiner, B. 2015. 'Subject pool recruitment procedures: organizing experiments with ORSEE', *Journal of the Economic Science Association* 1 (1): 114–25.

Grimmelikhuijsen, S. and A. Klijn 2015. 'The effects of judicial transparency on public trust: evidence from a field experiment', *Public Administration* 93 (4): 995–1011.

Grimmelikhuijsen, S., G. Porumbescu, B. Hong, and T. Im 2013. 'The effect of transparency on trust in government: a cross-national comparative experiment', *Public Administration Review* 73 (4): 575–86.

Harrison, G. W. and J. A. List 2004. 'Field experiments', *Journal of Economic Literature* 42 (4): 1009–55.

Hertwig, R. and A. Ortmann 2001. 'Experimental practices in economics: a methodological challenge for psychologists?' *Behavioral and Brain Sciences* 24 (3): 383–403.

Iyengar, S. 2011. 'Laboratory experiments in political science', in Druckman, Green, Kuklinski, and Lupia (eds.), pp. 73–88.

James, O. 2011. 'Performance measures and democracy: information effects on citizens in field and laboratory experiments', *Journal of Public Administration Research and Theory* 21 (3): 399–418.

Kim, S. H. and S. Kim 2014. 'National culture and social desirability bias in measuring public service motivation', *Administration and Society*, published online first.

Kittel, B., W. J. Luhan, and R. B. Morton (eds.) 2012. *Experimental Political Science: Principles and Practices*. Basingstoke: Palgrave Macmillan.

Knott, J. H., G. J. Miller, and J. Verkuilen 2003. 'Adaptive incrementalism and complexity: experiments with two-person cooperative signaling games', *Journal of Public Administration Research and Theory* 13 (3): 341–65.

Kruglanski, A. W. 1975. 'The human subject in the psychology experiment: fact and artifact', *Advances in Experimental Social Psychology* 8: 101–47.

Levitt, S. D. and J. A. List 2007. 'What do laboratory experiments measuring social preferences reveal about the real world?' *The Journal of Economic Perspectives* 21 (2): 153–74.

Lucas, J. W. 2003. 'Theory-testing, generalization, and the problem of external validity', *Sociological Theory* 21 (3): 236–53.

Luechinger, S., A. Stutzer, and R. Winkelmann 2010. 'Self-selection models for public and private sector job satisfaction', *Research in Labor Economics* 30: 233–51.

Maccoby, E. E. and N. Maccoby 1954. 'The interview: a tool of social science', in Lindzey and Aronsen (eds.), *Handbook of Social Psychology*, pp. 449–87.

Margetts, H. Z. 2011. 'Experiments for public management research', *Public Management Review* 13 (2): 189–208.

McCarty, N. and A. Meirowitz 2007. *Political Game Theory: An Introduction.* Cambridge: Cambridge University Press.

McCubbins, M. D., R. G. Noll, and B. R. Weingast 1987. 'Administrative procedures as instruments of political control', *Journal of Law, Economics, and Organization* 3 (2): 243–77.

Milgram, S. 1974. *Obedience to Authority: An Experimental View.* New York: Harper and Row.

Morrow, J. D. 1994. *Game Theory for Political Scientists.* Princeton, NJ: Princeton University Press.

Morton, R. B. 1999. *Methods and Models. A Guide to the Empirical Analysis of Formal Models in Political Science.* Cambridge: Cambridge University Press.

Morton, R. B. and K. C. Williams 2010. *Experimental Political Science and the Study of Causality: From Nature to the Lab.* Cambridge: Cambridge University Press.

Niskanen, W. A. 1971. *Bureaucracy and Representative Government.* Chicago: Aldine Atherton.

Nutt, P. C. 2006. 'Comparing public and private sector decision-making practices', *Journal of Public Administration Research and Theory* 16 (2): 289–318.

Ostrom, E. and J. Walker 2005. *Trust and Reciprocity: Russell Sage Foundation Series on Trust*, Vol. 6. New York: Russell Sage Foundation.

Pott, C. R. 1991. 'Will economics become an experimental science?' *Southern Economic Journal* 57: 450–61.

Remus, W. 1986. 'Graduate students as surrogates for managers in experiments on business decision making', *Journal of Business Research* 14 (1): 19–25.

Roth, A. E. 1995. 'Introduction to experimental economics', in J. H. Kagel and A. E. Roth (eds.), *The Handbook of Experimental Economics*. Princeton, NJ: Princeton University Press, pp. 3–109.

Scott, P. G. 1997. 'Assessing determinants of bureaucratic discretion: an experiment in street-level decision making', *Journal of Public Administration Research and Theory* 7 (1): 35–58.

Sell, J. 2008. 'Introduction to deception debate', *Social Psychology Quarterly* 71 (3): 213.

Shadish, W. R., T. D. Cook, and D. T. Campbell 2002. *Experimental and Quasi-Experimental Designs for Generalized Causal Inference*. Boston: Houghton Mifflin Company.

Shepsle, K. A. 1992. 'Bureaucratic drift, coalitional drift, and time consistency: a comment on Macey', *Journal of Law, Economics, and Organization* 8 (1): 111–18.

Smith, J. 2016. 'The motivational effects of mission matching: a lab-experimental test of a moderated mediation model', *Public Administration Review*, 76(4): 626–37.

Smith, V. L. 1976. 'Experimental economics: induced value theory', *The American Economic Review* 66 (2): 274–9.

Smith, V. L. 1982. 'Microeconomic systems as an experimental science', *The American Economic Review* 72 (5): 923–55.

Tepe, M. 2016. 'In public servants we trust? A behavioral experiment on public service motivation and trust among students of public administration, business sciences and law', *Public Management Review* 18 (4): 508–38.

Van de Walle, S. and G. G. Van Ryzin 2011. 'The order of questions in a survey on citizen satisfaction with public services: lessons from a split-ballot experiment', *Public Administration* 89 (4): 1436–50.

Webster, M. and J. Sell 2014. *Laboratory Experiments in the Social Sciences*. London: Elsevier.

Weingast, B. R. and M. J. Moran 1983. 'Bureaucratic discretion or congressional control? Regulatory policymaking by the federal trade commission', *Journal of Political Economy* 91 (5): 765–800.

Wilde, L. 1981. 'On the use of laboratory experiments in economics', in Joseph Pitt. (ed.), *The Philosophy of Economics*. Dordrecht: Reidel, pp. 137–43.

Wilson, R. and C. Eckel 2011. 'Trust and social exchange', in Druckman, Green, Kuklinski, and Lupia (eds.), pp. 243–57.

Woon, J. 2012. 'Laboratory tests of formal theory and behavioral inference', in Kittel, Luhan, and Morton (eds.), pp. 54–71.

PART III

Substantive Contributions

8 | Work Motivation

NICOLA BELLE AND PAOLA CANTARELLI

Significance and Context of the Topic

Work motivation is described 'as the psychological processes that direct, energise and maintain action toward a job, task, role, or project' (Grant and Shin 2012: 505). In line with previous research on the motives that drive prosocial behaviour (e.g., Grant 2008a; Grant and Berry 2011), we ground our chapter in self-determination theory (e.g., Deci and Ryan 1985), which features at its core the distinction between extrinsic and intrinsic motivation. Extrinsic motivation refers to the desire to expend efforts to obtain outcomes that are external to the activity and separable from it (e.g., Amabile 1993; Brief and Aldag 1977). Intrinsic motivation refers to the desire to expend efforts based on the interest in and enjoyment of an activity in and of itself (e.g., Amabile et al. 1994; Gagné and Deci 2005; Grant 2008a; Ryan and Deci 2000).

Ryan and Deci (2000) define extrinsic motivation as a continuum experienced by individuals, with four regions that involve progressively less control by others and increasing self-determination: external regulation, introjected regulation, identified regulation and integrated regulation. External regulation is a form of behavioural self-regulation triggered by external pressure; it refers to the desire to expend efforts to obtain an outside reward or to avoid an outside punishment. Introjected regulation is a form of behavioural self-regulation that is triggered by internal pressure; it refers to the desire to expend efforts based on internal feelings, including pride, guilt and/or a need for self-approval or approval from others. Identified regulation is a form of behavioural self-regulation that is caused by neither external nor internal pressure, but emanates from the need to act consistently with a personal value system. Finally, integrated regulation refers to identification with a given activity's value to the extent that it becomes

167

internalised as part of a person's habitual functioning and self-identity (Grant and Shin 2012).

While not native to the self-determination theory, the concept of Public Service Motivation has also generated enthusiasm and drawn extensive public management scholarship (e.g., Perry et al. 2010; Ritz et al. 2016; Vandenabeele 2007). Research on the related construct of prosocial motivation has blossomed in other disciplines like applied psychology and management (Belle 2013). The willingness to act to generate benefits for others is common to both concepts. Wright, Christensen and Pandey (2013) conclude that these two constructs are 'indistinguishable from each other' (2013: 211). Furthermore, scholars have shown that 'prosocial motivation can be distinguished from intrinsic motivation along three dimensions: self-regulation, goal directedness and temporal focus' (Grant and Berry 2011: 78).

The remainder of this chapter is organised into two main sections of experiments dedicated respectively to extrinsic motivation and intrinsic motivation. Each section summarises key design elements as well as key findings of a number of studies that meet three criteria. First, the study employs work motivation as a primary variable of interest, either independent or dependent. Second, the study uses an experimental design. Third, the study has direct implications for the advancement of public administration theory and practice. Some of the studies are from a growing subfield of public management that is focused on meeting these three criteria, but many are from related disciplines that show the potential of this approach. Our review is not meant to be exhaustive or systematic. Instead, our aim is to provide readers with an in-depth analysis of a series of selected studies that show the benefits of using experimental methods and that can inspire public administration scholars to use these methods for studying work motivation in mission-driven organisations. This chapter concludes with the theoretical and practical implications of the studies along with some challenges and suggestions for future experimental research.

Experimental Designs and Findings: Extrinsic Motivation

External Regulation

A well-established body of experimental research has investigated the effects of monetary incentives on external regulation. Many of these studies are from beyond public management but are directly relevant to it. Results suggest that monetary rewards are not unconditionally successful in boosting employee motivation and performance. Rather, the effectiveness of financial rewards seems to depend on such factors as the size of the incentives, their visibility, the time at which they are distributed and the type of task, as well as individual characteristics of the subjects performing the task. Table 8.1 summarises the main design features and results of the selected studies manipulating external regulation.

As far as the size of the financial incentive is concerned, for example, Gneezy and Rustichini (2000) conducted a field experiment with Israeli students involved in 'donation days' initiatives that take place yearly. In these days, students go from door to door to raise funds for organisations dedicated to causes like research for cancer or help for children with disabilities. Participants incentivised with a 10 per cent financial bonus raised the same amount of donations (Israeli new shekel 219.3) as unpaid students (Israeli new shekel 238.6) and significantly more money than students paid with a 1 per cent bonus (Israeli new shekel 153.6, *p-value* = 0.052). Students paid 1 per cent of the raised donations collected marginally less money than unpaid students did (*p-value* = 0.098).

Using a survey experiment administered to 186 part-time executive MBA students, Weibel and colleagues (2010 – Study 2) found that performance-related pay increased participants' intention to dedicate more hours to a work project (β = 0.24, *p-value* < 0.01). This effect was negatively moderated by participants' intrinsic motivation and positively moderated by individuals' extrinsic motivation. Using a similarly designed survey experiment, Belle and Cantarelli (2015) found that none of a 5 per cent, 10 per cent, 25 per cent or 50 per cent financial bonus to be added to the current base salary modified the intended job effort of a sample of 291 Italian government executives (*p-value* = 0.273). The effect of the bonus on respondents' intended job effort was negatively moderated by individuals' intrinsic motivation (*p-value* = 0.012), positively moderated by extrinsic motivation (*p-value* = 0.008) and unmodified by Public Service Motivation (*p-value* = 0.308).

With respect to the timing for the distribution of monetary rewards, Fryer and colleagues (2012) found that kindergarten through eighth grade students improved their math test scores between 0.201 and 0.398 standard deviations when their teachers were paid an upfront financial reward but were asked to give the money back if their

Table 8.1: *Studies on external regulation*

Study	Experimental design	Sample and task	Manipulated and measured variables	Main results
Ariely, Bracha and Meier 2009	Laboratory Randomised two-by-two-by-two between-subjects factorial	161 undergraduate students sequentially pressing X and Z on a computer keyboard for up to five minutes	**Manipulated:** nature of the cause (good/bad), payment scheme (donation/donation and private earnings), visibility of the nature of the cause, payment scheme, amount of money donated and kept for self (private/public) **Measured:** task performance (number of X-Z presses)	When exerting effort to donate to a good cause, participants in the public condition outperformed those in the private condition. When exerting effort for a good cause and earning money for themselves, participants in the private condition outperformed those in the public condition.
Belle 2015	Field Randomised three-by-two-by-two between-subjects factorial	300 nurses assembling surgical kits to be shipped to health care practitioners working in former war zone	**Manipulated:** reward (fixed pay/fixed pay and performance-contingent monetary reward/fixed pay and symbolic reward), visibility of performance achieved and reward (disclosed/secret), beneficiary contact (yes/no) **Measured:** task performance (number of surgical kits assembled correctly)	For the activity with a prosocial impact, monetary rewards had a larger performance effect when they were secret rather than disclosed. The negative interaction of performance-contingent monetary reward was stronger when nurses also had a contact with a beneficiary.

Study	Method	Sample	Manipulated/Measured	Findings
Belle and Cantarelli 2015	Survey (vignettes) Randomised between subjects	291 government executives	**Manipulated:** performance-related pay (5 per cent/10 per cent/25 per cent/50 per cent of the current salary) **Measured:** change in self-reported job effort, intrinsic motivation, extrinsic motivation, public service motivation	As compared to the performance-contingent monetary reward, the symbolic reward did not generate any crowding-out effects. None of the performance related-pay scheme changed intended job effort. The monetary rewards interacted negatively with participants' intrinsic motivation, negatively with participants' extrinsic motivation, and did not interact with participants' public service motivation.
Fryer, Levitt, List and Sadoff 2012	Field Randomised two-by-two between-subjects factorial	150 K-8 teachers performing their regular job	**Manipulated:** timing of monetary reward (beginning of the school year with requirement to return money if students' performance is below average /end of the school year), basis for the monetary reward (teacher's own	Pooling data across basis of the monetary reward, students obtained higher math scores when their teachers were paid the monetary incentive up front and were required to return money if

Table 8.1: (*cont.*)

Study	Experimental design	Sample and task	Manipulated and measured variables	Main results
			students/teacher's and teammate's students) **Measured:** job performance (students' scores in standardised tests)	students performed below average.
Gneezy and Rustichini 2000 (The donation experiment)	Field Randomised between subjects	180 high school students collecting donations	**Manipulated:** payment for self (none/ 1 per cent/10 per cent of the donations raised – all from funds additional to the donation) **Measured:** task performance (amount of money collected)	The monetary incentive reduced marginally the donations raised when students were paid a 1 per cent bonus and insignificantly when students were paid a 10 per cent bonus. Students in the 10 per cent bonus group collected more donations than students in the 1 per cent bonus group.
Mellström and Johannesson 2008	Field Randomised between subjects	262 students undergoing health examination to become blood donors	**Manipulated:** size and recipient of the monetary incentive (none/SEK 50/ SEK 50 that participants had to	Size and recipient of the monetary incentive did not change the percentage of men agreeing to donate blood.

		decide whether to keep for themselves or donate to charity) **Measured:** percentage of students undergoing the health examination, gender	Compared to the control group, the monetary payment led fewer women to undergo the examination required to donate blood (crowding-out effect). Compared to the SEK 50 group, the option to donate the financial bonus to charity led more women to undergo the health examination required to donate blood (alleviation of the crowding out effect).
Weibel, Rost and Osterloh 2010 (Study 2)	Survey (vignettes)	186 part-time executive MBA students	**Manipulated:** performance-related pay (yes/no) **Measured:** intended number of additional hours to dedicate to a project; intrinsic motivation; extrinsic motivation	Performance-related pay increased the willingness to invest more hours in the work project. Performance-related pay interacted negatively with respondents' intrinsic motivation and positively with respondents' extrinsic motivation.

students' performance on the test was below average. The study found no effect when teachers received an identical financial reward at the end of the school year. This suggests that financial rewards can be leveraged by providing them in a way that triggers individuals' tendency to value losses more than gains.

A meta-analysis of 46 experimental studies with 155 subgroups found that the effect of monetary rewards is bound to the task type. While raising work performance when the task was non-interesting (i.e., simple and/or boring), performance-related pay decreased performance when the task was interesting (i.e., difficult and/or interesting) (Weibel et al. 2010 – Study 1). This is consistent with predictions by self-determination theory that extrinsic rewards can crowd out intrinsic motivation, which tends to be higher for more interesting tasks.

As for gender differences, men and women reacted differently when offered the same financial incentive to undergo a health examination required to become a blood donor. In fact, experimental scholarship on gender differences in behaviour suggests that women tend to behave more prosocially than men (e.g., Mellström and Johannesson 2008). For women only, a monetary incentive crowded out the motivation to donate blood and the option to donate the financial bonus to a charity alleviated the crowding-out effect (Mellström and Johannesson 2008). The percentage of men agreeing to undergo the health examination was not statistically different when they received no financial incentive (29 per cent), Swedish krona 50 for themselves (37 per cent), or Swedish krona 50 and had to decide whether to keep the money or donate it to a charity (33 per cent). On the contrary, the percentage of women agreeing to undergo the health examination was smaller in the Swedish krona 50 payment condition as compared to the no payment condition: 30 per cent and about 52 per cent respectively (*p-value* = 0.024). Also, the percentage of women agreeing to undergo the health examination was higher in the Swedish krona 50 payment with charity option condition as compared to the Swedish krona 50 payment: about 53 per cent and 30 per cent respectively (*p-value* = 0.020).

Recent investigations of the interaction between extrinsic and reputational motivations hold the promise of shedding light on how the effect of financial bonus on task performance unfolds. Reputational motivation has been defined as an individual's tendency to be motivated by 'the desire to be liked and respected by others' (Ariely, Bracha and Meier 2009: 544). Because reputational motivation is triggered by external rewards and punishments – in the form of honour and shame, respectively – it is found towards the external regulation end of the extrinsic motivation continuum. Reputational motivation's dependency on visibility distinguishes it from the other typologies of motivations that drive human behaviour, such as intrinsic and prosocial motivation. Relative to reputational motivation, prosocial motivation and Public Service Motivation are positioned towards the opposite end of Ryan and Deci's (2000) extrinsic motivation continuum (i.e., near integrated regulation). Because reputational motivation is triggered by concern for one's social image, it comes into play only when an individual's actions are observable by others. Thus, an individual's image is affected by the degree to which people perceive him or her as prosocial (Bénabou and Tirole 2006).

Ariely, Bracha and Meier (2009) have shown that the effectiveness of monetary incentives for an activity aimed at raising donations is dependent on the nature of the cause as well as the visibility of the payment scheme. For a good cause, a monetary incentive for the self led to better performance on a task with prosocial consequences when the payment scheme was kept private as compared to when it was made public. Undergraduate students without any monetary incentives for themselves pressed X and Z sequentially on a computer keyboard more times in the public condition compared to the private condition, on average 822 versus 548, respectively (p-$value$ < 0.05). On the other hand, participants who could earn the financial bonus for themselves pressed X and Z sequentially more times in the private condition compared to the public condition, on average 740 versus 702, respectively (p-$value$ < 0.05). In other words, students in the private condition significantly increased their performance when offered a monetary incentive for themselves (on average 740 key-pairs) as compared to when they were not offered any monetary incentive (on average 548 key-pairs) (p-$value$ < 0.05). Students in the public condition did not perform statistically differently when offered a monetary incentive for themselves compared to when they were not (on average 822 versus 702, respectively).

In a related study, nurses receiving a fixed payment assembled correctly more surgical kits to be shipped to health care practitioners in former war zones when their performance and payment were disclosed rather than kept secret (+15.28, p-$value$ < 0.001). Nurses receiving performance-related pay in addition to the fixed pay, instead, assembled the same number of surgical kits in the two visibility conditions (*p-value* = 0.433). The contingent reward significantly increased the number of correctly assembled surgical kits when nurses' performance and payment were kept secret (+21.38, *p-value* < 0.001) and only marginally when nurses' performance and payment were publicly disclosed (+4.12, *p-value* = 0.095). Moreover, the negative interaction between financial rewards and visibility was stronger for participants who also interacted with a former beneficiary from the target area. The field experiment was carried out during a period of mandatory training for newly hired nurses (Belle 2015).

Introjected, Identified and Integrated Regulation

Experimental research on other-related motives that drive human behaviour has flourished in recent years. For instance, the concepts of prosocial motivation – in applied psychology and mainstream management – and Public Service Motivation – in public administration literature – have drawn abundant scholarship and raised enthusiasm among academics and practitioners alike. Drawing on self-determination theory, Grant (2007, 2008c) characterised prosocial motivation as a state of introjected or identified regulation and illuminated how the relational architecture of jobs shapes the motivation to make a prosocial difference. Recent experimental studies have converged in suggesting that contact with the beneficiaries of one's job improves task performance. This causal relationship has been robust across different operationalisations of performance, which include but are not limited to units produced, productivity, accuracy, persistence, job dedication and helping behaviour. Available literature has also investigated a number of boundary conditions under which the performance effect of beneficiary contact is stronger or weaker. Examples of such boundary conditions are individuals' Public Service Motivation, perceived prosocial impact, task significance and personality traits. Similar to contact with beneficiaries, self-persuasion interventions aimed at enhancing awareness of the task significance of one's job have also proven effective in improving task performance. Table 8.2 summarises the main design features and results of the selected studies manipulating introjected, identified and integrated regulation.

The longitudinal quasi-experimental study conducted by Grant (2008a) showed that one month after interacting for 15 minutes with

Table 8.2: *Studies on introjected, identified and integrated motivation*

Study	Experimental design	Sample and task	Manipulated and measured variables	Main results
Arieli, Grant and Sagiv 2014 (Study 2)	Laboratory Randomised between subjects	48 students	**Manipulated:** benevolence values **Measured:** benevolence values (Schwartz Value Survey on pre-test two weeks before intervention/Portrait Values Questionnaire on post-test), percentage of participants expressing willingness to voluntarily undertake community work	Benevolence values increased in the benevolence group and decreased in the control group. Forty-five per cent of the respondents in the benevolence values group expressed willingness to voluntary community work, as compared to 19 per cent in the control group. Change in benevolence values fully mediated the impact of the experimental intervention on willingness to volunteer.
Belle 2013	Field Randomised between subjects	90 nurses assembling surgical kits to be shipped to health care practitioners working in former war zone	**Manipulated:** beneficiary contact, self-persuasion **Measured:** task performance (surgical kits assembled correctly, minutes volunteered, productivity, error rate), public service motivation	Participants in both the beneficiary contact and self-persuasion interventions outperformed participants in the control condition across all task performance measures. Public service motivation partially

Table 8.2: (*cont.*)

Study	Experimental design	Sample and task	Manipulated and measured variables	Main results
				mediated the effect of both treatments on task performance.
Grant 2008a	Field Longitudinal quasi-experiment	45 fundraising callers collecting financial donations from alumni to fund scholarships	**Manipulated:** beneficiary contact **Measured:** job performance (number of pledges obtained per week, amount of donations raised per week)	Callers who interacted with a beneficiary of their work obtained more pledges and raised more money per week as compared to their own performance pre-intervention and to callers in the control group.
Grant 2008b (Experiment 1)	Field Longitudinal quasi-experiment	33 fundraising callers collecting financial donations from alumni to fund scholarships	**Manipulated:** task significance for others, personal benefit **Measured:** job performance (number of pledges obtained per week, amount of donations raised per week)	Callers who read stories written by former callers on how they have been able to benefit others through their work obtained more pledges and raised more donations per week as compared to their own performance pre-intervention, to callers in the personal benefit group, and to callers in the control group.

| Grant 2008b (Experiment 2) | Field | Longitudinal quasi-experiment | 32 paid lifeguards | **Manipulated:** task significance for others, personal benefit
Measured: job dedication (number of weekly hours that lifeguards voluntarily signed up to work), lifeguards' helping behaviour as rated by supervisors, lifeguards' perceived social impact, lifeguards' perceived social worth | Lifeguards who read stories about other lifeguards rescuing swimmers, dedicated more hours and showed more helping behaviour as compared to pre-intervention measures. Stronger perceived social impact mediated the effect of task significance for others on job dedication. Enhanced perceived social worth mediated the effect of task significance for other on helping behaviour.
Job dedication and helping behaviour did not change for lifeguards who read stories on the personal benefit from the job. |
| Grant 2008b (Experiment 3) | Field | Randomised between subjects | 34 fundraising callers collecting financial donations from alumni to fund scholarships | **Manipulated:** task significance for others
Measured: job performance (number of pledges earned), conscientiousness, prosocial values | Callers in the task significance for others group earned more pledges than callers in the control group. The relationship was negatively moderated by participants' conscientiousness and positively moderated by participants' prosocial values. |

Table 8.2: (*cont.*)

Study	Experimental design	Sample and task	Manipulated and measured variables	Main results
Grant, Campbell, Chen, Cottone, Lapedis and Lee 2007 (Experiment 1)	Field Randomised between subjects	39 fundraising callers collecting financial donations from alumni to fund scholarships	**Manipulated:** contact with beneficiary (interpersonal/through a written letter/no) **Measured:** job persistence (time on the phone), job performance (amount of donations raised)	Participants exposed to the interpersonal contact with the beneficiary outperformed participants in the other two groups as well as their own pre-intervention persistence and performance.
Grant, Campbell, Chen, Cottone, Lapedis and Lee 2007 (Experiment 2)	Laboratory Randomised between subjects	30 students editing cover letters written by other students applying for jobs	**Manipulated:** personal contact with a beneficiary **Measured:** task persistence (time spent editing), perceived prosocial impact	Personal contact with a beneficiary increased persistence through perceived prosocial impact.
Grant, Campbell, Chen, Cottone, Lapedis and Lee 2007 (Experiment 3)	Laboratory Randomised two-by-two between-subjects factorial	122 students editing cover letters written by other students applying for jobs	**Manipulated:** beneficiary contact (yes/no), task significance (high/low) **Measured:** job persistence (time spent editing), affective commitment	The contact with the beneficiary increased persistence when the task significance was high. Affective commitment to beneficiaries mediated the relationship.

| Grant and Hoffman 2011 (Study 2) | Laboratory Randomised between subjects | 103 students correcting and commenting a research paper | **Manipulated:** source of the ideological message (beneficiary/ leader/none) **Measured:** task performance (number of errors corrected successfully), citizenship performance (quality of the comments offered as rated by an external coder), perceived suspicion of the source | Ideological messages led to higher task and citizenship performance when delivered by the beneficiary rather than by the leader. The relationship was mediated by perceived suspicion of the source. Ideological messages delivered by a leader had no effect on task and citizenship performance compared to the absence of an ideological message. |
| Grant and Hoffman 2011 (Study 3) | Laboratory Randomised two-by-two between-subjects factorial | 371 students drafting a marketing campaign to highlight the benefits of switching from traditional pharmacy to the health care company's mail-order pharmacy | **Manipulated:** message source (leader/ beneficiary), message content (prosocial/achievement) **Measured:** task performance (overall quality of the campaign as rated by two business students majoring in marketing); citizenship performance (percentage of students participating voluntarily to a follow-up activity) | The beneficiary source generated better task performance and more citizenship performance when providing a prosocial rather than achievement message. |

a student who benefitted from a scholarship fund, fundraising callers for that fund made more pledges and raised more donations than callers in the control condition. The interaction with the beneficiary gave callers the opportunity to learn how the fellowship helped the graduate student to conduct her research and advance knowledge in her field of study, and gave them the chance to ask questions. One month after the intervention, callers in the treated group obtained about 364 pledges per week and about \$2,084 per week, while callers in the control group achieved only about 206 pledges and \$620 ($F(1, 43) = 11.17$, p-value < 0.01 and $F(1, 43) = 14.42$, p-value < 0.001, respectively). Moreover, in the contact with beneficiary condition, the number of pledges and donations raised per week increased as compared to pre-test measures (about 149 pledges per week, $t(21) = 4.87$, p-value < 0.001; and \$412 per week, $t(22) = 4.79$, p-value < 0.001, respectively). On the contrary, callers in the control condition did not change their level of pledges and donations per week as compared to pre-test performance (about 160 pledges per week, $t(21) = 1.34$; and \$455 per week, $t(21) = 1.86$, respectively). The same pattern of results was replicated in subsequent investigations. The experimental design added a personal benefit condition, where callers read stories written by former employees on how they benefitted from such a working experience in their own careers. Callers who read stories on how others benefitted from their work outperformed their pre-intervention measures as well as callers in the personal benefit and control groups in terms of number of pledges earned and amount of donations raised (Grant 2008b – Experiment 1). Fundraising callers' conscientiousness negatively moderated the effect of learning about how donations collected benefitted scholarship students on the number of pledges earned. Callers' prosocial values moderated positively the same relationship (Grant 2008b – Experiment 3).

In another study in the same article (Grant 2008b – Experiment 2), lifeguards volunteered more hours and showed more helping behaviours as rated by their supervisors after reading stories about colleagues rescuing swimmers, relative to pre-intervention performance (10.11 hours versus 7.06 hours, respectively, $t(8) = 3.13$, p-value < 0.01; 4.62 over a seven-point scale versus 3.81 over a seven-point scale, respectively, $t(10) = 2.16$, p-value $= 0.03$, respectively). When lifeguards instead read stories about the personal benefits of the job, job dedication did not change as compared to the pre-test (6.28 hours versus 7.39 hours, respectively, $t(17) = -1.51$) and helping behaviour decreased (3.57 over a seven-point scale versus 4.17 over a seven-point scale, respectively, $t(14) = -3.18$, *p-value* = 0.01). Perceived prosocial impact mediated the effect of task significance on job dedication. Moreover, perceived social worth mediated the effect of task significance on helping behaviours.

Belle (2013) also found that contact with a beneficiary improved task performance in a public service context. The study further showed that self-persuasion enhanced performance and that both relationships were partially mediated by participants' Public Service Motivation. A sample of 90 nurses assembling surgical kits to be shipped to former war zones was randomly divided into two treatment groups and one control group. Nurses in the beneficiary contact group met health practitioners from the beneficiary area and for 15 minutes listened to them sharing stories of successful interventions they conducted in the past thanks to the surgical kits. Nurses in the self-persuasion group wrote a short essay on how they thought their work was going to benefit health practitioners from the target area improve the quality of lives of their patients. They also were required to do their best in recruiting additional volunteers to perform the same task. As compared to the control condition, on average, participants in the contact with beneficiaries condition spent more minutes assembling kits voluntarily (+92.77, *p-value* < 0.01), assembled more kits (+131.43, *p-value* < 0.01), assembled more kits per minute (+.12, *p-value* < 0.05) and made fewer errors (−2.90 percentage points, *p-value* < 0.05). As compared to the control condition, on average, participants in the self-persuasion condition spent more minutes assembling kits voluntarily (+69.43, *p-value* < 0.05), assembled more kits (+104.17, *p-value* < 0.05), assembled more kits per minute (+.12, *p-value* < 0.05) and made fewer errors (−2.67 percentage points, *p-value* < 0.05). In the two treated groups, the level of nurses' Public Service Motivation increased in the after-treatment questionnaire as compared to the before-treatment questionnaire (+0.17 in the contact with beneficiaries condition, *p-value* < 0.05; +0.16 in the self-persuasion condition, *p-value* < 0.05). The change in Public Service Motivation partially mediated the effect of the experimental interventions on task performance measures.

Grant and colleagues (2007 – Experiment 1) showed that fundraising callers who had the chance to interact personally with a student who benefitted from a scholarship partially funded by their work spent more minutes on the phone per week ($F(2,30) = 4.74$, *p-value* = 0.02) and raised more donations ($F(2,28) = 5.07$, *p-value* = 0.01) one month after the intervention as compared to the other participants in the study, who either read a letter written by a beneficiary or were not exposed to any beneficiaries. Moreover, callers in the interpersonal contact condition improved their own persistence ($t(15) = 4.64$, *p-value* < 0.001) and performance ($t(15) = 3.45$, *p-value* < 0.01) one month after the experimental intervention relative to the same measures two weeks before the treatment. The pre- and post-intervention measures of persistence and performance did not vary for the other participants in the study. The same pattern of results was replicated by Grant and colleagues (2007) in Experiment 2. Students editing cover letters for job applications spent more time on the task when they personally met the students who wrote the applications than student who did not (31.39 minutes versus 23.85 minutes, respectively, ($F(1,29) = 5.16$, *p-value* = 0.03). This effect was mediated by participants' perceived prosocial impact. In Experiment 3 of Grant and colleagues (2007), students in the high task significance group learned that the beneficiary of their editing activity was looking for a job to pay college tuition and fees and rent. Participants in the low task significance group learned that the beneficiary of their editing activity was looking for extra income. Students exposed to contact with a beneficiary were more persistent in editing the cover letter only when the task significance was high ($t(113) = 2.60$, *p-value* = 0.01). Thus, task significance moderated the performance effect of contact with beneficiaries. Lastly, this relationship was mediated by the affective commitment of participants to beneficiaries.

Additional research has expanded these findings by investigating whether the effect of an ideological message on task and citizenship performance is conditional on the source and the content of the message. Grant and Hoffman (2011) showed that they are. As far as the source is concerned (Study 2), 103 students participated in a 60-minute online laboratory experiment in which they corrected grammatical errors and typos and provided comments on a research paper written by an international doctoral student in exchange for a \$10 Amazon.com gift certificate. Students in the beneficiary group were shown a video in which the actor presented herself as an international doctoral student who had previously benefitted from the programme. Students in the leader group were shown a video in which the same actor presented herself as the director of the programme and described how it has benefitted an international student in the past. Students in the control group were not shown any video. Participants in the beneficiary condition corrected, on average, more errors than participants in the leader condition (about 33 versus 25 errors respectively, *p-value* < 0.05) and provided, on average, higher-quality comments – as assessed by an expert coder – than participants in the leader condition (3.84 versus 3.18 scale points, respectively, *p-value* < 0.05). Participants in the beneficiary condition also outperformed the control group on both task performance (33 versus 2 errors, respectively, *p-value* < 0.05) and citizenship behaviour (3.84 versus 2.97 scale points, respectively, *p-value* < 0.05). Further analysis showed that the impact of the source of the ideological message on task and citizenship performance was mediated by participants' perceived suspicion of the source. Participants in the leader and control conditions did not differ in either task or citizenship performance. As far as the interaction between the source and content of the message is concerned, instead, Grant and Hoffman (2011 – Study 3) showed that a beneficiary, but not a leader, generated performance of better quality and more citizenship behaviour only when delivering a prosocial rather than an achievement message. A sample of 371 students was asked to draft a marketing campaign highlighting the benefit of switching from traditional pharmacy to the mail-order pharmacy offered by the company for which they were fictionally working. Participants read a message written by a company's patient in the beneficiary source group and by the company's vice president of marketing in the leader source group. Students read about how the company helped the patient in the prosocial message group and about how the switch was relevant to the company's success in the achievement message group. The study used two dependent variables. Task performance was measured as the quality of the marketing campaign as rated on a 1 to 7 scale by two business students majoring in marketing and blind to the research design. Citizenship performance was measured as the participation of students in a voluntary follow-up activity to help the company's marketing team. Task performance improved when the prosocial message was delivered by the beneficiary rather than by the leader ($F(1, 367) = 6.94$, *p-value* < 0.01) and did not change when the achievement message was delivered by the beneficiary or by the leader ($F(1, 367) = -1.67$). The same pattern of results emerged for citizenship performance. The portion of students' participating in the voluntary activity was higher when the prosocial message was delivered by the beneficiary rather than by the leader (χ^2 (1) = 7.65, *p-value* < 0.01) and did not change when the achievement message was delivered by either the beneficiary or the leader (χ^2 (1) = 0.00).

Arieli, Grant and Sagiv (2014 – Study 2) provided preliminary evidence that short interventions can change individuals' attention and care for benevolence values and, consequently, willingness to volunteer for community work. Forty-eight participants were instructed to perform several exercises over a 30-minute period. The intervention evoked both effortful and automatic mental processes through priming, consistency maintenance and self-persuasion. In the treated group, all exercises were meant to augment the salience of benevolence values. For instance, participants read a summary of scientific research suggesting that, on average, people tend to be more other-focused than believed, and that this benefits the self in the long term. They also reflected on how often they have shown benevolence towards others in their recent past, told a story about an occasion in which they positively affected others, and wrote a persuasive essay to convince others of the relevance of behaving benevolently. As compared to pre-test measures, benevolence values increased in the treated condition (t(21) = 2.27, *p-value* = 0.03) and decreased in the control condition (t(23) = –1.63, *p-value* = 0.12). As compared to 19 per cent of the students in the control group, 45 per cent of the participants in the treatment group expressed their willingness to volunteer for community work (χ^2 (1)= 4.08, *p-value* = 0.04). The pre-post change in benevolence values fully mediated the effect of the experimental manipulation on willingness to volunteer.

Experimental Designs and Findings: Intrinsic Motivation

Intrinsic motivation refers to the desire to expend efforts based on the interest in and enjoyment of an activity in and of itself (e.g., Amabile et al. 1994; Gagné and Deci 2005; Grant 2008a; Ryan and Deci 2000). Grant and Berry (2011 – Study 3) conducted a lab experiment to investigate whether, how and under what contingencies intrinsic motivation fuels creativity. Table 8.3 summarises its main design features and results. Participants in the study were 100 undergrads who were asked to generate ideas to increase a music band's revenues. The experiment used a two-by-two between-subjects factorial design in

Table 8.3: *Studies on intrinsic motivation*

Study	Experimental design	Sample and task	Manipulated and measured variables	Main results
Grant and Berry 2011 (Study 3)	Laboratory Randomised two-by-two between-subjects factorial	100 students generating ideas to increase a music band's revenues	Manipulated: intrinsic motivation (low/high) and prosocial motivation (low/high) Measured: creativity (as rated by two experts)	Intrinsic motivation increased creativity when prosocial motivation was high, but not when prosocial motivation was low. Perspective taking mediated the moderating effect of prosocial motivation on the relationship between intrinsic motivation and creativity.

which the researchers independently manipulated intrinsic and pro-social motivations. The manipulation of intrinsic motivation featured a combination of task interest and task choice. Although all partici-pants performed the same task, subjects in the high intrinsic motiva-tion condition were allowed to choose a task framed as interesting, whereas students in the low intrinsic motivation condition were required to perform a task framed as boring. To manipulate partici-pants' prosocial motivation, half of the students were told that the band members were in need of money (high prosocial motivation condition) and the other half were told that the band members were not in need (low prosocial motivation). Two independent experts rated the creativity of participants' ideas on a scale anchored at 1, 'not at all creative', 4, 'somewhat creative' and 7, 'very creative'. The authors found a significant interaction effect of the intrinsic and prosocial motivation manipulations on creativity ($F(1, 96) = 4.78$, *p-value* $= 0.03$). Analyses of simple effects showed that intrinsic motivation fuelled creativity only among participants in the high prosocial motivation condition ($F(1, 96) = 6.70$, *p-value* $= 0.01$), but not for students in the low prosocial motivation group ($F(1, 96) = 0.50$, *p-value* $= 0.48$). The data revealed that perspective taking (i.e., an individual's ability to adopt others' viewpoints in an attempt to understand their preferences) mediated the moderating effect of prosocial motivation on the relationship between intrinsic motivation and creativity.

Theoretical and Practical Implications

Based on our review of experimental scholarship on work motiva-tion, we propose four main implications for theory and practice in public management. Firstly, the studies summarised in this chapter suggest that we already know more than we probably think we do about work motivation in public service. Practitioners in public organisations and policy makers in public institutions can already make good use of the actionable knowledge already available, some of which has been described in the present chapter, to craft more effective organisational routines and more comprehensive reforms. For instance, the results of the experiment by Fryer and colleagues (2012) can easily translate into effective compensation schemes for teachers. Additional evidence (e.g., Ariely et al. 2009; Belle 2015) goes a long way in disentangling the conditions under which monetary incentives can be effective in improving performance for tasks with a prosocial impact, which are pervasively present in the public sector. Moreover, public organisations and their managers can design jobs to leverage the effects of beneficiary contact on employees' motivation and performance (e.g., Belle 2013; Grant and Hoffman 2011).

Secondly, the tasks employed by the studies described in our review show that conducting experiments in real organisations is potentially beneficial to both practitioners and scholars in our field. 'Field experiments are ... attractive to the practitioner because the setting is one that the consumer of the research understands and trusts' (Perry 2012: 480). Also, field experiments can be used to solve concrete organisational problems, like low productivity (e.g., Grant 2008a) and unsatisfactory kindergarteners' test scores (Fryer et al. 2012). Scholars in public administration and management can leverage the fact that the experiment has been conducted in real public sector organisations to address questions of realism and external validity, which are two weaknesses that often plague other kinds of experimental studies.

Thirdly, our review of experimental studies investigating work motivation demonstrates how public administration and management scholars need to draw on other disciplines. Although integrating contributions from different fields into public management theory may be challenging, we cannot overlook the abundant body of experimental research on work motivation that already exists in other disciplines, such as business management, social psychology and behavioural economics. Our need to build on literature coming from other branches of knowledge is even more pressing considering that a number of studies from those disciplines have in fact been conducted in the context of public organisations (e.g., Belle and Cantarelli 2015; Grant 2008b) or in organisations that directly affect the public interest (e.g., Belle 2015; Grant and Hoffman 2011; Mellström and Johannesson 2008).

Lastly, and as a strategic follow-up to the previous point, our review reveals that public management theory needs to develop strategies suited for investigating facets of public institutions that mainstream research has neglected so far. This is a unique opportunity for public management scholars to contribute to broader social science.

Challenges and Suggestions for Future Experimental Research

Our review of selected experimental studies on work motivation in jobs that affect the public interest – described following the paradigms of self-determination theory and connected to the Public Service Motivation construct – reveals avenues for future research as well as core challenges in conducting experiments. From a substantive perspective, our understanding about the determinants and the nature of work motivation is still incomplete. For instance, it is still debated whether motivation is a dynamic state or a stable personality trait. Also, research on the interplay between work motivation and other variables is still nascent. In particular, the mechanisms that mediate or moderate the causal relationship between motivation and performance remain largely unknown. To fill this gap, we urge public management scholars to experimentally manipulate the factors that theories indicate as mediators and moderators. In fact, none of the studies reviewed in this chapter did so.

From a methodological standpoint, our review suggests that construct validity is one of the main challenges when conducting experimental research about the causal effects of work motivation on job performance. For both these constructs, finding valid operationalisations may be daunting. As for work motivation (i.e., the independent variable), difficulties arise from the fact that motivation cannot be manipulated directly. Indeed, only a few indirect manipulations have been validated; selectively targeting one type of motivation is difficult; and there are not universally agreed upon measurement scales and manipulation checks. Also, the majority of available studies primarily focuses on short-term effects of motivation manipulations. Overcoming these limitations to investigate the effects of work motivation over extended periods seems a formidable challenge that public administration scholars will face. As for job performance (i.e., the outcome variable), finding meaningful and comprehensive indicators is a daunting task in general and even more so in the context of public organisations, in which the concept of performance is multifaceted and therefore more difficult to measure than in private organisations (e.g., Boyne 2002; Boyne et al. 2005; Perry et al. 2006).

As for the unique aspects of civil servants' work motivation, our review uncovers two main challenges and avenues for future studies. On one side, scholars in our field need to test whether and to what extent the findings of existing experimental research into work motivation carry over to the institutional peculiarities of public administration and management as well as real public sector workers. On the other side, public administration scholarship should find a way to contribute to current experimental evidence on work motivation in other fields. To do so, scholars can draw on a significant body of research about Public Service Motivation, which is native to our field. Addressing both challenges will require the integration of theories as well as the alignment of constructs and terminology that currently differ between and within disciplines.

References

Amabile, T. M. 1993. 'Motivational synergy: toward new conceptualizations of intrinsic and extrinsic motivation in the workplace', *Human Resource Management Review* 3(3): 185–201.

Amabile, T. M., K. G. Hill, B. A. Hennessey and E. M. Tighe 1994. 'The work preference inventory: assessing intrinsic and extrinsic motivational orientations', *Journal of Personality and Social Psychology* 66(5): 950.

Arieli, S., A. M. Grant and L. Sagiv 2014. 'Convincing yourself to care about others: an intervention for enhancing benevolence values', *Journal of Personality* 82(1): 15–24.

Ariely, D., A. Bracha and S. Meier 2009. 'Doing good or doing well? Image motivation and monetary incentives in behaving prosocially', *The American Economic Review* 99: 544–55.

Belle, N. 2013. 'Experimental evidence on the relationship between public service motivation and job performance', *Public Administration Review* 73 (1): 143–53.

Belle, N. 2015. 'Performance-related pay and the crowding out of motivation in the public sector: a randomized field experiment', *Public Administration Review* 75(2): 230–41.

Belle, N. and P. Cantarelli 2015. 'Monetary incentives, motivation, and job effort in the public sector: an experimental study with Italian government executives', *Review of Public Personnel Administration* 35(2): 99–123.

Bénabou, R. and J. Tirole 2006. 'Incentives and prosocial behavior', *American Economic Review* 96(5): 1652–78.

Boyne, G. 2002. 'Public and private management: what's the difference?' *Journal of Management Studies* 39: 97–122.

Boyne, G., K. J. Meier, L. J. O'Toole and R. M. Walker 2005. 'Where next? Research directions on performance in public organizations', *Journal of Public Administration Research and Theory* 15(4): 633–9.

Brief, A. P. and R. J. Aldag 1977. 'The intrinsic-extrinsic dichotomy: toward conceptual clarity', *Academy of Management Review* 2(3): 496–500.

Deci, E. L. and R. M. Ryan 1985. *Intrinsic Motivation and Self-Determination in Human Behavior.* New York: Plenum Press.

Fryer Jr., R. G., S. D. Levitt, J. List and S. Sadoff 2012. 'Enhancing the efficacy of teacher incentives through loss aversion: a field experiment', *National Bureau of Economic Research*, No. w18237.

Gagné, M. and E. L. Deci 2005. 'Self-determination theory and work motivation', *Journal of Organizational Behavior* 26(4): 331–62.

Gneezy, U. and A. Rustichini 2000. 'Pay enough or don't pay at all', *Quarterly Journal of Economics* 115(3): 791–810.

Grant, A. M. 2007. 'Relational job design and the motivation to make a prosocial difference', *Academy of Management Review* 32(2): 393–417.

Grant, A. M. 2008a. 'Employees without a cause: the motivational effects of prosocial impact in public service', *International Public Management Journal* 11(1): 48–66.

Grant, A. M. 2008b. 'The significance of task significance: job performance effects, relational mechanisms, and boundary conditions', *Journal of Applied Psychology* 93(1): 108–24.

Grant, A. M. 2008c. 'Does intrinsic motivation fuel the prosocial fire? Motivational synergy in predicting persistence, performance, and productivity', *Journal of Applied Psychology* 93(1): 48–58.

Grant, A. M. and J. W. Berry 2011. 'The necessity of others is the mother of invention: intrinsic and prosocial motivations, perspective taking, and creativity', *Academy of Management Journal* 54: 73–96.

Grant, A. M., E. M. Campbell, G. Chen, K. Cottone, D. Lapedis and K. Lee 2007. 'Impact and the art of motivation maintenance: the effects of contact with beneficiaries on persistence behavior', *Organizational Behavior and Human Decision Processes* 103: 53–67.

Grant, A. M. and D. A. Hofmann 2011. 'Outsourcing inspiration: the performance effects of ideological messages from leaders and beneficiaries', *Organizational Behavior and Human Decision Processes* 116(2): 173–87.

Grant, A. M. and J. Shin 2012. 'Work motivation: directing, energizing, and maintaining effort (and research)', in R. M. Ryan (Ed.), *The Oxford Handbook of Human Motivation.* Oxford: Oxford University Press.

Mellström, C. and M. Johannesson 2008. 'Crowding out in blood donation: was Titmuss right?' *Journal of the European Economic Association* 6(4): 845–63.

Perry, J. L. 2012. 'How can we improve our science to generate more usable knowledge for public professionals?' *Public Administration Review* 72(4): 479–82.

Perry, J. L., A. Hondeghem and L. Recascino Wise 2010. 'Revisiting the motivational bases of public service: twenty years of research and an agenda for the future', *Public Administration Review* 79(5): 681–90.

Perry, J. L., D. Mesch and L. Paarlberg 2006. 'Motivating employees in a new governance era: the performance paradigm revisited', *Public Administration Review* 66(4): 505–14.

Ritz, A., G. A. Brewer and O. Neumann 2016. 'Public service motivation: a systematic literature review and outlook', *Public Administration Review*. Early view. doi: 10.1111/puar.12505.

Ryan, R. M. and E. L. Deci 2000. 'Self-determination theory and the facilitation of intrinsic motivation, social development, and well-being', *American Psychologist* 55(1): 68.

Vandenabeele, W. 2007. 'Toward a public administration theory of public service motivation: an institutional approach', *Public Management Review* 9(4): 545–56.

Weibel, A., K. Rost and M. Osterloh 2010. 'Pay for performance in the public sector. Benefits and (hidden) costs', *Journal of Public Administration Research and Theory* 20(2): 387–412.

Wright, B. E., R. K. Christensen and S. K. Pandey 2013. 'Measuring public service motivation: exploring the equivalence of existing global measures', *International Public Management Journal* 16(2): 197–223.

9 | Experimenting with Leadership in Public Organisations

LOTTE BØGH ANDERSEN, LOUISE LADEGAARD
BRO, ANNE BØLLINGTOFT, AND JACOB
LADENBURG

Significance and Context of the Topic

It has been argued that 'virtually all of management and organization theory concerns performance and effectiveness, at least implicitly' (Rainey 1997: 125), and organisational leadership is a promising place to look for ways to influence performance. Testing the effects of leadership on performance is difficult, however, as the two concepts influence each other in complex and reciprocal ways, creating a potential endogeneity problem in non-experimental leadership research. Consequently, the extent to which leadership actually affects performance is unclear despite the large number of leadership studies (Antonakis et al. 2010; Knippenberg and Sitkin 2013). Experimental designs can provide more systematic knowledge about the causal effects of leadership, enabling us to decrease absenteeism, increase performance, and attract and retain more motivated employees to the public sector (Park and Rainey 2008). It is therefore important to discuss how we best can use experiments to study leadership in public administration and management.

Vogel and Masal find that 'Transformational public leadership' and 'Outcomes of public leadership' are dominant themes (Vogel and Masal 2014: 8). The literature on the outcomes of public leadership typically analyses various performance measures on which public leadership may have an impact, while the transformational leadership literature focuses more on measuring specific aspects of leader behaviour. Studies of transformational leadership and performance reflect both of these strands of leadership literature, and we will therefore pay special attention to these lines of research.

A transformational leader develops a vision with core goals for the organisation, strives to share this vision with the employees, and works to sustain the shared vision in the short and long run (Jacobsen and

194

Andersen 2015: 4). Existing research has consistently found transformational leadership is positively associated with employee performance (Trottier et al. 2008; Wofford et al. 2001), but few studies (e.g., Bellé 2014; Dvir et al. 2002) are able to make causal conclusions. Such conclusions should be based on an experimental design. As Blom-Hansen and colleagues (2015) noted, studying transformational leadership in observational studies is notoriously difficult, because leaders may react to past performance by adjusting their leadership strategies, and external factors may affect both leadership strategy and performance. Using experiments to estimate the effects of transformational leadership is therefore extremely relevant. Still, it can be very important to have observational studies from the same geographical area showing positive associations between leadership and performance to find out whether it is relevant to carry out a leadership experiment and gain support from key stakeholders to do the experiment. As discussed in greater detail later, the finding from a Danish (observational) study of transformational and transactional leadership and organisational performance (Jacobsen and Andersen 2015) helped convince decision makers that they should support a large-scale field experiment in Denmark: LEAP (Leadership and Performance).

This chapter discusses how we can conduct experimental investigations of leadership effects with a focus on transformational leadership and performance. It also examines what we can learn from existing leadership experiments in terms of handling relevant challenges. This is based on a review of (i) non-experimental and (ii) experimental studies of leadership in public organisations. In the section about field experiments, we use our own experience from the LEAP project, where more than 500 leaders and their 20,000 employees were randomised into three different treatment groups (transformational, transactional, and combined leadership training) and a control group. The purpose of this experiment was to see how leadership training affects leadership and ultimately organisational performance. It thus illustrates many of the characteristic challenges for leadership field experiments.

Non-experimental Research of Public Administration Leadership

According to an influential study by Van Wart (2003: 214), leadership received relatively little attention in the public administration literature in previous decades, but much progress has since been made (Van Wart 2013: 536). Much of this research has, however, been non-experimental. Later, we discuss examples from the non-experimental literatures on transformational, transactional, distributed, and collaborative leadership.

Transformational leadership is a very important part of public administration leadership research (Van Wart 2013: 532; Wright and Pandey 2010: 75). Several studies examine the antecedences and potential effects of transformational leadership in the context of functional and deputy/assistant managers in US local governments. Wright and Pandey (2010) analyse the relationships between transformational leadership, organisational characteristics, lateral/upward communication, and the use of performance measures. In a later article, Wright and colleagues (2012) proceed to investigate the consequences of transformational leadership, showing that transformational leadership is positively related to vision valence through public service motivation and goal clarity. Furthermore, Moynihan and colleagues demonstrate how transformational leadership is related to performance information use, mediated by goal clarity and developmental culture (2012: 156). These results are in line with earlier studies, which also include transactional leadership. A transactional leader uses contingent rewards and sanctions to make individual employees pursue their own self-interest in a manner that is beneficial to the organisation (Jacobsen and Andersen 2015: 4). Getting US federal employees to rate their leaders, Trottier, Van Wart, and Wang conclude that 'neither transactional nor transformational factors clearly predominate, although transformational factors have an edge in followers' perception of importance for job satisfaction and leadership effectiveness' (2008: 328). Furthermore, Park and Rainey find that although transformation-oriented leadership is more strongly correlated with job satisfaction, perceived performance, and work quality than is the case with transactional-orientated leadership, the combination of the two strategies enhances positive results (2008: 130).

In addition to transformational and transactional leadership, the existing non-experimental public sector leadership literature has also investigated distributed leadership and collaborative leadership (Van Wart 2013: 532). Collaborative leadership concerns 'collaborative processes leading to shared outcomes among agencies and sectors, and greater democratic accountability to ensure responsiveness and inclusiveness' (Van Wart 2013: 531). The public management literature has explored the determinants and types of – as well as barriers to – collaboration (see McGuire and Silvia 2009: 34 for an overview), and it has also begun investigating the effectiveness of such collaboration. In a quantitative study of US emergency managers, McGuire and Silvia (2009) emphasise how they work collaboratively with other agencies and non-profit and for-profit organisations. They find that how the managers perceive the extent to which their emergency management network meets the needs of their county depends on the extent to which they engage in different types of mobilising, synthesising, and framing behaviours (McGuire and Silvia 2009).

While collaborative leadership is focused on cross-boundary activities (McGuire and Silvia 2009), distributed leadership concerns 'the sharing of generic leadership tasks to influence resource availability, decision making, and goal setting *within* an organisational perspective' (Kjeldsen et al. 2015: 3, italics added). The effects of distributed leadership have mainly been investigated within a public school sector setting (Harris 2008: 179–80); both quantitatively (e.g., Silins and Mulford 2002) and qualitatively (Timperley 2005). Recently, qualitative studies have also been carried out in hospital settings (Chreim et al. 2010; Kjeldsen et al. 2015).

There are several methodological challenges in existing non-experimental leadership studies in public administration. Many of the previously mentioned studies of transformational leadership measure both independent and dependent variables in the same questionnaire (and therefore also at a single point in time). Consequently, common source bias may be a problem, leading to potentially biased estimates of the investigated associations (Favero and Bullock 2015). Measuring the independent and dependent variables simultaneously also renders it difficult to say whether leadership affects performance or the other way around. McGuire and Silvia, for example, are surprised to find that framing behaviours are negatively correlated to how managers perceive network effectiveness. As the authors hint, this could be due to reverse causality, because managers 'who engage in framing behaviours more frequently do so *because* they sense the network is not operating as effectively as it should or could' (2009: 54, italics added). Distributed leadership studies, however, have begun including multiple data sources (Chreim et al. 2010; Kjeldsen et al. 2015; Silins and Mulford 2002; Timperley 2005) and in some cases also longitudinal data (Kjeldsen et al. 2015; Timperley 2005). By applying a longitudinal design, Kjeldsen and colleagues contribute to a more complex and dynamic understanding of distributed leadership by showing that this is 'both affected by planned [organisational] changes *and* affecting ongoing changes in collaboration and organisation to emerge' (2015: 23, italics added). Including panel data is not enough to draw causal conclusions, because other variables might change over time, affecting the independent and dependent variables alike. Many of the studies are aware of these potential limitations in relation to causal inference. Moynihan and colleagues note that the proposed (transformational) empirical model itself 'does not prove causation; instead, it merely suggests a pattern of relationship between variables consistent with the theory' (2012: 158). Given that an aspect of public administration is making recommendations about effective leadership, it is essential to know more about causality. Experimental designs can contribute to this.

Experimental Designs and Findings

This section discusses field, laboratory, and survey experiments in public administration on leadership. In addition to this distinction between different experimental designs, we also distinguish between the content of the experiments, namely leadership training, managerial tools and communication. Table 9.1 illustrates the two distinctions and some examples of studies in each category.

Table 9.1: *Combinations of experimental designs and types of leadership experiments*

Experimental design	Leadership training experiment	Managerial tool experiment	Leadership communication experiment
Field experiment	Dvir et al. 2002	Bellé 2015	Bellé 2014
Lab experiment			Bono and Judge 2003
Survey experiment		Nielsen and Jacobsen 2014	Kovjanic et al. 2013

Leadership Field Experiments

One of the most promising types of field experiments is leadership training experiments. Given that aspects of leadership can be taught (Day 2013; Doh 2003), systematic leadership training can induce a difference in the behaviour of leaders (e.g., Barling et al. 1996; Dvir et al. 2002). The number of experimental studies reporting on the effect of transformational leadership training is not overwhelming, and to the best of our knowledge only six studies have been published (Barling et al. 1996; Dvir et al. 2002; Hardy et al. 2010; Hassan et al. 2010; Kelloway et al. 2000; Parry and Sinha 2005). These studies all investigate the effect of transformational leadership training and report significant increases in the use of transformational leadership strategies by participants (Barling et al. 1996; Hardy et al. 2010; Hassan et al. 2010; Kelloway et al. 2000; Parry and Sinha 2005) or significant effects on performance through the enhancement of transformational strategies (Dvir et al. 2002). Transformational leadership training has also proven to have an impact on employee attitudes and behaviours, such as employee commitment (Barling et al. 1996), employee development (Dvir et al. 2002), satisfaction with leadership (Hassan et al. 2010; Parry and Sinha 2005), employee effort (Parry and Sinha 2005), and performance (Dvir et al. 2002; Kelloway et al. 2000). The properties and characteristics of the studies are summarised in Table 9.2.

The leadership training field experiments are conducted in different countries and different organisational settings. The investigated public organisations and settings include health care in Canada (Kelloway et al. 2000), military leaders in Israel (Dvir et al. 2002), and marine recruit trainers in the UK (Hardy et al. 2010). Only one study includes leaders from both public and private organisations (Parry and Sinha 2005), the findings of which indicate that transformational leadership training is equally effective for organisations in the public and private sectors. The leadership training field experiments vary with respect to the number of leaders, length of treatment, and the form and content of the treatment. The maximum number of leaders included in existing studies is 54 (32 for treatment and 22 for control) (Dvir et al. 2002), with no more than 50 receiving training (all of the included leaders, no control group) (Parry and Sinha 2005). Parry and Sinha (2005) have the strongest treatment in terms of length: a three-month programme consisting of four days of intervention. Dvir and colleagues (2002) have

Table 9.2: *Overview of leadership training studies (see also Jacobsen et al. 2015)*

Study	Country and sector	Design	Length of treatment	Content in treatment	Measure of leadership	Findings
Barling et al. 1996	Canada Bank branch managers	Experiment N = 20 Randomly assigned to: Training (9) Control group (11)	One-day group session and four individual booster sessions (feedback and action plans) monthly basis	Group session: presentation of central concepts of transformational leadership, discussions, role play, plenary sessions	Five subordinates rating each leader two weeks before and five months after training	Training significantly affects transformational leadership strategy, employee commitment and two objective performance measures
Kelloway et al. 2000	Canada Department managers in Provincial health care corporation	Experiment, N = 40 Randomly assigned to: Training (10) Counselling (10) Training and counselling (12) Control group (8)	One-day workshop training and/or one-hour counselling with author	Workshop: behaviours displayed by effective/ineffective leaders, action plans Counselling: rating of leader's transformational leadership and feedback	180 subordinates rating the leaders before and six months after the intervention	Training, counselling and a combination of the two significantly affects transformational leadership strategy, but the combination does not generate more of the strategy than either training or counselling alone

	Military leaders	N = 54 Randomly assigned: Training (32) Control (22)	workshop	transformational leadership, role playing, group discussions, video cases, peer and trainer feedback	and 724 'indirect' followers rating the leader before and after training	leadership – enhanced by training – significantly affects followers development and objective performance measures
Parry and Sinha 2005	Australia Public and private sector mid-level managers	Quasi-experiment N = 50 Public (28) Private (22) No control group	Three-month programme consisting of four days of training	Introduction to full-range leadership development programme Actual workplace experience, coaching, self-analysis	500 raters before and three months after the initial two-day training	Training significantly affects transformational leadership, decreases passive leadership behaviour, increases satisfaction with leadership and extra effort of followers
Hassan et al. 2010	Country not specified Managers of private health care company	Experiment N = 24 Training (12) Control group (12)	Four sessions. Session 1: three days, remaining session length not reported	Introduction to transformational leadership, goal setting and revision of goals	Three subordinates rating each leader 10 days prior to and 90 days after training intervention	Training significantly affects employee satisfaction with trained leader

Table 9.2: (*cont.*)

Study	Country and sector	Design	Length of treatment	Content in treatment	Measure of leadership	Findings
Hardy et al. 2010	USA Military leaders	Experiment N = 6 troops Training (3) Control (3)	Three-phase programme: one day of interactive workshop four half-day workshops Field support to section commanders	Application of transformational leadership (the role of vision, support and vision) in relation to using four coaching skills (observations, effective questioning, constructive feedback and goal-setting)	Reported leadership behaviour and self-reported conditions (self-confidence, resilience and satisfaction)	Training significantly affects leadership behaviour and self-reported conditions

a three-day leadership workshop, while Barling and colleagues (1996) and Kelloway and colleagues (2000) both have one-day workshops, four follow-up sessions (Barling et al. 1996), and/or a one-hour counselling session (Kelloway et al. 2000), respectively. Hardy and colleagues (2010) report a one-day interactive workshop and four half-day workshops. Hassan and colleagues (2010) report four sessions, but the article does not include information about the total training time.

Along with colleagues at Aarhus University, Copenhagen Business School, Copenhagen University, University of Southern Denmark, Aalborg University, and KORA in Denmark, we are part of LEAP, an ongoing field experiment (see Jacobsen et al. 2015 and www.leap-project.dk for more details), which aims to add to existing leadership training field experiments in several ways. It includes the training of transformational, transactional, and a combined transformational–transactional leadership strategy. The treatments are more intense than previous experiments (four whole days with two months between the teaching days and activities between the teaching days), and the number of participants (672 leaders from both public and private organisations) is much higher, thus enabling the LEAP experiment to provide much more statistical power and opportunity to probe for heterogeneous treatment effects. As in previous experiments, leaders and their employees are surveyed twice (before and after the leadership treatment), and the questionnaires include questions about perceived leadership strategies, goal prioritisation, motivation, job satisfaction, and other relevant variables. The employees' personal identification numbers are collected, which makes it possible to follow important variables over time, including absence due to illness and stress. Given that we can identify individuals, we can get register data both from employees who remain in the organisations and those who retire, quit, or are dismissed. Objective and subjective performance data are being gathered.

Key considerations in the LEAP project were who to include as subjects, how to get distinct treatments, and how to avoid self-fulfilling prophecies and contamination across groups. We chose to focus on the leaders of employees in organisations where performance could be objectively measured. We did, however, include a group of leaders of mid-level managers in order to compare their different leadership tasks, but it was very important for us to have exact information about each leader's work. Concerning our effort to design district treatments, a calibration of all teaching and the joint creation of all teaching materials helped us considerably. Specifically, we calibrated all of the teaching with a class of political science and psychology graduate students, and all of the teachers were present for all of this teaching. We also had a didactical expert present during this teaching (associate professor in psychology, Ann-Louise Holten), who ensured that the three treatments were clearly different on substantial content but as similar as possible on form and didactical methods (see also Holten, Bøllingtoft, and Wilms 2015). Truthfully for all of the treatment groups, we informed the participating leaders that the leadership training was aimed to improve their abilities to improve organisational performance, but we did not tell them what exact type of leadership strategy we were teaching. Some of them observed that their colleagues (e.g., the neighbouring school principal) had received slightly different teaching material, and we told them honestly that there were different 'shadings' of how we taught the leaders to improve organisational performance. This also prevented severe contamination between the treatment groups. In our communication to the leaders, everything was similar (also to the control group) except when it had a differentiated training purpose. Our communications with the employees were exactly similar for all employees so that they would only experience a difference linked specifically to their leaders' changed behaviour due to the training. The fact that the trained leaders were absent from their organisations for four days and the control group leaders were not makes our test slightly conservative, but as a test of leadership training it actually makes the short-term impact more valid. In our opinion, there would be ethical problems with a placebo training group, as these leaders would have spent their time on leadership training without expected positive effects.

The LEAP project is not without challenges. Although the training programmes significantly affected the employee-perceived use of leadership strategies (Jacobsen et al. 2015), we have been very aware of attrition. Although the project succeeded in terms of having a 75 per cent completion rate and while most of the dropping out was due to organisational turnover or long-term sickness among the leaders, it was important to ask whether this attrition was random. Leaders might have dropped out of a given treatment group because they felt that they had already mastered the strategy and did not need to finish the training. The comparison of the leaders who dropped out with those who completed the training suggests that attrition did not create serious bias. Attrition was even lower in the control group. The repeated measures design of the project also allows us to handle potential bias by comparing exactly the same employees before and after and by controlling for the initial leadership strategy. Still, it is important to stress that attrition is a serious concern in experiments requiring long-term, active participation from employees and leaders.

Field experiments also allow us to test the effect of managerial tools, such as pay for performance. As discussed by Bellé in Chapter 8 of this book, these tools can be important for employee performance and are often relevant to discuss in relation to leadership behaviour (especially leadership communication). Exemplifying how leadership communication experiments can be carried out, Bellé (2014) analyses how a transformational speech affects the performance of nurses in a hospital setting. The participants were 138 Italian nurses who (as part of their mandatory training) were required to spend four hours readying surgical kits. They were randomly assigned to different groups, including a control group and a transformational leadership group in which the director of nursing talked for approximately 15 minutes, explaining why the project was meaningful to her and communicating her enthusiasm. She also gave the participants some practical tips and encouraged them to identify ways to improve the assembly process. She urged the participants to contact her directly with any feedback or suggestions for improvements. Bellé (2014) found that nurses who were exposed to the transformational leadership speech alone marginally outperformed the control group (12 per cent increase), while the performance effects of the speech were much greater if the nurses were exposed to either beneficiary contact or self-persuasion interventions in addition to the speech (66–69 per cent increase).

Another relevant leadership communication field experiment was done by Antonakis and colleagues (2014). It investigated whether charisma (which is conceptually close to the dimension of transformational leadership labelled 'idealised influence'), in the form of a stylistically different motivational speech, can lead to higher effort and performance on the part of workers. A total of 106 temporary workers was hired to prepare envelopes for a fundraising campaign conducted on behalf of a hospital. An actor was hired to brief the workers about the importance of their task. Antonakis and colleagues manipulated (a) the degree of charisma the actor demonstrated, and (b) the financial incentives they gave to the workers. The conditions were: i) the baseline condition, where 35 workers received a fixed wage for their work and were given a standard motivational speech; ii) the piece-rate condition, where 30 workers in addition to the standard motivational speech received piece-rate pay of GBP 0.12 for each additional envelope completed); and iii) the charisma condition, where 41 workers received a charismatic speech instead of the standard motivational speech (but no piece-rate pay). Antonakis and colleagues (2014) show that charisma increased worker output by 17 per cent relative to the baseline condition. This effect was statistically significant and comparable in size to the positive effect of the piece-rate condition.

Laboratory Experiments

Leadership communication experiments have also been conducted in the laboratory (i.e., under controlled conditions unrelated to the participants' normal jobs). Bono and Judge (2003) asked 162 students to participate in a business simulation in which the students performed the following tasks: coming up with names for a new restaurant, proofreading a menu draft, listing possible slogans and an optional task (thinking what could be done to best serve college students). The treatments were transformational and non-transformational leadership speeches. The results indicated that the transformational leader speech, relative to the non-transformational speech, increased creative performance by 0.25 (number of names and slogans) and extra-role performance by 0.21 (number of ideas in the voluntary task), which should be seen relative to the sample means of 4.8 (number of names and slogans) and 0.40 (number of ideas in the voluntary task). Interestingly, the results also suggest that self-concordance partly mediates the effect of the transformational speech on these two performance outcomes. The transformational speech did not influence accuracy (number of identified mistakes in the menu).

The Bono and Judge laboratory experiment (2003) was carried out in a private sector setting. Anderson and Edwards (2014) find that none of the public administration and management experiments on leadership published in leading journals between 2010 and mid-2014 were laboratory experiments, which makes learning from related disciplines relevant. Kirkpatrick and Locke (1996) tested three core components (vision, vision implementation through task cues and communication style) among 282 upper-level business students, who were asked to carry out simulated production tasks. The test results suggest that vision implementation (task cues) significantly affected performance quality and quantity. However, the vision of high quality only weakly influenced performance, while communication style did not influence performance.

Leadership Survey Experiments

Finally, it is possible to use survey experiments to study leadership effects. Such approaches give rise to higher validity in the estimated association between factors of interest and management outcomes and enable the estimation of stronger causal effects compared to cross-sectional studies. In a study by Deluga and Souza (1991), answers from 46 police officers who were presented with a vignette description of a hypothetical leader (male/female) that was either transformational (N = 23) or transactional (N = 23), the relation between type of leader and how the officer would respond to the vignette leader was analysed. The respondents were told to imagine that the leader was their own. The response strategies were divided into three types: soft (friendliness strategy), hard (assertiveness, coalition, and higher authority strategy), and rational strategy (bargain and reason strategy). Overall, the type of leadership in the vignettes significantly influenced the choice of response strategies. Based on answers on 27 items using a five-point scale (5 = almost always, 1 = never), the estimated effect ranged between a 6.9 and 17.5 per cent higher tendency to influence the transformational vignette officer relative to the transactional vignette. Particularly, those police officers presented to the transformational leader used rational strategies to a higher extent (17.5 per cent more). Using almost the same vignettes, Levy and colleagues (2002) tested the effect of the leadership vignettes on the intention to seek feedback from the leader among 132 students. The students were randomly presented with either a transformational (N = 64) or transactional leader (N = 68) and told to imagine them as their own leader. Subsequently, the respondents were asked questions about their intentions to seek feedback from the leader using seven 5-point Likert scale (1 = unlikely, 5 = very likely) items aimed at measuring the intention to seek feedback. The analysis found an approximately 25 per cent higher intention to seek feedback from the transformational vignette relative to the transactional vignette.

Kelloway and colleagues (2003) show how leadership communication experiments can be implemented in surveys. Using 132 undergraduate students as participants, three types of vignettes were tested in a remote transformational leadership experiment. The experiment focused on the feedback from receiving vignette emails from a leader. The emails represented a transformational leader type ($N = 45$), a management by exception leader type ($N = 42$), and a laissez-faire leader type ($N = 43$). Each respondent received only one email vignette and was asked to express satisfaction with the supervision, interpersonal justice, and continuance commitment. A multivariate analysis found that the transformational leadership and management by exception emails increased interpersonal judgment and job satisfaction in the range of 24–129 per cent, but not continuance commitment. Another example of survey experiments of leadership communication can be found in Kovjanic, Schuh, and Jonas (2013), who compared the effect of transformational and non-transformational leadership vignettes in an online experiment among 190 individuals recruited at different German-language websites. The participants were told to imagine that they worked in a research and development team in a paper manufacturing company. Based on leader instructions (one of the two vignettes), they were asked to generate as many ideas as possible about the future use of paper in four minutes. The performance was measured in terms of the quantity of ideas, quality of ideas, and persistence. The effect of the transformational treatment was estimated in a structural equation model. The transformational treatment had an estimated direct effect on the quality of the generated ideas of 0.65 and positive mediated effects of varying size through relatedness and competence need satisfaction on the quality, quantity, and persistence of the effect of the transformational treatment.

It is also possible to experiment with managerial tools in survey experiments. Nielsen and Jacobsen (2014) thus investigated the relationship between performance information and the acceptance of leadership. For 2,000 Danish teachers, they tested whether the acceptance of leadership was affected by the presence of true information about their school's performance (i.e., performance information as a managerial tool). Because leadership acceptance could also be proposed to affect performance, Nielsen and Jacobsen applied a survey experiment in which teachers were randomly assigned into treatment and control groups, with only the treatment group receiving (true) performance data about their school (Nielsen and Jacobsen 2014: 9). The randomisation was clustered within schools to ensure even variation within organisations. The results showed a nonlinear pattern of acceptance of leadership, where information about either low or high school performance increased the employees' acceptance of leadership by 6.4–10.8 per cent. Information about average performance had a significantly negative effect compared to no information (approximately 6 per cent). This experiment is relevant for public administration leadership research, because acceptance of leadership can be expected to affect the ability of leaders to increase goal attainment, making it important to study the antecedents of high and low acceptance.

In a recent study, Pedersen and Stritch (2015) focused on both leadership communication and managerial tools. They tested six (including a control vignette) different vignette leaders on a sample of 1,829 recruited US residents in an assessment of managerial trustworthiness (MTW). Data were collected using a crowd source platform (MTurk). The respondents were told to imagine that they were an employee at a public service organisation and had the described vignette Benjamin/Kathrine as their immediate supervisor. The vignette part of the experiment and the control (no further information) followed a general description of the leader. Five distinct characteristics and a control description of Benjamin/Kathrine were randomised among the respondents. The five experimental descriptions were (italics added by the authors):

In particular, Benjamin/Kathrine prioritises . . .
1) setting clear *goals* that are feasible but somewhat challenging to achieve,
2) communicating clearly and fully following through on *commitments*,
3) ensuring employee *participation* in decision making,
4) providing frequent *feedback* to employees on their job performance,
5) *rewarding* high-performing employees.

MTW was measured in three dimensions, Ability, Benevolence, and Integrity, with three items for each answered on a seven-point Likert-type scale. The study found that *goals* and *commitments* increased MTW Ability significantly, whereas *participation* and *feedback* increased MTW Benevolence significantly. *Goals, commitments*, and *feedback* increased MTW Integrity significantly. The effects are in the range of 0.15 to 0.33 of a standard deviation. There were no significant effects from *rewarding*.

The alignment between actual leader type and employee preferences for leadership might also be important, and this can be investigated in a new type of leadership survey experiment, which enables us to study which leadership attributes employees prefer. Employees' leader type preferences are estimated by asking employees to choose between hypothetical leadership types with variation in the relevant leadership attributes. This approach is called *discrete choice experiments* and is inspired by Luce and Turkey (1964), conjoint analysis in the marketing literature (Green and Rao 1971; Green and Srinivasan 1978) and economic valuation methods (Adamowicz et al. 1994; Louviere and Woodworth 1983; Propper 1990; Train 1998). Based on the work of Lancaster (1966) and Rosen (1974), the argument is that the attributes of goods drive demand, not the good itself. The simultaneous trade-offs inherent in the choice between leadership attributes therefore make it possible to model and interpret preferences cardinally; that is, one leader attribute is twice as important as another attribute. In addition to obtaining descriptive knowledge about employee preferences for leadership, differences in employee preferences can help explain variations in leadership training effects. A mismatch between experimentally induced leadership (through leadership training) and employee preferences for leader attributes can thus be expected to decrease the positive effect of leadership training on employee outcomes. In other words, employees with weaker preferences for an experimentally induced leadership attribute may respond more negatively to a leader who, due to training, starts exhibiting this leadership attribute to a higher extent.

As part of the pre-treatment survey in the LEAP project, a subsample of 1,503 respondents was asked to make choices between two hypothetical leadership leader types and their own leader's leadership type. The leadership types were described using four leadership attributes: how often the leader expresses a clear vision for the organisation and keeps the employees focused on joint goals; how often the leader keeps the employees focused on joint goals; how often the leader rewards the employees who perform as required; how often the leader demands high performance from the employees. Each attribute could take the intensity levels: 'Always', 'Sometimes', or 'Never'. In total, this gives $4^3 = 256$ different types of leadership. This was reduced to 48 leadership types using an orthogonal fractional main effect design (Kuhfeld 2010), which were grouped two and two in choice sets and divided in six choice blocks. Each employee thus made four choices regarding the preferred leadership type among two hypothetical leadership types and their actual leader's leadership type. Based on a mixed logit model regression (Train 2003), the results show that most employees prefer leader types who 'Always' or 'Sometimes' express a clear vision and/or keep the employees focused on joint goals, reward employees, and have high demands for performance. Leaders who 'Always' or 'Sometimes' showed these leadership behaviours were thus chosen more than twice as often as those who 'Never' did. That said, however, the results also reveal substantial variation in the preferences among the employees and between different public and private sectors. Interestingly, combining the stated leadership preferences with the subsample of teachers in Nielsen and Jacobsen (2014) reveals that preferences are significantly influenced by performance information. For example, giving teachers performance information about their (true) low level of performance reduced their preferences for a leader who always rewards employees compared to a control group of teachers with similar organisational performance who did not receive any performance information.

Theoretical and Practical Implications

Having described both non-experimental and experimental studies of leadership, we turn now to the theoretical and practical implications of this research. First, most of the experimental studies to date have focused on transformational leadership and performance. It is noteworthy that there are no experimental studies of the 'new' leadership concepts in public administration, such as distributed and collaborative leadership. The Collignon and Detrain (2010) experiment with distributed leadership and adaptive decision-making was performed for ants – not human beings. Generalising their conclusions from ants to humans would suggest that a minority of individuals can influence collective decisions in societies based on distributed leadership. This should be tested experimentally. It does, however, seem to take some time before experimental public administration research starts using new concepts. This is understandable, given that experimental designs must be very well thought out. A 'conservative bias' towards testing well-established concepts should not limit the theoretical development of new relevant leadership concepts.

Second, experiments within public administration are able to capture much of the complexity discussed in other types of public administration research. One concern may be that the need to specify exact experimental treatments would mean that conditional relationships were not analysed, although the experiments performed by Bellé (2014, 2015) put this concern to rest. Testing and finding significant interactions between three variables is seldom seen in public administration research, and Bellé (2015) also successfully combines insights from several different scientific disciplines in one experimental study.

Third, the leadership experiments tend to find the same results as other types of public administration research, indicating that the key strength of experiments (internal validity) supplements the typical key strength of observational research (external validity), although field experiments can also assist in this latter regard. Although the time and form of the encounters with leaders are restricted in most leadership experiments, consistent effects on participants' satisfaction, work engagement, and performance have been identified (e.g., Kovjanic et al. 2013). This strengthens our confidence in the relationships and shows that experimental research is a valuable extension of the evidence provided by non-experimental studies. Experiments in public leadership research thus allow us to move beyond 'a pattern of relationships between variables consistent with the theory' (Moynihan et al. 2012: 158). This is very useful, especially since the experimental design also rules out common source bias.

Challenges and Suggestions for Future Experimental Research

While experiments have many advantages, challenges still remain. As argued by Blom-Hansen and colleagues (2015), not everything is amenable to experimental manipulation. Gender is an example of a variable that cannot be manipulated experimentally. For some variables (e.g., leadership appointments), natural experiments might be possible, as illustrated in the Choudhury and Khanna (2014) design, where they use the fact that bureaucratic rules ensure that the timing of leadership change is uncorrelated with organisational characteristics.

Quasi-experiments can also enable the investigation of the effects of phenomena that are difficult to manipulate by the researcher. Arthur and Hardy (2014) employed a quasi-experimental design in an infantry training programme for new recruits in the UK to evaluate the effectiveness of transformational leadership intervention in terms of remediating poor performance. The danger of using natural experiments and quasi-experiments, however, is that we will restrict our investigations to that in which there is already variation (the natural experiment) or in which the decision-makers want variation (the quasi experiment). For example, the intervention in the Arthur and Hardy study was only conducted on those elements of the organisation that senior management perceived as underperforming.

Obtaining permission and support from decision-makers to assign organisations randomly to control and treatment groups can often be difficult. In the LEAP project, it took considerable time and effort to convince the relevant decision-makers concerning the merits of the experimental approach. Our approach was to start with a small-scale leadership study (done for high schools and published in, e.g., Jacobsen and Andersen 2015) so that stakeholders could see these promising results before committing to participate. We approached both employer and employee representatives, and examples of the relevant stakeholders were ministries, the association of municipalities, the central part of the taxation authority, HR departments in banks, individual municipalities, the professional associations for leaders, and the trade unions organising the employees. Based on our experience, it was hard work to get all these stakeholders to commit to the project, and some of the stakeholders did not deliver all they had promised (e.g., the tax agency had promised to deliver personal identification numbers but changed its mind due to a turbulent year in the media). Still, we see this early work in the project as essential for its success and we have spent much time talking to the aforementioned stakeholders. Their input has improved the project substantially, and we would probably never have been allowed to do the randomisation without their support.

The Achilles' heel of experimental research has long been said to be external validity; that is, realism, and therefore the generalisability of the results to real-world settings. We agree with Blom-Hansen and colleagues (2015) in that there is no logical contrast between internal and external validity. But optimising external validity in an experimental setting can be difficult, as it requires the researchers to think carefully about the potential moderators of the investigated relationships and choose contexts and participants in experiments in ways that enable them either to test these moderating effects or argue, theoretically, that the relationships are expected to be similar in the relevant real-world settings. In laboratory experiments, the context (and often the participants) can be very different from the real-world settings in which the studied phenomena take place. Survey experiments often involve hypothetical or artificial scenarios and typically focus on short-term effects. Field experiments are becoming increasingly integrated in the leadership of real public managers (as in the LEAP project), but even this type of experiment has its limitations. Ethically, participation in experiments is mostly voluntary, and it might not be possible to generalise some of the LEAP project findings to organisations where the manager would never attend voluntary leadership training (despite the education credit it provides). Furthermore, the attrition of leaders can be expected to be higher, the longer the duration of the experiment. Leaders also change jobs, making it difficult to assess the long-term impact of leadership correctly. And contamination between the treatment and control groups is possible when the experiment takes place in real-world public organisations. On the other hand, there is much to gain in terms of the causal understanding of the relationship between variables. While the most important relationship in this connection is between leadership and performance in public organisations, the leadership training field experiments also contribute with knowledge about the effects of different types of leadership training. Survey experiments are very well suited to test the (short-term) impact of different information, and laboratory experiments clearly provide the strongest internal validity due to the controlled context. All in all, experiments complement other types of leadership research, and we can only encourage new and innovative types of leadership experiments in public administration.

References

Adamowicz, W., Louviere, J., and Williams, M. 1994. 'Combining revealed and stated preference methods for valuing environmental amenities', *Journal of Environmental Economics and Management* 26(3), 271–92.

Anderson, D. M. and Edwards, B. C. 2014. 'Unfulfilled promise: laboratory experiments in public management research, *Public Management Review*, DOI: 10.1080/14719037.2014.943272.

Antonakis, J., Bendahan, S., Jacquart, P., and Lalive, R. 2010. 'On making causal claims: a review and recommendations', *The Leadership Quarterly* 21(6), 1086–1120.

Antonakis, J., d'Adda, G., Weber, R., and Zehnder, C. 2014. 'Just words? Just speeches? On the economic value of charismatic leadership'. Working paper. Department of Organizational Behavior, University of Lausanne.

Arthur, C. A. and Hardy, L. 2014. 'Transformational leadership: a quasi-experimental study', *Leadership & Organization Development Journal* 35(1), 38–53.

Barling, J., Weber, T., and Kelloway, E. K. 1996. 'Effects of transformational leadership training on attitudinal and financial outcomes: a field experiment', *Journal of Applied Psychology* 81(6), 827–32.

Bellé, N. 2014. 'Leading to make a difference: a field experiment on the performance effects of transformational leadership, perceived social impact, and public service motivation', *Journal of Public Administration Research and Theory* 24, 109–36.

Bellé, N. 2015. 'Performance-related pay and the crowding-out of motivation in the public sector: a randomized field experiment', *Public Administration Review* 75(2), 230–41.

Blom-Hansen, J., Morton, R., and Serritzlew, S. 2015. 'Experiments in public management research', *International Public Management Journal*. Posted online 11 March 2015.

Bono, J. E. and Judge, T. A. 2003. 'Self-concordance at work: toward understanding the motivational effects of transformational leaders', *Academy of Management Journal* 46, 554–71.

Choudhury, P. and Khanna, T. 2014. 'Do leaders matter? Natural experiment and quantitative case study of Indian state owned laboratories'. Harvard Business School Working Paper 14–077. www.hbs.edu/faculty/Publication %20Files/14–077_49ce3a1b-0f07-4bb0-9d8b-70bbaa7590ec.pdf Accessed 24 May 2015.

Chreim, S., Williams, B. E., Janz, L., and Dastmalchian, A. 2010. 'Change agency in a primary health care context: the case of distributed leadership', *Health Care Management Review* 35(2), 187–99.

Collignon B. and Detrain C. 2010. 'Distributed leadership and adaptive decision-making in the ant Tetramorium caespitum', *Proceedings: Biological Sciences* 277, 1267–73.

Day, D. V. 2013. 'Training and developing leaders: theory and research', in M. G. Rumsey (ed.), *The Oxford Handbook of Leadership* (New York: Oxford University Press), pp. 76–93.

Deluga, R. J. and Souza, J. 1991. 'The effects on transformational and transactional leadership styles on the influencing behavior of subordinate police officers', *Journal of Occupational Psychology* 64, 49–55.

Doh, J. P. 2003. 'Can leadership be taught? Perspectives from management educators', *Academy of Management Learning and Education* 2(1), 54–67.

Dvir, T., Eden, D., Avolio, B. J., and Shamir, B. 2002. 'Impact of transformational leadership on follower development and performance: a field experiment', *The Academy of Management Journal* 45(4), 735–44.

Favero, N. and Bullock, J. B. 2015. 'How (not) to solve the problem: an evaluation of scholarly responses to common source bias', *Journal of Public Administration Research and Theory* 25(1), 285–308.

Green, P. E. and Rao, V. R., 1971. 'Conjoint measurement for quantifying judgemental data', *Journal of Marketing Research* 8, 355–63.

Green, P. E. and Srinivasan, V. 1978. 'Conjoint analysis in consumer research: issues and outlook', *Journal of Consumer Research* 5, 103–23.

Hardy, L., Arthur, C. A. et al. 2010. 'The relationship between transformational leadership behaviors, psychological, and training outcomes in elite military recruits', *The Leadership Quarterly* 21(1), 20–32.

Harris, A. 2008. 'Distributed leadership: according to the evidence', *Journal of Educational Administration*, 46(2), 172–88.

Hassan R. A., Fuwad, B. A., and Rauf, A. I. 2010. 'Pre-training motivation and the effectiveness of transformational leadership training: an experiment', *Academy of Strategic Management Journal* 9(2), 123–31.

Holten, A. L., Bøllingtoft, A., and Wilms, I. 2015. 'Leadership in a changing world: developing managers through a teaching and learning programme', *Management Decision* 53(5), 1107–24.

Jacobsen, C. B. and Andersen, L. B. 2015. 'Is leadership in the eye of the beholder? A study of intended and perceived leadership practices and organizational performance', *Public Administration Review* 75(6), 829–41.

Jacobsen, C. B., Bøllingtoft, A., and Andersen, L. B. 2015. 'Can leadership training teach leaders to LEAP? Experimenting with leadership training and leadership strategies'. Paper presented at APPAM conference, 12–14 November 2015, Miami, USA.

Kelloway, E. K., Barling, J., and Helleur, J. 2000. 'Enhancing transformational leadership: the roles of training and feedback', *Leadership & Organization Development Journal* 21(3), 145–9.

Kelloway, K. E., Barling, J., Kelley, E., Comtois, J., and Gatien, B. 2003. 'Remote transformational leadership', *Leadership & Organization Development Journal* 24(3), 163–71.

Kirkpatrick, S. A. and Locke, E. A. 1996. 'Direct and indirect effects of three core charismatic leadership components on performance and attitudes', *Journal of Applied Psychology* 81, 36–51.

Kjeldsen, A. M, Jonasson, C., and Oversen, M. S. 2015. 'Distributed leadership in organizational change processes: a qualitative study in public hospital units'. Paper prepared for the 2015 IRSPM Conference. Panel B102: Contemporary Leadership Issues.

Knippenberg, D. V. and Sitkin, S. B. 2013. 'A critical assessment of charismatic-transformational leadership research: back to the drawing board?', *The Academy of Management Annals* 7(1), 1–60.

Kovjanic, S., Schuh, S. C., and Jonas, K. 2013. 'Transformational leadership and performance: an experimental investigation of the mediating effects of basic needs satisfaction and work engagement', *Journal of Occupational and Organizational Psychology* 86, 543–55.

Kuhfeld, W. 2010. *Marketing research methods in SAS: Experimental design, choice, conjoint and graphical techniques* (Cary, NC: SAS Institute).

Lancaster, K. J. 1966. 'A new approach to consumer theory', *Journal of Political Economy* 74, 132–57.

Levy, P. E., Cober, R. T., and Miller, T. 2002. 'The effect of transformational and transactional leadership perceptions on feedback-seeking intentions', *Journal of Applied Social Psychology* 32(8), 1703–20.

Louviere, J. J. and Woodworth, G. 1983. 'Design and analysis of simulated consumer choice or allocation experiments: an approach based on aggregate data', *Journal of Marketing Research* 20, 350–67.

Luce, D. R. and Turkey, J. W. 1964. 'Simultaneous conjoint measurement: a new type fundamental measurement', *Journal of Mathematical Psychology* 1, 1–27.

Marvel, J. D. 2015. 'Unconscious bias in citizens' evaluations of public sector performance'. Online before print in *Journal of Public Administration Research and Theory*.

McGuire, M. and Silvia, C. 2009. 'Does leadership in networks matter? Examining the effect of leadership behaviors on managers' perceptions of network effectiveness', *Public Performance and Management Review* 33(1), 34–62.

Moynihan, D. P., Pandey, S. K., and Wright, B. E. 2012. 'Setting the table: how transformational leadership fosters performance information use', *Journal of Public Administration Research and Theory* 22(1), 143–64.

Nielsen, P. A. and Jacobsen, C. B. 2014. 'The role of performance information in explaining employee acceptance of leadership'. Paper presented at the Public Administration Review 75th Anniversary International Conference, 'Next Steps for Public Administration in Theory and Practice: Looking Backward and Moving Forward'. 16–18 November, 2014, Sun Yat-sen University, Guangzhou, China.

Park, S. M. and Rainey, H. G. 2008. 'Leadership and public service motivation in U.S. federal agencies', *International Public Management Journal* 11(1), 109.

Parry, K. W. and Sinha, P. N. 2005. 'Researching the trainability of transformational organizational leadership', *Human Resource Development International* 8(2), 165–83.

Pedersen, M. J. and Stritch J. M. 2015. 'Effects of internal management on managerial trustworthiness', Paper presented at the Public Management Research Association (PMRA) Conference, Minneapolis, MN, 11–13 June 2015.

Propper, C. 1990. 'Contingent valuation of time spent on NHS waiting lists', *The Economic Journal* 100(400), 193–9.

Rainey, H. G. 1997. *Understanding and Managing Public Organizations* (San Francisco, CA: Jossey-Bass).

Rosen, S. 1974. 'Hedonic prices and implicit markets: product differentiation in pure competition', *Journal of Political Economy* 82, 34–55.

Silins, H. and Mulford, W. 2002. 'Leadership and school results', in K. Leithwood and P. Hallinger (eds.), *Second International Handbook of Educational Leadership and Administration* (Kluwer: Dordrecht), pp. 561–612.

Timperley, H. 2005. 'Distributed leadership: developing theory from practice', *Journal of Curriculum Studies* 37(4), 395–420.

Train, K. 1998. 'Recreation demand models with taste differences over people', *Land Economics* 74(2), 230–9.

Train, K. 2003. *Discrete Choice Methods with Simulation* (Cambridge: Cambridge University Press).

Trottier, T., Van Wart, M., and Wang, X. H. 2008. 'Examining the nature and significance of leadership in government organizations', *Public Administration Review* 68(2), 319–33.

Van Wart, M. 2003. 'Public-sector leadership theory: an assessment', *Public Administration Review* 63, 214–28.

Van Wart, M. 2013. 'Administrative leadership theory: a reassessment after 10 Years', *Public Administration* 91(3), 521–43.

Vogel, R. and Masal, D. 2014. 'Public leadership: a review of the literature and framework for future research', *Public Management Review*. Published online 20 March 2014 DOI: 10.1080/14719037.2014.895031.

Wofford, J. C., Whittington, J. L., and Goodwin, V. L. 2001. 'Follower motive patterns as situational moderators for transformational leadership effectiveness', *Journal of Managerial Issues* 13, 196–211.

Wright, B. E., Moynihan, D. P., and Pandey, S. K. 2012. 'Pulling the levers: transformational leadership, public service motivation, and mission valence', *Public Administration Review* 72, 206–15.

Wright, B. E. and Pandey, S. K. 2010. 'Transformational leadership in the public sector: does structure matter?', *Journal of Public Administration Research and Theory* 20(1), 75–89.

10 Prospects for Experimental Approaches to Research on Bureaucratic Red Tape***

SANJAY K. PANDEY, SHEELA PANDEY,
AND GREGG G. VAN RYZIN

Introduction

Red tape (or, more precisely, red ribbons or strings), an attractive and useful physical artifice for securing official documents in the late Middle Ages, ceased to be a symbol of order and efficiency long ago (Bozeman 2000; Brewer and Walker 2010). Instead, modern lexical usage of the term *bureaucratic red tape* has been unequivocally pejorative, leading Goodsell (1983: 63) to call it a 'classic condensation symbol' and Pandey (1995: 5–6) to highlight the term's connotative and evocative usefulness to critics of bureaucracy. Despite the pervasive and sustained use of the term *red tape* in everyday language, encapsulating different implicit explanations for dysfunctions of bureaucracy and its impact on a variety of stakeholders, neither policy makers nor scholars paid serious attention to bureaucratic red tape until about 25 years ago.

This state of affairs began to change in the 1990s in both policy making and academic domains. The reinventing government movement, spearheaded by then Vice President Al Gore, promised results by cutting red tape (Osborne and Gaebler 1992; Thompson and Riccucci 1998). Reinventing government was of course the American version of new public management, a global good government movement targeting bureaucracy and advertising the benefits of 'business-like' methods to counter bureaucracy and achieve results (Hood 1991;

*** Acknowledgments: We are grateful to Leisha DeHart-Davis, Mary Feeney, David Giauque, Stephan Grimmelikhuijsen, Oliver James, Sebastian Jilke, Wesley Kaufmann, Lars Tummers, and Richard Walker for comments on earlier versions of this chapter. Needless to say, we are responsible for any errors, omissions, interpretations, or other shortcomings.

219

Moynihan and Pandey 2006; Pandey et al. 2014; Pollitt and Bouckaert 2011).

Contemporaneously, the dominant academic view in public management scholarship regarding bureaucratic red tape as an epiphenomenon and a second-order event began to come apart in the 1990s. Barry Bozeman's insightful and frame-breaking scholarship provided the fillip to disintegration of the dominant academic view that regarded red tape as an epiphenomenon and also laid the foundation for a new way of looking at bureaucratic red tape in public management scholarship (Bozeman 1993, 2000; Bozeman and Scott 1996). In this chapter, we begin by providing an overview of advancements in public management theory on red tape. We furnish sufficient detail in this overview to provide insight into key perspectives and findings from the recently resurgent research on red tape. This also sets the stage for our review of the nascent body of work using the experimental method to study red tape and for our recommendations for further research.

Non-experimental Academic Research on Bureaucratic Red Tape

The bulk of non-experimental research on red tape, indeed the bulk of all research on red tape, has used survey questionnaires as the dominant methodological tool (Pandey and Marlowe 2015). Different waves of the National Administrative Studies Project, as well as other survey projects, have done much to advance the state of knowledge. We highlight two major contributions of these studies. The first of these is sorting out of conceptual and empirical issues surrounding measurement of red tape. The second contribution is specifying two unique pathways for red tape concept development.

Sorting Out of Conceptual and Empirical Matters in Measuring Red Tape

Sustained theoretical and empirical developments since the 1990s have prompted scholars to pronounce bureaucratic red tape as a native concept in public management research (e.g., Brewer and Walker 2010; Giauque et al. 2012). Before the stage was set for these developments, there were significant theoretical and empirical controversies about the status of red tape concepts and measures. One of the more cited empirical articles reported empirical findings that ran against the grain of common sense. Buchanan (1975) provided evidence showing that private managers faced more red tape than public managers.

This counterintuitive finding cast a long shadow on red tape research with early empirical studies attempting to verify if this finding held in other samples. A number of studies, using different measures of red tape conducted on different samples, produced results contradicting Buchanan's findings (e.g., Baldwin 1990; Bretschneider 1990; Coursey and Pandey 2007; Rainey, Pandey, and Bozeman 1995). This empirical controversy also led to the acknowledgment of and engagement with more important conceptual questions. Rainey and Bozeman (2000), for example, argued that in order to detect public-private differences, questionnaire items needed to focus on aspects of public organisations that are overrun with rules and procedures (e.g., personnel management). Pandey and Scott (2002) suggested that Buchanan's questionnaire items did not measure the red tape concept and there was a need to conceptually distinguish red tape from related concepts. Indeed, relying on survey data from Phase I of the National Administrative Project, they provided evidence for both convergent validity of red tape measures in use and divergent validity when compared with widely used formalisation measures. In a later study, Kaufmann and Feeney (2012) provided additional evidence to validate the distinction between red tape and formalisation using perceptual as well as rule-count measures. Furthermore, studies using well-validated measures of red tape and formalisation have produced divergent findings on similar dependent variables (e.g., DeHart-Davis and Pandey 2005; Lambert, Paoline, and Hogan 2006).

The sorting out of empirical and conceptual issues during the 1990s thus ushered in an interest in the study of bureaucratic red tape as a phenomenon in its own right. Arguing against the tendency to conflate bureaucratic red tape with other potentially benign (or neutral) concepts, Bozeman asserted that rules – and by implication formalisation, an essential aspect of administrative processes – could be and should be distinguished from bureaucratic red tape. Thus, he defined red tape as a rule that imposes 'compliance burden for the organisation but makes no contribution to achieving the rule's functional object' (2000: 82). Although Bozeman offered a useful redirection and clarification, this definition was not amenable to ready operationalisation for two reasons. First, the criterion of 'no contribution' is a strong one for almost any rule and is hard to meet. Second and more importantly, this definition required a focus on individual rules as the unit of analysis (Pandey and Scott 2002: 565).

To overcome these challenges, Pandey and Kingsley (2000) proposed an alternative approach. Instead of a focus on individual rules as the unit of analysis, they proposed that red tape be defined in terms of *managerial perceptions* of the extent to which formalisation has a negative effect. This redirection has had both positive and unintended consequences on red tape scholarship. On the positive side, red tape studies based on managerial perception measures have proliferated and produced significant insights (see Bozeman and Feeney 2011 for a recent synthesis). The unintended consequence is that red tape experienced by citizens and clients, and other stakeholder groups, has not received much attention in public management literature.

Divergent Concept Development Paths: Rules Pathway versus Individual Social Roles Pathway

The first concept development path, which we call the *rules pathway*, emphasises rules as the unit of analysis (Bozeman 1993, 2000). Bozeman advanced significant ideas about the origin and impact of red tape in organisations. He drew a distinction between rule-inception red tape and rule-evolved red tape, with the latter describing rules that become dysfunctional over time. Bozeman (1993: 290) also offered a useful analytical device in terms of a two-way classification with one axis being the origin of rules (internal or external to the organisation) and the other axis identifying the actor facing the compliance burden of rules (internal or external to the organisation).

The most influential part of Bozeman's concept development work has been the distinction he drew between organisational red tape and stakeholder red tape (1993). Working with the basic idea of compliance burden that has no benefit for rule's functional object, he drew this distinction on the basis of the stakeholder entity experiencing the compliance burden – in one case it was the organisation and in the other case it was a named stakeholder group. Although this distinction has served its purpose in stimulating research, it is based on an important implicit assumption. The definition of organisational red tape implicitly subscribes to the notion that there is a *punctum Archimedis* (i.e., an Archimedean point) from which one can obtain an organisational perspective on compliance burden that sits above the different perspectives associated with different organisational roles.

Walker and Brewer (2008) offer evidence that organisational role has significant influence on red tape perceptions, casting doubt on the plausibility of Archimedean point assumption. One implication of this finding is that the organisational-stakeholder distinction is untenable. Indeed, the most commonly used single-item global measure of organisational red tape proposed by Bozeman and investigated by others (e.g., Borry 2016; Feeney 2012) simply taps into perceptions of organisational employees at different levels. Thus, the organisational-stakeholder distinction provides information from a specific set of stakeholders in the organisation. Bozeman (2012: 257) acknowledges this point about the organisational-stakeholder distinction thus:

When I developed the organizational and stakeholder red tape concepts ... I was well aware of their limitations. ... At the same time as empirical research on red tape has proceeded apace, a number of scholars, especially Sanjay Pandey and his colleagues ... have worked hard to identify methodological problems with red tape research and to suggest new approaches to improving research and empirically based theory.

This research has led to the second concept development path, which we call the *individual social roles pathway*. This research builds on Bozeman's work but accords a central role to how dysfunctional rules are perceived through the lens of individual social roles (Pandey 1995; Pandey and Kingsley 2000; Pandey and Marlowe 2015; Pandey and Scott 2002). Using this approach and also recognising the difficulties in implementing the *rules pathway*, Pandey and Kingsley (2000: 782) defined red tape as 'impressions on the part of managers that formalisation (in the form of burdensome rules and procedures) is detrimental to the organisation'. It should be noted that the concept of formalisation, referring to the extent to which rules and procedures govern individual action inside an organisation, had been used as an organisation theory concept for a long time. The concept of formalisation has been measured through both survey questions and organisational documents that focused on a variety of properties such as the extensiveness of recordkeeping, specification of job roles, and rules regulating workplace behaviour (DeHart-Davis 2017; Hall 1996).

The *individual social roles pathway* relying on managerial perceptions continued in Coursey and Pandey (2007), who identified different organisational domains (personnel, procurement, information systems, and budgeting) and developed measures of red tape focusing on these domains. This concept development path, however, is focused on managerial experiences and does not step out of different managerial roles to propose definitions for other salient social roles. Pandey and Marlowe (2015: 3) note in this regard that 'Red tape [should] be examined as socially constructed reality that is dependent on the individual's social role ... we should study red tape that managers face and also red tape that clients (or other stakeholders) face rather than continue the quixotic quest to label something red tape if and only if managers and other stakeholders can come to full agreement.' However, studies that look at the client/citizen perspective on red tape remain rare (e.g., Moynihan and Herd 2010).

Research on red tape now covers a wide variety of public management themes such as organisational performance (e.g., Brewer and Walker 2010; de Jong and Van Witteloostuijn 2015; Pandey and Moynihan 2006; Van den Bekerom, Torenvlied, and Akkerman 2015), use of new information technologies in government (e.g., Bretschneider 1990; Heintze and Bretschneider 2000; Pandey and Bretschneider 1997; Welch and Pandey 2007), and employee motivation (e.g., DeHart-Davis and Pandey 2005; Giauque et al. 2012; Moynihan and Pandey 2007; Pandey and Welch 2005; Torenvlied and Akkerman 2012). The research stream exploring relationships between different aspects of employee motivation and bureaucratic red tape is perhaps the most vibrant and voluminous proportion of red tape research. Most often, this stream of research views red tape as the cause of work motivation and other salient attitudes and behaviours as the effect. For example, red tape research has shown that perceived red tape has negative effects on a range of different employee motivation variables such as organisational commitment, job satisfaction, and public service motivation (DeHart-Davis and Pandey 2005; Moynihan and Pandey 2007; Stazyk, Pandey, and Wright 2011). Whereas earlier work focused on the negative effects of red tape on positive motivational states, recent research has shown that red tape also induces a state of resigned satisfaction in which employees cut back their aspirations (Giauque et al. 2012; Quartulain and Khan 2013).

An important issue with stark theoretical and methodological implications that has emerged is the likelihood of endogeneity in the relationship between red tape and employee motivation. Indeed, when employees experience work alienation (or reduced job satisfaction), they are likely to report higher levels of red tape (Pandey and Kingsley 2000; Torenvlied and Akkerman 2012). This implies that a form of reverse causation may underlie many observed red tape effects. Pandey and Welch (2005) used cognitive dissonance theory to illustrate how job dissatisfaction/work alienation combined with minimal experience of red tape will lead to dissonance, which can be resolved if the individual revises his/her cognition to include a higher level of red tape. Torenvlied and Akkerman (2012) extend this perspective to examine the effect of work engagement on perceptions of red tape, arguing that managers who are more engaged with their work will perceive lower levels of red tape. Thus, this stream of research views work motivations as the cause and red tape perceptions as the effect. Experimental techniques are ideal for probing the direction and nature of the causal link between red tape and work motivation/attitudes. It is therefore important that public management researchers use experimental methods to investigate questions about how red tape shapes attitudes and behaviour.

A Review of Experimental Research on Bureaucratic Red Tape

Experimental research on red tape is still at an early stage. Even though the earliest experimental study on red tape we report on was published more than 15 years ago, there are only a handful of studies to report on. Therefore, we include both published studies, papers presented at leading public management conferences, and an unpublished study conducted by the authors. We summarise key details, on seven reviewed studies, in Table 10.1 – the research question, the experimental context, design of the red tape treatment, and the findings. Two of the studies are survey experiments, both conducted in the local government context, and have methodological goals (Feeney 2012; Pandey and Marlowe 2015). Of the remaining five, two are set in the personnel management context (Grimmelikhuijsen, Pandey, and Deat 2015; Kaufmann and Tummers 2014), two examine red tape at the citizen/client interface (Kaufmann and Feeney 2014; Tummers et al. 2015),

Table 10.1: *Experimental studies on red tape**

Research Question	Experimental Context	Red Tape Treatment	Findings
1. Grimmelikhuijsen, Pandey, and Deat 2015 The effect of counter-attitudinal behaviour, involving red tape, on work attitudes	– Personnel management – Between-subjects laboratory experiment (conducted at a US university) – Executive MPA students	Red tape measured as an inflexible rule requiring that *even badly performing employees cannot be fired for an undecided period of time*	'The perceived impact of red tape on job satisfaction strongly increased, but we did not find an actual impact on job satisfaction. One way of coping with a counter-attitudinal situation may be to *exaggerate* the importance of a cognition (i.e., importance of red tape for job satisfaction)'.
2. Tummers et al. 2015 The effect of red tape on citizen satisfaction	– Citizen experience – Between-subjects laboratory experiment (conducted at two universities in the Netherlands) – Applying for passport – Focus on citizens	Red tape measured by requiring applicants to provide duplicative and irrelevant information in the application	Red tape has a negative effect on citizen satisfaction and this relationship is stronger in respondents who have limited/lower knowledge of politics.

Study	Details	Operationalisation	Findings
3. Pandey and Marlowe 2015 The validity of survey measures of personnel red tape	– Personnel Management – Within-subjects survey experiment administered to a random subset of study participants – Senior managers in city government	Red tape operationalised in vignettes by varying the <u>amount of time for promotion and the outcome</u>	Survey measure of personnel red tape is valid and does not suffer from systematic sources of error.
4. Kaufmann and Tummers 2014 The effect of red tape on procedural quality and procedural justice	– Personnel management – Between-subjects survey experiment – Online (MTurk) – US-based respondents	Red tape measured by <u>number of steps in the procedure and amount of time required to complete the procedure</u>	Red tape has a negative effect on procedural quality and procedural fairness.
5. Kaufmann and Feeney 2014 Red tape perceptions – the influence of rule burden and outcome	– Client perspective – Between-subjects laboratory experiment – MPA students – University procedures; registering for a course	Red tape operationalised as a combination of procedural <u>length and outcome</u>	Procedural length and outcome favourability have comparable effects on red tape perception.

Table 10.1: (*cont.*)

Research Question	Experimental Context	Red Tape Treatment	Findings
6. Feeney 2012 The validity of survey measure of general red tape	– Wording choices for general red tape measure – Between-subjects survey experiment – Local government managers	Use variations of Bozeman measure of red tape. Four variations used are: original measure, original measure without the term *red tape*, named outcomes other than performance, no definition provided	Specificity in definition has an impact. Highest red tape rating when least specificity provided.
7. Scott and Pandey 2000 The effect of red tape on benefits provided to clients	– Caseworker recommendation on client case files – Within-subjects design with counterbalancing – Laboratory experiment – MPA/MSW students	Procedural burden in terms of forms to be filled out and environmental cues about the organisation's work environment	Red tape has a negative effect on benefits provided to similar clients. Effect of red tape on caseworker behaviour stronger for male recipients.

*Studies are summarised chronologically in the table with the latest appearing first. We use the term *laboratory experiment* to designate experiments using university students as subjects in a university building rather than *in situ* in an actual public organisation, even though public management scholars generally do not have typical laboratories like psychologists (but see Chapters 7 and 20).

and one examines how caseworkers respond to red tape (Scott and Pandey 2000). Some of these experiments use red tape as the dependent variable and others use red tape as the independent variable.

Using a question wording experiment embedded in a larger survey, Feeney (2012) tested the validity of the most commonly used single-item measure of global red tape devised by Bozeman. Feeney provides a detailed account of the critique of this measure, chief among them being the appropriateness of the use of the phrase *red tape* in the question and whether respondents paid attention to the definition offered as part of the question. This measure has been used widely in the red tape literature and there is some concern that the use of the phrase *red tape* in the question can have the effect of introducing an upward bias. Feeney used the original Bozeman measure, which provides a definition of red tape, and also three additional variants of the Bozeman measure to assess whether respondent evaluations of organisational red tape are influenced by the choice of wording.

The Bozeman measure asks respondents to rate organisational red tape on an 11-point scale (0 to 10) in response to the question, 'If red tape is defined as "burdensome administrative rules and procedures that have negative effects on the organisation's effectiveness," how would you assess the level of red tape in your organisation?' Using a between-groups design with random assignment to one of the four variants, she obtained ratings from nearly 900 respondents. She found that one variant that merely deletes the term *red tape* does not produce a statistically significant difference in rating, thus providing evidence against possible upward bias introduced by use of the phrase *red tape* in the question. Interestingly, when respondents are asked to rate organisational red tape without a definition, they provided higher ratings of red tape (10.7 percent higher than the original measure). Again, this seems to indicate that the definition offered in the question is useful and facilitates attentive processing of the question by identifying tangible referents for the attitudinal assessment.

The Pandey and Marlowe (2015) study used a within-subjects design in which a random subset of study participants (n = 307) provided ratings of anchoring vignettes. The purpose of the study was to test the validity of personnel red tape measures used in prior literature. The validity concern was whether personnel red tape measures truly reflected underlying reality of personnel red tape or were compromised by systematic biases rooted in individual 'experiences, values and other cognitive shortcuts'.

Personnel red tape items have been used extensively in the red tape literature, almost as often as Bozeman's single-item measure of global red tape. These questionnaire items were originally constructed by Rainey (1979), who labelled these items 'personnel rules constraints', and have been used with minor or no modification in a number of other studies (e.g., Feeney and Rainey 2010; Stazyk et al. 2011; Walker and Brewer 2008). These items link a poor personnel outcome with an inflexible rule or process and focus on common tasks in personnel administration such as recruitment, discipline, termination, administration of pay raises, and promotions. The Pandey and Marlowe study focused on the domain of promotion, designing anchoring vignettes that were used to generate a differential item functioning (DIF) measure to correct for systematic bias. They conclude, 'measures of red tape perceptions are subject to DIF, but the causes of that DIF are more random than systematic' (2015: 16). Consistent with Feeney (2012), the Pandey and Marlowe (2015) study provides assurance about the validity of survey measure of personnel red tape concept.

Tummers and colleagues (2015) assessed the effect of red tape on citizen satisfaction. They conducted an experiment in which 179 subjects completed a simulated passport application. They used a simple between-group design in which the treatment group receiving the high red tape condition was required to enter the requested information a second time in a 'large computer readable grid' and also provide additional information that on the face of it seemed duplicative or irrelevant. For example, respondents were asked to enter age after they had provided a date of birth. The respondents provided information about attitudes such as emotional reactance and their knowledge of local politics in a posttest questionnaire. Predictably, they found that red tape led to lower satisfaction (4.87 as compared with 6.08 on a 1–10 scale). In the study context, this processing was done at the local government level and the study found that knowledge of local politics had a moderating effect on the satisfaction level.

Kaufmann and Feeney (2014) sought to understand the extent to which clients' perceptions of red tape were shaped by procedure length and outcome favourability. The study was conducted in the context of a US university in which students were registering for courses. The study used a basic between-group design in which 81 study participants were exposed to one of the following four conditions: positive outcome and short procedural length, positive outcome and long procedural length, negative outcome and short procedural length, negative outcome and long procedural length. The reference group in the analysis was the one with positive outcome and short procedural length. The standardised regression coefficients for the three scenarios reflecting the difference from the reference group were 0.30 for negative outcome and short procedural length, 0.32 for positive outcome and long procedural length, and 0.46 for negative outcome and long procedural length. On balance, the analyses indicate that both outcome favourability and procedural length have an effect on perceptions of red tape.

Kaufmann and Tummers (2014) used Amazon's MTurk online platform (described in more detail in Chapter 6) to recruit experimental subjects for a survey experiment. In their online experiment with 141 subjects providing complete data, respondents were presented with a personnel management scenario in which number of steps (two versus eight) and time (one hour versus eighteen hours) were varied for the red tape treatment. They found that red tape produced lower assessments of procedural fairness (3.21 for high red tape as compared with 3.71 on a 1–5 scale) and procedural quality (2.80 for high red tape as compared with 3.53 on 1–5 scale).

Grimmelikhuijsen and colleagues (2015) carried out another personnel management experiment in which they operationalised red tape as an inflexible personnel rule. One hundred forty-five participants were recruited from an executive master's program. In the experiment, the control group was asked to provide a balanced assessment of an inflexible rule and the treatment was asked to come up with a defence of the inflexible rule. The expectation was that the process of defending an unpopular rule would elicit dissonance. The treatment group reported higher dissonance (3.49 as compared with 2.41 on a 1–7 scale). Whereas this dissonance did not lead to lower job satisfaction as cognitive dissonance theory might predict, it induced participants to elevate the importance of red tape in determining job satisfaction.

Finally, the oldest study in this review (Scott and Pandey 2000) used a within-subjects design with complete counterbalancing. Ninety-six study participants assumed the role of caseworkers and processed client case files, awarding benefits to clients. The red tape treatment was made up of two components – procedural burden and environmental cues. In terms of procedural burden, the caseworker was required to complete additional paperwork for awarding benefits and to provide narrative justification instead of using a simple checklist. The experimental task was to award benefits to two pairs of cases with similar client needs; one in each pair was portrayed as more sympathetic. One of the most striking findings of the study is the difference in benefits awarded – a high-compassion female client in the low red tape scenario was awarded $512 more than in the high red tape scenario (56 per cent higher than the low red tape scenario).

Red Tape and Reverse Causality: Two New Experiments

Taken together, these previous experimental studies on red tape ask interesting research questions and make valuable contributions. None of these studies, however, examined the reverse causality question that has become important in light of the accumulation of survey-based studies examining the relation between work motivation and individual perceptions of red tape. Given the dominance of red tape evidence from surveys (observational studies) that remain ambiguous as to causality, we carried out an experimental test to assess the direction of causation between red tape and job satisfaction (Pandey and Welch 2005). Perceptions of red tape may be endogenous – influenced by job satisfaction (reverse causation) or linked to red tape perceptions through some common cause (such a person's mood or personality). To better understand the causal order of these variables, we embedded two experiments about red tape in an online survey of 175 public service professionals from across the United States. The survey was conducted in December 2013, using the Public Service Research Panel, a research panel of public service professionals recruited online using LinkedIn, GovLoop, and other social networks, professional listservs, and other online outreach efforts.

In Study 1, we ran a 2 × 2 factorial experiment in which we tried to induce perceptions of dissatisfaction in order to test whether this would increase perceptions of red tape. Respondents were then asked to rate their job satisfaction in each situation. As expected, respondents presented with the low job satisfaction situation rated their likely satisfaction as much lower than respondents given the high job satisfaction situation. Having provoked this big difference in satisfaction, we then randomly assigned respondents to one of two descriptions of a hiring process at the same hypothetical organisation, distinguishing the low red tape process and high red tape process on the basis of number of

Table 10.2: *Mean ratings of red tape*

| Factor 2: Red Tape Scenario | Factor 1: Satisfaction Situation | | |
	Low Job Satisfaction	High Job Satisfaction	Total
High Red Tape	75.6	75.4	75.5
Low Red Tape	43.4	49.9	47.1
Total	63.2	61.8	62.5

approvals and the duration of the hiring process. As expected, those presented with the low red tape scenario gave a lower rating than did those presented with the high red tape scenario. But the aim of the experiment again was to test if prior job satisfaction would influence, or moderate, later ratings of red tape. As Table 10.1 shows, those who were given the low job satisfaction situation gave only slightly higher red tape ratings (mean = 63.2) than did those who had the high job satisfaction situation (mean = 61.8), but this difference was insignificant statistically ($p = 0.46$). Furthermore, there was little interaction effect ($p = 0.43$). Thus, despite our efforts to frame the hypothetical organisation as a good or bad place to work, the respondents rated red tape similarly. These results, while not conclusive, suggest that job satisfaction may have a limited causal influence on red tape ratings.

In Study 2, we aimed to probe this causal question further and in a different way. While Study 1 relied on a hypothetical organisation, in Study 2 we primed respondents to think either positively or negatively about their own, real work organisations before asking about red tape. Specifically, we randomly allocated respondents to one of two simple priming tasks:

- In your own words, what are some of the things you like the most about your job?
- In your own words, what are some of the things you dislike the most about your job?

These primes were designed to activate either positive or negative associations participants have about their current jobs. Having primed the participants in this way, we then asked this standard red tape question: if red tape is defined as burdensome administrative rules and procedures that have negative effects on the organisation's performance, how would you assess the level of red tape in your organisation? Respondents then gave a 0–100 rating.

The results again showed no influence of satisfaction on red tape. In fact, those primed to think positively about their job gave slightly higher red tape ratings (mean red tape = 56.2) than did those primed to think negatively about their job (mean red tape = 53.5), although this difference was not significant statistically (p = 0.56). Again, despite our efforts, we could not induce a reverse causal process wherein job dissatisfaction would lead to higher red tape ratings.

In sum, the results of these two new experiments provide some initial evidence against the reverse causality hypothesis – that is, they suggest that job satisfaction (and analogous work motivations and attitudes) do not significantly influence red tape perceptions. These new studies are admittedly limited, and more research needs to be done to confirm these results. But if the results hold, they would suggest that red tape perceptions might indeed cause lower motivation rather than the other way around.

Implications and Future Research

Experimental research presents previously unexplored research opportunities for advancing our understanding of red tape, its effects, and its relationship with other concepts. Before discussing these opportunities, we want to acknowledge that experimental research also comes with risks. There is the risk that experimental research will remain disconnected and unintegrated with prior research and/or reality. At its worst, it is also possible that rather than pursue substantive questions of significant import, we mistake the novelty of experimental method for significant research, as Chapter 22 by Van de Walle warns us. These trends are already sweeping some areas of public management research where methodological novelties (at least novel to public management research) are leading to a 'methodologisation' that is either disconnected from substantive research questions or makes too much of minute methodological improvements (Pandey et al. 2017). A field like public management, without dedicated methodologists in its ranks to debate pros and cons of new methodological concerns, is particularly vulnerable in this regard.

It is therefore important for public management researchers to stay cognisant of these risks and be open to other disciplines to advance rigor and relevance of experimental approaches. Although there are differences in experiment design preferences, protocols, analytic methodologies, and reporting styles across the disciplines (e.g., Dickson 2011; List, Sadoff, and Wagner 2011), researchers agree there is no substitute for the kind of hypothesis testing experiments allow us to do (e.g., Druckmen et al. 2011). Experimental research in public management can benefit by learning from other disciplines like economics, political science, and psychology that have longer traditions of experimental research. We close this chapter with a set of recommendations for future experimental research on red tape.

Exploit New Possibilities Opened up by Experimental Research

Experimental research techniques open up new possibilities for future research. To some extent, this is already happening. The survey experiment of Feeney (2012) and Pandey and Marlowe (2015), for example, investigated long-standing debates on the validity of two of the most commonly used measures of red tape. In this chapter, we provided a test of the reverse causation hypothesis – whether work motivations influence perceptions of red tape. The tests we report offer a good beginning. However, for these results to be persuasive, experimental tests of reverse causal pathway and a better understanding of causal mechanisms are needed. Survey-based research on red tape and related topics also has thrown up interesting hypotheses that are better tested in experiments. DeHart-Davis, Chen, and Little (2013), for example, make the case for studying unwritten rules to better understand intra-organisational power dynamics. One interesting implication of their research is that perceptions of red tape at the front lines reflect 'unpalatable' power differentials in the organisation rather than the extent of formalisation and routinisation. Experimental techniques are well suited to testing such propositions.

Experiments also open up the possibility of examining the influence of red tape on behaviours. Observational/cross-sectional research on red tape is limited – from the perspective of dependent variables that can be studied – and there is a preponderance of attitudinal variables as the dependent variable. This tendency is replicated to some extent in some of the experimental studies. Part of this is understandable because red tape is an attitudinal construct and similar objective circumstances can give rise to differing perceptions of red tape. The important question, therefore, is the best way to connect perceptions of red tape with behaviour – to understand how perceptions of red tape drive behaviour and how behaviours influence perceptions. The Scott and Pandey (2000) study shows a clear impact of red tape perceptions on caseworker behaviour – the research opportunity here is to devise studies that provide an insight into causal mechanisms. If we better understand the causal mechanisms, that understanding can be used to better train caseworkers. Grimmelikhuijsen and colleagues (2015) show that behavioural engagement with red tape in the form of inflexible rule causes dissonance (3.49 on a 1–7 scale). This study offers a proof of concept about the dissonance-arousing function of red tape, but experimental treatment needs further refinement for the level of dissonance aroused to have material effect.

Clarify Conceptual Approach to Focus on Explaining Perceptions and Behaviours

Pandey and Scott's (2002: 554) observation in this regard rings true even today: 'The variety in theoretical specifications and operational measures of red tape may present significant obstacles to further research progress.' Whereas there is much to celebrate about the two concepts development paths – the *rules pathway* and the *individual social roles pathway* – it is also time to take stock of the value of this distinction. The *individual social roles pathway* is consistent with the venerable perspective in social sciences expressed in the oft-quoted Thomas Theorem from sociology, which states that 'If men define situations as real, they are real in their consequences' (Merton 1995; Smith 1999; Thomas and Thomas 1928). Using this pathway can provide a productive avenue for progress with a clearer focus on compliance burden (posed by rules and procedures) and resultant perceptions and behaviours.

Indeed, one way to view the experimental treatments of red tape (summarised in Table 10.1) is as different ways of operationalising compliance burden such as rule inflexibility, length of time, and irrelevant and/or duplicative procedural requirements. From an experimental perspective, conceptualising red tape, simply as compliance burden, can make it easier to design red tape treatments. This approach can also be complemented with recent developments in 'green tape theory' that advance the idea that rules can be designed so as to minimise compliance burden and to encourage cooperation from different stakeholders (DeHart-Davis 2017). Perhaps, future experimental research that develops crosscutting standard protocols for compliance burden and provides guidance on their sensitivity in terms of giving rise to perceptions of red tape can be useful. We believe that the *individual social roles pathway* offers a better approach to take advantage of the experimental method to advance our understanding of attitudes and behaviours relevant to red tape.

Devise Field Experiments and Extend Red Tape Research in other Domains and Contexts

Public organisations have much to gain by better communicating the value of the public services they provide. The commitment to serve the public often comes with compliance burden that can either undermine the ability to serve the public or give the organisation an ill-deserved reputation for red tape. Either outcome is unacceptable because the organisational purpose is to serve the public and to minimise compliance burdens. Given the increasing interest and openness to harnessing the power of social science research in government – as evidenced by creation of entities such as the Social and Behavioral Sciences Team in the United States, or the Behavioural Insights ('Nudge') Team in the United Kingdom – there is a chance to create opportunities for collaboration between academics and public organisations. Academic theories about how individual employees or citizens process and cope with bureaucratic red tape can be used to devise interventions that differ from the standard official procedures. Thus, exploration of opportunities for public organisations and public management scholars to collaborate on field experiments has the potential to improve citizen experience and to diminish red tape perceptions.

It is important to sustain the interest in experimental studies on red tape. Given the early and formative stage of research, there is potential for red tape researchers to learn from each other. This will require setting an ambitious research agenda that asks relevant questions of import and also matches the rigor of published studies in other disciplines. We believe this can be accomplished, especially if there are frequent and open public exchanges of data and information on red tape experimental work. Red tape research is bound up in organisational context in more ways than one. There are so few studies that look at client or citizen experiences. We know little about how citizen/ client experiences are shaped by social and political standing. We know even less about how the particularly vulnerable (e.g., the poor, the homeless, racial and ethnic minorities, undocumented immigrants, the elderly) cope with different forms of red tape and if individual coping strategies can even make a difference. In the public management scholarship on red tape, there is even less attention paid to how other actors (e.g., small businesses or entrepreneurs) experience red tape and the impact it has on them. There is evidence, for example, that even simple interventions such as publicising rules and regulations on a government website make it easier for small businesses to prosper (Pandey 2012). Research that examines how small business founders and entrepreneurs perceive and cope with red tape can therefore be very useful. In sum, red tape researchers should adopt a more applied focus by embracing real-world contexts and conducting field experiments in collaboration with different stakeholders.

References

Baldwin, J. N. 1990. 'Perceptions of public versus private sector personnel and informal red tape: their impact on motivation', *The American Review of Public Administration*, 20(1), 7–28.

Borry, E. 2016. 'A new measure of red tape: introducing the three-item red tape (TIRT) scale', *International Public Management Journal*. DOI: 10.1080/ 10967494.2016.1143421.

Bozeman, B. 1993. 'A theory of government "red tape"', *Journal of Public Administration Research and Theory*, 3(3), 273–304.

Bozeman, B. 2000. *Bureaucracy and Red Tape*. Upper Saddle River, NJ: Prentice Hall.

Bozeman, B. 2012. 'Multidimensional red tape: a theory coda', *International Public Management Journal*, 15(3), 245–65.

Bozeman, B. and Feeney, M. K. 2011. *Rules and Red Tape: A Prism for Public Administration Theory and Research*. ME Sharpe.

Bozeman, B. and Scott, P. 1996. 'Bureaucratic red tape and formalization: untangling conceptual knots', *The American Review of Public Administration*, 26(1), 1–17.

Bretschneider, S. 1990. 'Management information systems in public and private organizations: an empirical test', *Public Administration Review*, 50(5), 536–45.

Brewer, G. A. and Walker, R. M. 2010. 'Red tape: the bane of public organizations?' In R. M. Walker, G. A. Boyne, and G. A. Brewer (eds.), *Public Management and Performance: Research Directions*. Cambridge, UK and New York: Cambridge University Press, pp. 110–26.

Buchanan, B. 1975. 'Red-tape and the service ethic: some unexpected differences between public and private managers', *Administration & Society*, 6(4), 423–44.

Coursey, D. H. and Pandey, S. K. 2007. 'Content domain, measurement, and validity of the red tape concept: a second-order confirmatory factor analysis', *The American Review of Public Administration*, 37(3), 342–61.

de Jong, G. and Van Witteloostuijn, A. 2015. 'Regulatory red tape and private firm performance', *Public Administration*, 93(1), 34–51.

DeHart-Davis, L. 2017. *Creating effective Rules in Public Sector Organizations*. Washington, DC: Georgetown University Press.

DeHart-Davis, L., Chen, J., and Little, T. D. 2013. 'Written versus unwritten rules: the role of rule formalization in green tape', *International Public Management Journal*, 16(3), 331–56.

DeHart-Davis, L. and Pandey, S. K. 2005. 'Red tape and public employees: does perceived rule dysfunction alienate managers?' *Journal of Public Administration Research and Theory*, 15(1), 133–48.

Dickson, E. S. 2011. 'Economics vs. psychology experiments: stylization, incentives, and deception'. In J. N. Druckmen, D. P. Green, J. H. Kuklinski, and A. Lupia (eds.), *Cambridge Handbook of Experimental Political Science*. New York: Cambridge University Press, pp. 58–69.

Druckmen, J. N., Green, D. P., Kuklinski, J. H., and Lupia, A. 2011. 'Experimentation in political science'. In J. N. Druckmen, D. P. Green, J. H. Kuklinski, and A. Lupia (eds.), *Cambridge Handbook of Experimental Political Science*. New York: Cambridge University Press, pp. 3–9.

Feeney, M. K. 2012. 'Organizational red tape: a measurement experiment', *Journal of Public Administration Research and Theory*, 22(3), 427–44.

Feeney, M. K. and Rainey, H. G., 2010. 'Personnel flexibility and red tape in public and nonprofit organizations: distinctions due to institutional and political accountability'. *Journal of Public Administration Research and Theory*, 20(4), 801–26.

Giauque, D., Ritz, A., Varone, F., and Anderfuhren-Biget, S. 2012. 'Resigned but satisfied: the negative impact of public service motivation and red tape on work satisfaction', *Public Administration*, 90(1), 175–93.

Goodsell, C. T. 1983. *The Case for Bureaucracy*. Chatham, NJ: Chatham House.

Grimmelikhuijsen, S., Pandey, S. K., and Deat, F. 2015. 'Defending inflexible rules: an experiment on the effect of counter attitudinal behavior on work-related perceptions of public managers', Paper presented at the 2015 *Public Management Research Association Conference*, Minneapolis, MN, June 11–13, 2015.

Hall, R. H. 1996. *Organizations: structures, processes, and outcomes*, Upper Saddle River, NJ: Prentice Hall.

Heintze, T. and Bretschneider, S. 2000. 'Information technology and restructuring in public organizations: does adoption of information technology affect organizational structures, communications, and decision making?' *Journal of Public Administration Research and Theory*, 10(4), 801–30.

Hood, C. 1991. 'A public management for all seasons', *Public Administration*, 69(1), 3–19.

Kaufman, H. 1977. *Red Tape: Its Origins, Uses, and Abuses*. Washington, DC: Brookings Institution Press.

Kaufmann, W. and Feeney, M. K. 2012. 'Objective formalization, perceived formalization and perceived red tape: sorting out concepts', *Public Management Review*, 14(8), 1195–1214.

Kaufmann, W. and Feeney, M. K. 2014. 'Beyond the rules: the effect of outcome favourability on red tape perceptions', *Public Administration*, 92(1), 178–91.

Kaufmann, W. and Tummers, L. 2014. 'More than words: experimental evidence on the negative effects of red tape on quality and procedural justice', Paper presented at the IRSPM Conference, Ottawa, Canada.

Kelman, Steven. 2008. 'The "Kennedy school" of research on innovation in government', In S. Borins (ed.), *Innovations in Government: Research, Recognition, and Replication*. Washington, DC: Brookings Institution Press, pp. 28–52.

Lambert, E. G., Paoline, E. A., III, and Hogan, N. L. 2006. 'The impact of centralization and formalization on correctional staff job satisfaction and organizational commitment: an exploratory study', *Criminal Justice Studies*, 19(1), 23–44.

List, J. A., Sadoff, S., and Wagner, M. 2011. 'So you want to run an experiment, now what? Some simple rules of thumb for optimal experimental design', *Experimental Economics*, 14(4), 439–57.

Luton, L. S. 2007. 'Deconstructing public administration empiricism', *Administration and Society*, 39(4), 527.

Merton, R. K. 1995. 'The Thomas theorem and the Matthew effect', *Social Forces*, 74(2): 379–422.

Moynihan, D. and Herd, P. 2010. 'Red tape and democracy: how rules affect citizenship rights', *The American Review of Public Administration*, 40(6), 654–70.

Moynihan, D. P. and Pandey, S. K. 2006. 'Creating desirable organizational characteristics: how organizations create a focus on results and managerial authority', *Public Management Review*, 8(1), 119–40.

Moynihan, D. P. and Pandey, S. K. 2007. 'The role of organizations in fostering public service motivation', *Public Administration Review*, 67(1), 40–53.

Osborne, D. and Gaebler, T. 1992. *Reinventing Government: How the Entrepreneurial Spirit Is Transforming Government*. Reading, MA: Adison Wesley.

Pandey, S. K. 1995. 'Managerial perceptions of red tape', Unpublished PhD dissertation, Syracuse University, Syracuse, NY.

Pandey, S. 2012. 'E-government and small business activity'. In M. A. Shareef et al. (eds.), *Transformational Government through Egov Practice: Socio-economic, Cultural, and Technological Issues*. Emerald Group Publishing Limited, pp. 369–86.

Pande, S. and Bretschneider, S. 1997. 'The impact of red tape's administrative delay on public organizations' interest in new information technology', *Journal of Public Administration Research and Theory*, 7(1), 113–30.

Pandey, S. K., Coursey, D. H., and Moynihan, D. P. 2007. 'Organizational effectiveness and bureaucratic red tape: a multimethod study', *Public Performance & Management Review*, 30(3), 398–425.

Pandey, S. K., Dwivedi, Y. K., Shareef, M. A., and Kumar, V. 2014. 'Introduction: markets and public administration'. In Y. K. Dwivedi, M. A. Shareef, S. K. Pandey, and V. Kumar (eds.), *Public Administration Reformation: Market Demand from Public Organizations*. Routledge/Taylor and Francis, pp. 1–6.

Pandey, S. K. and Kingsley, G. A. 2000. 'Examining red tape in public and private organizations: alternative explanations from a social psychological model', *Journal of Public Administration Research and Theory*, 10(4), 779–800.

Pandey, S. K. and Marlowe, J. 2015. 'Assessing survey-based measurement of personnel red tape with anchoring vignettes', *Review of Public Personnel Administration*, 35(3), 215–37.

Pandey, S. K. and Moynihan, D. P. 2006. 'Bureaucratic red tape and organizational performance: testing the moderating role of culture and political support'. In G. A. Boyne, K. J. Meier, L. J. O'Toole Jr., and R. M. Walker (eds.), *Public Services Performance: Perspectives on Measurement and Management*. Cambridge University Press.

Pandey, S. K., Pandey, S., Breslin, R., and Broadus, E. 2017. Public Service Motivation Research Program: Key Challenges and Future Prospects. In J. Raadschelders and R. Stillman (eds.), *Foundations of Public Administration*. Irvine, CA: Melvin and Leigh, Chapter 19, pp. 314–332.

Pandey, S. K. and Scott, P. G. 2002. 'Red tape: a review and assessment of concepts and measures', *Journal of Public Administration Research and Theory*, 12(4), 553–80.

Pandey, S. K. and Welch, E. W. 2005. 'Beyond stereotypes a multistage model of managerial perceptions of red tape', *Administration & Society*, 37(5), 542–75.

Pollitt, C. and Bouckaert, G. 2011. *Public Management Reform: A Comparative Analysis – New Public Management, Governance, and the Neo-Weberian State*. Oxford University Press.

Quratulain, S. and Khan, A. K. 2013. 'Red tape, resigned satisfaction, public service motivation, and negative employee attitudes and behaviors: testing a model of moderated mediation', *Review of Public Personnel Administration*, 0734371X13511646.

Rainey, H. G., 1979. 'Perceptions of incentives in business and government: implications for civil service reform', *Public Administration Review*, 39(5), pp. 440–8.

Rainey, H. G. and Bozeman, B. 2000. 'Comparing public and private organizations: empirical research and the power of the a priori', *Journal of Public Administration Research and Theory*, 10(2), 447–70.

Rainey, H. G., Pandey, S., and Bozeman, B. 1995. 'Research note: public and private managers' perceptions of red tape', *Public Administration Review* 55(6): 567–74.

Scott, P. G. and Pandey, S. K. 2000. 'The influence of red tape on bureaucratic behavior: an experimental simulation', *Journal of Policy Analysis and Management*, 19(4), 615–33.

Smith, R. S. 1999. 'Contested memory: notes on Robert K. Merton's "the Thomas theorem and the Matthew effect"', *The American Sociologist*, 30(2), 62–77.

Stazyk, E. C., Pandey, S. K., and Wright, B. E. 2011. 'Understanding affective organizational commitment: the importance of institutional context', *The American Review of Public Administration*, 41(6), 603–24.

Thomas, W. I. and Thomas, D. S. 1928. *The Child in America: Behavior Problems and Programs*. Knopf.

Thompson, F. J. and Riccucci, N. M. 1998. 'Reinventing government', *Annual Review of Political Science*, 1(1), 231–57.

Torenvlied, R. and Akkerman, A. 2012. 'Effects of managers' work motivation and networking activity on their reported levels of external red tape', *Journal of Public Administration Research and Theory*, 22(3): 445–71.

Tummers, L., Weske, W., Bouwman R., and Grimmelikhuijsen, S. 2016. 'The impact of red tape on citizen satisfaction: an experimental study', *International Public Management Journal*, 19(3), 320–41.

Van den Bekerom, P., Torenvlied, R., and Akkerman, A. 2015. 'Managing all quarters of the compass? How internally oriented managerial networking moderates the impact of environmental turbulence on organizational performance', *The American Review of Public Administration*, 46(6), 639–59.

Walker, R. M. and Brewer, G. A. 2008. 'An organizational echelon analysis of the determinants of red tape in public organizations', *Public Administration Review*, 68(6), 1112–27.

Welch, E. and Pandey, S. K. 2007. 'E-government and bureaucracy: toward a better understanding of intranet implementation and its effect on red tape', *Journal of Public Administration Research and Theory*, 17(3), 379–404.

11 | Managerial Use of Performance Data by Bureaucrats and Politicians

DONALD P. MOYNIHAN, POUL A. NIELSEN,
AND ALEXANDER KROLL

Introduction

This chapter examines experimental evidence on performance information use by public officials – including both bureaucrats and politicians – charged with managing public services. Unlike topics covered in many of the chapters in this book, the topic is relatively new, and while observational studies of performance information use precede experimental work, the temporal gap is small. The topic therefore allows us to consider how experimental and observational work approach the same empirical phenomenon in approximately the same time frame.

In some respects, the study of performance information use is a natural fit with the broader trend towards experiments discussed in this book, as it reflects a behavioural approach to studying public management. Moynihan and Pandey (2010: 852) 'conceptualise performance information use as a form of organisational behaviour' that could be explained by studying individual, job, organisational, and environmental factors. By contrast, the study of performance management more broadly has traditionally centred on the study of particular reforms and initiatives, and broad assessments on whether they appeared to have been working or not (e.g., Radin 2012). A shortcoming of such work is that it typically excluded attention to micro-foundational bases for how public officials actually make use of performance data.

Performance management reforms have consistently sought to improve government effectiveness and accountability, but the central and frequently unspoken assumption is that such improvement requires a particular type of behaviour: that public officials incorporate performance data into their judgments and decisions. But whether and how public officials use data, and under what conditions, are questions which until recently were virtually unaddressed. This is why performance information use has been characterised as a 'big question' (Moynihan and Pandey 2010) for the broader study of performance management, reflecting Van Dooren's (2008: 22) claim that 'if we want to study the successes and failures of performance movements, we have to study the use of performance information.'

The question of performance information use is important not just for the study of performance management, or even administration generally, but also for policy and governance. Performance data have become the central mechanism by which many fundamental governance changes are expected to work, altering the basic structural and cultural conditions of both front-line and managerial work, affecting the motivations of those who enter public work (Moynihan and Soss 2014).

A simple illustration of the importance of performance data comes from the field of education, where many studies of performance information use have taken place. Schools were once treated as exemplars of 'coping' organisations: that is, organisations where the outputs and outcomes are difficult to observe (Wilson 1989). Today, schools, principals, and teachers are increasingly held directly accountable for performance metrics. Such a leap is possible only with the growing existence and sophistication of performance measures, the assumption that such measures appropriately capture the value of public work, and the expectation that managers will proactively make use of measures. In such a context, gaining a better understanding of performance information use among public employees is increasingly essential to understanding more fundamental shifts in governance (Moynihan et al. 2011).

Observational Studies: Antecedents of Performance Information Use

To put the contributions of experimental work on performance information use in context, we first briefly summarise what has been gleaned from observational studies. The relatively recent turn to experiments is reflected by the fact that the only systematic analysis of the use of performance data by managers features no experiments, but relies exclusively on observational analyses (Kroll 2015a).[1]

---

[1] Kroll specifically excludes politicians from his analysis, but we include local elected officials who have direct oversight of programmes.

Kroll points to six variables that are deemed to be 'important drivers of use' in that there is consistent evidence of an association between their presence and performance information use. These are a) measurement system maturity (a well-developed performance system with available data), b) stakeholder involvement, c) leadership support, d) support capacity (investment of resources into the performance system), e) innovative organisational culture, and f) goal clarity.

With the exception of goal clarity and culture, these factors are largely about how the organisation, its leaders, and stakeholders view and support a performance system. In this respect, the findings are consistent with intuition and prior research on organisational reform or policy implementation: when key political actors champion and invest in an organisational system, it is more apt to engender behavioural change.

Goal clarity and culture reflect basic organisational conditions that interact with performance systems in more specific and nuanced ways. Where goals are experienced as clearer, the relevance of information to evaluate goal achievement also becomes clearer. A developmental culture – an openness to innovation and experimentation – is assumed to spur the use of performance data largely to facilitate organisational improvement. The findings on culture are also consistent with findings about social processes that influence data use (Kroll 2015a). Data are not used in isolation, but are a social phenomenon, part of the dialogue among public actors (Moynihan 2008). Therefore, social prompts such as 'peer pressure' facilitate use in multiple ways, increasing managers' intention to conform with a general norm of use, but also pressuring them to do so, even if this effect is not mediated by their intentions (Kroll 2015b). Similarly, the creation of social routines can facilitate use. For example, learning forums, which are routines where managers and employees deliberately engage in a collective reflection about how changes in performance data are associated with the use of data for decisions (Moynihan and Kroll 2015).

Organisation–environment relations also matter. Managers in agencies with strong political support are more enthusiastic data users because for these managers information use is less risky. They can experiment with performance data, and are less likely to face political blame if data-driven decisions do not lead to expected results or if information portrays poor performance (Yang and Hsieh 2007). A second variable is the fragmentation of an agency's environment, which has also been found to facilitate data use. In contexts where managers deal with various groups of competing stakeholders, performance data are likely to be used to justify government decisions and needed as an additional feedback source to tailor specific solutions for diverse problems (Bordeaux and Chikoto 2008).

With respect to politicians, some research, based on case studies as well as survey results, suggests that data use within this group is less pronounced than use by public managers (Johnson and Talbot 2007; Moynihan 2008). One explanation is that politicians favour performance management reforms due to symbolic gains, but they have few incentives to give up established control mechanisms and replace them with number-driven performance monitoring practices (Moynihan 2008). However, studies also identify a great deal of variation in data use among politicians. For example, performance information use seems to vary across policy fields and sectors, though initial findings appear to be somewhat idiosyncratic.

A document analysis of queries of parliament members in Flanders (Belgium) addressed to executive departments showed that politicians, working in the areas of mobility and public works, employment, welfare, and public health, were particularly interested in using performance information (Van Dooren 2004). This has been found to be different in Norway, where survey results suggest that data use is high among politicians working in the areas of elderly care, administrative affairs, and educational affairs (Askim 2007). In addition, frontbenchers (mayors and members of the executive committee) more frequently use performance information than backbenchers, and inexperienced politicians use such data more than long-established ones (Askim 2009). Politicians are unlikely to read performance reports themselves, but will make use of performance information if they receive it through policy networks maintained by key committee staff (Bordeaux 2008) and if quantitative data can be transformed into richer, more qualitative information that can be disseminated through verbal conversations (ter Bogt 2004).

Cumulatively, observational studies have been helpful in identifying important organisational and environmental drivers of performance information use, but have told us relatively little about relevant user-related characteristics. Individual-level variables have been found to be insignificant or inconclusive. There is evidence, however, that managers' general attitudes towards performance management reforms determine information use and that their early involvement in the measurement process (creating ownership) has a positive effect on use (Kroll 2014).

Observational studies have thus made significant progress in terms of explaining when managers are likely to use performance information. In contrast, less attention has been paid to how the actual performance data themselves affect specific managerial or political decisions. Whereas general performance information use is measured through survey self-reports, examining the impact of actual performance data that public officials attend to is often more challenging. No standardised performance metrics exist to compare performance across different types of organisations, and in many cases performance metrics differ even within similar types of organisations. Most performance systems also include multiple measures that might provide conflicting views on how well an organisation performs. Moreover, managers are likely to interpret the same data differently depending on, for instance, how well their organisations did the previous year, how well their neighbouring peers perform, organisational task difficulty, or performance targets set by their hierarchical superiors. Studying how performance data affect decision-making therefore typically requires making fairly strong assumptions about both the data and the data interpretation process.

The few existing observational studies of how performance data affect managerial decision-making have been insightful. These include studies by Salge (2011) and Nielsen (2014) that suggest that hospital and school managers were more motivated to pay attention to performance data when they fell below a target, previous performance, or peer performance. Rutherford and Meier (2015) generally do not find effects of similar performance gaps on managerial goal setting in US higher education, which they partly attribute to the lower salience of any one specific goal in this context. A few additional studies have focused on budgetary decision-making by elected officials (Gilmour and Lewis 2006; Heinrich 2012), but these fail to find any discernible impact of performance metrics on US congressional budget allocations.

Apart from the challenges of measuring the specific performance signals that decision-makers are expected to respond to, endogeneity concerns are also generally difficult to overcome in observational studies, as discussed in Chapter 4 and elsewhere in this volume. The key challenge is that the performance scores reflect the same organisational performance that managerial and political responses to the data are deliberately trying to affect. As organisational performance is likely to be correlated over time, it becomes unclear whether performance scores are a cause or an effect of the types of organisational decisions studied. Regarding both measurement and causal identification, experimental designs have offered new possibilities. Finally, observational research has not been able to provide insights into user-related biases, the role of advocacy, or the actual decision-making process, mainly because such variables are difficult to measure through traditional survey designs. Experiments, on the other hand, have the ability to probe these aspects of information use, and we summarise some of the major experimental findings in the next section.

Experimental Findings: Manipulating and Framing Performance Data

The range of available experimental studies in this area that we are aware of is relatively limited, partly a testament to the difficulty of running experiments with public officials relative to the general public or convenience samples such as students. We therefore include studies which use graduate students in public affairs asked to engage in public employee tasks (Moynihan 2015). As Chapter 3 argues, professional graduate students can be a reasonable proxy for public managers (and indeed many are already practising public managers). The body of existing papers includes:

- A survey experiment of US graduate students (N = 140) in public affairs and other fields who are given performance data about a series of programmes and asked to make a series of decisions on a budget (Moynihan 2015).
- A field experiment of Danish school principals (N = 230) who are exposed to an organisational change (hiring a new set of employees) and who self-report on performance information use (Andersen and Moynihan 2016a). A related study examines if the same set of principals exposed to different types of performance data are likely to download more performance data anonymously (Andersen and Moynihan 2016b).

- A survey experiment of Danish local elected officials (N = 844) exposed to varying levels of actual performance data about local schools, and then asked to make decisions on resource allocation and management restructuring (Nielsen and Bækgaard 2015). This study was subsequently replicated among Flemish local elected officials (N = 1,413) (George et al. 2016).
- A survey experiment of local Danish election officials (N = 1,016) who are exposed to varying levels of actual performance data about schools, and advocacy about that performance data, and asked to make judgments about responsibility that school principals have for outcomes (Nielsen and Moynihan 2015).

Despite the limited number of studies, there is an impressive array of theoretical frameworks employed. Table 11.1 summarises the key treatments, the findings, and the theoretical frameworks employed by these studies, which we narrate in greater detail.

Blame Avoidance

Nielsen and Bækgaard (2015) randomly assigned true performance data to elected officials showing that local schools are performing below, around, or above the national average (relative to a control that received no performance data). They find that both treatments indicating low and high performance make elected officials more inclined to increase educational spending in their municipality by around 30 per cent of one standard deviation of the Likert-scaled attitudinal measure. The findings also suggest that the receipt of performance data matters differently for different types of decisions. When asked about willingness to reform schools, politicians were less likely to support organisational reform (20 per cent of a standard deviation) when told that their schools were performing well.

These patterns, argue the authors, align with the logic of blame avoidance theory: politicians feel pressure to do something to help poor performers in a salient policy area, but are happy to leave high performers alone. They caution that the finding on financial support in case of low performance may be specific to core governmental functions like education – in cases where a programme is viewed as less salient, policy makers may respond by cutting resources rather than investing more.

Table 11.1: *Overview of experimental studies*

Treatment	Dependent Variable	Theoretical Framework	Author(s)
Performance data indicating high performance	Increase in resource allocation Blocks general tendency to support managerial reform	Blame avoidance	Nielsen and Bækgaard (2015) Nielsen and Bækgaard (2015); George et al. (2016)
Performance data indicating low performance	Increase in resource allocation Increase in willingness to hold bureaucrats personally responsible	Blame avoidance Negativity bias, responsibility attribution	Nielsen and Bækgaard (2015); George et al. (2016) Nielsen and Moynihan (2015)
Provision of comparative performance information	Downloading of more performance data	Expertise model	Andersen and Moynihan (2016b)
Advocate interprets performance data in way supportive of programme	Increase in resource allocation	Interactive dialogue	Moynihan (2015)
Advocate interprets performance data in way critical of programme	No effect	Interactive dialogue	Moynihan (2015)

Table 11.1: (*cont.*)

Treatment	Dependent Variable	Theoretical Framework	Author(s)
Advocate criticises nature of performance data	Reduces willingness to hold bureaucrats personally responsible, but only for politicians aligned with advocate	Responsibility attribution, motivated reasoning	Nielsen and Moynihan (2015)
Targets set above actual achievement level	Reduction in resource allocation	Expectancy disconfirmation	Moynihan (2015)
Outcomes instead of outputs to measure performance	Increase in resource allocation	Goal ambiguity	Moynihan (2015)
Additional performance metrics that portrayed less positive outcomes relative to primary measure	Reduction in resource allocation	Goal ambiguity	Moynihan (2015)
Organisational change in the form of hires of new and more diverse employees	School principals use performance data in response to new hires if they view organisational culture as lacking innovation	Diversity theory, developmental culture	Andersen and Moynihan (2016a)

This study was subsequently replicated among Flemish local elected officials by George and colleagues (2016) using identical survey experimental treatments and response items with the only slight difference concerning the exact type of performance data represented by the treatments. In this new context, the findings for organisational reform and the positive effect of low performance on spending attitudes were replicated, albeit with *p-values* slightly above the 0.05 threshold, whereas the authors found no indications that the high performance treatment made elected officials more inclined to increase spending.

Negativity Bias in Responsibility Attribution

The findings of Nielsen and Bækgaard suggest that policy makers are more attentive and responsive to performance data that are unusual, but they may be especially responsive to data showing poor performance, as is indicated by the replication study. This finding is consistent with growing evidence that the electorate, politicians, and managers might not be responsive to performance data as a whole, but are mainly responsive to negative performance data. Both survey experiments (James and Moseley 2014) and actual elections offer evidence of this pattern (Kogan, Lavertu, and Peskowitz 2015). For example, incumbent UK local government officials tended to lose vote share when local governments were publicly rated as poorly performing, but did not gain equivalent votes in cases of positive ratings (Boyne et al. 2009).

A follow-up study to the Nielsen and Bækgaard study again surveyed local Danish council officials who oversaw school services (Nielsen and Moynihan 2015). Once again these officials were provided with school performance data in the treatment groups. They were then asked to assess the degree to which school principals controlled school performance, based on Likert scale responses to two items: 'The school principals do not have much influence on how well their schools are performing' (reversed) and 'The individual school principals are to a great extent responsible for how well their students are doing academically.'

Such a judgment represents a form of responsibility attribution – a topic that has been studied in mainstream political science in terms of voter attributions of elected officials' control over outcomes, but that has not been examined in terms of how bureaucrats are assessed (Tilley and Hobolt 2011). The experiment showed that only the provision of performance data showing low performance triggered attribution processes, making council officials more likely to judge that school principals controlled outcomes by one third of a standard deviation. The authors therefore propose that a negativity bias shapes how performance data trigger attribution processes.

Advocacy: Motivated Reasoning in an Interactive Dialogue

As policy makers and stakeholders engage in an interactive dialogue about what constitutes performance, they can be expected to both unconsciously and strategically select and interpret information in a way that accords with their worldviews and institutional goals (Moynihan 2008). But for such a strategic approach to work, it assumes that individuals are actually amenable to different policy narratives that will alter their interpretation of performance data.

To test some of the basic claims of interactive dialogue theory, Moynihan (2015) examines whether the comments of advocates about performance data affect hypothetical resource allocation decisions. The subjects were public administration and other graduate students who played a budget game. The dependent variable was percentage of budgetary change on previous budget allocations (subjects were given previous year budget allocations). In order to replicate one basic characteristic of actual budget decisions – resource constraints – subjects were told that the county executive expected the upcoming budget to increase by approximately 3 per cent overall, although some programmes might see larger budget increases, and some might be reduced. The average proposed change in budget subjects offered was even lower, below 1 per cent.

Two experiments were used. In one, the treatment was an advocate statement from a county sheriff commenting on a rise in crime figures, making the case for the need for more resources *because* of the increase in crime: 'The County Sheriff acknowledges that drug use and related crime may be up, but says "we usually see this sort of thing spike when the economy is in recession. This means that the Narcotics Task Force needs more money to tackle this problem."' This advocate was successful in making subjects more generous to the programme, resulting in a 0.1 per cent budgetary decline versus a 1.1 per cent decline for the control group. However, another advocacy treatment failed to generate a significant difference in budget allocations. In this treatment, the advocate was critical of customer satisfaction data that appeared to show improving performance in a local parks system: 'But the head of the local taxpayers association suggests that [the] parks system is not a good use of public resources. "You see a relatively small number of people using the park system again and again. Of course they give the system good ratings – they are getting a free service that the rest of us are paying for."' Not only did this negative advocacy fail to generate the expected reduction in resources, the sign for the treatment was in the wrong direction – as it seemed to make subjects more generous, though not at a statistically significant level.

The curious implication from the experiment is that advocacy may sometimes work, but not always. More precisely, these findings raised the question of how the effects of advocacy are contingent on characteristics of the advocate, the target audience, and the interaction between these two factors. Such characteristics may include the advocates' position and the content of the information they provide. Target audiences may vary in prior knowledge about a policy area, policy preferences, or ideological beliefs.

Nielsen and Moynihan (2015) also test the role of advocacy, focusing on one specific variable suggested by the interactive dialogue framework: political ideology. Within political science growing attention is being paid to how political ideology, and especially the ideological distance between political actors, shapes voter responses to political messages and economic performance. For example, partisans tend to be less likely to attribute responsibility for negative outcomes to fellow partisans, but are more willing to blame those who have different ideological beliefs (Tilley and Hobolt 2011).

Observational studies have also pointed to the role of ideology in how politicians apply performance management reform and use performance data. Such a pattern became evident during the conservative George W. Bush administration, whose Programme Assessment Rating Tool (PART) assessed almost all federal programmes on a five-point scale from ineffective to effective. Liberal agencies were subject to more assessments per dollar of spending, were more likely to receive lower scores, found the process more burdensome, and were more likely to be given corrective recommendations to restructure their programmes (Lavertu et al. 2013; Moynihan 2013).

Nielsen and Moynihan (2015) employed a survey experiment of local elected officials to test the role of ideology in shaping how advocacy matters. As explained previously, local council members were provided with performance data about local schools (with a control group receiving no information). The performance data were based on actual performance of local schools, employing a value-added-based measure used by the Education Ministry and reported in the press. Based on these indicators, council members were told if local school performance was in the top, middle, or lowest third of municipalities. A second treatment group was also provided with an advocacy treatment. Here, the advocate was the teachers' union casting doubt on the validity of test scores: 'The use of quality measurements has also been criticised, however. For instance, the Danish Teachers' Union has argued that national test scores provide an incorrect picture of the quality of public schools.' In the Danish context and elsewhere, teachers' unions are associated with liberal parties and seen as ideologically distant from conservatives.

For liberal politicians the interest group and politician shared the same ideological space, resulting in liberal politicians becoming less likely to use test scores showing low performance to attribute responsibility to school principals, not only compared to conservatives but even to the similar liberal control group that received no performance data. By contrast, conservative politicians ignored the comments of teachers' unions. The result is that conservative and liberal politicians, when exposed to performance data and data advocacy consistent with actual policy processes, arrive at very different judgments about what bureaucrats should be held responsible for. In short, advocacy about performance data can increase pre-existing polarisation between actors, in this case with a difference in marginal treatment effects for conservatives and liberals of more than one standard deviation of the dependent variable. The underlying causal mechanism is consistent with the theory of motivated reasoning (Taber and Lodge 2013), with politicians more trusting and receptive of advocates who share the same ideological space.

Organisational Change: Diversity

In a relatively rare field experiment for the topic, Andersen and Moynihan (2016a) assessed the effects of organisational change on performance information use by organisational leaders. To do so, they embedded a survey in a broader field experiment in Danish schools, where resources were provided to make actual hires but with varying degrees of constraints on the type of employee that could be hired. In one treatment, new employees were hired with the same educational background as existing teachers in a classroom to fulfil an existing organisational role of co-teacher in a classroom ('status quo' treatment). In the second treatment, schools hired an employee from any other educational background to fulfil the same co-teacher role ('educational diversity' treatment). In the third treatment, schools hired an individual who shares the educational background of existing teachers to fulfil a novel organisational role: observing and providing advice to teachers ('role diversity' treatment). Both the educational and role diversity treatments provided two different types of employee diversity, bringing in new employees who have a different background or fulfil a different role relative to existing employees. The effects of these treatments were compared to schools that were assigned no additional resources (the control group).

The dependent variable was a set of self-reports on performance information use, similar to those used in observational studies, completed by school principals months after the treatment was put in place. The results found that leaders tended to become more likely to use performance data in response to the introduction of diverse new employees (as opposed to the control or status quo treatment), but this finding was contingent on perceptions of organisational culture (based on survey responses collected at the outset of the experiment). When leaders did not see an innovative culture, the addition of diverse hires tended to increase performance information use. One way of considering the results is to ask in what proportion of organisations we find a statistically significant positive effect of diversity on performance information use. The answer to that question depends on the level of significance used and the distribution of innovative culture in the sample, but it is a non-trivial amount, ranging from 16 per cent using 95 per cent confidence interval, to 31 per cent using 90 per cent confidence interval.

The results are interesting for a couple of reasons. One is that they use an experimental design to test precisely the sort of temporal questions that cross-sectional studies cannot. In particular, the authors suggest that organisational change will spur leadership attention to performance data for three related purposes: to understand if change is having an effect, to manage change, and to explain it. Performance information becomes more important as a way of knowing when organisational actors know relatively little about a phenomenon.

A second implication of the result is the degree to which organisational treatments may be contingent on underlying organisational conditions – in this case, organisational culture. Prior research (Kroll 2015a) has pointed to a positive relationship between developmental culture and performance information use for managers (and indeed, Andersen and Moynihan find such a relationship in the control group, but, unlike prior studies, document this relationship using two different surveys rather than a single survey collected at one point of time). The results from the experimental treatment are slightly different, suggesting that the way in which organisational leaders make use of performance data depends on their pre-existing beliefs (which were collected in a survey before the treatments were provided) about the organisation. If the research design had also not sought to measure these underlying conditions prior to the introduction of treatments, the role of pre-existing beliefs would have been missed.

Comparative Performance Data

A number of survey experiments also directly consider how the nature or presentation of data alters how public officials use it. For example, Andersen and Moynihan (2016b) test if providing comparative information – data that rank an organisational unit relative to peers – makes respondents more likely to consume information. Here, the dependent variable is not actually performance information use, but willingness to invest time and effort in acquiring information, which the authors argue is representative of expertise acquisition in the sense of Gailmard and Patty's (2012) formal model of bureaucracy.

In the experiment, respondents were school principals who were offered the opportunity to download performance data about their school on a website. The control group received performance data only about their school, while the treatment group were also offered comparative data showing how their school ranked compared to others. The rate of downloads was monitored, unbeknownst to the subjects.

At the most basic level, absolute performance scores do not communicate whether the level of performance is good or bad, or what to do next. Some data may be more helpful than others, providing a key for the user to unlock the value of other information. In the case of performance data, comparative information is more useful than absolute scores, because it provides a reference point that helps the agent understand if their unit is doing relatively well or not, and anchors aspirational levels (Cyert and March 1963; Greve 2003).

The results provide evidence that comparative data do indeed increase the general willingness of bureaucrats to acquire information. School principals were likely to download 15 percentage points more of the proportion of performance data they were offered when they were provided with comparative information (an increase of 45.8 per cent compared to the 32.5 per cent in the control group). The practical implication is that elected officials can make bureaucratic investments in expertise more attractive by providing agents with tools that alter the relative costs and benefits of information acquisition. Specifically, if school principals were offered comparative performance data that helped to contextualise the performance data for their own school, they were likely to acquire more data.

Outcomes versus Outputs: Evaluative Goal Ambiguity

Performance reformers have argued that outcome measures are more helpful than outputs in assessing public sector performance. Some observational studies offer support for this claim. Heinrich (2012) finds programmes from the federal Department of Health and Human Services that relied more on outcomes received higher budgets. Outcomes are expected to provide greater goal clarity, which has been consistently associated with performance information use (Kroll 2015a). The flip side of goal clarity is goal ambiguity – the 'interpretive leeway that a statement of organisational goals allows in evaluating the progress toward the achievement of the mission' – which has been shown to undercut efforts to improve performance (Chun and Rainey 2005: 533).

Moynihan (2015) tests this by examining two types of goal ambiguity among a group of graduate students. Evaluative goal ambiguity has been measured in terms of the relationship between outcomes and outputs, with a higher ratio of outcomes to outputs associated with lower evaluative goal ambiguity (Jung 2012). In the experiment, one group of students was given a set of output measures while the other was given an outcome. Both showed positive performance. However, recipients of the outcome measure were more likely to show support for the programme by allocating resources to it. While the control group provided a 1.5 per cent increase over prior year funding, the treatment group proposed a 5 per cent increase.

Contradictory Performance Data: Priority Goal Ambiguity

The second aspect of ambiguity Moynihan (2015) examines is priority goal ambiguity, defined as 'the level of interpretive leeway in deciding on priorities among multiple goals' (Chun and Rainey 2005: 535). This type of ambiguity captures the common tendency of public programmes to feature multiple and potentially competing goals. For a performance system, this creates a very real potential that multiple measures will offer contradictory accounts of organisational performance.

At a psychological level, contradictory performance data created by priority goal ambiguity is expected to create a sense of dissonance, which subjects may resolve by ignoring the information that contradicts their views, or by altering their beliefs about the programme. In the experimental treatment, subjects are given two sets of measures that capture the performance of a job-training programme (Moynihan 2015). For one measure, which is also shared with the control group, subjects are provided the rate of job placement, which shows positive and improving performance. But the second measure – actual pay received by placed employees – shows a less positive picture. In the experiment, those who received both types of measure, and therefore were provided a more complex though more comprehensive understanding of the programme, were significantly less likely to allocate resources to the programme, providing a 2 per cent increase to the programme relative to 3.2 per cent for the treatment group, reflecting the general tendency of respondents to alter their beliefs when shown dissonant information about a programme.

Unmet Performance Targets: Expectancy Disconfirmation

Another potential circumstance that will affect the perception of and response to performance data is the expectations that individuals have about what performance could or should be. This claim draws from the expectation disconfirmation model, which proposes that an individual's sense of satisfaction with services is shaped by their expectations. A frequently evoked implication of this theory for public managers is the need to limit citizen expectations to avoid disappointment (James 2009; Van Ryzin 2006). How can governments shape expectations about performance? One of the primary tools at their disposal are performance targets. Targets communicate the expectations that governments set for themselves and invite others to hold them accountable. Targets might alter expectations about what constitutes programme success and failure.

The same actual underlying performance may be perceived as more or less impressive if accompanied by performance targets that are respectively modest or ambitious. If targets anchor expectations to a level that is not achieved in practice, this is likely to reduce support for the programme. Moynihan (2015) finds support for this proposition. A control group of graduate students received performance data showing consistently improving performance for a programme. The treatment group also received performance data, but in addition received performance targets that were higher than the achieved goals. Even though the underlying performance was improving over time, it failed to match targets. This resulted in lower support for the programme; with treatment subjects likely to increase budgets above previous allocations 2.1 relative to control groups increased budgets by 3.2 per cent.

The use of targets may create a risk for programmes, for when those targets are not met – even if performance scores are improving – this reduce support for a programme among subjects. If such a risk is apparent to practitioners, they may wish to not publicly report targets, set modest targets they know they can achieve, or limit performance in one time period so as to curb higher expectations in the future.

Conclusion: A Research Agenda for Performance Information Use

In comparing the body of knowledge from experimental work versus observational analyses, it is worth emphasising that there have not been multiple experimental studies of the same variables we have seen in observational work, and therefore the usual cautions about external generalisability of experiments, as discussed in Chapter 4, are especially relevant. What remains true is that different approaches have different strengths. Experimental designs have cast the greatest light on variables that are most easily represented by treatments, especially in the form of a survey experiment. Experiments have therefore been most persuasive at uncovering how individual biases and perceptions alter how managers respond to information, and how manipulations of performance information itself affects its use. The design of experimental treatments, apart from aiding in causal identification, thus also helps solve some of the measurement problems in observational research regarding the precise content and circumstances surrounding the use of performance information.

Such work is valuable, partly because it complements a parallel and growing experimental body of knowledge on how citizens engage with performance data, as discussed in Chapter 12. We are therefore coming to know more about how citizens and public officials compare in their use of performance data, but more work that directly makes such comparisons with identical treatments would be valuable. On one hand, it is plausible that officials more familiar with performance data are less subject to systematic biases and errors. On the other hand, they may be more exposed to the pressures and motivations that prompt biases. For example, there is growing evidence of a negativity bias among citizens and politicians in how they respond to data. In addition to being subject to the same underlying bias, public managers may be even more responsive to data about poor performance precisely because they know that citizens and politicians are attentive to negative outcomes.

Another advantage of an experimental approach relative to observational studies is the ability to craft the dependent variable in a variety of ways. While observational studies mainly rely on self-reports of performance information use, experimental designs can use actual decisions or judgments (e.g., responsibility attribution, resource allocation, assessment of programme quality), and assess how performance data and other treatments affect those. This has a number of benefits. The most obvious is that self-reports have the potential for some form of bias, although Meier and O'Toole (2013) suggest that self-reported performance information use is less subject to the problems associated with common method bias relative to other variables. More importantly, it grounds performance information use in an actual decision or judgment rather than the respondents' beliefs about their general tendencies to make decisions or judgments. This increases confidence in causal attribution, but also sheds light on *how* performance information use occurs.

While initial studies have made only broad distinctions between types of performance information use, this approach allows for a more fine-grained link to particular behaviours, which in turn are of interest to other research literatures. For example, the relationship between performance data and responsibility attribution offers new insights to an existing literature in political science on responsibility attribution, as well as to studies of blame avoidance more generally. A few observational studies have also sought to link performance data to particular behaviours, but it is difficult both to identify the exact content of the performance signals that managers are expected to respond to, and to overcome the endogeneity problem that may arise from organisational performance being a result of these same types of behaviours.

Experiments also have an advantage in determining if the type and format of the information affects use. A key premise of performance management reforms has been that measurement routines produce quantitative data that are more systematically collected, analysed, and reported than other feedback information and therefore more influential. Experiments that provide participants with information presented in different ways and drawn from different sources (routine and non-routine performance data) could help to better understand whether certain types of information are really more influential than others and complement existing observational research (Kroll 2013).

In public management, as in surrounding disciplines, the issue of replication has become more important, as Chapter 21 discusses. This effort at replication has already been present in observational studies of performance information use, where similar antecedents have been examined in different contexts. However, exact replications are difficult to conduct in observational research, as many factors are likely to vary across settings, including the nature and relevance of the performance data and the sophistication of the measurement system. By contrast, experimental designs and treatments can be transferred more directly to other contexts, at least among organisations dealing with similar tasks. The study by George and colleagues (2016) is an example of this, where the experimental design was replicated among fairly similar local elected officials in a different country. Conducting such replications should be encouraged to generate more robust findings and knowledge for the practice of performance management. To facilitate this, a high level of transparency is needed, and authors should be willing to share the details of their experimental designs, issues that are discussed at more length in Chapter 21.

Limitations of Experimental Research and Potential Solutions

The study of performance information use also points to limitations on experimental work. Some key variables – organisational culture is perhaps the best example – are not easy to capture or manipulate in an experimental design. This is a real limitation, since experiments cannot persuasively model factors where the effect of the variable accumulates over time on the subject. Observational studies may also be the best way to observe government-wide reforms where there is no variance in the introduction of the treatment (the reform). Such reforms are rarely implemented in a way that allows for experimental designs, or multiple data sources, leaving researchers with less-than-perfect foundations for making causal inferences (e.g., Moynihan and Kroll 2015). The alternative, however, is that clearly important reforms are left unexamined by scholars, who instead focus on empirical questions that lend themselves to cleaner causal inference but often have less external generalisability. Policy makers want to understand progress on the type of reforms that fuel an interest in the study of performance data, and this demand will be met by think-tanks and oversight bodies likely using even less rigorous approaches. To be relevant in such policy debates in areas of limited data implies doing the best analysis with the data available, rather than waiting for the perfect causal research design.

Another potential limitation of the experimental study of performance information use is that the focus on individual biases and heuristics also displaces attention away from the possibility of studying issues of organisational design and aggregate decision outcomes in multi-actor settings, such as agencies or legislatures. With relatively simple survey experiments, it is possible to demonstrate how, for example, negativity bias or ideology affects the processing of data by individuals. Such findings are clearly important, contributing to our understanding of how performance data are used in governance, but policy makers also want actionable advice. What are the practical implications of demonstrating that we are flawed and subjective users of data? Perhaps it helps to tamp down the heightened expectations that policy makers have about performance management, and to compensate for such biases. Studies that show the effects of framing data may also have practical implications for how government agencies present and describe performance information.

But there is also a need for more research that directly addresses institutional design issues – how altering some facet of government improves performance information use. As a matter of research design, experimental work is best suited to addressing institutional design issues, offering clear causal inferences about what happens when a new approach is tried. The problem is a practical one, as Chapter 3 on the history of experimentation in public administration and management points out. Field experiments that include some manipulation of the organisational setting are inherently more difficult than survey experiments. They usually require not just more resources, but partnerships with governments, who historically have not been willing to employ experimental designs in the workplace. However, things may be changing here also, as Peter John shows in Chapter 23. As governments have become more enamoured with the promise of behavioural economics, they have also become willing to use the tools of simple field experiments to examine how different 'nudges' alter citizens' behaviour in their interactions with the state. Examples include the Behavioural Insights Team in the United Kingdom and the Social and Behavioral Sciences Team in the United States.

It is the job of public management scholars to convince governments to apply the tools of field experiments not just on citizens, but on public organisations and their employees, examining how alterations in work conditions alter performance information use. Similarly, if governments remain intent on introducing new performance reforms, this offers an opportunity for a field experiment (e.g., Andersen and Moynihan 2016a). Even if such reforms are implemented government-wide, a staggered introduction allows the variation needed for an experimental or at least quasi-experimental design. In this respect, scholars of performance management are fortunate, because governments are consistently interested in new reform ideas on performance issues. For example, we have observational studies that suggest that exposure to and the quality of learning routines are associated with greater use of data (Moynihan and Kroll 2015). The introduction and nature of such routines could be easily tested experimentally.

A final suggestion for future research is to attempt to combine the relative strengths of observational studies and experiments. For example, Andersen and Moynihan (2016a) combine survey data from multiple points in time and the introduction of a treatment into a field setting, as well as administrative data on teachers and students. Such an approach is relatively rare, but in this case was enabled because of a partnership with the government to understand the implementation of an educational reform, where performance data was not the primary purpose. A similar approach is described in Chapter 9 by Lotte Andersen and colleagues, where they describe an ambitious field experiment to examine the effects of transformational leadership on government. The benefit of such longitudinal, mixed-mode, and mixed methods studies is that they can identify underlying organisational factors that may interact with the experimental treatment to generate a variety of outcomes.

References

Andersen, S. and Moynihan, D. 2016a. 'How leaders respond to diversity: the moderating role of organizational culture on performance information use', *Journal of Public Administration Research and Theory* 26(3): 448–60.

Andersen, S. and Moynihan, D. 2016b. 'Bureaucratic investments in expertise: evidence from a randomized controlled field trial', *Journal of Politics* 78(4): 1032–1044.

Askim, J. 2007. 'How do politicians use performance information? An analysis of the Norwegian local government experience', *International Review of Administrative Sciences* 73(3): 453–72.

Askim, J. 2009. 'The demand side of performance measurement: explaining councillors' utilization of performance information in policymaking', *International Public Management Journal* 12(1): 24–47.

Bourdeaux, C. 2008. 'Integrating performance information into legislative budget processes', *Public Performance and Management Review* 31(4): 547–69.

Bourdeaux, C. and Chikoto, G. 2008. 'Legislative influences on performance management reform', *Public Administration Review* 68(2): 253–65.

Boyne, G., James, O., John, P., and Petrovsky, N. 2009. 'Democracy and government performance: holding incumbents accountable in English local governments', *Journal of Politics* 71(4): 1273–84.

Chun, Y. and Rainey, H. 2005. 'Goal ambiguity and organizational performance in U.S. federal agencies', *Journal of Public Administration Research and Theory* 15(4): 529–57.

Cyert, R. and March, J. 1963. *A Behavioral Theory of the Firm*. Hoboken, NJ: Willey-Blackwell.

Gailmard, S. and Patty, J. 2012. *Learning while Governing: Information, Accountability, and Executive Branch Institutions*. Chicago: University of Chicago Press.

George, B., Deschmidt, S., Nielsen, P., and Bækgaard, M. 2016. 'Rational planning and politicians' attitudes to spending and reform: replication and extension of a survey experiment', forthcoming in Public Management Review.

Gilmour, J. and Lewis, D. 2006. 'Assessing performance budgeting at OMB: the influence of politics, performance, and program size', *Journal of Public Administration Research and Theory* 16(2): 169–86.

Greve, H. 2003. *Organizational Learning from Performance Feedback: A Behavioral Perspective on Innovation and Change*. Cambridge: Cambridge University Press.

Heinrich, C. 2012. 'How credible is the evidence, and does it matter? An analysis of the program assessment rating tool', *Public Administration Review* 72(1): 123–34.

James, O. 2009. 'Evaluating the expectations, disconfirmation and expectations anchoring approaches to citizen satisfaction with public services', *Journal of Public Administration Research and Theory* 19(1): 107–23.

James, O. 2011. 'Performance measures and democracy: information effects on citizens in field and laboratory experiments', *Journal of Public Administration Research and Theory* 21(3): 399–418.

James, O. and Moseley, A. 2014. 'Does performance information about public services affect citizens' perceptions, satisfaction and voice behaviour? Field experiments with absolute and relative performance information', *Public Administration* 92(2): 493–511.

Johnson, C. and Talbot, C. 2007. 'The UK Parliament and performance: challenging or challenged?', *International Review of Administrative Sciences* 73(1): 113–31.

Jung, C. 2012. 'Developing and validating new concepts and measures of program goal ambiguity in the U.S. federal government', *Administration and Society* 44: 675–701.

Kogan, V, Laverty, S. and Peskowitz, Z. 2015. 'Performance federalism and local democracy: theory and evidence from school tax referenda', *American Journal of Political Science* 60(2): 418–35.

Kroll, A. 2013. 'The other type of performance information: nonroutine feedback, its relevance and use', *Public Administration Review* 73(2): 265–76.

Kroll, A. 2014. 'Why performance information use varies among public managers: testing manager-related explanations', *International Public Management Journal* 17(2): 174–201.

Kroll, A. 2015a. 'Drivers of performance information use: systematic literature review and directions for future research', *Public Performance and Management Review* 38(3): 459–86.

Kroll, A. 2015b. 'Explaining the use of performance information by public managers: a planned-behavior approach', *American Review of Public Administration* 45(2): 201–15.

Lavertu, S., Lewis, D., and Moynihan, D. 2013. 'Administrative reform, ideology, and bureaucratic effort: performance management in the Bush era', *Public Administration Review* 73(6): 845–56.

Meier, K. and O'Toole, L. 2013. 'Subjective organizational performance and measurement error: common source bias and spurious relationships', *Journal of Public Administration Research and Theory* 23(2): 429–56.

Moynihan, D. 2008. *The Dynamics of Performance Management: Constructing Information and Reform*. Washington, DC: Georgetown University Press.

Moynihan, D. 2013. 'Advancing the empirical study of performance management: what we learned from the program assessment rating tool', *American Review of Public Administration* 43(5): 499–517.

Moynihan, D. 2015. 'Uncovering the circumstances of performance information use', *Public Performance and Management Review* 39(1): 33–57.

Moynihan, D., Fernandez, S., Kim, S., LeRoux, K., Piotrowski, S., Wright, B. and Yang, K. 2011. 'Performance regimes amidst governance complexity', *Journal of Public Administration Research and Theory* 21 (suppl 1): i141–55.

Moynihan, D. and Kroll, A. 2015. 'Performance management routines that work? An early assessment of the GPRA Modernization Act', *Public Administration Review* 76(2): 314–23.

Moynihan, D. and Pandey, S. 2010. 'The big question for performance management: why do managers use performance information?', *Journal of Public Administration Research and Theory* 20(4): 849–66.

Moynihan, D. and Soss, J. 2014. 'Policy feedback and the politics of administration', *Public Administration Review* 74(3): 320–32.

Nielsen, P. 2014. 'Learning from performance feedback: performance information, aspiration levels, and managerial priorities', *Public Administration* 92(1): 142–60.

Nielsen, P. and Bækgaard, M. 2015. 'Performance information, blame avoidance, and politicians' attitudes to spending and reform: evidence from an experiment', *Journal of Public Administration Research and Theory* 25(2): 545–69.

Nielsen, P. and Moynihan, D. 2015. 'How do politicians attribute bureaucratic responsibility for performance? Negativity bias and interest group advocacy.' Forthcoming in *Journal of Public Administration Research and Theory*.

Radin, B. 2012. *Federal Management Reforms in a World of Contradictions*. Washington, DC: Georgetown University Press.

Rutherford, A. and Meier, K. 2015. 'Managerial goals in a performance-driven system: theory and empirical tests in higher education', *Public Administration* 93(1): 17–33.

Salge, T. 2011. 'A behavioral model of innovative search: evidence from public hospital services', *Journal of Public Administration Research and Theory* 21(1): 181–210.

ter Bogt, H. 2004. 'Politicians in search of performance information? Survey research on Dutch aldermen's use of performance information', *Financial Accountability and Management* 20(3): 221–52.

Taber, M. and Lodge, C. 2013. *The Rationalizing Voter*. Cambridge: Cambridge University Press.

Tilley, J. and Hobolt, S. 2011. 'Is government to blame? An experimental test of how partisanship shapes perceptions of performance and responsibility', *The Journal of Politics* 73(2): 1–15.

Van Dooren, W. 2004. 'Supply and demand of policy indicators: a cross-sectoral comparison', *Public Management Review* 6(4): 511–30.

Van Dooren, W. 2008. 'Nothing new under the sun? Change and continuity in the twentieth-century performance movements', in Van Dooren, W. and Van de Walle, S. (eds.), *Performance Information in the Public Sector – How is it used?*, Basingstoke: Palgrave, pp. 11–23.

Van Ryzin, G. 2006. 'Testing the expectancy disconfirmation model of citizen satisfaction with local government', *Journal of Public Administration Research and Theory* 16(4): 599–611.

Wilson, J. Q. 1989. *Bureaucracy: What Government Agencies Do and Why They Do It*. Jackson: Basic Books Classics.

Yang, K. and Hsieh, J. Y. 2007. 'Managerial effectiveness of government performance measurement: testing a middle-range model', *Public Administration Review* 67(5): 861–79.

12 Citizens and Public Performance Measures: Making Sense of Performance Information

OLIVER JAMES AND ASMUS LETH OLSEN

Introduction: Making Sense of Performance Information

There has been a huge growth in published performance information about public organisations and services in recent years aimed at citizens and users, including scorecards, league tables, and other published metrics. This information potentially affects citizens' perceptions of services and their interaction with services and their associated institutions, especially political voice, including voting and lobbying, and choice of service (Dowding and John 2012; Hood 2006; James 2011a; Olsen 2015c). Recently a strand of experimental research has developed on this topic analysing citizens and users' contact with performance information, how they make sense of it, the effects on them, and their responses (Bækgaard and Serritzlew 2016; James 2011a, 2011b; James and Van Ryzin 2017a, 2017b; Olsen 2015a, 2015c). This chapter identifies the contribution made by experimental methods, including in combination with psychologically informed public administration theory, towards understanding these processes and outcomes and the potential of this approach.

The experimental method is especially valuable in this context because non-experimental, observational, methods struggle to identify the causal effects of performance information on citizens. Performance information varies in its availability, format of presentation, and incorporation of benchmarks for comparison in ways that are often correlated with a range of factors. Notably, differences in performance information are often related to variation in service sector, type of audience, saliency of the measure, policy makers' incentives for presenting data in a certain manner, or citizens' use of information. These factors are often themselves correlated with the effects of performance information per se, making it difficult for researchers using observational methods to disentangle the effects of the information from the influence of these other factors. For example, citizens who are already favourably disposed towards a public service may be more likely to seek out information about it. An observational study unable to control for this latent characteristic risks conflating citizens' initial disposition with the effect of being exposed to performance information about the service.

Experimental research offers a promising way of understanding how citizens are influenced by performance information. This information is a factor that is relatively easy to manipulate experimentally, in contrast to both macro-institutional features of the public sector, for example the form of governmental system, and citizens' own personal characteristics, for example socioeconomic status or gender. This chapter sets out the contribution of recent experiments to understanding citizens' interaction with performance information. We compare the results to what has been found by observational studies and show the benefits and limitations of experimental work on four important topics.

The first section focuses on the reception of performance information by citizens, highlighting findings about the credibility of performance information, the influence of different sources of information, and the role of motivated reasoning in how it is processed. The second section examines how numerical factors influence citizens' perception, focusing on numerical biases. The third section examines how variation in reference points influences the benchmarks citizens use for judgments, especially whether they compare performance across time and/or between different organisations and services. The fourth section assesses citizens' knowledge about the valance (positive or negative) of performance information and its consequences, including the role of negativity bias. Relatedly, Chapter 17 focuses on experimental research about citizen and users' responses to the failure of public services, extending this interest in negativity bias. The final section of the current chapter draws conclusions. We call for more use of experiments, especially those informed by psychological theory, as complements to observational research, and set out some key topic areas for the study of performance information and citizens.

Information Sources, Credibility, and Motivated Reasoning

Citizens get information about public organisations and services from many sources regarding different aspects of performance. The dimensions of performance information include economy, efficiency, and effectiveness across a range of outcomes. A central tenet of new public management attempts to publish performance information is based on the view that governments' reporting of good performance will increase trust in government and support for public service provision (Hatry 1999; Hood 2006). However, citizens and users may not always believe published information. General distrust of government found in observational studies (Bevan and Hood 2006; Chanley, Rudolph, and Rahn 2000; Van Ryzin 2011) suggests a lack of trust in performance measures developed by government for self-reporting. This being said, observational studies are limited by the fact that citizens select information sources for good reasons, which in turn makes it very difficult to infer how the effect of different sources might be conditional on citizens' predispositions.

Experiments have begun to address the reception and use of published performance information by citizens and service users. Information provided by independent public auditors has been found to be effective in influencing citizens' perceptions of the performance of public services provided by local governments (James 2011a; James and Mosely 2014). However, experiments also reveal that citizens are sometimes sceptical about performance self-reports provided by government agencies themselves. Part of this lack of credibility may be the result of prejudice against the public sector on some dimensions of performance. In an experimental design, changing the sector cue from private to public made respondents perceive otherwise identical hospital organisations as having a higher level of red tape and being less capable of containing its costs (Hvidman and Andersen 2015). Performance information is also received against a background of unconscious, sometimes negative, attitudes towards the public sector, measured using the psychological implicit association test, which experimental research has found influences the evaluation of the information (Marvel 2015).

The credibility of government agency self-reports varies; when the metric for measuring performance is relatively simple and for a straightforward service area, as in the example of street cleanliness, the credibility of self-reported performance is as high as other sources (Van Ryzin and Lavena 2013). The credibility problem is greater for more complex services, which citizens find less straightforward to verify and consequently have a higher potential to misrepresent.

The problem is especially found where good performance is being reported, which citizens may fear organisations have an incentive to misrepresent in this way. In an experimental study, citizens were given information about reported good performance on a measure of customer satisfaction with the Veterans Affairs and Citizenship and Immigration departments in the US federal government. They viewed the information as more credible when it came from the independent American Customer Satisfaction Index than when it came from the government agencies themselves (James and Van Ryzin 2017a). These findings suggest that independent, nongovernmental sources such as public audit bodies and private sector bodies that monitor government have the highest potential for reports about good performance to build trust in government services.

Citizens' responses to performance information, including their concerns about misrepresentation of performance, are further influenced by their motivation for engagement with the information. While 'accuracy' goals related to uncovering an actual level of performance sometimes predominate, there are often a range of other motives that contribute to biases of a kind found in controversial areas of public policy (Lodge and Taber 2013). Where public services and programs are related to citizens' motives for retaining their group identity or have implications for deeply held values, citizens' information search, processing, and use of information is influenced by these motives rather than searching for accuracy. Experiments giving information to citizens have found that the effects vary according to the partisan viewpoint of the receiver. When given information about the relatively good performance of a local government, citizens who supported the party in control of the local government exhibited a more favourable shift in their perceptions of performance relative to those who did not support that party (James 2011a). This finding is consistent with research that finds party supporters have group-based motivations to appear loyal to the policy line and position of 'their' party (Petersen et al. 2012) and more general findings of partisan-motivated reasoning (Leeper and Slothuus 2014; Lodge and Taber 2013).

Experiments have found that citizens given a prime to encourage party political thinking, in contrast to a prime about their needs as service users, engage in more partisan-motivated reasoning. Using the example of the Affordable Care Act (often called Obamacare) in the United States, James and Van Ryzin (2017b) show that, under the political prime, Democrats rate evidence favourable to the health care program's performance more strongly than Republicans. Similarly, under the political prime, when Democrats are given a choice of indicators from a basket of such measures to inform their assessment of the program's performance, they choose indicators that report more positive performance than those chosen by Republicans.

Differences in attitudes to public and private provision have also been found to lead to motivated reasoning about performance reports. Bækgaard and Serritzlew (2016) compared experimental subjects' ability to correctly interpret performance information about hospitals when they were presented with a comparison of the performance of a public and private organisation in two scenarios. In one scenario they were presented with information about the organisations' sector affiliation (public or private) while in the other scenario the organisations' affiliation was unknown to participants. They found that those previously sympathetic to the private sector delivery of services were more likely to rate the private provider better than the public provider, showing the influence of their prior beliefs.

Numerical Cognition and Biases in Understanding of Performance Information

Most scholars stress the importance of the *quantitative* element of much contemporary performance information (Hood 2007; James 2011a; Moynihan 2008; Perrin 1998; Van Dooren, Bouckaert, and Halligan 2015).Performance measurement assigns numbers to organisational activities, outputs, and outcomes, which in turn is presumed to inform citizens about performance on these measures and relative to each other. This simple fact has inspired theoretical work on how the quantification of the public sector affects leaders, employees, and citizens (Espeland and Sauder 2007; Herbst 1993; Stone 1997). However, only recently have we seen experimental work on citizens' perception and interpretation of numerical performance data, for example, how citizens draw on symbolic reference numbers and extract meaning out of performance numbers.

Round numbers tend to serve as cognitive reference points) and performance information is often evaluated on the basis of being below or above some salient yet arbitrary number. Malhotra and Margalit (2010) show this in a simple survey experiment that randomly assigns the overall costs of a potential stimulus bill. They show that

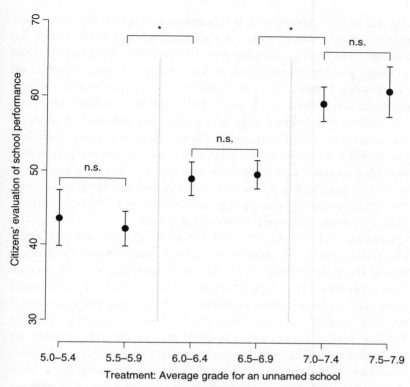

Figure 12.1: Mean school evaluations with 95%–CIs for grade decimals in the intervals 0.0–0.4 and 0.5–0.9 for each of the leftmost grades 5, 6, and 7. A star indicates significance at p < 0.001 (see Olsen (2013a) for details).

opposition to the bill shifts discontinuously upward as the costs rise above $1 trillion. However, opposition remains unaffected for increases from $800 billion to $900 billion or from $1 trillion to $1.4 trillion. In other words, citizens rely on salient round numbers when evaluating budgetary information.

Olsen (2013a), along the same lines, randomly assigned school grades to a representative sample of Danish citizens in a survey setting. Subjects were asked to rate the school based on the information they were provided. Grades were presented with one decimal and ranged between 3.0 and 10.0. The results showed a very robust pattern consistent with a leftmost-digit bias: citizens exclusive rely on the leftmost digit in their evaluations of schools. The results are provided in Figure 12.1. Here we can see how a school with a 6.0 grade average receives the same evaluation as a school with a 6.9 average, while schools with a 7.0 average see a large positive jump in the evaluation. Specifically, while a change *within* the same grade of 0.9 grade points has zero effect on evaluations, a shift of 0.1 grade points *between* two grades changes evaluations of the school with about half a standard deviation. The finding of a leftmost-digit bias aligns with incentivised observational data on educational and economic decision making, including that round numbers in performance scales act as reference points, that individuals exert effort to perform just above rather than just below such numbers (Pope and Simonsohn 2011), and that large and discontinuous drops occur in sale prices of used cars at 10,000-mile thresholds in odometer mileage (Lacetera et al. 2012).

Experimental studies draw on the more general theories about numerical cognition in order to understand the quantitative characteristic of much performance information. A natural question is to contrast experiments that explicitly compare how numerical performance information affects citizens relative to more idiosyncratic and qualitative sources of information (Olsen 2017a). Here the results point to the fact that, while citizens prefer numerical performance information over single case stories if explicitly asked to make a choice, their evaluations of services actuality remain more strongly influenced by stories than statistics. Furthermore, single cases elicit a stronger emotional response and are much more easily recalled than dry statistics. These findings remind us that while citizens are exposed to a wealth of numerical performance data, they remain easily affected by casual observations and case stories that capture a more vivid account of public services.

Reference Point in Performance Comparisons

Performance information is not evaluated in a vacuum; in particular, judgment and decision making has a strong relative component where people compare information to some reference point (Mussweiler 2003). Observational research on the general use of benchmarking and relative performance evaluation recognises the importance of this issue (Ammons and Roenigk 2014). However, most of the existing work has not looked into how citizens rely on reference points in comparison. Instead, most empirical work has focused on how policy makers and organisations use comparisons

(Askim 2007; Askim et al. 2008; Kroll 2013; Moynihan and Pandey 2010). However, recent experiments have moved this focus to the level of citizens to assess whether and how citizens respond to information about absolute and/or relative performance and the reference points that citizens draw on.

The first set of studies assessed the effects of relative performance information and the relative importance of relative and absolute forms of information (Hansen, Olsen, and Bech 2015; James 2011a; James and Moseley 2014). Using real data from performance reports, James (2011a) found that a cue about the relatively good performance of a local government compared to other local governments raises citizens' perceived performance and satisfaction with services (on a scale ranging from 1 to 5 as shown in Figure 12.2a and 12.2b). A cue about relatively bad performance had the opposite effect.

Separating out absolute and relative performance measures reveals that both kinds of information are influential on citizens' perceptions in the direction of the information provided (James and Moseley 2014). The same study also found that relative information makes citizens judge local providers as being more responsible for outcomes in the case of relatively high performance. These findings suggest that systems for comparative performance reporting across multiple units, as is common in many jurisdictions' health care, education, and local public service systems, increase the extent to which citizens hold local providers to account for outcomes.

Another way of comparing relative and absolute performance information was utilised by Hansen, Olsen, and Bech (2015), who adopted a conjoint method (Hainmueller et al. 2014). The conjoint method allows for many sources of performance information to be manipulated in the same experiment. This is often useful in the study of performance information as different dimensions of absolute and relative performance will tend to be correlated. In the conjoint framework, subjects are provided packages of performance information and asked to choose the one they prefer. The researchers can then disentangle how much value citizens assign to different performance attributes by studying the relative prevalence of attributes in the choice combinations that are preferred. Hansen, Olsen, and Bech's (2015) findings indicated that Danish voters valued combinations of performance information in which Denmark performed better than Sweden, an important reference point for this group of citizens.

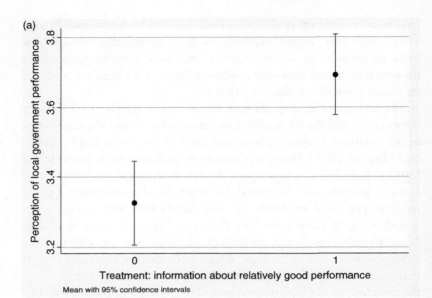

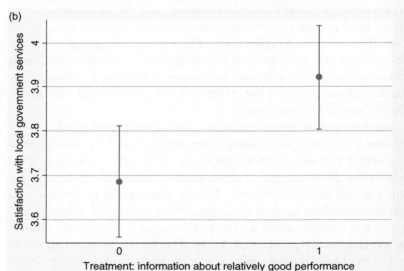

Figure 12.2: Citizens' responses and information cues about relatively good performance: 12.2a perceptions of performance; 12.2b satisfaction with services.

The different *types* of reference points matter to citizens' judgments of performance to varying degrees. Assessing the effect of reference points is difficult without clear guidance about the potential reference points that citizens adopt in the first place. Accordingly, studies focus on experimentally manipulating the different types of reference point that citizens are exposed to. Here we can rely on Simon (1939: 106), who pointed to two fundamental sources of comparisons: 'The only sound basis for decisions about numbers is numerical factual information about past experiences or the experiences of others nothing more nor less than comparative statistics.' Olsen (2017b) makes a direct test of Simon in a survey experiment of how important social comparison (i.e., with others) is relative to historical comparison (i.e., with own past). By randomly assigning subjects to performance data from an organisation and either a social or historical reference point, the study finds that social reference points have about a twice as strong impact on citizens' evaluations than historical ones. This finding is similar to experimental evidence from Charbonneau and Van Ryzin (2015) from a US context, who also find that social comparisons dominate historical comparisons.

Negativity Bias and Framing of Information

Negativity bias has gained considerable attention in public administration research and is important in blame of managers and politicians for poor performance, and in blame avoidance among policy makers (Hood 2010; James et al. 2016; Weaver 1987). Negativity bias denotes how 'negative events are more salient, potent, dominant in combinations and generally efficacious than positive events' (Rozin and Royzman 2001: 297). Experimental work on negativity bias is a good example of how experimental research builds on and extends work from observational studies in public management, along with research in neighbouring fields of political psychology and behavioural economics.

In the study of performance information, negativity bias changes our naïve understanding of performance data as asserting a symmetrical effect on citizens' evaluations, which cause both credit and blame to be assigned. The observational evidence clearly and consistently shows that poor performance affects the incumbent's popularity while excellent performance often brings about no more praise than mere average performance (Boyne et al. 2009; James and John 2007). However, observational studies are limited by the difficulty of identifying negative and positive performance in the real world that is in fact of comparable magnitude. Maybe negative and positive information varies on other dimensions than pure valence? For instance, negative input is often highly distinct and is characterised as being less frequent, more unexpected, and potentially more extreme (Rozin and Royzman 2001). Within an experimental setting we get the opportunity to carefully design treatments with negative and positive information that differ only in their valence and not on other confounding dimensions.

There are two main forms of assessing negativity bias that have been assessed in the experimental literature. The first, examined by Olsen (2015a), concerns framing of performance information that is logically equivalent. The second, examined by James (2011a, 2011b), concerns how performance below the centre value of a distribution of performance (for example, the mean value) has a bigger effect on citizens' perceptions, attitudes, and behaviour than equivalently sized performance above the mean. Experimental evidence reveals that both forms of negativity bias are important in citizens' reception of performance information.

Olsen (2015a) shows how performance information valence in the form of negative and positive wording of information affects citizens' associative memory of public services. Exposing citizens to a patient *dissatisfaction* measure led to more negative views of public service than exposing them to a logically equivalent *satisfaction* metric. The difference in effect of the two labels is plotted in Figure 12.3 for a large range of different satisfaction and dissatisfaction rates. For instance, the evaluation of a hospital with a 90 per cent satisfaction rate was almost one standard deviation better than if subjects were exposed to a 10 per cent dissatisfaction rate. For comparison, the effect of switching the valence of the labels was equivalent to an actual improvement in the satisfaction rate of 22 percentage points. This finding is in line with studies of equivalence framing and loss aversion in psychology (Levin et al. 1998; Tversky and Kahneman 1991).

In a more direct test of negativity bias, the difference in impact of negative and positive frames is compared with a neutral frame. This allows for separating the effect of the negative and the positive treatment and thereby determines which one is driving the asymmetry in evaluations. In the neutral frame, subjects are exposed to

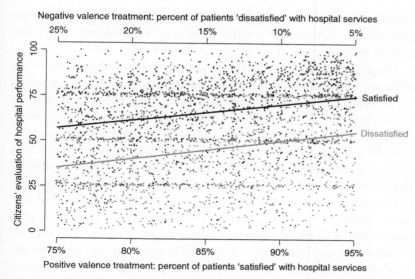

Figure 12.3: Effect of satisfied percentage label and dissatisfied percentage label (N = 3,443). Ordinary least squares estimated slopes for the satisfied (black line and dots) and dissatisfied (grey line and dots) frames. The lower horizontal axis shows the treatment per cent received under the satisfied frame. The upper horizontal axis shows the treatment per cent assigned under the dissatisfied frame. See Olsen (2015a) for further details on the study.

a combination of the information of the positive and negative frame. This reveals that the neutral and positive frame obtains a very similar evaluation while the negative frame induces a very negative evaluation (Olsen 2015d). This asymmetrical difference between the positive-neutral and the neutral-negative frame is highly consistent with a negativity bias.

In the second form of negativity bias, information about low performance reduces citizens' expectations of what performance will be, but information about high performance does not raise expectations as much, in the case of overall services provided by local governments (James 2011b). In the case of an individual service, information about low absolute performance of local recycling services reduces citizens' satisfaction, but information about high performance does not raise satisfaction (James and Moseley 2014). These findings provide the individual-level underpinning of findings from observational studies of aggregate political behaviour that show local incumbent politicians are punished for poor service performance but are not rewarded for good performance above the middle range (Boyne et al. 2009; James and John 2007).

The studies also show some of the strengths and limitations of different forms of experimental method and the need to use a range of different kinds of experiment. James (2011a) used real performance information about a local government that was performing relatively well compared to other local governments that provided similar services. Extending this analysis to study negativity bias it is necessary to have an equivalently sized, but oppositely signed, performance level for a local government below the mid-range of performance. In a laboratory study, a hypothetical version of the performance of the local government was presented to participants and, while it lowered perceived performance and satisfaction, no evidence of negativity bias was found. However, as was noted in the published study, the hypothetical poor performance information conflicted with what at least some of the experimental participants might have known about the actual, good performance of that local government. This conflict might have subdued the negativity bias effect because 'the form of information about bad performance used in the study was not consistent with the actual performance of the local unit ... information effects may differ if information about bad performance is given to citizens for a local unit that is actually performing badly' (James 2011a: 414). Such information is not simultaneously available for the same real case at the same point in time. To use conditions more similar to such a context, a later study (James and Moseley 2014) used real performance data for two similar local governments that differed on their levels of performance. One experiment was in an area below the mid-range of performance and one experiment in an area broadly symmetrically above the mid-range. This approach has the limitation of needing to compare results of experiments in two different sites, but provides evidence about citizens' responses under these two circumstances. The effects of information about low relative performance were greater in reducing citizens' perceived performance than the effects of high relative performance were in raising perceived performance. While low absolute performance reduced citizens' satisfaction, information about high performance did not raise satisfaction.

Conclusions and Directions for Future Research

Reviewing the existing studies reveals the contribution that experiments are making to understanding citizens and performance information. Experiments have shown that performance information can influence citizens and service users' perceptions and attitudes. However, its credibility is influenced by the source, with some scepticism of governments reporting about their own good performance. Accuracy-based motives in reasoning are sometimes supplanted by other motivations that can lead to selective use and interpretation of information, including partisan-motivated reasoning and motivated reasoning influenced by attitudes towards the public sector. In understanding numerical cognition and biases, experiments on leftmost-digit bias show the potential of applying fundamental psychological insights about numerical cognition in a context of performance information research. The importance of reference points is another example of this, but at the same time an example in which experiments can be evaluated against an existing body of broader experimental and observational evidence in public administration. The research on reference points has provided empirical support for the importance of relative comparisons (over absolute performance evaluations) and also found social comparisons to be more powerful than historical ones. Experimental evidence largely confirms strong negativity bias in citizens' response to performance information that bolsters similar findings from observational studies, proving support for the larger body of research linking negativity bias with blaming behaviour and blame avoidance strategies used by politicians and public managers.

Current experimental research findings point to four particularly promising themes for future experimental research. First, experiments are making use of existing theories from social, cognitive, and political psychology (notably motivated reasoning, source cues, numerical cognition, reference dependence, and negativity bias). This trend follows Simon's (1955) largely forgotten call to place a firm marking stone between public administration and psychology to help travellers in both directions. It also follows a general path in the public management field towards a more psychologically informed behavioural public administration (Grimmelikhuijsen et al. 2017; Tummers et al. 2016; Olsen 2015b). Psychologically informed theory is especially amenable to experimental method because it seeks to understand processes and outcomes at the individual citizen level. Much more research can be done where psychological theories and experimental methods go hand in hand with a range of outcome measures to further our understanding of how performance information affects citizens. For example, the different factors affecting motivated reasoning could be extended beyond partisan influences (James and Van Ryzin 2017b) and ideological beliefs about the public sector (Bækgaard and Serritzlew 2016) to consider, for example, the influence of individuals' personality or their shared or different group identity with those providing public services. There should also be research on the implications of the biases found for how well citizens and users reason about public organisations and services. For example, while partisanship influences citizens' ratings of information and their selection of indicators that are deemed useful, some authors suggest that partisan bias is not a bias in a normative sense because relying on party cues can sometimes be consistent with Bayesian updating (Gerber and Green 1999). In a similar way, current findings do not yet reveal whether negativity bias is just contesting our naïve symmetrical view of information processing or is in fact a highly unproductive bias that leads to less optimal decisions (Olsen 2015d). In pursuing this agenda, public management research should be open to considering conflicting evidence that can sometimes arise when concepts from other disciplines are tested in administrative-political systems, especially where this evidence challenges long-standing presumptions about how these systems operate.

Second, experimental research should make full use of the various types of experiment, combing insights from laboratory, survey, and field experiments. Much of the research agenda of public management relates to understanding institutions and their effects on politicians, public managers, and citizens, so it is important to have experiments that make such structures as realistic as possible for participants in experiments. Field experiments are helpful in this regard because they assess the effects of real performance regimes being used by governments (James 2011a; James and Moseley 2014). Relatedly, while much experimental research to date has concentrated on perceptual and attitudinal outcomes, which are important to study, some of these field studies also made use of behavioural outcome measures that tie directly to political action. For example, James and Moseley (2014) used experimental participants' agreement to be involved in a consultation about service performance following their receipt of performance information as an outcome measure. This consultation entailed a real-time cost to those undertaking this action that was made apparent to participants, giving the behavioural outcome a true opportunity cost. More use of behavioural outcome measures is an important way to expand the domain of findings from experiments.

While field contexts have benefits as set out discussed earlier, hypothetical cases are sometimes necessary in experimental research and these can sometimes be better if undertaken outside the field. For example, to examine the effects of presenting information about poor performance that is symmetric to information about good performance, some laboratory and survey experiments have used hypothetical cases to facilitate presentation of high- and low-performing organisations while holding other factors constant (James 2011a; Olsen 2015a). Similarly, experiments have used hypothetical cases where the public or private organisational status of an otherwise identical organisation is varied (Bækgaard and Serritzlew 2016). Some research questions are difficult to study ethically using field experiments; for example, it might be easier to justify the use of potentially misleading performance information in laboratory contexts where participants can be fully informed at the end of the study. It would risk unethical practice knowingly to release false information in a field context where it is difficult to correct.

Third, public management involves the interplay between individuals and broader macro-level administrative and political institutions. Often, experimental micro-level studies help generate macro-level hypothesis that can be assessed using evidence at the macro level from observational studies. For example, evidence from experiments on negativity bias among citizens is the micro-level foundation, which generates an expectation of citizens and users' tendency to blame rather than give credit to those providing public services, which is consistent with observational findings (Boyne et al. 2009). The importance of blame encourages the use of blame avoidance strategies by managers and politicians (Hood 2010; Weaver 1986). Experimental studies of citizens' response to public service failures have assessed the effect of different macro-level institutional structures on individual citizens' blame of politicians. Information cues about delegation of service delivery by politicians to public managers reduces blame compared to cues explicitly stating politicians' role in managing delivery of the failing service (James et al. 2016). Relatedly, politicians' strategic setting of tax rates has been found to conform with leftmost-digit bias as a means for lowering citizens' perceptions of the tax burden (Olsen 2013b). These findings point to the potential in linking experimental work on how citizens make sense of performance information and how elites manipulate, game, or design performance information. Future experimental research should consider how to integrate micro- and macro-level evidence so that evidence found at one level generates expectations about what should be found at the other level.

Fourth, there is great potential for using observational and experimental methods in combination. Conflicting evidence may, for example, highlight that some observational studies suffer from endogeneity or suggest that an experiment has poor design or implementation. However, in other instances, comparison may reveal that observational and experimental studies diverge because, on detailed inspection, they are found to be addressing different research questions. The methods will often be differentially suited to addressing some questions. The effect of introducing a system of performance measures in a country is an example of an institutional design question that is challenging to experimentalists because of the difficulty of randomising the institution across a sufficient number of country units, compounded by potentially heterogeneous treatment effects in different country contexts. In this way, comparison and discussion of both observational and experimental evidence offers the best potential for accumulating knowledge.

References

Ammons, D. N. and Roenigk, D. J. 2015. 'Benchmarking and interorganizational learning in local government'. *Journal of Public Administration Research and Theory* 25(1), 309–35.

Askim, J. 2007. 'How do politicians use performance information? An analysis of the Norwegian local government experience', *International Review of Administrative Sciences* 73(3): 453–72.

Askim, J., Johnsen, A., and Christophersen, K. A. 2008. 'Factors behind organizational learning from benchmarking: experiences from Norwegian municipal benchmarking networks', *Journal of Public Administration Research and Theory* 18(2): 297–320.

Bækgaard, M. and Serritzlew, S. 2016. 'Interpreting performance information: motivated reasoning or unbiased comprehension', *Public Administration Review* 76(1): 73–82.

Bevan, G. and Hood, C. 2006. 'What's measured is what matters: targets and gaming in the English healthcare system', *Public Administration* 84(3): 517–38.

Boyne, G. A., James, O., John, P., and Petrovsky, N. 2009. 'Democracy and government performance: holding incumbents accountable in English local governments', *Journal of Politics* 71(4): 1273–84.

Chanley, V. A., Rudolph, T. J., and Rahn, W. M. 2000. 'The origins and consequences of public trust in government: a time series analysis', *Public Opinion Quarterly* 64(3): 239–56.

Charbonneau, É. and Van Ryzin, G. G. 2015. 'Benchmarks and citizen judgments of local government performance: findings from a survey experiment', *Public Management Review* 17(2): 288–304.

Dowding, K. M. and John, P. 2012. *Exits, Voices and Social Investments: Citizens' Reaction to Public Services*. Cambridge: Cambridge University Press.

Espeland, W. N. and Sauder, M. 2007. 'Rankings and reactivity: how public measures recreate social worlds', *American Journal of Sociology* 133(1): 1–40.

Gerber, A. and Green, D. 1999. 'Misperceptions about perceptual bias', *Annual Review of Political Science* 2(1): 189–210.

Grimmelikhuijsen, S., Jilke, S., Olsen, A. L., and Tummers, L. 2017. 'Behavioral public administration: combining insights from public administration and psychology', *Public Administration Review* 77(1): 45–56.

Grimmelikhuijsen, S. G. and Meijer, A. J. 2014. 'The effects of transparency on the perceived trustworthiness of a government organization: evidence from an online experiment', *Journal of Public Administration Research and Theory* 24(1): 137–57.

Hainmueller, J., Hopkins, D., and Yamamoto, T. 2014. 'Causal inference in conjoint analysis: understanding multidimensional choices via stated preference experiments', *Political Analysis* 22(1): 1–30.

Hansen, K. M., Olsen, A. L., and Bech, M. 2015. 'Cross-national yardstick comparisons: a choice experiment on a forgotten voter heuristic', *Political Behavior* 37(4): 767–89.

Hatry, H. P. 1999. *Performance Measurement: Getting Results*. Washington, DC: Urban Institute Press.

Herbst, S. 1993. *Numbered Voices: How Opinion Polling Has Shaped American Politics*. Chicago: University of Chicago Press.

Hibbing, J. R., Smith, K. B., and Alford, J. R. 2014. 'Differences in negativity bias underlie variations in political ideology', *Behavioral and Brain Science* 37: 297–350.

Hood, C. 2006. 'Transparency in historical perspective'. In C. Hood and D. Heald (Eds.), *Transparency: The Key to Better Governance?* 3–23. Oxford: Oxford University Press.

Hood, C. 2010. *The Blame Game: Spin, Bureaucracy and Self-Preservation in Government*. Princeton, NJ: Princeton University Press.

Hvidmand, U. and Andersen, S. 2015. 'Perceptions of public and private performance: evidence from a survey experiment', *Public Administration Review*.

James, O. 2011a. 'Performance measures and democracy: information effects on citizens in field and laboratory experiments', *Journal of Public Administration Research and Theory* 21: 399–418.

James, O. 2011b. 'Managing citizens' expectations of public service performance: evidence from observation and experimentation in local government', *Public Administration* 89(4): 1419–35.

James, O., Jilke, S., Petersen, C., and Van de Walle, S. 2016. 'Citizens' blame of politicians for public service failure: experimental evidence about blame reduction through delegation and contracting', *Public Administration Review* 76(1): 83–93.

James, O. and John, P. 2007. 'Public management at the ballot box: performance information and electoral support for incumbent English local governments', *Journal of Public Administration Research and Theory* 17(4): 567–80.

James, O. and Moseley, A. 2014. 'Does performance information about public services affect citizens' perceptions, satisfaction, and voice behaviour? Field experiments with absolute and relative performance information', *Public Administration* 92(2): 493–511.

James, O. and Van Ryzin, G. G. 2017a. 'Incredibly good performance: an experimental study of source and level effects on the credibility of government', *American Review of Public Administration* 47(1): 23–35.

James, O. and Van Ryzin, G. G. 2017b. 'Motivated reasoning about public performance: an experimental study of how citizens judge the Affordable Care Act', *Journal of Public Administration Research and Theory* 27(1): 197–209.

Kroll, A. 2013. 'The other type of performance information: non-routine feedback, its relevance and use', *Public Administration Review* 73(2): 265–76.

Lacetera, N., Pope, D. G., and Sydnor, J. R. 2012. 'Heuristic thinking and limited attention in the car market', *American Economic Review* 102(5): 2206–36.

Lau, R. R. 1982. 'Negativity in political perception', *Political Behavior* 4(4): 353–77.

Lau, R. R. 1985. 'Two explanations for negativity effects in political behavior', *American Journal of Political Science* 29(1): 119–38.

Leeper, T. J. and Slothuus, R. 2014. 'Political parties, motivated reasoning, and public opinion formation', *Political Psychology* 35(S1): 129–56.

Levin, I. P. and Gaeth, G. J. 1988. 'How consumers are affected by the framing of attribute information before and after consuming the product', *Journal of Consumer Research* 16: 374–78.

Levin, I. P., Schneider, S. L., and Gaeth, G. J. 1998. 'All frames are not created equal: a typology and critical analysis of framing effects', *Organizational Behavior and Human Decision Processes* 76(2): 149–88.

Lodge, M and Taber, C. S. 2013. *The Rationalizing Voter*. Cambridge: Cambridge University Press.

Malhotra, N. and Margalit, Y. 2010. 'Short-term communication effects or longstanding dispositions? The public's response to the financial crisis of 2008'. *The Journal of Politics* 72(03): 852–67.

Marvel, J. D. 2015. 'Public opinion and public sector performance: Are individuals' beliefs about performance evidence-based or the product of anti-public sector bias?' *International Public Management Journal* 18(2): 209–27.

Moynihan, D. P. 2008. *The Dynamics of Performance Management: Constructing Information and Reform*. Washington, DC: Georgetown University Press.

Moynihan, D. P. and Pandey, S. K. 2010. 'The big question for performance management: why do managers use performance information?' *Journal of Public Administration Research and Theory* 20(4): 849–66.

Mussweiler, T. 2003. 'Comparison processes in social judgement: mechanisms and consequences', *Psychological Review*, (110)3: 472–89.

Olsen, A. L 2013a. 'Leftmost-digit-bias in an enumerated public sector? An experiment on citizens' judgment of performance information', *Judgment and Decision Making* 8(3): 365–71.

Olsen, A. L. 2013b. 'The politics of digits: evidence of odd taxation', *Public Choice* 154 1–2): 59–73.

Olsen, A. L. 2015a. 'Citizen (dis)satisfaction: an equivalence framing study', *Public Administration Review* 75(3): 469–78.

Olsen, A. L. 2015b. '"Simon said", we didn't jump', *Public Administration Review* 75(2): 469–78.

Olsen, A. L. 2015c. 'The numerical psychology of performance information – implications for citizens, managers, and policy makers', *Public Performance & Management Review* 39(1): 100–15.

Olsen, A. L. 2015d. 'Negative performance information causes asymmetrical evaluations and elicits strong responsibility attributions', 111th Annual Meeting of the American Political Science Association, San Francisco, September 2015.

Olsen, A. L. 2017a. 'Human interest or hard numbers? Experiments on citizens' selection, exposure, and recall of performance information', *Public Administration Review* http://dx.doi.org/10.1111/puar.12638.

Olsen, A. L. 2017b. 'Compared to what? experimental evidence on social and historical reference points in performance evaluation', Forthcoming in *Journal of Public Administration Research and Theory*.

Perrin, B. 1998. 'Effective use and misuse of performance measurement', *American Journal of Evaluation* 19(3): 367–79.

Petersen, M. B., Skov M., Serritzlew, S., and Ramsøy, T. 2012. 'Motivated reasoning and political parties: evidence for increased processing in the face of party cues', *Political Behavior* 35(4): 831–54.

Pope, D. and Simonsohn, U. 2011. 'Round numbers as goals evidence from baseball, SAT takers, and the lab', *Psychological Science* 22(1): 71–9.

Rabin, M. 1998. 'Psychology and economics', *Journal of Economic Literature* 36(1): 11–46.

Rozin, P. and Royzman, E. B. 2001. 'Negativity bias, negativity dominance, and contagion', *Personality and Social Psychology Review* 5(4): 296–320.

Simon, H. A. 1939. 'The administrator in search of statistics', *Public Management*, 21: 106–9.

Simon, H. A. 1955. 'A behavioral model of rational choice', *The Quarterly Journal of Economics* 69(1): 99–118.

Soroka, S. N. 2006. 'Good news and bad news: asymmetric responses to economic information', *Journal of Politics* 68(2): 372–85.

Stone, D. A. 1997. *Policy Paradox: The Art of Political Decision Making*. New York: WW Norton.

Tummers, L., Olsen, A. L., Jilke, S., and Grimmelikhuijsen, S. 2016. 'Introduction to the virtual issue on behavioral public administration', *Journal of Public Administration Research and Theory*, Virtual Issue (3): 1–3.

Tversky, A. and Kahneman, D. 1991. 'Loss aversion in riskless choice: a reference-dependent model', *The Quarterly Journal of Economics*, 1039–61.

Van Dooren, W., Bouckaert, G. and Halligan, J. 2015. *Performance Management in the Public Sector*. London, Routledge.

Van Ryzin, G. G. 2011. 'Outcomes, process, and trust of civil servants', *Journal of Public Administration Research and Theory*, 21(4): 745–760.

Van Ryzin, G. G. and Lavena, C. F. 2013. 'The credibility of government performance reporting', *Public Performance & Management Review*, 37(1): 87–103.

Weaver, R. K. 1986. 'The politics of blame avoidance', *Journal of Public Policy* 6(4): 371–98.

13 | Public Sector Transparency

STEPHAN GRIMMELIKHUIJSEN, ULRIKE WESKE, ROBIN BOUWMAN, AND LARS TUMMERS

Transparency in the Limelight

Attention to government transparency has increased greatly in the past 15 years. For instance, US president Barack Obama[1] stated, 'We're not going to change America unless we change the culture that has dominated Washington for far too long. And that means shining a bright light on how Washington works.' Subsequently, the Open Government Directive, which President Barack Obama issued in 2009, has highlighted the importance of transparency for policy makers, politicians, and scholars. Institutional transparency has gained 'quasi-religious significance' (Hood 2006), and has become a key feature in modern governance (Erkkilä 2012; Etzioni 2010; Keane 2009). Moreover, transparency is seen as a way to increase trust in government (Grimmelikhuijsen 2012; Porumbescu 2015a), state legitimacy (De Fine Licht 2011), citizen participation (Porumbescu 2015b), and to reduce corruption (Bauhr and Grimes 2014).

Two societal developments have contributed to the strong appeal of transparency nowadays. First, the rise of the Internet and communication technologies has greatly increased the amount of government information accessible to the public (Meijer 2009). The information technology revolution and the consequential vast increase in the amount of information stored and gathered by government have also increased the importance of transparency: if more information can be stored, there is more potential for disclosure and increased transparency. This partly coincides with a second development: the rise of New Public Management (NPM) as way of organising governments (Hood 1991). Public sector reforms inspired by NPM urge a greater degree of transparency of government services and activities, with the idea that

[1] Barack Obama, speech in New Hampshire, 4 September 2007.

increased visibility of how these services operate will improve their performance. In addition, it is commonly agreed that a certain extent of transparency is essential for democratic accountability to flourish: without information about political or administrative decision making, it is impossible to keep officeholders to account (Florini 2007; Roberts 2006).

These developments have given government transparency a heightened relevance; and with its increased technological and administrative possibilities, transparency has been looked to by many as a panacea for better governance. But what is transparency? The term is often used in different ways by different people (Meijer 2009). Transparency in this chapter is defined generally as 'the extent to which a (public) organisation allows external actors to monitor and assess its internal workings and performance' (Grimmelikhuijsen and Meijer 2014: 139). Note that this is a fairly broad definition, including both procedural – visibility of decision-making procedures, for instance – and outcome elements – visibility of the effects of certain policies and actions. One specific aspect of transparency is the growth of public reporting of public organisations and public services' performance. Experimental work on this topic is covered in Chapters 11 and 12.

In this chapter we will focus on two foci in transparency research: the causes of transparency and the effects of transparency. Scholars looking for the determinants of government transparency look at this question from either an institutional perspective or a micro-level perspective. The first type of research looks more broadly at, for instance, the strength of Freedom of Information (FOI) laws or website information. The second type of research looks at whether particular information and how information is disclosed by asking: what are the effects of government transparency? Research addressing this question empirically studies the normative claims surrounding government transparency. These normative claims are twofold. On one hand, there is the idea that transparency will discipline public officials: if behaviour is out in the open, there will be more 'good' behaviour (less corruption, more efficiency, better performance). On the other hand, there is the idea that citizens or other external stakeholders use government information and process it properly, which then results in more positive perceptions of government (e.g., trust, satisfaction, legitimacy).

We will review experimental and non-experimental research on government transparency broadly addressing these two questions. We will assess what experimental work has contributed to the academic debate on transparency and remaining lacunae.

Non-experimental Research on Transparency

We will first focus on what we can learn from non-experimental research on the two key research questions mentioned earlier. Next, we will briefly discuss the limitations of this kind of research.

Politicians, some interest groups, and scholars have been strong promoters of the idea of shedding 'sunlight' on government organisations in order to reduce corruption, enhance performance, and restore or strengthen citizen trust in government (Florini 2007; Meijer 2009). According to Hood and Heald (2006), transparency has even acquired a 'quasi-religious status' and it has become suspect to oppose calls for increased transparency. Therefore, transparency has become an important part of the political vocabulary (Coglianese 2009). Arguments for secrecy in public affairs are still made by some, yet usually for particular – and exceptional – circumstances, mainly related to security issues (Roberts 2006).

Nevertheless, there are critics of increased government transparency. First, scholars argue that although transparency leads to a great deal of available information, this does not necessarily result in increased levels of trust. Indeed, O'Neill (2002: 77) argues that transparency may even erode trust. She states that the Internet makes it possible to disclose a great deal of information, which not only leads to a cascade of information, but also to a flood of misinformation. Furthermore, public officials could 'massage' or 'spin' the messages. Second, transparency pessimists stress that increased transparency could lead to increased and unjustified blaming of government (e.g., Worthy 2010: 575–6). A third 'dark side' of transparency might be that when people can see everything behind the scenes of government, they may become disenchanted with it. Governing is often a messy and uncertain activity, and exposing this may erode citizen trust and legitimacy of government operations.

This normative debate has sparked a string of empirical studies that have attempted to find evidence for the various alleged effects of government transparency. To begin with, we will review some studies that looked at the causes/determinants of transparency; next, we look at studies regarding the effects of transparency.

In the wake of the desirable connotation of transparency, scholars have tried to pin down what its potential drivers are. Mostly quantitative studies have focused on explaining variation in transparency statistics across countries (e.g., Pina et al. 2007; Relly and Sabwarhal 2009; Welch and Wong 2001) or between local governments (Cucciniello and Nasi 2014; Grimmelikhuijsen and Welch 2012). Furthermore, qualitative case studies have provided an in-depth investigation of what shapes transparency (Grimmelikhuijsen and Kasymova 2015; Meijer 2013; Zyl 2014). Case study research by Zyl (2014), for example, emphasises the importance of external stakeholders as intermediaries and as a lever to further improve transparency. In addition, Meijer (2013) provides case studies that show how changes in transparency regimes link with broader societal developments. These findings highlight that a combination of government capacity and external pressures are important in determining the degree of transparency.

With regard to research on the effects of transparency – most studies assess the relation between transparency and outcomes such as trust, legitimacy, and participation. Campbell (2003) argues that one cause of the lack of trust in government is that citizens are not provided with factual documentation about government processes and performance. In this sense, disclosing information about government activities is crucial to increasing citizen trust. Overall, results suggest that there are moderately positive effects of transparency on trust and other perceptions of government. Using survey data, Tolbert and Mossberger (2006) found a significant relationship between trust and website transparency. Likewise, Porumbescu (2015a) found neutral to positive correlations between (electronic) transparency and perceptions of government trustworthiness. Welch and colleagues (2005), using survey data from the Council of Excellence in Government, studied whether there was a correlation between transparency satisfaction, e-government satisfaction, and trust. No direct relation between transparency and trust in government was found. However, results showed a weak but significant correlation between transparency satisfaction and e-government satisfaction. In contrast, Worthy (2010) found mixed results. He analysed the impact of the rather recent enactment of the Freedom of Information Act (FOIA) in the United Kingdom, but concludes that although FOI has increased transparency and accountability, it did not result in increased participation or improved trust in government.

Furthermore, there have been studies of the link between transparency and (reduced) corruption. Bauhr and Grimes (2014) analysed data from the World Values Survey. Their empirical analyses appear to confirm that a gain in transparency in highly corrupt countries tends to increase the chances that corrupt regimes will resign. Contrary to this, a comparative study by Lindstedt and Naurin (2010) shows that transparency (the availability of information on rulers' behaviour) is not enough to combat corruption.

Overall, non-experimental work has provided valuable insights about the determinants and effects of transparency. With regard to determinants of transparency, a combination of survey and qualitative research has shown that external pressure is needed to create transparency, such as from the media or other major stakeholders. Furthermore, sufficient budget and personnel are also needed for a government to become more transparent. Research on the effects of transparency has found relatively optimistic results regarding its effect on trust, legitimacy, and corruption.

However, some lacunas can be identified due to the nature of the research methodologies used in non-experimental work on transparency. First, there is the obvious concern of endogeneity associated with cross-sectional, observational research. For instance, the finding that external pressure is important to create a lever for increased transparency may be prone to reverse causality. Instead of creating more transparency, a more transparent government could already be more open and cause stronger external pressure groups.

In research on transparency as the cause of an effect, this concern is probably even stronger. Citizens with higher trust, for instance, may also perceive government as more transparent. Similarly, it is highly likely that societies with higher rates of corruption will automatically be less transparent. Cause and effect are hard to separate.

In the next section we will discuss how experimental work in the area of transparency has dealt with these issues.

Experimental Designs and Findings on Transparency

We found 11 papers investigating transparency using an experimental design. Of these 11, 7 are based on a survey/vignette experiment. Four papers use a field experiment. Only one paper focuses on the antecedents of transparency and 10 on the effects. Next, we will discuss laboratory and survey experiments, followed by field and natural experiments. For each experiment, we discuss the research topic, the design, and the results.

Laboratory and Survey Experiments

We found seven experiments in this category. Most experiments focus on the effects of transparency in various contexts. First, Grimmelikhuijsen and colleagues have carried out a series of experiments on the effects of various dimensions of transparency on trust in government. In a similar vein, De Fine Licht looked at various policies to assess the effect of various degrees of transparency on perceived legitimacy.

To answer the question of whether balanced government information has different effects on citizen trust in government than do politically *spun* messages, Grimmelikhuijsen (2011) used an online experiment with a between-subjects design. Spinning is operationalised as the degree of positivity of the message content. Undergraduate students (N = 60) were asked to visit a fictitious municipality website that contained information on a municipal air pollution policy in three different levels of 'spin'. The treatments (level of 'spin') consisted of a balanced message, a slightly positive message, and a very positive message on the air pollution policy. After viewing the different websites, the subjects filled out a questionnaire asking about trust, which was operationalised as perceived benevolence, competence, and honesty. The results indicate that, indeed, there is some effect of message 'spin' on benevolence, competence, and honesty together. However, a balanced message on a government website will lead to negative evaluations of competence. Further, the results suggest that less 'spin' does not affect the honesty and benevolence of a government organisation.

In a larger online experiment on the link between transparency, knowledge, and trust, Grimmelikhuijsen (2012) tested two rival hypotheses (N = 658) (between-subjects design). One proposition predicts the link between citizen knowledge and trust whereas the second one argues that more or less subconscious and affective cues (such as the general image people have of the government) are relevant. In this experiment, a voluntary sample of citizens was asked to visit one of four government mock-up websites with varying degrees of government transparency as well as varying message contents. Again the case of air pollution in the municipality was used, and a posttest questionnaire measured trust in government. The results provide mixed evidence of the two rivaling hypotheses. The results indicate that the link between transparency and trust in a government organisation is determined by a mix of knowledge and feelings and that the overall effect of transparency is limited. Preexisting ideas about what government does and whether it is benign are far more determining than a single experience with a government organisation. A takeaway from this article is that knowledge about performance outcomes is only part of the link between transparency and trust, and that more realistic views about transparency's effects should be developed.

Grimmelikhuijsen and Meijer (2014) employed an experiment to develop a more specific expectation of the relation between transparency and trust, looking at how different types of citizens respond to various degrees of transparency. The participants were assigned randomly to one of three conditions: In a 'high transparency' condition, subjects were informed timely and comprehensibly on air pollution policy outcomes of their municipality. Timeliness is operationalised as the amount of time between the actual measurement or determination of the policy outcome and the disclosure of the data (Grimmelikhuijsen and Meijer 2014: 141). Comprehensibility is regarded as the simplicity and clarity of the disclosed information. In a 'low transparency' condition, the subjects were not informed timely and comprehensibility was low. In a control condition, participants read some general information about the city government. After reading the information subjects filled out a posttest questionnaire with measurements of trust, predisposition to trust government, knowledge, and demographic variables.

In this study, Grimmelikhuijsen and Meijer showed there is a limited effect of transparency on trust, but they fleshed out the transparency–trust link further by testing two moderating effects: predisposition to trust and knowledge. The results indeed show that general predisposition to trust government and prior knowledge (issue specific) moderate the relation between transparency and trust. More knowledge makes citizens less likely to change their trust, whereas citizens with a high predisposition do not increase their trust because their trust is high already.

In an effort to compare effects of transparency on trust across nations, a series of three experiments with university students (N = 660) in South Korea and the Netherlands was carried out by Grimmelikhuijsen and colleagues (2013). A national culture may influence how people think and act; the relationship between transparency and trust may also be affected.

The three experiments each used a different operationalisation/ manipulation of transparency, namely, completeness, colour, and usability. Completeness refers to whether the information is disclosed fully (Grimmelikhuijsen et al. 2013: 576). Colour is thought of as the degree of positiveness of the information. Finally, one experiment used usability of information, which is conceived as the comprehensibility of the information disclosed. A remarkable result is that the experiments in South Korea yielded negative effects on trust in government, whereas this was hardly the case in the Netherlands. While many factors could influence this effect, one tentative explanation proffered by the authors are the differences in cultural values in both countries.

Building on Hofstede's work on cultural values (2001), the authors theorise that the differences in effect sizes might be explained as a result of the differences in power distance. Power distance is thought of as the extent to which power inequalities in society are accepted and seen as normal. Power distance is one of the cultural dimensions of Hofstede that is much higher in South Korea than in the Netherlands. Government transparency is supposed to reduce information asymmetry between the 'rulers' and the 'ruled', and as such it mitigates power distance. In a country where power distance is high, transparency may go against this cultural value.

In 2011, De Fine Licht employed a survey experiment (N = 210) that provided counterintuitive evidence that transparency of decision-making processes does not necessarily lead to more perceived legitimacy. De Fine Licht designed a refined experiment in which participants (a heterogeneous sample of citizens) were presented with a description of priority setting between two groups with different health care needs. She used seven experimental groups to test two types of manipulations. Next to one control group, six groups were presented with different descriptions of the decision-making procedure, including decision making through representation, direct participation, and expert decision making. In addition, to also gauge the effect of media framing, a second manipulation framed the decision-making procedure in positive or negative terms. De Fine Licht demonstrates that transparent decision-making procedures tend to weaken rather than strengthen general legitimacy of decision making in health care. Another interesting contribution of this experiment was that while the form of decision making seemed to have no significant impact on perceived legitimacy, the framing of a decision-making procedure did influence public perceptions.

Later, De Fine Licht (2014) built on this experiment, adding various conditions and nuances. She tested the effect of different policy areas as a moderator on transparency effects in a large online experiment (N = 1,032). De Fine Licht uses the psychological concept of 'taboo trade-offs' (Tetlock et al. 2000) to show how citizens respond more sceptically to government decision-making transparency in areas that relate to human life and death, compared with less controversial areas. According to this theory, human life and well-being are considered 'sacred' and cannot be traded off against 'secular' values, such as money. Government transparency can expose decision making of these trade-offs. This was tested by including one area with taboo trade-offs – traffic security – and one area without taboo trade-offs – culture and leisure – in an experimental setting. Participants were randomly assigned to one of these two policy areas and to one of three conditions of transparency: no transparency, transparency in rationale, and transparency in process. Participants who were exposed to decision making about a taboo trade-off, such as traffic security, perceived the decision maker as less legitimate than non-taboo decisions (such as about parks and recreation). It illustrates that transparent government decisions about such trade-offs will therefore encounter much more resistance than trade-offs that do not violate this taboo.

Furthermore, De Fine Licht and colleagues (2014) employed a vignette experiment related to the same question (N = 400). High school students (aged 17–19) were asked to read a piece of text and answer questions. The text contained scenarios in which 'new rules of conduct for the school were to be decided' (De Fine Licht et al. 2014: 119). Two issues were central to this code of conduct: 1) the use of mobile phones in classrooms and 2) the possibility to make formal complaints against teachers. There were five manipulations of transparency: 1) no transparency, 2) transparency in rationale (justifying a decision in retrospect), 3) transparency in process (opportunity), 4) transparency in process (exposing bargaining), and 5) transparency in process (exposing deliberation). The students answered questions about legitimacy in a posttest questionnaire. Results indicated that indeed transparency may lead to improved legitimacy, particularly in the transparency in rationale condition, but not in the process conditions of transparency. Hence, this experiment showed that it might be better not to expose too much information about the decision-making process when it regards legitimacy.

Field Experiments

Four experiments in this category were found mostly looking into the effects of transparency.

To answer the question of whether the Right to Information Act (RTIA) can be used to obtain greater access to basic public goods that are otherwise attainable through bribery, Peisakhin and Pinto (2010) employed a field experiment on access to ration cards among New Delhi's slum dwellers. The RTIA mandates that all government institutions must take the necessary steps to enable information disclosure and thus transparency. The idea is that greater availability of information will result in a drop in corruption. In their experiment, they asked slum dwellers (N = 86) to apply for ration cards, randomly assigning them to one of the three treatment groups (RTIA request, support letter from a local NGO, and bribing a middleman) or the control group (using the standard application procedure). All ration card applications were filed at a local office responsible for an area. Applicants randomised into the RTIA group filed a request for information under the Act shortly after submitting their ration card application. In their RTIA request, the slum dwellers asked for information about the status of their applications and the average processing time for ration card applications in this district. Applicants in the NGO experimental group submitted a letter of support from a local NGO with their ration card application. This letter showed that the applicant was eligible for a ration card and urged prompt administrative action. Applicants in the bribe money group submitted their applications to a middleman active at the office rather than leaving it directly with the officials. The middleman requested a bribe with each application. Their findings demonstrate that 94 per cent of the individuals in the RTIA and bribery groups received their ration cards within one year, as opposed to 21 per cent in NGO and control conditions. Median processing time was 82 days for the bribery group, 120 days for the RTIA group, and 343 days for the NGO and control groups. While the RTIA is not as effective as bribery, it is considerably more effective than the standard application procedures or reliance on NGO support. These findings indicate that greater transparency can reduce the need for bribery and corruption.

In a similar experiment, Peisakhin (2012) tests how effective RTIA is in comparison to bribery for both slum dwellers and middle-class individuals in India as they apply for basic public services. Slum dwellers (N = 61) and middle-class individuals (N = 60) were asked to apply for a registration to vote. Individuals were randomly assigned to one of the two treatment conditions: RTIA or bribery and a standard procedure. Like in the previous experiment, the RTIA group was asked to file a RTIA request shortly after submitting paperwork to register to vote. The RTIA asked about the status of the individual's application and the average waiting time to be added to the electoral roll in the district. The bribe intervention consisted of an illicit payment submitted with an individual's electoral roll application. The amount paid was based on interviews with middlemen. The control group submitted its applications in accordance with the standard procedure. Applications in all groups were staggered so that government officials would not suspect the research study. Applications in the RTIA and bribe groups did very well compared to the control group; however, the only group with a 100 per cent success rate was the bribe group. While bribing is still the most effective intervention, the RTIA still halves standard processing times.

Grimmelikhuijsen and Klijn (2015) investigated to what extent transparency affects trust in judges and asked: how is this effect related to individual predispositions to trust and knowledge? To investigate this question, the study used a field experiment and consisted of two groups that both completed a pretest and a posttest. The treatment group received the instruction to watch a nationally broadcasted TV series about judges (n = 585) and a control group did not receive such an instruction (n = 464). The television series consisted of eight episodes and in each episode several judges were televised in different types of cases to present different realms of the judicial practice. In addition to informing the public about the actual work of judges, the episodes clearly express the symbols and values of the judiciary. Looking at the effect of the series on the overall sample, the authors carried out an instrumental variables analysis and found a main effect of the number of shows watched on trust in judges. Moreover, the analysis demonstrates that it has the strongest effect on people with medium prior knowledge about the judiciary. However, they also found that a higher predisposition to trust mitigated the effect of transparency, potentially because of a ceiling effect.

Cuillier (2010) conducted an experiment about access to government information, focusing on the effect of persuasion tactics to obtain information through Freedom of Information requests. He used a basic randomised posttest-only design. Cuillier reports on two experimental studies. In the first experiment, a journalist requested use-of-force reports from all police agencies in a state, mailing agencies either friendly (N = 53) or threatening (N = 53) letters, randomly assigned. In the second experiment, a journalist requested superintendent contacts from school districts (N = 219), mailing agencies friendly, threatening, or neutral letters (all groups N = 73). The threatening letter ends with a threat of litigation for noncompliance. The friendly letter was created by incorporating elements that foster liking, such as subordinating language and sincere compliments. In this letter, the public records law and threat of litigation for noncompliance were not mentioned. The letters were identical, except for changes in wording and tone – the experimental manipulation. In both experiments, a control group was not possible because there is no standard request letter in which one can compare different wording. When needed, a third letter was sent after four weeks. In both experiments, the threatening letter resulted in slightly higher response rates, lower copy fees, and faster response times; however, the friendly letters resulted in more helpfulness.

Implications

What have these experiments shown so far? Table 13.1 provides an overview of main experimental findings and how they match with previously existing assumptions from observational studies.

The general pattern is that experimental findings tend to nuance and contextualise non-experimental findings. As such, they contribute to further specification of theory formation about transparency and have proven to be an important complementary methodology for transparency research.

Table 13.1: *Overview of experiments of transparency*

Topic	Main findings	Implications for theory
Five experiments on effect of transparency on trust Type: Online survey and one field	Transparency has subdued and sometimes negative effect on citizen trust in government. Effect depends on the type of citizen; preexisting images, predisposition, and knowledge moderate the effect of transparency on trust. There may vast be cross-national differences in how government transparency is valued.	*Expectation from observational studies:* Indicate linear positive relation between transparency and trust. *Experimental findings:* Effect of transparency is highly contingent and depends on how different types of citizens process information differently.
Three experiments on effects of transparency on legitimacy Type: Survey	Decision-making transparency has subdued and sometimes negative effect on perceived legitimacy. Media framing matters and also the policy area is a contextual factor that affects how transparency affects perceived legitimacy of decision making.	*Expectation from observational studies:* Indicate linear positive relation between transparency and legitimacy. *Experimental findings:* The effect of transparency is highly contingent and depends on how the type of policy area and how it is framed by the media.

Table 13.1: (*cont.*)

Topic	Main findings	Implications for theory
Two experiments on effectiveness of transparency in corrupt regimes Type: Field	Using transparency in application for social services in corrupt regimes can be a way to limit corruption.	*Expectation from observational studies:* Transparency reduces corruption. *Experimental findings:* Transparency forces services delivery without bribery and thus indeed has potential to reduce the need for bribery.
One experiment on determinants of transparency Type: Field	Approaching government organisations more aggressively leads to more forthcoming information disclosure.	*Expectation from observational studies:* Various determinants are mentioned, mostly institutional. *Experimental findings:* Add to literature that certain micro-level determinants can also improve transparency.

First, it is evident that the experimental evidence shows that transparency does not lead to positive effects by definition. In the political realm and popular press, transparency is often lauded. Surveys also often point out that there are moderately positive effects of transparency on various perceptual outcomes. However, there is the obvious concern of endogeneity associated with cross-sectional research. For instance, reverse causality can play a major role. In a governmental organisation where there is a great deal of corruption, there will probably not be very much transparency. Hence, corruption and transparency are related, but corruption may be the *cause* of low transparency, not the *effect*. Experimental research is uniquely suited to separate cause and effect. The experimental studies reviewed earlier show that transparency does not always lead to 'positive' effects. Sometimes, there are no effects. For instance, in their study on transparency and trust across nations, Grimmelikhuijsen and colleagues (2013) found no significant differences between high transparency (complete information provided) and the control group on trust for the Dutch student sample. In other experiments, even negative effects of transparency were found (e.g., De Fine Licht 2011).

Second – and highly related to the previous point – experimental studies can be beneficial in teasing out what type of transparency has which kind of effects. Transparency is a very broad concept and it can be comprised of various dimensions of information, such as understandable information, timely information, and usable information. Further, the object of transparency can vary, such as decision making or performance. Randomised experiments are especially suited to specifically test what type of transparency has what type of effects. For instance, various conditions can be created, such as providing transparency about the decision-making process or only about the outcome of this process. For instance, De Fine Licht and colleagues (2014) differentiate in their experiment between transparency in rationale, transparency in process (opportunity), transparency in process (bargaining), and transparency in process (deliberation). She also includes the control condition 'no transparency'. She shows that transparency in rationale improves procedure acceptance more than process transparency or not being transparent at all.

Third, experiments can provide insights on the boundary conditions regarding the effects of transparency. Hence, the antecedents and effects of transparency are highly dependent on the particular context.

For instance, Grimmelikhuijsen and colleagues (2013) show that transparency increases trust in certain countries, while not in others. Furthermore, De Fine Licht (2014) provides experimental evidence that that transparency is less effective in sensitive policy areas that involve trade-offs of human life (traffic security) as compared to more 'mundane' policy areas (like leisure and culture). Also Grimmelikhuijsen and Meijer (2014) show how different types of citizens are affected differently by transparency.

Challenges and Suggestions for Future Experimental Research

Overall, this chapter showed that the number of experiments conducted in the area of transparency is still limited and – given the important empirical and theoretical contributions of experimental work on transparency – more systematic experimental evidence on the effects and causes of transparency is necessary. Based on this general premise, we offer four conclusions and subsequent recommendations for future experimental research:

1. There is much more experimental research on the effects of transparency than on the determinants of transparency. Future experimental work could look into the determinants of public sector transparency.
2. Survey experiments are predominant in testing the effects of transparency. We recommend scholars use a greater diversity of experimental types, such as field experiments and laboratory experiments.
3. There are many other normative claims still understudied by experiments, such as the effect transparency on participation and voice behavior by citizens, or the effect of transparency on the behavior of civil servants. Experiments are useful to investigate causal relationships for these assumed relations as well.
4. Experiments have shown the contingency of transparency effects; we should further and more systematically explore the contextual and boundary conditions that are relevant for the effects of transparency.

These recommendations are further explained next. We would like to see more diversity in the type of experiments. First, it is important to carry out more field experiments as a means of establishing the external validity of key findings on one hand, but also more lab experiments to very rigorously determine internal validity of findings. As noted previously, some field experiments on transparency issues have been done. One looked at how using persuasion tactics influenced the compliance of government bodies to FOI requests, which thus looks at which determinants foster transparency. The two other field experiments we found viewed transparency as the independent variable, with trust (Grimmelikhuijsen and Klijn 2015) and social benefits (Peishakin 2012) as dependent variables. These field experiments show a more optimistic picture of the effect of transparency than many of the lab and survey experiments. Whereas survey experiments have nuanced the overly optimistic view of the potential of transparency, field experiments show that transparency has a positive effect on judicial legitimacy and handing out of social benefits to disadvantaged groups in society. The question remains of whether these more positive findings in field experiments are due to the context-sensitivity of transparency or are artefacts of the type of experiment. Currently, the number of experiments is limited and there are no replications of survey experiments in the field, so there is no answer to this question as of yet. The first recommendation therefore is to replicate survey experiments, which are more common in transparency research, as field experiments. For instance, researchers could collaborate with local government to vary the degree of dimensions of transparency when informing citizens about policy projects. This would need to address various ethical considerations, but would be a highly interesting way to assess the effects of transparency in the field instead of in survey experiments.

Furthermore, the absence of laboratory experiments is striking. We envision that artificial lab settings are suitable to determine the effect of transparency on behavioural elements, for instance, one alleged negative effect of government transparency on decision makers (e.g. Bannister and Connolly 2011). A computerised laboratory experiment could help to determine whether decision makers indeed behave differently under transparent conditions.

Our second recommendation is for more work to be done on the causes or determinants of transparency. We found 11 experimental studies focused on the effects of transparency, but little work on the determinants of transparency. Of course, determinants are often sought and found in the institutional environment of governments (e.g., Relly and Sabharwal 2009). Still, the dearth of experimental research in this area limits our ability to answer key causal questions about how to promote transparency. It may not be possible or feasible to manipulate institutional factors experimentally at the macro level; however, other factors may be manipulated experimentally. For instance, lack of organisational support and perceived risk have been identified as a barrier to government transparency (Wirtz et al. 2015). In a bold field experimental setting, leadership support can be manipulated. For instance, public managers or leaders can be randomly assigned to receive training and instruction about the value of openness (and then compared to a control group without such training or instruction). Next the level of transparency can be monitored by, for instance, looking at proactive information provision on websites or by responsiveness to FOI requests.

Our third suggestion is to focus more effort on substantive areas that so far have received less experimental attention. For example, there have been a series of experimental studies in the area of citizen trust and legitimacy. However, there are other normative claims, for example, transparency as a means to increase citizen participation and citizen voice (e.g., Porumbescu 2015b). Also, experiments have predominantly focused on its effects on citizens, whereas there are potentially important effects on public sector organisations, their managers, or professionals. For example, transparency could enhance government performance or affect decision making of managers. The debate about whether transparency positively or negatively affects performance and decision making can be of much interest in the field of public management (Bannister and Connolly 2011), potentially with lab experiments such as mentioned before.

Our fourth recommendation is to experiment across various policy areas and types of transparency. Experimentation in two different policy areas has shown that the effect of transparency is context-bound (e.g., De Fine Licht et al. 2014). However, the contextual conditions have not yet been explored in a systematic manner. The context could consist of policy area, such as suggested by De Fine Licht (2014), implying that we can extend experimentation to underexplored areas such as education, safety, and health care.

Furthermore, various types of transparency have not been systematically tested. For instance, transparency can regard procedural elements, such as how decisions have been made (De Fine Licht 2011); yet it can also concern policy outcomes (Grimmelikhuijsen and Meijer 2014). Both types of transparency have a different nature and yield different effects. Hence, we propose two potential lines of varying the contextual conditions of transparency: extending the policy domain and extending to various types of transparency.

Finally, note that experimentation has its limits in terms of what it can test as transparency is interwoven with its institutional context, and as such considerable attention should be paid to 'macro-level' dynamics (Meijer, 't Hart, and Worthy 2015). Experimental research is not very suitable to assess transparency at this level. Therefore, in the pursuit of empirical evidence, a balanced approach is needed: macro-level work to assert how transparency is embedded in its institutional environment (e.g., Erkkilä 2012; Grimmelikhuijsen and Kasymova 2015; Meijer 2013; Piotrowski 2008) and micro-level research to assess transparency effects on individuals. That being said, even though the number of experimental studies on public sector transparency is small, this chapter shows how these studies have already improved our understanding of the effects of transparency tremendously.

References

Bannister, F. and Connolly, R. 2011. 'The trouble with transparency: a critical review of openness in e-government', *Policy and Internet* 3(1): 1–30.

Bauhr, M. and Grimes, M 2014. 'Indignation or resignation: the implications of transparency for societal accountability', *Governance* 27(2): 291–320.

Campbell, A. L. 2003. *How Policies Make Citizens: Senior Political Activism and the American Welfare State.* Princeton, NJ: Princeton University Press.

Coglianese, C. 2009. 'The transparency president? The Obama administration and open government', *Governance* 22(4): 529–44.

Cucciniello, M. and Nasi, G. 2014. 'Transparency for trust in government: how effective is formal transparency?' *International Journal of Public Administration* 37(13): 911–21.

Cuillier, D. 2010. 'Honey v. vinegar: testing compliance-gaining theories in the context of freedom of information laws', *Communication Law and Policy* 15(3): 203–29.

De Fine Licht, J. 2011. 'Do we really want to know? The potentially negative effect of transparency in decision making on perceived legitimacy', *Scandinavian Political Studies* 34: 183–201.

De Fine Licht, J. 2014. 'Policy area as a potential moderator of transparency effects: an experiment', *Public Administration Review* 74(3): 361–71.

De Fine Licht, J., Naurin, D., Esaiasson, P., and Gilljam, M. 2014. 'When does transparency generate legitimacy? Experimenting on a context-bound relationship', *Governance*, 27(1): 111–34.

Erkkilä, T. 2012. *Government Transparency: Impact and Unintended Consequences*. Basingstoke, UK: Palgrave Macmillan.

Etzioni, A. 2010. 'Is transparency the best disinfectant?' *The Journal of Political Philosophy* 18(4): 389–404.

Florini, A. 2007. 'Introduction: the battle over transparency', in A. Florini (ed.), *The Right to Know: Transparency for an Open World*, pp. 1–16. New York: Colombia University Press.

Grimmelikhuijsen, S. G. 2011. 'Being transparent or spinning the message? An experiment into the effects of varying message content on trust in government', *Information Polity* 16(1): 35–50.

Grimmelikhuijsen, S. G. 2012. 'Linking transparency, knowledge and citizen trust in government: an experiment', *International Review of Administrative Sciences* 78(1): 50–73.

Grimmelikhuijsen, S. and Kasymova, J. 2015. 'Not so universal after all: exploring the meaning and use of government transparency in consensual and majoritarian democracies', *Public Integrity* 17(4): 389–407.

Grimmelikhuijsen, S. and Klijn, A. 2015. 'The effects of judicial transparency on public trust: evidence from a field experiment', *Public Administration* 93(4): 995–1011.

Grimmelikhuijsen, S. G. and Meijer, A. J. 2014. 'The effects of transparency on the perceived trustworthiness of a government organization: evidence from an online experiment', *Journal of Public Administration Research and Theory* 24(1): 137–57.

Grimmelikhuijsen, S. G., Porumbescu, G., Hong, B., and Im, T. 2013. 'The effect of transparency on trust in government: a cross-national comparative experiment', *Public Administration Review* 73(4): 575–86.

Grimmelikhuijsen, S. G. and Welch, E. W. 2012. 'Developing and testing a theoretical framework for computer-mediated transparency of local governments', *Public Administration Review* 78(1): 562–71.

Hofstede, G. 2001. *Culture's Consequences. International Differences in Work-Related Values*. Thousand Oaks, CA: Sage Publications.

Hood, C. 1991. 'A public management for all seasons?' *Public Administration* 69(1): 3–19.

Hood, C. 2006. 'Transparency in historical perspective', in C. Hood and D. Heald (eds.), pp. 3–23.

Hood. C, and D. Heald (eds.) 2006. *Transparency: The Key to Better Governance?* Oxford: Oxford University Press.

Keane, J. 2009. *The Life and Death of Democracy*. Norton: New York.

Lindstedt, C. and Naurin, D. 2010. 'Transparency is not enough: making transparency effective in reducing corruption', *International Political Science Review* 31(3): 301–22.

Meijer, A. J. 2009. 'Understanding computer-mediated transparency', *International Review of Administrative Sciences* 75(2): 255–69.

Meijer, A. J. 2013. 'Understanding the complex dynamics of transparency', *Public Administration Review* 73(3): 429–39.

Meijer, A. 't Hart, P., and Worthy, B. 2015. 'Assessing government transparency: an interpretive framework', *Administration and Society*. DOI: https://doi.org/ 10.1177/0095399715598341

O'Neill, O. 2002. *A Question of Trust: The BBC Reith Lectures 2002.* Cambridge: Cambridge University Press.

Peisakhin, L. 2012. 'Transparency and corruption: evidence from India', *Journal of Law and Economics* 55(1): 129–49.

Peisakhin, L. and Pinto, P. 2010. 'Is transparency an effective anti-corruption strategy? Evidence from a field experiment in India', *Regulation and Governance* 4(3): 261–80.

Pina, V., Torres, L., and Royo, S. 2007. 'Are ICTs improving transparency and accountability in the EU Regional and local governments? An empirical study', *Public Administration* 85(2): 449–72.

Piotrowski, S. J. 2008. *Governmental Transparency in the Path of Administrative Reform.* Albany: State University of New York Press.

Porumbescu. G. 2015a. 'Comparing the effects of e-government and social media use on trust in government: evidence from Seoul, South Korea', *Public Management Review*. DOI: 10.1080/14719037.2015.1100751.

Porumbescu. G. 2015b. 'Linking transparency to trust in government and voice', *American Review of Public Administration*. DOI: 10.1177/ 0275074015607301.

Relly, J. E. and Sabharwal, M. 2009. 'Perceptions of transparency of government policymaking: a cross-national study', *Government Information Quarterly* 26(1): 148–57.

Roberts, A. 2006. *Blacked Out: Government Secrecy in the Information Age.* Cambridge: Cambridge University Press.

Tetlock, P. E., Kristel, O. V., Elson, S., Green, M. C., and Lerner, J. S. 2000. 'The psychology of the unthinkable: taboo trade-offs, forbidden base rates, and heretical counterfactuals', *Journal of Personality and Social Psychology* 78(5): 853–70.

Tolbert, C. J. and Mossberger, K. 2006. 'The effects of e-government on trust and confidence in government', *Public Administration Review* 66(3): 354–69.

Welch, E. W., Hinnant, C. C., and Moon, M. J. 2005. 'Linking citizen satisfaction with e-government and trust in government', *Journal of Public Administration Research and Theory* 15(3): 371–91.

Welch, E. W. and Wong, W. 2001. 'Global information technology pressure and government accountability: the mediating effect of domestic context on website openness', *Journal of Public Administration Research and Theory* 11(4): 509–38.

Wirtz, B., Piehler, R., Thomas, M., and Daiser, P. 2015. 'Resistance of public personnel to open government: a cognitive theory view of implementation barriers towards open government data', *Public Management Review*. DOI:10.1080/14719037.2015.1103889.

Worthy, B. 2010. 'More open but not more trusted? The effect of the freedom of information act 2000 on the United Kingdom central government', *Governance* 23(4): 561–82.

Zyl, A. 2014. 'How civil society organizations close the gap between transparency and accountability', *Governance* 27(2): 347–56.

14 Representative Bureaucracy: An Experimental Approach

GREGG G. VAN RYZIN AND NORMA
M. RICCUCCI

Introduction

Representative bureaucracy as a topic within the field of public administration and management reaches back more than half a century to the work of J. Donald Kingsley (1944). The initial work approached the topic descriptively and normatively, asking to what extent is the bureaucracy representative of the people it serves and to what extent should it be. More recent research has examined the positive effects or outcomes of a representative bureaucracy, with much of the work focused on the consequences for women and racial minorities (see, e.g., Meier and Nicholson-Crotty 2006; Riccucci and Meyers 2004; Selden 1997; Sowa and Selden 2003; Wilkins 2007). In our joint work, which we review in this chapter, we have attempted to take an experimental approach to the study of representative bureaucracy. This experimental work, which to date has focused on gender representation, aims to better understand the causal mechanisms linking representativeness of an agency with changes in the attitudes and behaviours of citizens.

This chapter begins with an overview of the previous research on representative bureaucracy within the field of public administration and management. We then discuss our methodological and theoretical motivation for trying an experimental approach to representative bureaucracy. This is followed by a summary of three experiments that we have designed and implemented to test representation effects, with a focus on gender representation.[1] This chapter concludes with our

---

[1] Experimentation has also become more popular in recent years in the field of political science to study, for example, gender stereotyping of political candidates (Aalberg and Jenssen 2007; Matland 1994) and gender differences in voting behaviour (Morton and Williams 2008; Wantchekon 2003).

reflections on the advantages and limitations of experimentation in this topic area, as well as suggestions for future research.

Overview of the Previous (Non-experimental) Literature

Representative bureaucracy has been an important area of research in public administration and management for decades. First advanced by Kingsley in 1944, the theory holds that bureaucracies that are representative of the people they serve will be more effective in meeting the needs and interests of the citizenry. At its core is the notion that not only elected bodies but the bureaucracy as well has the institutional power to engage in public policy making, thus fulfilling representational obligations to the public. Kingsley's original work focused on the restricted social background of the UK Civil Service, calling this elite the 'new aristocracy' and arguing that for bureaucracies to be truly democratic they instead needed to represent the groups whom they served (1944: 305). The theory further holds that elective bodies, such as parliaments or the US Congress, are not completely effective in representing the needs of certain segments of the population (e.g., lower-income socioeconomic groups or African Americans). Thus, to the extent the bureaucracy shares social characteristics with various segments of the population, bureaucrats will more effectively represent their needs and values. Thus, representative bureaucracy fulfils an important democratic function in our society to embody the broader population and in so doing represent their needs and interests.

Mosher (1968) further advanced the theory by offering two forms of representativeness: passive and active. The former refers to bureaucracies whose social characteristics mirror those of the population it serves. So, for example, if the city of Midvale U.S.A. has a population of 14 per cent African Americans, the city's bureaucracy would likewise be comprised of 14 per cent African Americans. Studies have shown that passive representation can lead to diversity gains and enfranchise various social groups (Kellough 1990; Kellough and Elliott 1992; Meier 1993b; Riccucci and Saidel 1997; Selden 1997). Active representativeness, on the other hand, exists when the African Americans in the Midvale bureaucracy push for the needs and interests of their counterparts in the city. In this sense, passive and active representation are linked. Kenneth Meier, a pioneer of systematic empirical representative bureaucracy research, was the first scholar to examine the linkage between passive and active representation, and has made major contributions to the literature (Meier 1975, 1993a; Meier and Nigro 1976). A good deal of research further demonstrating and elaborating this linkage has followed (see, e.g., Meier and Stewart 1992; Meier 1993b; Selden 1997; Sowa and Selden 2003; Riccucci and Meyers 2004; Meier and Nicholson-Crotty 2006; Wilkins 2007; Bradbury and Kellough 2011). Importantly, certain conditions must be present in order for passive and active representation to be linked. For example, Keiser and colleagues (2002) argue that bureaucrats must have a certain amount of discretionary authority to develop and implement public policies. They also argue that the policy domain within which bureaucrats work must be linked to the interests of those being served (e.g., women seeking child support; see Wilkins and Keiser 2006). For women, according to Keiser and colleagues (2002: 556), the policy area must be 'gendered', whereby 'the policy directly benefits women as a class ... the gender of the bureaucrat changes the client–bureaucrat relationship ... or the issue has been defined as a women's issue through the political process'.

More recent research has uncovered another type of representation: symbolic. Here, passive representation itself can produce positive outcomes for the citizenry without specific actions being taken on the part of bureaucrats (Gade and Wilkins 2013; Meier and Nicholson-Crotty 2006; Theobald and Haider-Markel 2009). For example, Theobald and Haider-Markel's (2009) research shows that the presence of African American police officers in a community enhances trust in the police force, thereby creating greater legitimacy for the police department within the community. Atkins and Wilkins' (2013) study moved the representative bureaucracy theory further in that they found that outcomes linked to bureaucratic representation are not necessarily tied to the mission of the organisation. They found that the presence of women or minority teachers was associated with lower teen pregnancy rates, suggesting that outcomes not directly linked to the primary mission of the agency or organisation can still be influenced by representativeness. In another study, Gade and Wilkins (2013) found that shared identities between bureaucrats and citizens, which are not linked to gender, race, or ethnicity, can also lead to positive outcomes for clients of the bureaucracy. Their research shows that veterans who know or believe their counsellors in Veterans Affairs are themselves veterans report greater satisfaction with services. Andrews, Ashworth, and Meier's (2014) study found that the representation of women and ethnic minorities in fire services in England was linked to organisational effectiveness. Their research also showed that performance impacts were greater in non-mission-specific tasks that presented opportunities for coproduction, suggesting a possible mechanism through which representation influences outcomes.

Methodological and Theoretical Motivations for Experimentation

Our decision to attempt an experimental approach to representative bureaucracy emerged from both methodological and theoretical motivations. Methodologically, as discussed elsewhere in this volume, randomised experiments offer the distinct advantage of more clearly demonstrating cause and effect. Given that most of the findings in the public administration literature about representativeness effects were derived from non-experimental (observational) studies, in which lurking variables likely confound the relationship between representativeness and outcomes, we perceived a need for alternative studies with stronger evidence that these observed representativeness effects were indeed causal. Moreover, theoretically, we saw an opportunity to examine the particular causal mechanism of symbolic representation, which, as noted earlier, had recently been suggested in the public administration literature. To reiterate, passive representativeness could potentially influence how clients or citizens construe the situation and in turn respond behaviourally – including enhancing their effort, compliance, or other behaviours that lead to desired outcomes – independent of any active representation on the part of bureaucrats.

To experimentally test the active representation hypothesis is quite difficult, to be sure, because this would involve experimentally varying the real gender or racial composition of functioning agencies. We will return in the last section to the challenges of working with real agencies to experiment with representativeness. But it was more feasible, we realised, to experimentally test the symbolic representation hypothesis. This would simply require experimentally manipulating a description of an agency, in our case the gender composition of the agency, and then ask survey respondents about their attitudes or behavioural intentions. This basic insight – that we could probe symbolic representation effects by merely manipulating the description of an agency – led us to a series of three survey experiments that we have conducted together with our graduate students at Rutgers University.

Three Experiments about Gender Representativeness

We present our three experiments about gender representativeness in the chronological order in which we designed and implemented them. For each study, we give an overview of the theory, methods, and key findings.

Experiment 1: Policing and Domestic Violence

In our first experiment, we examined gender representation in the context of policing and domestic violence (Riccucci, Van Ryzin, and Lavena 2013). This made sense as a starting point because various prior studies had looked at representativeness effects in this policy context (Meier and Nicholson-Crotty 2006; Theobald and Haider-Markel 2009), and symbolic representation was clearly a plausible mechanism for the observed effects. That is, a greater representation of women in a police agency might influence how women construe the agency, for example, by judging it to be fair and trustworthy, which in turn might influence their willingness to report domestic abuse or sexual violence. We were also interested in the interaction of gender representativeness and performance of the agency. Specifically, we speculated that a police agency with a reportedly high arrest rate (high performance) might be judged even more favourably when it was also more representative in terms of gender.

Thus, we designed a 2 × 2 factorial experiment, with gender representativeness of the agency as the first factor and performance as the second. After being instructed to imagine themselves as residents of a typical city named 'Middletown', participants were shown a 100-word description of a police domestic violence unit in which we varied the number of male and female officers (mentioning six females and four males, or alternatively, one female and nine males) and the unit's arrest rate of domestic violence perpetrators (either 70% or 30%). This description was then followed by questions that asked respondents to rate the agency's job performance (from 1 = very poor to 5 = very good), trust in the agency to do what's right (1 = never to 5 = almost always), and fairness of the agency in its handling of

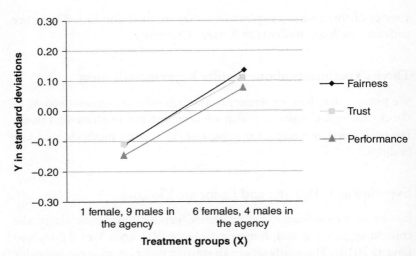

Figure 14.1: Main effects of gender representativeness on women in experiment 1
Note: Adapted from Riccucci, Van Ryzin, and Lavena (2013)

domestic violence cases (1 = very unfair to 4 = very fair). Participants were n = 789 US adults in the CivicPanel project, an Internet research panel at Rutgers University that is broadly representative of the US adult population (Van Ryzin 2008).

Our results were quite clear: the gender representativeness of the domestic violence agency influenced people's judgments of the agency's fairness, trustworthiness, and performance, all else equal. Figure 14.1 shows the results for women in the experiment (n = 508), and it can be seen that the more representative agency (with six females and four males) was rated higher in fairness, trustworthiness, and job performance, compared to the less representative agency (with just one female and nine males). The effects on all three measures are statistically significant (p < 0.05) and about equal in magnitude, with a roughly 0.20 standard-deviation difference between treatment groups. We found these results very encouraging, as they clearly indicated that the gender composition of the agency – which was the only difference between descriptions of the police domestic violence unit – causally influenced people's judgments of the agency.

Note that we also observed large performance effects, with people judging the agency with a 70 per cent arrest rate as doing a much better job and as being fairer and more trustworthy, compared to the agency with a 30 per cent arrest rate. But we found no evidence of a performance-by-representativeness interaction effect; in other words, the representativeness effect was entirely independent of the performance effect.

Experiment 2: Recycling and Coproduction

Encouraged by the results of our first experiment, we decided to try a new experiment in the policy domain of recycling (Riccucci, Van Ryzin, and Li 2016) that contained some important modifications. To begin with, we selected an area that is not specifically tied to gender issues, as discussed previously. Also, we tried a more subtle way to vary gender representativeness than by simply telling people outright about the number of males and females in the agency. When people encounter an agency in daily life, after all, they are exposed to names and faces of actual agency representatives – not statistics on gender composition. We did not have the means to manipulate a real agency's staffing, of course, so we relied on presenting a description of a hypothetical agency in a survey experiment. But rather than present numbers, we decided to vary the first names of the officials in the program description. Thus we crafted a description of a local recycling initiative in which four public officials were named: the mayor, the sanitation commissioner, the deputy mayor for operations, and the director of organics recycling. We then simply varied the first names of these officials; so for example, the sanitation commissioner was named either William Smith or Linda Smith (we used common names as reported by the US Census). This simple variation in first names of the four government officials was the only difference across treatment groups.

We chose a recycling initiative for several reasons. First, it allowed us to ask people about specific cooperative behaviours, namely their willingness to recycle hard plastics and engage in food composting, rather than assess attitudes. Although in the context of a survey we could gauge only behavioural intentions – not real behaviours – still these intentions are important indicators of people's actual willingness to cooperate with government. This leads to our second motivation, which was to examine a policy area in which government-citizen coproduction of a public service was especially critical and potentially modifiable by symbolic representation effects. Indeed, we based our description of our hypothetical recycling initiative on the example of

New York City and other large American cities that are grappling with ways to reduce the costs and environmental impacts of household waste disposal. Third, we wanted to test if gender representation mattered in a public service domain that was not explicitly gendered, in the sense of serving only women or dealing with a largely women's issue, as in our previous study of domestic violence. Both men and women produce household waste, after all, and both men and women stand to gain from the financial and environmental benefits of recycling.

So with these aims in mind, we designed a basic dose-response experiment with three treatment groups as indicated earlier: all male names (i.e., 0% female), half male and half female names (i.e., 50% female), and all female names (i.e., 100% female). Specifically, after instructing participants to read and consider the information carefully, as if it were a real recycling initiative in their own communities, we presented them with a 200-word description of a city recycling initiative in which the focus was on expanding recycling to include hard plastics (such as toys, hangers, and shampoo bottles) and on introducing food waste composting, for which special brown plastic bins would be issued for citizens to use to save food and other organic materials for weekly pickup. Again, the first names of the officials were all that varied experimentally in the descriptions presented to the different treatment groups. The dependent variables consisted of three follow-up questions (on a 0–100 scale) about the respondents' willingness to recycle hard plastics, to do light composting (coffee grounds, tea bags, etc.), and to do heavy composting (meat, fish, bones, etc.). Participants in the experiment were n = 754 US adults recruited from the CivicPanel project, as in our first experiment, and were broadly representative of the US population, although not a probability sample (Van Ryzin 2008).

So what did we find from this second experiment? For women in the study, the findings were clear and consistent with our first study: when the description of the recycling initiative included more female names of public officials, women's willingness to recycle increased – by quite a lot, in some cases. Figure 14.2 shows the key results, and it is especially interesting to note that the greatest gain in willingness to recycle is evident for heavy recycling, which is perhaps the most arduous and unpleasant form of coproduction in our study (as confirmed by the generally lower levels of willingness to do heavy recycling). Only

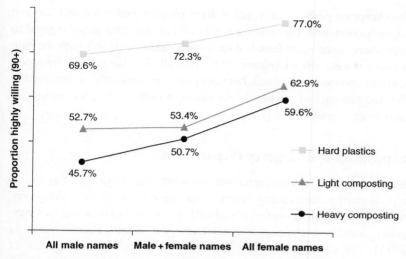

Figure 14.2: Effects of gender representation on willingness to recycle
Note: Adapted from Riccucci, Van Ryzin, and Li (2015)

about 46 per cent of women in the study reported being highly likely to recycle (defined as a rating of 90 or above on the 0–100 willingness scale) when the officials had all male first names. But this rate increased to nearly 60 per cent when the officials had all female first names, representing a 30 per cent gain in the share of participants highly willing to recycle (which was clearly significant statistically). For light composting, the effect was a 20 per cent gain in the willingness to recycle (from 53% to 63%), which is still quite large (and statistically significant). For the less arduous task of recycling hard plastics, willingness went up only about 10 per cent (from 70% to 77%, which was not significant statistically). Together, these results demonstrate the influence of female officials in the leadership of a government initiative on the willingness of women to cooperate and hence coproduce an important policy outcome, especially when such coproduction is more demanding.

We should say a few words about the effects on men in the study, which we analysed separately. Overall, men expressed less willingness to recycle and to engage in composting than women. And when more female names were included in the description, men's expressed willingness declined a slight amount (although not significant statistically) – with the exception perhaps of recycling hard plastics. For this easier form of coproduction, men expressed a nearly 20 per cent gain in willingness to coproduce when more female names were mentioned, although the gain was not statistically significant. Thus, overall, the effect of gender representation on men was mixed. But note that there was little evidence either that the presence of women in the ranks of public officials discouraged men in any significant way.

Experiment 3: Emergency Preparedness

Because our first two experiments provided clear evidence of symbolic representation effects using different operationalisations and policy contexts, we confidently moved ahead with yet a third experiment in a new policy context: emergency preparedness (Van Ryzin, Riccucci, and Li 2015). We chose this policy because (like recycling) the success of emergency preparedness depends a great deal on the cooperation and coproduction of citizens. We also selected emergency preparedness because it is quite different from recycling, which is much more part of the daily lives of the citizenry. Indeed, recycling has almost become a cultural norm in the United States. On the other hand, despite major disasters that have occurred in the United States in recent history (e.g., the 9/11 terrorist attacks, Hurricane Katrina, and Superstorm Sandy), efforts by governments to respond to emergencies or disasters remain far removed from the daily routines and even consciousness of the American people. Thus, we were interested in learning whether a more obscure policy domain would lead to a finding of symbolic representation. Also, this was another relatively non-gendered policy area and thus a chance to test the generalisability of the gender representation effects we had observed so clearly in our recycling experiment. Note, however, that it can be argued that most policy areas have at least some gendered aspects or connotations to them, a point we return to in our discussions later on.

Our emergency preparedness experiment was a fairly direct replication of the recycling experiment, in that we once again randomised the first names of four government officials mentioned in the program description. We used a description of a real emergency preparedness program called Citizens Corps, which was started by the Federal Emergency Management Agency (FEMA) in the aftermath of the 9/11 terrorist attacks in the United States and operates through a network of locally organised Citizen Corps in communities across the country. Although benefitting from federal support, local Citizen Corps also engage in fundraising and other community engagement activities. Following some brief instructions to read and consider the information carefully, participants were presented with a 270-word description of Citizen Corps adapted directly from the federal government's Ready.gov website. As before, we experimentally varied the first names of the four public officials mentioned such that the names were all male, half male and half female, or all female. The officials, in order of mention, were the FEMA director, the Citizens Corps administrator, an outreach coordinator, and a local council leader.

The dependent variables were questions about how many hours a month respondents would be willing to volunteer for Citizen Corps, how much money they would be willing to donate monthly, and how likely they would be to donate blood as part of a blood drive by Citizen Corps (on a 0–100 willingness scale). We chose these behaviours because at least some local Citizen Corps make such requests of community members, and because they have been used to gauge prosocial behaviours in prior studies (Houston 2004). Once again, participants in the experiment were n = 604 US adults from the CivicPanel project and were broadly representative of the US population, although not a probability sample (Van Ryzin 2008). Many of the participants were likely the same individuals as in the recycling experiment; however, we are unsure of the extent of overlap because participants' identities are confidential.

Surprisingly, we found no effects at all in this experiment. Gender representation did not influence women or men for any of the three behaviours (time, money, blood). No matter how we examined the data, there was simply no relationship between the gender of the names of officials and the responses of participants. Although not statistically significant, the trends in the data suggested a slight negative relationship – women were less likely to volunteer, donate money, or give blood when the names of officials were all female. In any event, our emergency preparedness experiment found no evidence at all for a symbolic representation effect on citizens' cooperative behaviors.

Reflections and Ideas for Future Research

What have we learned and what are the implications of our attempt to apply an experimental approach to the study of representative bureaucracy? Despite our null finding in the emergency preparedness experiment, our two previous experiments did uncover some fairly convincing evidence that the gender composition of the bureaucracy can influence women's attitudes and behavioural intentions. And we found little or no effects on men in our experiments. Thus, it appears that symbolic representation can have a causal influence on intervening variables like trust and the willingness to cooperate with government that, at least in some policy contexts, are important prerequisites for achieving vital outcomes. Moreover, we think the results of our first two experiments should convince other scholars to probe representative bureaucracy effects using experimental methods in other social and policy contexts. Indeed, we hope that we have at least succeeded in inspiring a new trend of experimental representative bureaucracy research that will continue on for some years to come in the field of public administration.

We were somewhat surprised and unclear about what to make of our null findings from the Citizens Corps experiment. At the very least, given the similarity in method and sample to the recycling experiment, we can say that the discrepancy in findings may have something to do with the different policy contexts. Perhaps women simply care or respond less to the need for emergency preparedness, although there was no effect for men either. Alternatively, emergency preparedness may not be as salient an issue as recycling, which as mentioned has become a dominant value in society. Thus, for symbolic representation effects to emerge, it may be that the policy domain must incorporate values that are widely shared or that a broad spectrum of people identify with, such as policing and recycling. Relatedly, perhaps this kind of difference in policy salience led participants to engage with and pay more attention to the written description of the recycling program, compared to the emergency management scenario, and thus notice the gender of names more readily. Another possibility is that, in the recycling experiment, the program description contained an explicit appeal to citizens to recycle hard plastics and to engage in food composting. In the emergency preparedness experiment, Citizens Corps was described in terms of its broad purpose and emphasis on local organising, but only volunteering was mentioned explicitly and not donating money or giving blood. Still, there was no symbolic representation effect on volunteering when looked at separately.

Certainly, the surprising null findings of our emergency preparedness experiment, contrasted with the strong and intriguing findings of our recycling experiment, points to the importance of replication in testing and developing theory, as discussed in Chapter 21 on replication. Indeed, as mentioned, it is our hope that these first three studies are only the beginning of what will become a stream of experimental representative bureaucracy research in the field of public management and administration. In future studies, as we have suggested, it will be important to examine a wider variety of policy and public service contexts in which citizen cooperation and coproduction play a role. Possibilities include parental involvement in education, public health behaviours, traffic safety, water conservation, and tax compliance, to name a few. Moreover, experimental work on representative bureaucracy should examine race and ethnicity, as well as gender, as critical dimensions of representativeness. Studies of employment discrimination have successfully used names in résumés as cues about racial identity (Bertrand and Mullainathan 2004), and thus our method of varying the gender of names of public officials can be extended to varying racial or ethnic identity as well. We look forward to pursuing some of these avenues of investigation in our own work, and we hope others join us.

Finally, note that the experimental approach to representative bureaucracy we have introduced and advocated can address only some of the many important causal questions posed by representative bureaucracy theory. Namely, the approach seems most readily suited to studying the symbolic effect of passive representation on clients and citizens. Studying active representative experimentally is more difficult. Indeed, this would entail some sort of large field experiment in which the actual gender or racial composition of real government agencies was somehow manipulated, perhaps through changes in hiring policies, in order to observe the consequences. It is possible some kind of natural experiment along these lines may present itself, such as the rapid diversification of an agency in response to a court order, allowing a before-after comparison (perhaps with a non-random control agency). Or a government agency may be persuaded to vary work assignments at the sub-agency level in an effort to experimentally vary gender or racial composition of field offices or work units, although such changes could well be politically and ethically difficult to implement. Another approach might be to attempt to vary the race or gender of the clients or citizens by using matched pairs of testers, as has been done in audit studies of discrimination in lending, home buying, and employment (Fix and Struyk 1993). Such testers could be

randomly allocated to visit or make a service request of a real government administrator, and the bureaucratic response – along with the
characteristics of the bureaucrat – could be recorded or observed. But
again, political and ethical complications are involved in researchers
posing as clients or citizens in order to probe the behavioural response
of real government officials.

In conclusion, despite the null findings from our replication, we remain
enthusiastic about the promise of an experimental approach to the study
of representative bureaucracy. The topic is not only long-standing, but
also rich and complex, and indeed a range of methods – including
observational studies, qualitative methods, and case studies – is required
to fully investigate representative bureaucracy and its effects.
Experimental research adds another, useful approach to this important
area of public management research.

References

Aalbert, T. and A. Todal Jenssen 2007. 'Gender stereotyping of political
    candidates: an experimental study of political communication', *Nordicom
    Review* 28(1): 17–32.
Andrews, R., R. Ashworth, and K. J. Meier 2014. 'Representative bureaucracy and
    fire service performance', *International Public Management Journal* 17: 1–24.
Atkins, D. N. and V. M. Wilkins 2013. 'Going beyond reading, writing, and
    arithmetic: the effects of teacher representation on teen pregnancy rates',
    Journal of Public Administration Research and Theory 23: 771–90.
Bertrand, M. and S. Mullainathan 2004. 'Are Emily and Greg more employable
    than Lakisha and Jamal? A field experiment on labor market discrimination',
    American Economic Review 94(4): 991–1013.
Bradbury, M., and J. E. Kellough 2011. 'Representative bureaucracy: assessing
    the evidence on active representation', *American Review of Public
    Administration* 41:157–67.
Fix, M. and R. J. Struyk 1993. *Clear and Convincing Evidence: Measurement
    of Discrimination in America*. Washington, DC: Urban Institute Press.
Gade, D. M. and V. M. Wilkins 2013. 'Where did you serve? Veteran identity,
    representative bureaucracy, and vocational rehabilitation', *Journal of Public
    Administration Research and Theory* 23: 267–88.
Houston, D. J. 2004. '"Walking the Walk" of public service motivation: public
    employees and charitable gifts of time, blood, and money', *Journal of Public
    Administration Research and Theory* 16(1): 67–86.

Keiser, L. R., V. M. Wilkins, K. J. Meier, and C. Holland 2002. 'Lipstick and logarithms: gender, institutional context, and representative bureaucracy', *American Political Science Review* 96: 553–64.

Kellough, J. E. 1990. 'Integration in the public workplace: determinants of minority and female employment in federal agencies', *Public Administration Review* 50: 557–66.

Kellough, J. E. and E. Euel 1992. 'Demographic and organizational influences on racial/ethnic and gender integration in federal agencies', *Social Science Quarterly* 73: 1–11.

Kingsley, J. D. 1944. *Representative Bureaucracy: An Interpretation of the British Civil Service*. Yellow Springs, OH: The Antioch Press.

Matland, R. E. 1994. 'Putting Scandinavian equality to the test: an experimental evaluation of gender stereotyping of political candidates in a sample of Norwegian voters', *British Journal of Political Science* 24(2): 273–92.

Meier, K. J. 1975. 'Representative bureaucracy: an empirical analysis', *American Political Science Review* 69(2): 526–42.

Meier, K. J. 1993a. 'Latinos and representative bureaucracy: testing the Thompson and Henderson hypotheses', *Journal of Public Administration Research and Theory* 3: 393–414.

Meier, K. J. 1993b. 'Representative bureaucracy: a theoretical and empirical exposition', *Research in Public Administration* 2: 1–35.

Meier, K. J. and J. Nicholson-Crotty 2006. 'Gender, representative bureaucracy and law enforcement: the case of sexual assault', *Public Administration Review* 66: 850–60.

Meier, K. J. and L. G. Nigro 1976. 'Representative bureaucracy and policy preferences', *Public Administration Review* 36: 458–69.

Meier, K. J. and J. Stewart 1992. 'The impact of representative bureaucracies: educational systems and public policies', *American Review of Public Administration* 22: 157–71.

Morton, R. B. and K. C. Williams 2008. 'Experimentation in political science'. In Janet M. Box-Steffensmeier, Henry E. Brady, and David Collier (eds.), *The Oxford Handbook of Political Methodology*. New York: Oxford University Press, pp. 339–56.

Mosher, F. C. 1968. *Democracy and the Public Service*. New York: Oxford University Press.

Riccucci, N. M. and M. Meyers 2004. 'Linking passive and active representation: the case of front-line workers in welfare agencies', *Journal of Public Administration Research and Theory* 14: 585–97.

Riccucci, N. M. and J. R. Saidel 1997. 'The representativeness of state-level bureaucratic leaders', *Public Administration Review* 57: 423–30.

Riccucci, N. M., G. G. Van Ryzin, and H. Li 2016. 'Representative bureaucracy and the willingness to coproduce: an experimental study', *Public Administration Review* 76(1): 121–30.

Riccucci, N. M., G. G. Van Ryzin, and C. F. Lavena 2014. 'Representative bureaucracy in policing: does it increase perceived legitimacy?' *Journal of Public Administration Research and Theory* 24: 537–51.

Selden, S. C. 1997. *The Promise of Representative Bureaucracy: Diversity and Responsiveness in a Government Agency.* Armonk, NY: Sharpe.

Sowa, J. E. and S. C. Selden 2003. 'Administrative discretion and active representation: an expansion of the theory of representative bureaucracy', *Public Administration Review* 63: 700–10.

Theobald, N. A. and D. P. Haider-Markel 2009. 'Race, bureaucracy, and symbolic representation: interactions between citizens and police', *Journal of Public Administration Research and Theory* 19: 409–26.

Van Ryzin, G. G. 2008. 'Validity of an on-line panel approach to citizen surveys', *Public Performance and Management Review* 32(2): 236–62.

Van Ryzin, G. G., N. M. Riccucci, and H. Li 2015. 'Representative bureaucracy and public engagement in emergency preparedness: a replication experiment', Paper presented at the 2015 Association for Public Policy Analysis and Management (APPAM) Research Conference, Miami, FL.

Wantchekon, L. 2003. 'Clientelism and voting behavior: evidence from a field experiment in Benin', *World Politics* 55(3): 399–422.

Wilkins, V. M. 2007. 'Exploring the causal story: gender, active representation, and bureaucratic priorities', *Journal of Public Administration Research and Theory* 17: 77–94.

Wilkins, V. M. and L. R. Keiser 2006. 'Linking passive and active representation by gender: the case of child support enforcement', *Journal of Public Administration Research and Theory* 16: 87–102.

15 | Coproduction of Public Services

SIMON CALMAR ANDERSEN, MORTEN
JAKOBSEN, SØREN SERRITZLEW, AND
METTE KJÆRGAARD THOMSEN

Introduction

Many public services rely on inputs from the public sector and from citizens, and indeed efficient service provision requires that citizens participate in service delivery in some way. Classic examples include citizens reporting crimes to the police and parents helping students with school attendance and homework. A growing literature shows that citizen participation in public service delivery – also known as citizen coproduction – can in fact increase the quality and efficiency of public services (Brudney 1983; Jakobsen and Andersen 2013).

We still know little about what motivates citizens to participate in public service delivery. Some scholars simply assume that citizens are more likely to coproduce if it mainly benefits themselves (Percy 1984). If this is true, simply informing citizens about the personal benefits of coproducing should motivate them to coproduce more. In this chapter, we discuss three sources of citizen coproduction. First, we discuss how information about personal benefits can motivate citizens to coproduce. Second, we argue that citizen coproduction can be increased by providing citizens with the necessary resources to engage in coproduction. Third, we argue that changes in the level of public input may have an independent effect on citizen coproduction due to substitution or complementary effects.

However, studying the antecedents of citizen coproduction is challenging. Problems of endogeneity weaken the internal validity of empirical studies based on observational data. Public initiatives aimed at enhancing citizen participation in the production and delivery of public services may target specific groups of citizens (either the most needy or the most resourceful in terms of coproduction), which will

329

introduce selection bias in the identification of a causal effect. For
example, if a school seeks to increase parents' involvement in homework
for children with low test scores, it is quite likely that we will observe
a negative correlation between exposure to the initiative and test scores,
even if the increased involvement has a positive effect – simply because
the targeted children had lower scores to begin with. We argue that these
problems can be addressed through the use of experimental methods.
Based on a discussion of three field experiments conducted by the
authors, we find that the more expensive initiatives (providing resources
and increasing public sector input) can be effective, while the cheaper
and frequently used alternative (providing information) is not.

We begin by introducing and defining the concept of coproduction
and review central studies that demonstrate its potential. We discuss
how the three initiatives (resources, public input, and information) can
affect the level of citizen coproduction and how field experiments can
solve problems of endogeneity inherent in observational studies of
citizen coproduction. Finally, we present the results of three experiments and discuss the utility of nesting several field experiments within
a single research agenda.

Theoretical Background

The Concept of Coproduction

The concept of coproduction was introduced in public administration
research in the late 1970s and early 1980s and conceptualises how
public services involve a mix of inputs from different actors such as
public employees, citizens, and private providers (Ostrom 1996). For
example, police officers fight crime, but they need input from citizens to
do it effectively; a surgeon performs an operation, but the patient often
has to provide input in the form of rehabilitation training to benefit
from the procedure (thus, the inputs of citizens and public employees
are often complementary). An early definition of the concept presented
by Parks and colleagues (1981: 1002) reads: 'Coproduction involves
a mixing of the productive efforts of regular and consumer producers.
This mixing may occur directly, involving coordinated efforts in the
same production process, or indirectly through independent, yet
related efforts of the regular producers and consumer producers.'
The 'regular producers' in this definition are public organisations and

Table 15.1: *Types of coproduction*

	The citizen benefits from coproduction	
	Individually enjoyed	Collectively enjoyed
Individually provided	A	C
	Private individual coproduction	*Philanthropic individual coproduction*
	(Alford 2009 – 'users-clients' and 'single' volunteers)	(Alford 2009 – individuals acting as 'members of the community')
Collectively provided	B	D
	Private collective coproduction	*Philanthropic collective coproduction*
	(Brudney and England 1983 – 'group' coproduction)	(Alford 2009 – groups acting as 'members of the community')
	(Alford 2009 – 'group' volunteers)	(Thomas 2012 – 'public as citizen')
	(Pestoff 2012 – 'collective self-help groups' providing benefits of 'individual self-interest')	(Pestoff 2012 – 'collective self-help groups' providing benefits of 'collective self-interest', especially through collective interaction)

Citizen input to coproduction (row axis label)

Note: Reproduction of Bovaird et al. (2015).

their employees, and 'consumer producers' are the service users. Hence, in this understanding of public service delivery, citizen participation is an important part of the production process.

From the early 1980s onward, a vast literature has explored the role of citizen input in public service delivery, and the concept of coproduction has been used to label different ways in which citizens may participate in and benefit from service delivery. Table 15.1 reproduces a typology developed by Bovaird and colleagues (2015), which outlines the different types of coproduction studied in the literature. First, the typology distinguishes between coproduction in which citizen input to the production process is delivered by individual citizens (e.g., service users or individual volunteers) or by a collective of citizens (e.g., a group of users or a group of volunteers). The second dimension categorises coproduction according to citizen benefits of the coproduction efforts. In some cases the benefits are mainly allocated to individual service users (e.g., a patient after knee surgery). In other cases the benefits are collective (e.g., a service that benefits a community or society). In sum, this categorisation of coproduction produces four types of coproduction.

Our studies of coproduction (presented in the following sections) include cases where individual service users provide input to services and individually enjoy the benefits. Our empirical case is coproduction of education and more specifically parents' input to their children's school-based development of skills (e.g., parents reading with their children, helping them with homework, and contributing to school activities). This is predominantly a *private individual* type of coproduction (see Table 15.1), and our experimental results are mainly applicable to this type of citizen coproduction in service delivery.

The Benefits of Citizen Coproduction

Research on coproduction has emphasised different types of societal benefits related to citizen participation in public service delivery. First, because citizen coproduction increases the total input to the production of services, it is expected to increase the quantity and quality of services, which benefits the service users (Alford 2009; Bovaird 2007; Percy 1984; Vamstad 2012). This is perhaps the most direct and most frequently recognised benefit of coproduction.

Second, citizen participation in service delivery is expected to increase the efficiency of service production. In many cases, input by public employees and service users is complementary in the sense that one type of input increases the effect of the other (Ostrom 1996). In the example of teaching, the teacher's input is more effective when the students (and the parents in the case of pre- and primary schools) provide input in the form of doing homework, participating in class, helping organise school activities, etc. Thus, if citizen input is low, an increase will not only increase the quantity or quality of services because it increases the total input, but also because it makes the public employees' input more effective.

Third, several studies have argued that citizen coproduction may improve citizenship and civic participation. That is, citizen coproduction may lay the groundwork for a positive relationship between government and citizens and increase citizens' knowledge about services and government structure, which is fundamental to their participation in the community and its political life (Levine 1984; Wilson 1981). Hjortskov, Andersen, and Jakobsen (2015) argue that including citizens in service delivery affects their self-image as being part of or related to government, which is expected to increase civic participation as well.

Fourth, increasing citizen coproduction may, depending on how and among whom coproduction efforts are increased, enhance equity in service delivery. Citizens with high socioeconomic status tend to coproduce more than people with lower socioeconomic status and therefore benefit differentially from coproduction. However, programmes that increase participation among citizens who otherwise would provide a limited input to the production of services they consume may increase equity in the outcomes of services (Jakobsen and Andersen 2013).

Why Do Citizens Coproduce?

What induces citizens to coproduce? Research on coproduction emphasises two factors as particularly important (Alford 2002; Jakobsen 2013; Porter 2012): ability and motivation. According to the coproduction literature, initiatives targeted at enhancing citizens' ability or motivation to coproduce, such as providing them with information, training, education, or materials and tools, are means for local governments to increase citizen coproduction (e.g., Alford 2002; Brudney 1983; Jakobsen 2013; Percy 1984). As argued later in this chapter, initiatives to increase input from public employees may also influence citizen coproduction. The rest of this section outlines the theoretical arguments behind three public initiatives to enhance citizen participation in public service delivery. The two first initiatives are targeted at increasing input from citizens, the third at increasing input from public employees.

The first type of initiative rests on the theoretical assumption that increasing citizens' ability to coproduce may enhance their participation in the coproduction of public services (Alford 2002; Brudney 1983; Percy 1984). The argument is that lifting constraints on citizens' ability to coproduce by providing resources in the form of knowledge and materials necessary for coproduction may enhance their level of coproduction (Jakobsen 2013; Jakobsen and Andersen 2013).

The second type of initiative draws on some of the same theoretical assumptions, namely that informing citizens about the benefits of coproduction will encourage them to coproduce (Brudney 1983; Rosentraub and Sharp 1981). Citizens who do not know how to coproduce are less likely to participate, and an initiative that informs citizens via booklets or leaflets will affect their ability and motivation (Thomsen and Jakobsen 2015). Moreover, providing knowledge of that and how citizens' input matters may encourage them to coproduce.

As mentioned, an initiative to increase input from public employees may also influence citizen participation in coproduction activities. The third initiative draws on the two-input production function developed by Ostrom (1996). Depending on whether citizens perceive an increase in input from public employees as complementary to or as a substitute for their own, they may increase or decrease their participation in public service delivery (Andersen, Nielsen, and Thomsen 2015). For instance, if a school increases its efforts to involve parents more in their children's education, parents may experience a greater return from helping their child with homework. If parents respond to the increased school effort by increasing their own effort, it suggests that parents perceive the two inputs as complementary. If they respond by reducing their own input, it suggests that they perceive the two inputs as substitutes.

Research Design

Isolating the effect of citizens' input to public service delivery is a challenge. Coproduction is by definition an interactive process, and thus it is difficult to distinguish cause and effect. If citizens are actively engaged in coproduction, public authorities may be encouraged to attempt to expand coproduction through targeted initiatives. As a result, any association between government initiatives to enhance coproduction and service outcomes may be a reflection of an already more cooperative public, rather than a cause of citizen behaviour. Alternatively, public authorities may prioritise new initiatives in areas where citizens are not participating because there is more need for coproduction in these areas, resulting in a negative association between government action and citizen coproduction. In other words, we cannot be sure whether existing correlations over- or underestimate the true effect of coproduction initiatives on citizens' behaviour.

On the other hand, citizens' coproduction may be an unanticipated effect of programmes that are difficult to account for in observational studies. Increased coproduction may be the intent of new programmes, but citizens may also react in unintended ways, for example, if they see increased public input as a substitute for their own input and therefore reduce their effort (Das et al. 2013; Pop-Eleches and Urquiola 2013). Research on policy feedback has shown how public policies may influence citizens' interpretation of and role in the political system (Campbell 2012). All such endogenous processes make it difficult to isolate the effect of a public programme on citizens' participation in coproduction.

Experiments are a strong solution to these methodological challenges (Blom-Hansen, Morton, and Serritzlew 2015). The general advantages of the experimental approach are covered elsewhere in this volume (see especially Chapters 1 and 44). We just note here that these advantages are especially relevant for phenomena like coproduction that by definition involve endogenous relationships. We now turn to several challenges to the experimental approach in coproduction research.

One challenge is external validity, i.e., whether the intervention, the participants, and the setting in general resemble the real-world situations being studied. Laboratory experiments may have high implementation fidelity, but they do not necessarily test treatments and time periods that are relevant to real-world situations. Furthermore, study participants in laboratory experiments may not be representative of a broader population. Survey experiments may be better suited than laboratory experiments in terms of the representativeness of the participants, but the treatments may not be realistic. Thus, it may be difficult to examine the effect of public interventions on coproduction and service outcomes in survey experiments. The advantage of field experiments is that they typically test the effects of real-world interventions in real-world settings (see Chapter 5). While implementation fidelity may be lower than in laboratory experiments, for many issues relevant to public administration imperfect implementation is almost inevitable. Indeed, the interesting question is often about the policy effect of an intervention in a real-world setting where implementation is in fact not perfect. This produces a more relevant answer to the question: *what is the likely effect of this intervention if it were scaled up?* Field experiments typically involve cooperation with public organisations. This can be a practical challenge, but it can also strengthen the external validity and practical relevance of the research findings.

The external validity can further be strengthened by analysing the intent-to-treat effect rather than, for instance, the effect on the treated. As Chapter 4 noted, the intent-to-treat effect compares the outcome for subjects assigned to the treatment and the control group, regardless of whether they complied with or took up the treatment. Citizens assigned to a coproduction intervention may not participate, so the intent-to-treat may underestimate the effect of the intervention on the treated. However, it still provides an estimate of the policy effect: the net effect of a treatment in similar real-world situations where citizens (or street-level bureaucrats) do not always comply with a programme or intervention. In addition to providing a more correct estimate of the policy effect, the intent-to-treat effect has the advantage of not requiring additional assumptions about compliance.

Another aspect of external validity relates to generalising results from the specific participants in a study to a broader population. This is a generic challenge to most empirical work in the social sciences: can results from a study in one country be generalised to other countries – or from one point in time to another? It may, however, be a particular challenge to field experiments, which are often conducted on relatively small and select groups of participants and within a limited time frame. For example, only some public organisations or citizens may sign up for enrolment in the experiment (before they are randomised to treatment or control status). We argue that a single experiment is not the definite answer to issues in public administration, as Chapter 21 on replication discusses. Instead, experiments should ideally be used within a research agenda that builds on several experiments and thereby combines the high internal validity of each single experiment with an ambition to understand the robustness and generalisability of the findings through a process of replication and extensions. If the results of a field experiment can be replicated in a different setting, it would increase the confidence in the results significantly. If they cannot, the 'failed' replication study provides better opportunities for theorising about why the intervention was effective in one setting and not in another, especially what support factors are needed for the intervention to produce its effects (Cartwright and Hardie 2012). New replications varying these support factors systematically may clarify where interventions will work. Another advantage of conducting field experiments within a common research agenda is the ability to consider dose–response relationships. In the case of coproduction, an important question would be: *how intensive should a public initiative be to induce citizens to coproduce?* If a public initiative has been found to be effective in one trial, the next trial may be designed to examine the effect of different 'doses'. Perhaps the same effect could be achieved by a less expensive intervention, which would have important policy implications. A third advantage of conducting several experiments within a research agenda is the ability to examine the external validity of the findings by testing the intervention in very different settings, for example, different political or geographical units, or by comparing different service areas, different client groups, etc.

Working in this way will take time, of course. The three field experiments presented next represent only a first step in this approach, but taken together they provide a much better understanding of coproduction processes than any one study.

Empirical Evidence

Coproduction Experiment I: Resources and Interaction

The first field experiment was conducted in 2009–11 in cooperation with the local government in the city of Aarhus, Denmark. Its purpose was to examine whether increasing citizens' ability to coproduce by providing service users with resources (materials and knowledge) necessary to coproduce would enhance their input to coproduction and improve service delivery. Results from this experiment are reported in Jakobsen (2013), Jakobsen and Andersen (2013), and Hjortskov and colleagues (2015).

Specifically, the experiment examined the effect of providing immigrant parents with tools and knowledge about the coproduction of their children's development of Danish language skills. In Denmark, public child care centers provide children who learn Danish as their second language with targeted language support, and even parents who do not speak much Danish can also do a lot to enhance their children's Danish language skills. The government coproduction initiative provided the parents with relevant materials and knowledge, as described by Jakobsen (2013: 36): 'Each child in the treatment group received a "language suitcase", developed by language development experts, containing children's books, a game, and a video tutorial on how parents can help their children learn Danish. The childcare employees presented the suitcase to the families, suggested how they could use it, and included the suitcase as a part of the regular discussions with the families about their children's language development.' More than 600 families were included in the experiment (coproduction intervention and control group).

The results showed an effect of the initiative on the parents' coproduction, but it was moderated by characteristics of the parents. In particular, the initiative was effective among parents with low Danish proficiency (i.e., those most in need of the initiative) and time available to increase their coproduction input (thus time is an important resource for coproduction) (Jakobsen 2013). The initiative was also effective in increasing the educational outcomes of the children, mainly children from families with low socioeconomic status (Jakobsen and Andersen 2013). Moreover, analyses showed that the coproduction initiative increased the extent to which parents voiced their opinions about the delivery of education services to children (Hjortskov et al. 2015).

Coproduction Experiment II: Sending Information

The second experiment investigated whether providing parents of schoolchildren with information about how to coproduce and its value for their children's educational development would increase their input to this coproduction process. The experiment was undertaken in November and December 2012, and results from the experiment are reported in Thomsen and Jakobsen (2015), Jakobsen and Serritzlew (2016), and Jakobsen and Thomsen (2015).

The empirical investigation was designed as a field experiment conducted in cooperation with the government of the city of Aarhus, Denmark. More than 1,400 families with children in first grade to third grade participated. One half of the families were randomly assigned to the coproduction intervention, the other half to the control condition. The aim of the intervention was to increase the extent to which parents read with their children (which benefits the children's reading abilities) by increasing their knowledge about the value of this activity and providing insights on how different ways of reading with children may develop their cognitive skills. The information was included in booklets, which were sent to the parents in the intervention condition by mail. The school administrations were the senders of the information, and the information was sent to the parents as under non-experimental circumstances.

The results showed that the intervention was successful in enhancing knowledge among parents (Jakobsen and Serritzlew 2016), but, as reported in Thomsen and Jakobsen (2015), not their coproduction efforts (reading with their children). This is somewhat surprising since a number of contributions to research on coproduction suggest that information is an effective means to increasing citizen coproduction (e.g., Brudney 1983; Rosentraub and Sharp 1981). Of course, sending information may work differently in other settings or in relation to other types of coproduction; the applied treatment may not have been strong enough (although it did substantially affect knowledge); or the way the information was delivered (one-way information from school administration to citizens) and the implicit control message may have reduced the intrinsic motivation to coproduce among some parents. An analysis by Jakobsen and Thomsen (2015) indicates that a negative effect on parents' intrinsic motivation may partially explain the lacking effect on coproduction efforts by parents.

Coproduction Experiment III: Increasing Input by Public Employees

The third experiment examined whether increasing input from public employees affects citizen participation in public service delivery. In the intervention, a teacher aide was assigned to a number of lessons per week in sixth grade classes. The experiment included almost 10,200 children and was conducted during the school year 2012/13. The result on behavioural responses by parents is reported in Andersen, Nielsen, and Thomsen (2015). The intervention included three types of teacher aides who differed with regard to qualifications and number of lessons spent in class: a co-teacher with a teaching degree, a teaching assistant without a teaching degree, and a supervisor who mainly assisted the regular teacher.

The results showed that the intervention with a teaching assistant and a supervisor increased the school's efforts to involve parents of the academically weakest students by assigning the children significantly more homework. Compared to the supervisor, the teaching assistant focused directly on improving children's education performance and spent the most lessons in the class, and this intervention was expected to have a positive effect on coproduction efforts by parents of the academically weakest children (measured by how often these children experienced that their parents helped them with homework). The expectation was confirmed by the empirical results, which suggest that these parents may perceive the increased input from the school as complementary and therefore respond by increasing their coproduction efforts. Moreover, the results underline that not only public initiatives directly targeting citizen input, but also public initiatives targeting public input may increase citizens' coproduction efforts in a way that strengthens rather than weakens the effect of such initiatives (Andersen et al. 2015).

Conclusions and Prospects for Future Research

Although coproduction has great potential, citizens do not automatically participate in public service delivery. We have discussed three initiatives that are likely to be antecedents of citizen participation in public service delivery: providing citizens with resources, sending information, and increasing public input to service provision. We argue that field experiments can handle methodological problems of endogeneity and spuriousness, and we present the results of three field experiments that all contribute to the same research agenda.

In the field experiment in which citizens were provided with resources necessary for participating in service delivery, we found a clear effect on citizens' contributions, especially among those who need the service most. Parents who received tools and knowledge about language development did in fact engage more in coproduction, which led to better educational outcomes for their children. We infer from this that providing resources can be an effective initiative.

In the second field experiment, we studied the effect of sending information about the benefits of participation. This is a common public initiative, typically in the form of booklets. We found that although sending information by means of traditional booklets to citizens did in fact increase knowledge, it had no effect on citizens' coproduction behaviour. Parents who received a booklet explaining the benefits of reading with their children did learn more about reading strategies, but they did not spend more time reading with their children.

The third field experiment examined the effect of increased public sector input, which may be a double-edged sword: on one hand, it may, via substitution effects, lead to a decrease in citizens' contributions to public service provision. On the other hand, it may be a signal to citizens about the importance of a given service and lead to an increase in coproduction. The experiment showed that such interventions have some positive effects.

These three field experiments belong to the same research agenda: how can the public sector secure citizen participation in service delivery? External validity is usually a limitation to isolated field experiments. It is difficult to generalise results from a single field experiment to cover a broad range of initiatives. Based on the first experiment and third field experiment presented here, where coproduction was found to have positive effects, it is tempting to conclude that citizen participation in service delivery can in fact be secured, with great potential for outcomes. Based on the second experiment, it is tempting to draw the opposite conclusion. However, both conclusions are misleading, and integrating several field experiments allows us to reach a more nuanced conclusion: public initiatives can in fact increase citizen participation in service delivery, but it seems that only tangible – and relatively expensive – initiatives (such as the provision of resources and increased public sector input) are most effective. Merely explaining to citizens about the personal benefits of coproduction, which is a frequently used and relatively cheap initiative, does not affect participation in our studies. This implies that increasing citizens' participation is thus possible, but may be costly.

We infer from this that future research based on field experiments can benefit from conducting several experiments within a research agenda. In this particular case, the experiments summarised in this chapter mainly focus on coproduction in which service users individually provide input and individually enjoy the service outcomes, and the results are mainly applicable to this type of coproduction (what Bovaird et al. 2015 call private coproduction). More studies will be required to address whether similar logics apply to philanthropic coproduction. Furthermore, it is important to note that our experiments focus on educational coproduction within the specific setting of a Danish municipality. Whether similar results can be found in other areas and in other political systems will have to be settled by future research.

Experiments have been criticised for being too narrow in the sense that the external validity is low or that it is difficult to understand the mechanisms underlying the treatment effects. We argue that any single experiment cannot provide the definite answer to issues in public administration and management. Experiments should ideally be conducted within a research agenda that builds on several experiments in order to combine the high internal validity of each single experiment and with the ambition to understand the mechanisms and boundary conditions of the findings.

References

Alford, J. 2002. 'Why do public-sector clients coproduce? Toward a contingency theory', *Administration & Society* 34(1): 32–56.

Alford, J. 2009. *Engaging Public Sector Clients: From Service-Delivery to Co-production*. Houndmills, UK: Palgrave Macmillan.

Andersen, S. C., H. S. Nielsen, and M. K. Thomsen. 2015. 'Brugernes reaktion når det offentlige øger serviceniveauet. Resultater fra et lodtrækningsforsøg på skoleområdet', *Politica* 47(2): 125–43.

Blom-Hansen, J., R. Morton, and S. Serritzlew. 2015. 'Experiments in public management research', *International Public Management Journal* 18(2): 151–70.

Bovaird, T. 2007. 'Beyond engagement and participation: user and community coproduction of public services', *Public Administration Review* 67(5): 846–60.

Bovaird, T., G. G. Van Ryzin, E. Loeffler and S. Parrado. 2015. 'Activating citizens to participate in collective co-production of public services', *Journal of Social Policy* 44(1): 1–25.

Brudney, J. L. 1983. 'The evaluation of coproduction programs', *Policy Studies Journal* 12(2): 376–85.

Campbell, A. L. 2012. 'Policy makes mass politics', *Annual Review of Political Science* 15: 333–51.

Cartwright, N. and J. Hardie. 2012. *Evidence-Based Policy: A Practical Guide to Doing It Better*. Oxford: Oxford University Press.

Das, J., S. Dercon, J. Habyarimana, P. Krishnan, K. Muralidharan, and V. Sundararaman. 2013. 'School inputs, household substitution, and test scores', *American Economic Journal: Applied Economics* 5(2): 29–57.

Hjortskov, M., S. C. Andersen, and M. Jakobsen. 2015. 'Encouraging political voices of underrepresented citizens through coproduction: evidence from a randomized field trial'. Paper presented at the 2015 PMRA Conference, 11–13 June, Minneapolis.

Jakobsen, M. 2013. 'Can government initiatives increase citizen coproduction? Results of a randomized field experiment', *Journal of Public Administration Research and Theory* 23(1): 27–54.

Jakobsen, M. and S. C. Andersen. 2013. 'Coproduction and equity in public service delivery', *Public Administration Review* 73(5): 704–13.

Jakobsen, M. and S. Serritzlew. 2016. 'Effect on knowledge of nudging citizens with information', *International Journal of Public Administration* 39(6): 449–58.

Jakobsen, M. and M. K. Thomsen. 2015. 'Samproduktion, offentlige tiltag og servicebrugernes motivation til at deltage', *Politica* 47(2): 164–84.

Levine, C. H. 1984. 'Citizenship and service delivery: the promise of coproduction', *Public Administration Review* 44(SI): 178–87.

Ostrom, E. 1996. 'Crossing the great divide: coproduction, synergy, and development', *World Development* 24(6): 1073–87.

Parks, R. B., P. C. Baker, L. L. Kiser, R. J. Oakerson, E. Ostrom, V. Ostrom, S. L. Percy, M. B. Vandivort, G. P. Whitaker, and R. K. Wilson. 1981. 'Consumers as co-producers of public-services – some economic and institutional considerations', *Policy Studies Journal* 9(7): 1001–11.

Pestoff, V. 2012. 'Co-production and third sector social services in Europe: some concepts and evidence'. *Voluntas: International Journal of Voluntary and Nonprofit Organizations*, 23(4): 1102–18.

Percy, S. L. 1984. 'Citizen participation in the coproduction of urban services', *Urban Affairs Review* 19(4): 431–46.

Pop-Eleches, C. and M. Urquiola. 2013. 'Going to a better school: effects and behavioral responses', *American Economic Review* 103(4): 1289–1324.

Porter, D. O. 2012. 'Co-production and network structures in public education', in V. Pestoff, T. Brandsen, and B. Verschuere (eds.), *New Public Governance, the Third Sector and Co-production*, pp. 145–68. New York: Routledge.

Rosentraub, M. S. and E. B. Sharp. 1981. 'Consumers as producers of social services: coproduction and the level of social services', *Southern Review of Public Administration* 4(4): 502–39.

Thomas, J. C. 2012. *Citizen, Customer, Partner: Engaging the Public in Public Management*. Armonk, NY: ME Sharpe.

Thomsen, M. K. and M. Jakobsen. 2015. 'Influencing citizen coproduction by sending encouragement and advice: a field experiment', *International Public Management Journal* 18(2): 286–303.

Vamstad, J. 2012. 'Co-production and service quality: a new perspective for the Swedish welfare state', in V. Pestoff, T. Brandsen, and B. Verschuere (eds.), *New Public Governance, the Third Sector and Co-production*, pp. 297–316. New York: Routledge.

Van Eijk, C. J. A. and T. P. S. Steen. 2014. 'Why people co-produce: analysing citizens' perceptions on co-planning engagement in health care services', *Public Management Review* 16(3): 358–82.

Wilson, R. K. 1981. 'Citizen coproduction as a mode of participation: conjectures and models', *Journal of Urban Affairs* 3(4): 37–49.

16 Expectations of and Satisfaction with Public Services

JUE YOUNG MOK, OLIVER JAMES, AND
GREGG G. VAN RYZIN

Introduction

Citizen satisfaction with public services and organisations has been
a consistent topic of investigation for several decades in public management research. This interest is in large part because satisfaction has
become a key outcome that government agencies seek to measure as
a valuable indicator of performance (Roch and Poister 2006; Stipak
1980). However, criticisms of subjective measures of government
performance such as satisfaction are also long-standing, including
how various background and attitudinal factors, distinct from actual
government performance, can influence satisfaction judgments (Kelly
and Swindell 2002; Stipak 1979). As a result, various public management studies have looked at the correspondence between objective
government performance and subjective judgments by citizens
(Charbonneau and Van Ryzin 2012; Favero and Meier 2013; Licari,
McLean, and Rice 2005; Van Ryzin et al. 2008).

Insight into the relationship between performance and satisfaction
has been elaborated by expectancy disconfirmation (E-D) theory,
which originated in the study of consumer behaviour, but has also
developed as a way of better understanding citizens' satisfaction with
public services. E-D theory holds that citizens evaluate government
services not simply in terms of the level of service performance they
experience, but through a process of comparison with prior expectations. Figure 16.1 presents the general model (Oliver 2010; Van Ryzin
2004). According to this model, people not only experience the performance of a service (link B), but bring to this experience a set of prior
expectations (link A). The resulting comparison is referred to as
disconfirmation, which can be positive (with performance exceeding
expectations) or negative (with performance falling short of expectations) (link C). But the model suggests that performance can have

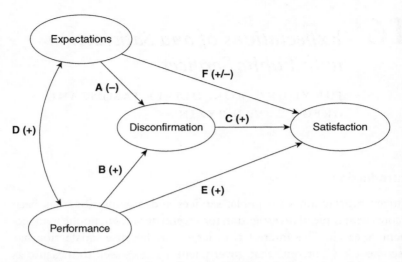

Figure 16.1: Expectancy disconfirmation (with performance) model

a direct effect on satisfaction (link E), and expectations also can have a direct effect as well (link F). More than a dozen studies using the E-D model to explore these various relationships have now been published in public management journals (e.g., James 2009; Morgeson 2013; Poister et al. 2011; Van Ryzin 2004, 2006).

Most of the studies on expectations disconfirmation are non-experimental and rely on surveys in which expectations, perceived performance, and satisfaction are self-reported perceptions or attitudes. Although support for the E-D model has been demonstrated this way across a variety of settings (including local, state, and federal government services), such observational studies have difficulty in convincingly demonstrating that the key relationships are causal. However, work has started to assess E-D theory using experimental designs (Van Ryzin 2013) and the factors influencing expectations of performance, especially the prior performance of public services (James 2011a). The first section of this chapter sets out the state of knowledge based on non-experimental studies. The second section shows the emerging contribution of experimental research on expectations and the E-D model. The third section sets out some challenges and an agenda for future experimental work arguing that there is much potential for an experimental approach and, more generally, that much remains to be learned about how citizens actually form their satisfaction judgments of public services.

Non-experimental Work on Expectations Disconfirmation and Satisfaction

Satisfaction is a core concept in social science and can be defined as a good feeling or sense of pleasure that results when a person has achieved some desired goal or state (Oliver 2010). In the consumer context, satisfaction can be defined as a person's subjective feelings about a consumed good or service. The approach generally adopted is that consumers can judge their satisfaction with individual elements of services and then make an overall satisfaction judgment from those elements. Through the process of comprehending and judging the qualities of consumed goods or services, consumers learn new information and incorporate it into their existing knowledge. Thus, satisfaction is not just a good feeling as a result of consumption. It is an indicator of a successful comprehension and incorporation of the environment and of successful decision making.

There are two dimensions sometimes used to understand satisfaction (Oliver 2010): vertical and horizontal dimensions. The vertical dimension refers to the level of aggregation of experiences, that is, the individual's satisfaction with a single event or observation versus the aggregation of overall satisfaction over many samples, situations, and time periods. For example, a researcher might study happiness (life satisfaction) over the course of a day, or alternately overall life satisfaction as a summative judgment of many past and present experiences. The horizontal dimension refers to the process or behavioural sequence involved in reaching a given satisfaction judgment, as well as the consequences that flow from being satisfied (or dissatisfied). Expectancy-disconfirmation theory is an example, as it focuses on the cognitive process involved in forming a satisfaction judgment.

Satisfaction has increasingly been used as a key measure of the performance of public services, because it reflects the subjective experience of outcomes. Citizen satisfaction has been shown to be positively related with perceived performance (Morgeson 2013; Poister and Thomas 2011; Swindell and Kelly 2000; Van Ryzin 2004) and as well as more objectively measured performance (Licari et al. 2005; Van Ryzin 2013). When citizens judge the quality of public services favourably, or when they are exposed to objectively better public services, they tend to be more satisfied. This implies that the local government successfully grasps citizens' needs and desires and effectively provides relevant public services. This performance–satisfaction link matters because many public services or outcomes are inherently difficult or costly to measure. As a result, citizen satisfaction surveys have become a feasible and increasingly employed method to gauge a variety of otherwise difficult-to-measure outcomes or aspects of government performance (Hatry 2006; Miller et al. 2009; Morgeson 2014).

Studying the relationship between citizen satisfaction with public services and government performance also matters because satisfaction affects other political attitudes and behaviours toward policies and governments. Citizens who are dissatisfied with public services are likely to "voice" (such as complaining or protesting) or "exit" (such as withdrawing from using a public service or even moving out of a jurisdiction) in response (Hirschman 1970; James and Moseley 2014; Lyons, Lowery, and DeHoog 1992). Dissatisfied citizens are likely to lobby and vote against incumbents (Boyne et al. 2009; James and John 2007). In addition, citizen satisfaction has been shown to have a positive relationship with trust in government (Van Ryzin et al. 2004) and willingness to pay taxes (Glazer and Hildreth 1999). Hence, it is hard for policy makers and public managers to ignore citizens' satisfaction judgments about public services.

However, the factors influencing satisfaction judgments are complex. Experiments have found that providing performance information influences perceptions of performance and satisfaction, and that there is negativity bias in satisfaction responses to performance (James and Moseley 2014; Olsen 2015). That is, information about good performance leads people to give more positive ratings of performance and satisfaction, as would be expected, yet information about poor performance results in disproportionately negative ratings of performance and satisfaction, that citizens are more sensitive and responsive to the low level than the high level of government performance. In other words, when delivering public services, doing poorly has much more of an influence on citizen satisfaction than doing well.

In addition, expectations play a role as a reference point for judging experienced or perceived performance (Oliver 1977, 1980, 2010). In particular, as the E-D model suggests, consumers or citizens tend to be satisfied when the quality of services exceeds their initial expectations, but dissatisfied when performance fall short of expectations. This implies a negative relationship between expectations and satisfaction; that is, all else equal, higher expectations lead to lower satisfaction (see Figure 16.1). But expectations can play an alternative role in the decision-making process as well. In particular, when the good or service is complex, unfamiliar, or difficult to judge, people sometimes seem to anchor on their expectations in forming a satisfaction judgment (Oliver 2010; Van Ryzin 2004). If there is uncertainty about how to judge a fine wine, for example, and you know in advance that it has a high price (and thus have high expectations), you may judge it more positively simply by anchoring on the price (your prior expectations). This can lead to a positive relationship in which higher expectations actually result in higher satisfaction. In this way, the formation of a satisfaction judgment is similar to Bayesian updating, with the judgment starting from the prior level set by expectations and updated with new experiences.

The role of expectations in the E-D model seems to differ depending on the types of expectations citizens hold at the moment. As the E-D model implies, expectations are another important influence on citizen satisfaction, including both positive and normative expectations. Positive expectations in the context of public services refers to the anticipation or prediction of what the quality of public services and outcomes *will be*. Normative expectations refer to what they should or *ought to be*, and apply to different aspects of services and their outcomes (James 2011a; Van Ryzin 2004). Positive expectations focus on the feasibility of public services, whether the anticipated outcomes will occur or not; whereas normative expectations focus on the desirability of the outcomes or end-states of public services. Hence, people may differently respond to and judge government performance when they hold different types of expectations.

In the observational studies to date, indeed, contradictory relationships have been found between expectations and satisfaction with public services. James (2009) and Poister and Thomas (2011) measured people's normative expectations by asking "how government performance *should* be." Their results show a negative relationship between normative expectations and satisfaction. On the other hand, Morgeson (2013) and Van Ryzin (2004) asked about citizens' positive expectations about what performance *will* be and found a positive relationship, suggesting an anchoring or updating process may be at work. These differences in findings call for a better understanding of how normative and positive expectations may operate differently, as well as what other factors may influence when expectations have negative or positive effects on satisfaction.

As mentioned, disconfirmation refers to the gap between expectations and the perceived performance of a good or service (Oliver 1980, 2010). Positive disconfirmation occurs when the level of perceived performance surpasses individuals' expectations, and negative disconfirmation emerges when a judgment about service qualities is less than their expectations. Disconfirmation can be calculated as the rating of expectations minus perceived performance, or it can be measured by directly asking citizens about whether performance exceeds or falls short of their expectations (Oliver 2010; Van Ryzin 2006). In one study, Van Ryzin (2006) structured the model so that subjective disconfirmation mediates the effects of calculated disconfirmation on satisfaction; his results showed that positive expectations had a negative relationship with subtractive disconfirmation, yet had a positive association with directly stated disconfirmation. These conflicting findings highlight the limitation of observational studies, in which expectations and performance are measured (albeit in various ways) as part of a citizen survey, rather than being manipulated experimentally.

Nevertheless, these studies have been important to the extent that they suggest that the E-D model, originally developed to analyse the determinants of consumer satisfaction with private services, can be extended to public services. Furthermore, these results indicate that the dynamic among the determinants may differ depending on how the concepts are defined and measured. Thus, as Stipak (1979, 1980) argued, researchers who study citizen satisfaction, as well as policy makers who want to use citizen satisfaction to evaluate government performance, should be aware of the complex nature of satisfaction and expectations and be cautious about interpreting such subjective measures.

Although the observational studies in the public management literature generally support the E-D model, the research has limitations in probing the causal relationships among the key factors. For instance, it is difficult to strictly separate expectations and perceived performance because they seem to positively influence each other (Van Ryzin 2004).

Commonly, observational survey studies ask about expectations and perceived performance at a single point in time, making it difficult to establish the causal order of influence. Some scholars have tried to minimise this problem by asking people to recall their past expectations before asking them to judge current performance and, later, satisfaction (Van Ryzin 2004). But of course, recall is often biased and in fact may well be coloured by current perceptions of performance. Others have evaluated the perceived performance of already consumed public services and compared these to future expectations (Oliver 2010). However, this approach also has a conceptual conflict in that the services for individuals' expectations and perceived performance may not be the same. In other words, the performance of garbage collection that an individual experienced a month ago may be different from the garbage collection they expect 12 months in the future. In short, it becomes very difficult to separate expectations, performance perceptions, and satisfaction judgments in the context of cross-sectional survey of citizens.

Experimental Studies of the E-D Model in the Context of Public Services

One of the advantages of experimental research is that it can better estimate the causal relationships in the E-D model. This section, therefore, introduces some of the new experimental research that has begun to evaluate the causal relationship among expectations, perceived performance, and citizen satisfaction with public services. In one of the first experimental studies of the full E-D model, Van Ryzin (2013) designed an online survey experiment to evaluate the expectancy disconfirmation model that minimises the correlation between individuals' expectations and perceived performance by using a priming method. The experiment follows a two-by-two design, with a manipulation of both expectations and performance to disentangle the possible correlation between them. First, participants were primed to form high or low expectations about their city government's performance by instructing them to read hypothetical public statements. Expectations were then measured with a survey question. Next, participants were shown photographs of either a fairly clean street (high performance condition) or a street that was less clean (low performance condition). Perceived performance was then measured with a question asking respondents to rate the cleanliness of the street in the photo. Finally, participants answered how much they were satisfied overall with the public service. On average, participants in the high expectations condition tended to express higher expectations, and people in the high performance condition rated the streets as cleaner. When combined in one model, expectations, perceived performance, and calculated disconfirmation had positive direct relationships with overall satisfaction with public services. Disconfirmation had a negative relationship with expectations, but a positive relationship with perceived performance. However, the positive direct effect of expectations on satisfaction was essentially cancelled out by the negative indirect effect of expectations on satisfaction through disconfirmation, resulting in only a small net effect of expectations on satisfaction.

By using an experiment, the Van Ryzin (2013) study provided clearer causal evidence for the key relationships in the expectancy disconfirmation model. The significant and positive direct effect of perceived performance on satisfaction indicates that subjective evaluations may well reflect objective public performance, as prior observational studies have suggested (Licari et al. 2005; Van Ryzin et al. 2004). Although the results of prior observational studies have been used to speculate that officials could influence satisfaction by managing citizens' positive (although not normative) expectations about their local governments' performance (James 2011a; Van Ryzin 2004), the small net effect of expectations on satisfaction in Van Ryzin's (2013) experimental study suggests that the ability of public officials to influence satisfaction through this route may be limited. More generally, these experimental findings cast some doubt on the importance of expectations in determining overall levels of satisfaction with public services.

In another early experiment in the public management literature related to E-D theory, James (2011a) conducted an experiment with manipulations to reveal how the provision of performance information affects both positive and normative expectations. Participants were randomly assigned to a treatment group, receiving information about prior local service performance, and a control group, receiving no information. One experiment instructed participants in the treatment group to read information about an excellent level of prior government performance, while the other experiment led participants in the treatment group to consider information about a poor level of prior government performance. Both experiments were conducted in field settings in order to increase the external validity of their results. Normative and positive expectations of individual participants were measured as outcomes after the treatments. The results demonstrated a different effect of information on positive and normative expectations and also provided evidence of negativity bias (James 2011a). Specifically, providing information in the treatment condition had a significant impact on positive expectations, but not on normative expectations about public services. Participants who received information about an excellent quality of local government services tended to have higher positive expectations, while people who read information about a poor quality of government services were likely to hold lower positive expectations, compared to the control groups. In addition, the effect sizes of information about poor qualities of government services were double the effect sizes of information about excellent qualities of public services.

By comparing the effects of information on both normative and positive expectations, the James (2011a) study provides robust evidence for the possibility of different roles of normative and positive expectations in the expectancy disconfirmation model. Also, there could be different sets of antecedents that influence these two types of expectations. For example, information about government performance tended to influence positive expectations (James 2011a), while personal attitudes toward services and personal needs are more likely to affect normative expectations (Zeithaml, Berry, and Parasuraman 1993). This finding concurs with the concept of positive and normative expectations: the information about prior government performance may act as a cue about the feasibility of public services, while the attitudes and needs are more related to the desirability of public services.

Several recent studies have attempted to replicate and extend experiments on expectations. Grimmelikhuijsen and Porumbescu (2016) conducted a series of replications of Van Ryzin's (2013) original experiment on expectations disconfirmation. They started with a strict replication of Van Ryzin's (2013) study, another involving a more extreme manipulation of expectations and performance, and a third conceptual extension in which expectations were manipulated after (rather than before) performance. The strict replication produced results similar to Van Ryzin's findings, and the more extreme manipulations resulted in larger performance effects. A study by Gaardboe and colleagues (2016) in Denmark also replicated Van Ryzin's (2013) study and found largely similar results for street cleanliness, schools, and libraries. However, their study found a generally positive total effect of expectations on satisfaction, which suggests that citizens may be anchoring on expectations when forming satisfaction judgments. In an important paper by Andersen and Hjortskov (2016), the E-D model was tested in three survey experiments aimed at probing the extent to which the relationships between expectations, performance perceptions, and satisfaction judgments and the actual public services citizens consumed. The findings suggest that people may not rationally judge expectations, perceived performance, and satisfaction in quite the way that the E-D model assumes, but may be more influenced by intuitive and emotional processes. Although the basic relationships in the core E-D model were replicated, the results also suggested that performance perceptions and satisfaction judgments can be influenced by priming and framing effects. Specifically, they find that recall of past performance can be influenced by priming future expectations, and that the order in which performance and satisfaction questions are asked influences the strength of their association. Andersen and Hjortskov (2016, p. 660) conclude that "the relationship between performance, experienced performance, and satisfaction is not as stringent as the basic EDM suggests [and] can better be interpreted as a result of a dual-process model of thinking," referring to the System 1 (fast, heuristic thinking) versus System 2 (slow, analytical thinking) framework for interpreting biases in human decision making (Kahneman 2011).

Conclusions and an Agenda for Research

Research in public management on the expectancy disconfirmation (E-D) model of citizen satisfaction with public services provides a good illustration of how experiments can play a role in theory development. The E-D model was introduced in the public management literature more than a decade ago (Van Ryzin 2004) and led to a series of studies testing the model in various contexts, all of which were based on surveys (observational studies). Uncertainty emerged about the extent to which some of the key relationships in the model were truly causal. This uncertainty inspired attempts to test the model experimentally, which confirmed aspects of the model, but also led to new insights about the role of expectations in the formation of satisfaction judgments (James 2011a; Van Ryzin 2013).

Importantly, these experimental studies have now begun to be replicated, and these replications have both added support to the model but also highlighted aspects of the model that may be contingent on policy and country contexts. The replications have also involved critiques and extensions of the E-D model. In particular, these studies have suggested alternative interpretations and deeper insights into the processes citizens use to form their satisfaction judgments by attempting to demonstrate the cognitive and psychological mechanisms underlying citizens' evaluations and judgments. In an important sense, this is how theory development in public management should proceed, building from initial observational studies to experiments, replications, and extensions of the original theory.

The experimental tests of E-D theory, although strong in terms of internal validity, have limitations as well. Expectations are difficult to simulate or manipulate in an experiment, and indeed the kind of expectations that can be influenced by reading a short statement may be quite different to the kinds of expectations about public services that citizens develop in the course of their daily lives. Similarly, the real-life experience of the performance of a public service, like street cleanliness, may be quite different than the brief inspection of a photograph in the context of a survey experiment. For instance, Petrovsky, Mok, and Cázares (2016) conducted a field experiment in Mexico to test the role of normative and positive expectations. Without any statement or information about government performance, one group of citizens was instructed to hold normative expectations, while another group was asked to form positive expectations. Although the researchers replicated the E-D model, they failed to demonstrate the different roles of normative and positive expectations as in the James (2011a) study. This is partly the problem of mundane realism, which is the extent to which the experimental materials and procedures resemble the real world. Because of the lack of mundane realism in many experiments, therefore, surveys that ask about people's actual expectations and their perceptions of real public services in their daily lives remain important methods for studying the E-D model and citizen satisfaction more generally. All of this is to say that experiments are often necessary for testing theory, but they are not sufficient for understanding a complex social phenomenon like citizen satisfaction with public services. A mix of methods including surveys, experiments, and in-depth qualitative research is likely to yield the most complete picture of reality.

There are several implications of these findings for future experimental research on E-D theory and citizen satisfaction with public services. One important line of inquiry concerns the nature and origins of expectations – where do they come from, and how might they be influenced? James (2011a) found experimental evidence for information about prior performance influencing citizens' positive but not normative expectations about performance. But much remains to be studied; expectations may well reflect long experiences with and deep-seated attitudes toward public services, but some of the evidence discussed earlier in this chapter suggest that expectations can in fact be influenced by more immediate information cues or frames. An additional issue concerns the proposition that people may have other kinds of expectations, in addition to normative and positive expectations (Jacobsen, Snyder, and Saultz 2015). Certainly, more experimental work is needed to probe the origins and manipulability of expectations. Relatedly, from a public management perspective, how should expectations be influenced (if at all) to enhance citizen satisfaction? The political intuition of public managers is often to dampen expectations, believing that this will lead to a more favourable judgment of government performance by the public (all else equal). Indeed, the basic E-D model would seem to imply as much. But as the empirical evidence reviewed previously indicates, the role of expectations in the formation of satisfaction judgments is often complex; indeed, raising expectations may even lead to more, not less, satisfaction (Filtenborg, Gaardboe, and Sigsgaard-Rasmussen 2017). More experimental evidence is needed to probe the influence of expectations on satisfaction levels.

Another line of investigation that would be useful for public managers in particular concerns ways to correct for expectations-related bias in satisfaction judgments. In other words, if citizen satisfaction is to be used as a performance measure, what types of anchors, cues, or frames might help citizens provide less biased and thus more valid ratings of government performance and satisfaction? But such research should remain open to the possibility that expectations may be found to inform, rather than bias, performance and satisfaction judgments to the extent that expectations capture important prior information and experiences with public services. Perhaps experiments could be devised to test the accuracy of citizens' performance and satisfaction judgments when expectations are either activated or mitigated. Finally, building on the work of Andersen and Hjortskov (2016), it would seem promising to continue investigating the ways in which citizens' expectations, performance perceptions, and satisfaction judgments may be influenced by more associative (fast) thinking rather than calculative (slow) thinking, as the E-D model tends to presume. Incorporating insights from dual-process theory could well help advance and extend our understanding of citizens' expectations of and satisfaction with public services.

References

Andersen, S. C. and Hjortskov, M. (2016). Cognitive biases in performance evaluations. *Journal of Public Administration Research and Theory*, 26(4), 647–62.

Boyne, G. A., James, O., John, P., and Petrovsky, N. (2009). Democracy and government performance: holding incumbents accountable in English local governments. *The Journal of Politics*, 71(4), 1273–84.

Charbonneau, E. and Van Ryzin, G. G. (2012). Performance measures and parental satisfaction with New York City schools. *The American Review of Public Administration*, 42(1), 54–65.

Favero, N. and Meier, K. J. (2013). Evaluating urban public schools: parents, teachers, and state assessments. *Public Administration Review*, 73(3), 401–12.

Filtenborg, A. F., Gaardboe, F. and Sigsgaard-Rasmussen J. Experimental Replication: An experimental test of the expectancy disconfirmation theory of citizen satisfaction. *Public Management Review* (forthcoming).

Glaser, M. A. and Hildreth, B. W. (1999). Service delivery satisfaction and willingness to pay taxes: citizen recognition of local government performance. *Public Productivity & Management Review*, 23(1), 48–67.

Grimmelikhuijsen, S. and Porumbescu, G. *Revisiting the Expectancy Disconfirmation Model: Confirmation instead of Disconfirmation?* Public Management Review (forthcoming).

Hatry, H. P. (2006). *How Effective Are Your Community Services? Procedures for Performance Measurement*. Washington, DC: International City/County Management Association.

Hirschman, A. O. (1970). *Exit, Voice and Loyalty: Responses to Decline in Firms, Organizations, and States*. Cambridge, MA: Harvard University Press.

Jacobsen, R., Snyder, J. W., and Saultz, A. (2015). Understanding satisfaction with schools: the role of expectations. *Journal of Public Administration Research and Theory*, 25(3), 831–48.

James, O. (2009). Evaluating the expectations disconfirmation and expectations anchoring approaches to citizen satisfaction with local public services. *Journal of Public Administration Research and Theory*, 19, 107–23.

James, O. (2011a). Managing citizens' expectations of public service performance: evidence from observation and experimentation in local government. *Public Administration*, 89(4), 1419–35.

James, O. (2011b). Performance measures and democracy: information effects on citizens in field and laboratory experiments. *Journal of Public Administration Research*, 21(3), 399–418.

James, O. and John, P. (2007). Public management at the ballot box: performance information and electoral support for incumbent English local governments. *Journal of Public Administration Research and Theory*, 17(4), 567–80.

James, O. and Moseley, A. (2014). Does performance information about public services affect citizen's perceptions, satisfaction, and voice behaviour? Field experiments with absolute and relative performance information. *Public Administration*, 92(2), 493–511.

Kahneman, D. (2011). *Thinking, Fast and Slow*. New York: Farrar, Straus and Giroux.

Kelly, J. M. and Swindell, D. (2002). A multiple–indicator approach to municipal service evaluation: correlating performance measurement and citizen satisfaction across jurisdictions. *Public Administration Review*, 62, 610–21.

Licari, M. J., McLean, W., and Rice, T. W. (2005). The condition of community streets and parks: a comparison of resident and nonresident evaluations. *Public Administration Review*, 65(3), 360–8.

Lyons, W. E., Lowery, D., and DeHoog, R. H. (1992). *The Politics of Dissatisfaction: Citizens, Services, and Urban Institutions*. Armonk, NY: M. E. Sharpe.

Miller, T. I., Miller, M. A., Kobayashi, M. M., and Hayden, S. E. (2009). *Citizen Surveys for Local Government: A Comprehensive Guide to Making Them Matter*. Washington, DC: International City/County Management Association.

Morgeson, F. V. (2013). Expectations, disconfirmation, and citizen satisfaction with the US federal government: testing and expanding the model. *Journal of Public Administration Research and Theory*, 23(2), 289–305.

Morgeson, F. V. (2014). *Citizen Satisfaction: Improving Government Performance, Efficiency, and Citizen Trust.* New York: Palgrave MacMillan.

Oliver, R. L. (1977). Effect of expectation and disconfirmation on postexposure product evaluations: an alternative interpretation. *Journal of Applied Psychology,* 62(4), 480–6.

Oliver, R. L. (1980). A cognitive model of the antecedents and consequences of satisfaction decisions. *Journal of Marketing Research,* 17(4), 460–9.

Oliver, R. L. (2010). *Satisfaction: A Behavioral Perspective on the Consumer* (2nd ed.). New York: Routledge.

Olsen, A. L. (2015). Citizen (dis)satisfaction: an experimental equivalence framing study. *Public Administration Review,* 75(3), 469–78.

Petrovsky, N., Mok, J., and Cázares, F. L. (2016). Citizen expectations and satisfaction in a young democracy: a test of the expectancy-disconfirmation model. *Public Administration Review.* Early view, DOI: 10.1111/puar.12623.

Poister, T. H. and Thomas, J. C. (2011). The effect of expectations and expectancy confirmation/disconfirmation on motorists' satisfaction with state highways. *Journal of Public Administration Research and Theory,* 21(4), 601–17.

Roch, C. H. and Poister, T. H. (2006). Citizens, accountability, and service satisfaction the influence of expectations. *Urban Affairs Review,* 41(3), 292–308.

Stipak, B. (1979). Citizen satisfaction with urban services: potential misuse as a performance indicator. *Public Administration Review,* 39(1), 46–52.

Stipak, B. (1980). Using clients to evaluate programs. *Computers, Environment and Urban Systems,* 5, 137–54.

Swindell, D., and Kelly, J. M. (2000). Linking citizen satisfaction data to performance measures: a preliminary evaluation *Public Performance & Management Review,* 24(1), 30–52.

Van Ryzin, G. G. (2004). Expectations, performance, and citizen satisfaction with urban services. *Journal of Policy Analysis and Management,* 23(3), 433–48.

Van Ryzin, G. G. (2006). Testing the expectancy disconfirmation model of citizen satisfaction with local government. *Journal of Public Administration Research and Theory,* 16(4), 599–611.

Van Ryzin, G. G. (2013). An experimental test of the expectancy-disconfirmation theory of citizen satisfaction. *Journal of Policy Analysis and Management,* 32(3), 597–614.

Van Ryzin, G. G., Immerwahr, S., and Altman, S. (2008). Measuring street cleanliness: a comparison of New York City's scorecard and results from a citizen survey. *Public Administration Review,* 68(2), 295–303.

Van Ryzin, G. G., Muzzio, D., Immerwahr, S., Gulick, L., and Martinez, E. (2004). Drivers and consequences of citizen satisfaction: an application of the American Customer Satisfaction Index model to New York City. *Public Administration Review*, 64(3), 331–41.
Zeithaml, V. A., Berry, L. L., and Parasuraman, A. (1993). The nature and determinants of customer expectations of service. *Journal of the Academy of Marketing Science*, 21(1), 1–12.

17 Citizen and Users' Responses to Public Service Failure: Experimentation about Blame, Exit, and Voice

OLIVER JAMES AND SEBASTIAN JILKE

Introduction

Citizens and users' responses to failures of public services has long been of interest to public management researchers, especially because of negativity bias, with responses to failure looming larger than citizens and users' reactions to well-performing services. Negativity bias is a general feature of political and organisational life and is reflected in responses to many dimensions of performance, including the economy and service performance (Boyne et al. 2009; Dowding and John 2012; Hirschman 1970; James 2011b; Lau 1982; Lyons, Lowery, and DeHoog 1992; Olsen 2015; Soroka 2006; Weaver 1986). This chapter sets out how experimental evidence is increasingly making a contribution to assessing the empirical implications of theories about responses to public service failure. Experiments have been particularly valuable for analysing the micro-foundations of aggregate-level results of prior observational studies into responses to failure by estimating the causal effects operating at the individual level.

The first section discusses research on blame in response to public service failure. There is a sizeable literature examining blame in more general politics, defined as the attribution of a 'bad' or 'wrong' outcome or action to a particular person, group, or organisational entity by an audience (Arceneaux and Stein 2006; Hood 2003, 2011; Malhotra and Kuo 2008; McGraw 1990, 1991). In the context of public services, experiments have begun to assess citizens' attribution of blame for service failure as part of the democratic control of these services (James 2011a; James et al. 2016; Marvel and Girth 2016).

The second section sets out the contribution that experiments are making to research on the use of services and political action in response to failure. Research in the tradition of Albert Hirschman (1970, 1980) distinguishes alternative ways of reacting to deterioration of performance and dissatisfaction with organisations. He identified exit through leaving the organisation or a customer switching a product, and voice for members or customers to express the need for change from within. Competitive mechanisms relying on exit, such as the introduction of competition within public service markets, were suggested as undermining voice whilst being unable to stop decline, with loyalty retarding exit and encouraging voice. These and closely related ideas have been extensively studied non-experimentally for public services (Dowding and John 2012; Lyons et al. 1992). However, experiments have recently begun more directly to address aspects of exit and voice in this context (James and Moseley 2014; Jilke, Van Ryzin, and Van de Walle 2016).

The third section concludes by setting out a research agenda for experimental work on responses to service failure. It seeks better integration of research on blame and responsibility with research on exit, voice, and loyalty. There is an opportunity for advancing both theory and empirical research by recognising how these theories relate to each other and using experiments to address this topic area.

Responsibility and Blame for Public Service Failure

Blame as the attribution of a 'bad' or 'wrong' outcome or action to a particular person, group, or organisational entity by an audience has considerable relevance to politics, public organisations, and services (Hood 2003, 2011; McGraw 1990, 1991; Tilley and Hobolt 2011). In general, individuals attribute outcomes to individuals and organisations, which affects their allocation of blame (Alicke 2000; Schlenker et al. 1994). For example, citizens' perceptions of politicians' blame for failure is partly about assessments of causality (the extent to which they caused, through their action or inaction, the failure) and partly about the severity of outcomes (which affects amount of harm as part of the blame). These judgements are in part informed by citizens' view of politicians' capacities for intending or foreseeing outcomes, taking into account relevant factors, including other actors and organisations involved. Blame can spur citizen and users' actions, including complaint or voting (voice) against those responsible, and blame has itself become a focus of research.

Hood (2003, 2011) considers blame in public organisations and discusses how it is affected by a range of institutional and related factors. He argues that the anticipation of blame by politicians and public managers is an important factor explaining the institutional design of public organisations. He identifies a set of blame-avoiding strategies: presentational techniques to shape impressions of responsibility, agency strategies involving the redistribution of formal responsibility to shift blame, and strategies to stay out of contentious areas of policy that might give rise to blame (2011: 18). These expectations about blame have received some empirical support from case study evidence put forward by Hood himself (2011) and are consistent with a similar type of evidence presented by Weaver (1987). Further observational evidence is consistent with the concept of presentational strategies; Mortensen (2012) found blame-shifting rhetoric in a content coding of accounts from elected regional officials blaming central government for cuts in public health care. Evidence that perceptions of responsibility are important in how citizens vote was found by Arceneaux and Stein (2006). They used a situation in which a prominent election in a large city followed a devastating flood to discover that voters punished the incumbent mayor for the flood if they believed the city was responsible for flood preparation.

As well as the observational studies discussed previously, experimental research has begun to look at individual-level citizen blame attribution for failures and the effects of different factors supposed to affect blame. Experiments began by examining blame and political accountability of public activity in general, rather than specifically blame as a response to public service failure. Malhotra and Kuo (2008) found that blame is affected by the extent to which political responsibility for a public activity is split across levels and branches of government, and that different descriptions of officeholders' responsibilities can further affect blame. In their study, they used a survey experiment in which respondents ranked seven public officials in order of blame for damage in New Orleans after Hurricane Katrina. They experimentally manipulated the information provided to respondents, with some receiving the officials' party affiliations, others their job titles, and others receiving both cues. They found that party cues caused individuals to blame officials of the opposite party, but that objective information about officials' responsibilities was also influential. However, not all experimental research on blame has found that structures matter for blame. Sulitzeanu-Kenan's (2006) survey experiment discovered that information about structural accountability did not affect individuals' blame attributions. Using the case of UK government ministers potentially avoiding blame for a government failure by initiating an independent public inquiry after the failure, he found that citizens' views about the credibility of the report's content affected their judgement of who was responsible for the failure.

Overall, the findings about blame reveal that only some structures are effective in reducing blame and the results depend on the structure *and* the context. The context of public services is not typically comparable to that of extreme, major events like Hurricane Katrina, although these findings are highly relevant to responses to disaster. Consequently, experimental methods have increasingly been used to consider blame in the specific context and structures that characterise the more routine delivery of public services. Experimental research has examined the effect of giving citizens information from systems publicly reporting the comparative performance of different local governments delivering the same service (where governments deliver services separately for their own, distinct local areas). When the level of service performance reported is much lower than the average, local citizens are more likely to see local politicians as being responsible for performance. Because local politicians differ between jurisdictions in a context of otherwise similar organisations and services provided they are seen by citizens as an important reason for the lower relative performance of the jurisdiction (James and Moseley 2014). These findings suggest that systems for reporting relative performance across jurisdictions, as well as changing citizens' perceptions of performance and satisfaction with services (James 2011a), can also increase the extent to which citizens hold local politicians responsible for performance outcomes. Holding politicians responsible for outcomes is an important part of blaming them for service failures. This experimental evidence at the level of the individual citizen helps provide a form of micro-foundation for aggregate-level responses to performance found in observational studies, including that voters punish incumbent politicians for relatively poor public service performance (Boyne et al. 2009; James and John 2007).

The extent of politicians' formal responsibility for service delivery sets the context within which citizens make their judgements about blame. In this way, the contracting of public service delivery by governments is a potential 'agency strategy' for politicians to use delegation in the management of delivery of the service to the contractor to avoid blame for service failures (Hood 2003, 2011: 67–89). Evidence about this issue, whether from observational or experimental sources, has been limited. Van Slyke and Roch (2004) used observational evidence in the form of a survey to find that citizens are often unsure who is responsible for public services and concluded that whom they see as responsible is important in the democratic control of these services.

Recent experimental research has estimated the effects of service delivery arrangements on different aspects of citizens holding politicians or managers to account. Taking the example of the failure of an important local public service, street maintenance, James and colleagues (2016) used vignettes about a realistic but hypothetical local government area to estimate the effects of different information cues about how politicians had chosen to have the service delivered. Using an online experiment, 1,000 citizens in the United Kingdom were randomly allocated to four experimental conditions (250 in each group), each with a different information cue about the management of delivery of a failing street maintenance service. The experiment used pictures of poorly maintained streets to give participants clear and easily understood presentation of the performance failure. This is the type of context that more generally has been found to stimulate people to take an interest in finding out why something has gone wrong (Wong and Weiner 1981).

The failure of street maintenance experiment gave participants materials describing service delivery arrangements and a realistic framing of the information cues about delivery, such as citizens might encounter it if they were to try and find out to whom they should complain or otherwise contact about the failing service. The experiment examined citizens' blame of politicians under four different cues about delivery, randomly allocated to participants. The outcomes for citizens' blame of politicians under each experimental condition were gathered through a survey of participants asking them about blame of politicians for the service (using multi-item measures to produce a single scale of 0 = not at all to blame to 100 = completely to blame).

In a first comparison data from the experiment was used to compare an information cue about contracting with a cue containing no information about the form of service delivery. The no information cue was used because, whilst some citizens may know about local management structures, in many cases their factual knowledge is limited (Van Slyke and Roch 2004). A second comparison compared the information cue about contracting with a cue in which citizens were told that politicians were involved in managing the day-to-day delivery of street maintenance, potentially linking politicians with the service failure more closely in the minds of citizens. The interest in this comparison was motivated by the observation that some politicians, for example many mayors, seek to link their role and responsibilities to the effective delivery of services, such as good preparedness for bad weather, having a safe city, or effective transportation.

There was little evidence in support of the agency model of reducing blame by use of contracted-out service delivery. In comparisons of blame following receipt of the cues, the contracting to a private company cue did not reduce blame compared to having no information about the form of service delivery. In addition, contracting did not reduce blame compared to being told that politicians manage service delivery. The authors suggested that well-publicised arguments between English politicians and private contractors about their respective contributions to causing service failures may have led respondents not to reduce their blame of politicians who used this form of delivery.

The research also compared the cue about contracting with a private firm with that of an alternative form of delegation using an alternative cue of delegation of management of service delivery to a unit within the local government. Many local governments use their own public managers and associated staff to manage delivery of services. In many senses this relationship between politicians and public managers is the heart of traditional public management. Including this alternative form of delivery in a cue enabled the research to contrast delegation through contracting with delegation within a public organisation. The experiment found support for delegation by politicians to managers as a blame reduction, agency strategy. The management of service delivery by a delegated unit within local government reduced blame by 4.16 percentage points, 95% CI: [-7.80, -0.53], from the cue of politicians involved in managing service delivery level of 80.60. The results show that the type of organisation politicians choose to manage service delivery matters for citizens' blame of them.

Politicians explicitly stating that they were involved in managing service delivery experienced higher blame; the information cue that politicians were involved in managing day-to-day delivery raised blame by 5.16 percentage points, 95% CI: [1.52, 8.80], from the cue of no information baseline of 75.44. This suggests that politicians, such as local mayors, who proclaim their role in management need to be especially careful about service performance if they do not want to have higher blame than if they had not made public statements of this kind.

Unusually for public management research, the service failure and information cues experiment has been subject to a replication, in the sense of another experiment using the same treatments and measurement instruments. The same protocols were followed, including the same scenario of failure and set of cues, but with a different online sample from the Netherlands (Jilke et al. 2016). Both studies used a multiple-item measure of the dependent variable of blame, to test and ensure the cross-replication measurement equivalence of the studies. This type of measurement equivalence is necessary to compare the results across the two studies, to rule out the possibility that differences in the findings occur through a lack of equivalence in the way the concept of blame was measured (which would be a legitimate concern in a replication in two different countries). Through a series of multiple group confirmatory factor analyses, Jilke and colleagues (2016) found that the studies' outcome measures were indeed equivalent across experiments.

Substantially, the study in the Netherlands replicated the finding from the UK study that the contracting-out cue did not reduce citizens' blame of politicians for the failure of the service (Jilke et al. 2016). However, it did not replicate the initial experiment's finding of an effect of increased blame from political involvement in managing services (compared to having no information) or delegation to an unit within local government reducing blame compared to the cue about politicians managing service delivery. The difference in findings is consistent with the theoretical rationale of the initial study that blame of politicians is most likely in political systems where politicians are directly associated with provision of services, as is typical in UK local government. The expectations differ for alternative systems that do not have the same framework of direct political control. In the Netherlands, politicians' direct involvement in local services of this kind is less common under typical institutional arrangements. This context leads to the expectation that participants in the Netherlands would be less responsive to the suggestion that politicians could be responsible for day-to-day management of service delivery. Consequently, the experiments show that the degree to which politicians associate themselves with managing services can have an effect on blame in systems where political control over public services is typically strong, but these effects are more muted in systems where politicians are not seen as being in such direct control of these services.

The findings about blame are consistent with those for citizens' blame of politicians for service delivery problems under the use of 'third party government'. Marvel and Girth (2016) conducted experimental research to evaluate the expectation that citizens would be more inclined to blame political principals for service delivery problems when a public agency is directly providing a government service than when it used third party government. They further expected that, as the distance between political principal and a service provider increased, citizens' blame of the political principal would decrease. Marvel and Girth (2016) describe their finding about the theory as 'mixed' and note that 'Individuals perceive political actors to have more control over a service provider when that provider is a public sector organisation (versus a private organisation), but this heightened perceived control does not fully translate to individuals' blame attributions' (Marvel and Girth 2016). When taken together with the findings from the James and colleagues (2016) study, this set of findings is consistent with citizens blaming politicians for using private contractors in the first place.

Exit, Voice, and Loyalty as Responses to Decline or Failure

Recent years have seen an increase in studies looking at how citizens respond to a decline and failure in organisations, including public services. Much of this research stands in the tradition of Albert Hirschman's (1970, 1980) work on exit, voice, and loyalty, as distinct, though interrelated, means of how individuals respond to organisational decline. For Hirschman, the key mechanism behind these behavioural responses is individuals' dissatisfaction with a given state of affairs. Indeed, if people would not be dissatisfied with the services they receive there would be no need to do anything. Dissatisfaction is of particular importance given that prior research has shown that citizens' responses to public service performance are influenced by negativity bias – humans' tendency to give a greater weight to negative events and information (Lau 1982; Weaver 1987). Here dissatisfaction is assumed to be caused by a decline in public service performance – although according to expectations-disconfirmation theory (discussed in Chapter 16), it could also be the result of an increase in individuals' expectations.

Citizen responses to service failure are important from a macro perspective, because these behavioural responses serve as signals that ought to give service providers information that would help them to adjust the delivery of their services in accordance to their users' needs and demands. This is especially important for many public sector organisations who deliver crucial public services that are in the general interest – such as public transport or road cleaning – and thus providers cannot easily go out of business if service quality declines, as would be the case for their private sector counterparts (Jilke 2015).

Exit and voice are in some ways functional equivalents; if service quality declines, users can either voice their dissatisfaction with the state of affairs, or they can leave the service provider in question. Yet both responses have different causes and effects, and changes in the institutional design of service delivery will affect the choice of which one to use (Dowding and John 2012). For example, if a certain service, such as municipal water provision, is provided by a monopolistic provider, service users have no such opportunity to exit, given they want to continue receiving water services. They will thus be more inclined to use their voice to express any discontent. However, if the same service would be delivered within a competitive market of multiple (public and private) providers, then exit (in this case choice between providers) would be much more likely to come into being. This example displays the dynamic relationship between exit and voice. In Hirschman's theory, the right combination between both can lead to overcome organisational decline and his work especially pointed to how limited exit can promote voice which is beneficial for the organisation and which might not occur if exit is too easy.

Perhaps slightly less well conceptualised in the context of public services is the notion of loyalty. It means that citizens have a feeling of attachment to an organisation and are thus less likely to exit. Not only would users' loyalty moderate the exit-voice trade-off, but loyal citizens would also be more inclined to passively wait until things improve. Thus it is kind of a psychological state (perhaps the result of past responses to exit and/or voice) and not a response to service failure as such. Yet it is possible that users alter their loyalty with public service organisations as a response to service failure. Nearly all of the work within the exit and voice tradition has been non-experimental, but an emerging set of experimental studies is making a contribution to the topic area, in terms both of exit (and relatedly choice) and voice processes.

Experiments on Exit and Choice Responses

There have been hardly any experiments on exit responses to service failure in public management. However, Jilke, Van Ryzin, and Van de Walle (2016) conducted an experiment on the effect of choice options on whether users exit a failing public service. Using electricity as a realistic case where users can choose among multiple service providers, they tested and extended the choice-overload hypothesis. The choice overload hypothesis states that increasing the number of alternatives reduces people's motivation to choose, and has received considerable attention within consumer psychology (Iyengar and Lepper 2000). Applied to the field of marketised public services, they investigated whether increasing the number of providers of electricity services reduced users' motivation to switch away from a poor service provider. Doing so, they used a large-scale survey experiment where the number of alternative providers (2 versus 17 alternative service providers) and users' dissatisfaction (high versus low) was randomly varied, resulting in a 2 by 2 factorial design. Respondents were shown a hypothetical service failure scenario and then asked whether they would switch to another service provider from a list of alternatives shown to them. The study found that increasing provider choice reduced people's likelihood of stating that they would switch away from a poor-performing (versus well-performing) provider by 10 percentage points. A direct replication among an independent online sample produced similar findings. Their findings suggest that users can become locked in to suboptimal service providers simply due to an overload of alternative choices available to them. On a more general level, these results show that public service delivery reforms that have been focussing on introducing choice and competition into public service delivery may be susceptible to overly positive assumptions about how users respond to service failure.

Experiments on Voice Responses

There is a large political science literature on a range of voice processes, including some using experimental methods, notably in the area of voter mobilisation (see Michelson and Nickerson 2011). There has also been some research on voice in research on consumers in markets (Goodwin and Ross 1992). However, there are fewer experimental studies on voice responses to public service failure. In the limited evidence to date, experiments have found that, despite poor performance affecting citizens' perceptions and lowering their satisfaction, there is little evidence that this leads to citizens responding to poor services through voice. James and Moseley (2014) conducted an experiment to evaluate a model of the effect of performance information on voice. The experiment gave citizens in a specific locality information about the relatively poor performance of their local government's services compared to that provided by other local governments. The information affected perceptions of performance, reducing the perceptions consistent with the information, and information about poor outcomes reduced satisfaction with the services. However, whilst there was evidence of these links in the chain from information to action, the citizens did not voice to the local government provider when given the opportunity to do so (in the form of participating in a consultation about local performance).

The lack of voice was found in a context that should have been favourable to it because of the limited exit options to citizens (with citizens unlikely to relocate just because of information about poor services – although this possibility might exist for a small subgroup of them or for particularly important services). Instead, the finding is consistent with citizens disengaging from and neglecting poor services, suggesting that some local providers, perhaps those needing citizen participation and pressure the most, do not get it.

Conclusions: An Experimental Research Agenda for Responses to Service Failure

Blame is part of the network of citizens' or service users' attitudes in response to service failure and should be better integrated with theories of exit, voice, and loyalty behavioural responses. Whilst this is an ambitious project, some elements include a more elaborated theory of perceptions of performance and whether citizens and users see services as failing, the degree of negativity of the failure, and the link between these perceptions and who is seen as responsible. These can then be related to judgements of dissatisfaction with not only the service, but the provider of the service and any blame following on from that. As the research findings about blame show, the provider is not limited to formal overall political accountability, but responsibility can be complex with a network of organisations and individuals involved in commissioning and delivering services. For example, as the research by James and colleagues (2016) and Marvel and Girth (2016) shows, simple contracting out of delivery does not necessarily insulate politicians from blame for service failure. There is considerable potential for future experiments to consider the effects on blame of other service structures in different service contexts. For example, responses to failure may vary according to whether citizens are taxpayers and/or users of a service. Taxpayer non-users may care primarily about the tax-financed cost rather than service failure.

The judgements and attitudes formed by citizens and users, including blame, and their views of the service and the structure of service provision, including expectations about future provision, then influence a range of behaviours, including exit or voice. The relationship between citizens and service users on one hand and politicians, public managers, and the range of other actors on the other hand affect how these turn into behaviour. As part of this process, service providers' strategies for giving accounts and excuses, and deflecting responsibility and blame, need to be taken into account, as well as citizen and users' assessments of the efficacy of their action, and the alternatives available to them. There is potential for experiments on these topics, including how they affect users' voice and choice and the trade-off between exit and voice behaviour that has been the focus of much interest in the Hirschman tradition but very little experimental research so far.

Research on voice should extend evidence about the failure to respond to poor performance which has so far been limited to giving citizens information about performance (James and Moseley 2014). This lack of voice could reflect citizens' views that they have low political efficacy in changing the performance of the service provider. The particular experiment was conducted for a local area with chronic low performance such that voice might have been seen as not being worthwhile to undertake. Future experiments could be undertaken for services that have dipped in performance, where the provider is seen as having the capacity to respond to voice and improve services.

References

Alicke, M. D. 2000. 'Culpable control and the psychology of blame'. *Psychological Bulletin* 126(4): 556–574. doi: 10.1177/0146167208321594.

Arceneaux, K. and R. M. Stein. 2006. 'Who is held responsible when disaster strikes? The attribution of responsibility for a natural disaster in an urban election'. *Journal of Urban Affairs* 28(1): 43–53.

Bartling, B. and U. Fischbacher. 2012. 'Shifting the blame: on delegation and responsibility'. *Review of Economic Studies* 79(1): 67–87.

Boyne, G. A., O. James, P. John, and N. Petrovsky. 2009. 'Democracy and government performance: holding incumbents accountable in English local governments'. *Journal of Politics* 71(4): 1273–84.

DeHoog, R. H., D. Lowery, and W. E. Lyons, 1990. 'Citizen satisfaction with local governance: a test of individual, jurisdictional, and city-specific explanations'. *Journal of Politics* 52(3): 807–37.

Dowding, K. M. and P. John. 2012. *Exits, Voices and Social Investments: Citizens' Reaction to Public Services.* Cambridge: Cambridge University Press.

Goodwin, C. and Ross, I. 1992. 'Consumer responses to service failures: influence of procedural and interactional fairness perceptions'. *Journal of Business Research* 25(2): 149–63.

Hirschman, A. O. 1970. *Exit, Voice, and Loyalty: Responses to Decline in Firms, Organizations, and States.* Cambridge, MA: Harvard University Press.

Hirschman, A. O. 1980. '"Exit, voice, and loyalty": further reflections and a survey of recent contributions. The Milbank Memorial Fund Quarterly'. *Health and Society* 430–53.

Hood, C. 2003. 'The risk game and the blame game'. *Government and Opposition* 37(1):15–37.

Hood, C. 2011. *The Blame Game: Spin, Bureaucracy, and Self-Preservation in Government.* Princeton NJ and Oxford: Princeton University Press.

Iyengar, S. S. and Lepper, M. R. 2000. 'When choice is demotivating: can one desire too much of a good thing?' *Journal of Personality and Social Psychology* 79(6): p.995.

James, O. 2011a. 'Performance measures and democracy: information effects on citizens in field and laboratory experiments'. *Journal of Public Administration Research and Theory* 21: 399–418.

James, O. 2011b. 'Managing citizens' expectations of public service performance: evidence from observation and experimentation in local government'. *Public Administration* 89(4):1419–35.

James, O. and P. John. 2007. 'Public management at the ballot box: performance information and electoral support for incumbent English local governments'. *Journal of Public Administration Research and Theory* 17(4): 567–80.

James, O. and A. Moseley. 2014. 'Does performance information about public services affect citizen's perceptions, satisfaction and voice behaviour? Field experiments with absolute and relative performance information'. *Public Administration* 92: 493–511.

James, O., Jilke, S., Petersen, C., and Van de Walle, S. 2016. 'Citizens' blame of politicians for public service failure: experimental evidence about blame reduction through delegation and contracting'. *Public Administration Review* 76(1): 83–93.

Jilke, S. 2015. 'Essays on the Microfoundations of Competition and Choice in Public Service Delivery'. PhD dissertation, Erasmus University Rotterdam.

Jilke, S., N. Petrovsky, B. Meuleman, and O. James. 2016. 'Measurement equivalence in replications of experimental findings: when and why it matters and guidance on how and when to determine equivalence'. *Public Management Review* http://dx.doi.org/10.1080/14719037.2016.1210906

Jilke, S., G. G. Van Ryzin, and S. Van de Walle. 2016. 'Responses to decline in marketized public services: an experimental evaluation of choice overload'. *Journal of Public Administration Research and Theory* 26(3): 421–32.

Lau, R. R. 1982. 'Negativity in political perception'. *Political Behavior* 4(4): 353–78.

Lyons, W. E., D. Lowery, and R. H. DeHoog. 1992. *The Politics of Dissatisfaction: Citizens, Services and Urban Institutions*. London: M.E. Sharpe.

Malhotra, N. and A. G. Kuo. 2008. 'Attributing blame: the public's response to Hurricane Katrina'. *The Journal of Politics* 70(1): 120–35.

Marvel, J. D. and A. M. Girth. 2016. 'Citizen attributions of blame in third-party governance'. *Public Administration Review* 76(1): 96–108.

McGraw, K. M. 1990. 'Avoiding blame: an experimental investigation of political excuses and justifications'. *British Journal of Political Science* 20(1): 119–42.

McGraw, K. M. 1991. 'Managing blame: an experimental test of the effects of political accounts'. *American Political Science Review* 85(4): 1133–57.

Michelson, M. R. and D. W. Nickerson. 2011 'Voter Mobilisation', in Druckman, J. N., Green, D. P., Kuklinski, J. H., and Lupia, A. eds., *Cambridge Handbook of Experimental Political Science*. Cambridge: Cambridge University Press, 228–40.

Mortensen, P. B. 2012. '"It's the central government's fault": elected regional officials' use of blame-shifting rhetoric'. *Governance* 25: 439–61.

Olsen, A. L. 2015. 'Citizen (dis)satisfaction: an experimental equivalence framing study'. *Public Administration Review* 75: 469–78.

Schlenker, B. R., T. W. Britt, J. Pennington, R. Murphy, and K. Doherty. 1994. 'The triangle model of responsibility'. *Psychological Review* 101(4): 632–52.

Soroka, S. N. 2006. 'Good news and bad news: asymmetric responses to economic information'. *The Journal of Politics* 68(2): 372–85.

Sulitzeanu-Kenan, R. 2006. 'If they get it right: an experimental test of the effects of the appointment and reports of UK public inquiries'. *Public Administration* 84(3): 623–53.

Tilley, J. and S. B. Hobolt. 2011. 'Is the government to blame? an experimental test of how partisanship shapes perceptions of performance and responsibility'. *The Journal of Politics* 73(2): 316–30.

Van Slyke, D. and C. H. Roch. 2004. 'What do they know, and whom do they hold accountable? Citizens in the government–nonprofit contracting relationship'. *Journal of Public Administration Research and Theory* 14(2): 191–209.

Weaver, R. K. 1986. 'The politics of blame avoidance'. *Journal of Public Policy* 6(4): 371–98.

Weaver, R. K. 1987. 'The politics of blame'. *The Brookings Review* 5(2): 43–7.

Wong, P. T. and B. Weiner. 1981. 'When people ask "why" questions, and the heuristics of attributional search'. *Journal of Personality and Social Psychology* 40(4): 650–63.

18 Assessing Public Support for Government Policy: Comparing Experimental and Attitudinal Approaches

SCOTT E. ROBINSON, JAMES
W. STOUTENBOROUGH, AND
ARNOLD VEDLITZ

Introduction

In a democratic policy system, the management and administration of policy requires attention to the desires of the democratic public. There are a variety of points in the policy process where this opinion could be relevant – including in the implementation stage that is the subject of much attention in public administration research. As policy makers and public managers choose from among various options, they may need information on the public support or opposition to these various options.

To assess public support, policy makers and public managers have access to a wide variety of tools. Most research into public support for policies has relied on traditional attitudinal research designs. However, an approach has emerged that makes use of experimental methods to provide specific assessments of support in the form of willingness-to-pay (WTP) for specific policy amenities. This chapter uses the case of public support for a variety of water policies to compare the traditional, attitudinal approaches to assessing policy support to the experimental, WTP approaches. The comparison will illustrate the types of policies and circumstances that best fit each approach.[1]

---

[1] It is important to note that this chapter will focus on a comparison of the methods of attitudinal and experimental approaches to assessing policy support rather than on the substance of water policy.

Traditional Approaches to Assess Policy Support

The traditional approach to assessing policy support is to ask direct attitudinal questions about specific policies. The respondent is presented with a scale to measure support. This scale can be as simple as allowing respondents to choose between 'support' or 'oppose' options. More complex scales can provide ordered options (e.g., 'strongly support', 'support', 'no opinion', 'oppose', 'strongly oppose')[2] or ratio measures (e.g., scales of 0–10 or even 0–100).

Public managers and policy makers can analyse the results of these attitudinal approaches in a variety of ways. One can provide a direct summary of the survey results. This may take the form of the percentage of the respondents who choose 'support' (or the combination of 'support' and 'strongly support') compared to 'oppose' (or the combination of 'oppose' and 'strongly oppose'). Of course, one can break out the ordered responses in full detail if there is a meaningful interpretation of the results that distinguishes the 'strong' versions of each response.

Directly interpreting the numerical scales is more difficult. There is no natural interpretation of any but the extreme points on the scale. If the average level of support is zero, it is clear opposition is strong. Similarly, average levels of support at the maximum of the scale indicate strong support. Between these extreme values, it is hard to interpret any specific number. Is a 7 (out of 10) evidence of strong support? It is hard to tell because the scale itself has no natural units.

With numerical attitudinal scales, the clearer alternative is to provide only comparative assessments. While it may be difficult to interpret a specific score like a 7, one can argue that a policy with an average support of 7 is more supported than one with an average support of 5. One can use relatively simple statistical techniques to compare the support scores of two or more policies and evaluate whether any differences are statistically significant.

The need to shift to a comparison of levels of support is an indication of the difficulty in interpreting attitudinal measures of support. The simplest measures ('support' vs. 'oppose') provide little nuance in the degrees of support (or opposition). Scales with the opportunity for more nuances create difficulty in interpretation. Most fundamentally, it

[2] To take a recent Pew poll as an example, various questions used ordered responses options such as: 'top priority', 'important but lower priority', 'not too important', 'should not be done', and 'don't know/refuse to answer' (Pew 2016).

is not obvious that all respondents mean the same thing by a support level of 7. If respondents have varying interpretations of these values, their choice of values is difficult to interpret. Two respondents may have the same underlying level of support but choose a 6 and an 8, respectively, because of the differences in how they interpret the scale. As a result, scales raise questions of inter-respondent comparability in proportion to the number of options the respondents have. The trade-off between nuance (with more scale options) and inter-respondent comparability issues is unavoidable in these cases.

The raw support scores are not the only way to analyse public support for policies. While the raw support may be the most important piece of information for public managers and policy makers, there may also be interest in how different factors are related to these levels of support. Does policy support vary based on the demographics of the respondents? For example, is support stronger or weaker among older respondents? Alternatively, one can assess whether levels of support vary based on other attitudes, ideological identification, and party identification. While policy makers may not be able to change the ideologies or party identifications of potential opponents of the policy (much less change the demographic composition of her or his commu-nity), this information may provide some insight into which commu-nities the policy maker will have to persuade to generate support.

The non-experimental nature of the multivariate models typically used to address such questions presents several well-understood (if some-times underappreciated) limitations of interpretation. For example, because there is a close relationship between ideological attitudes and party identification (even if this relationship is not perfect), including both variables in a multivariate model makes the interpretation of results difficult. The coefficients that emerge from the statistical analysis assume that all other variables are held constant. The effect of party identifica-tion, then, is based on the assumption that ideology is held constant. What does a one-unit change in party identification mean when holding ideology constant? Among the respondents, a close correlation between party identification and ideology would indicate that these values often change together. At the extreme ranges of ideology, for example, one may find very few people of the traditionally opposed party. Given the lack of independence between these variables, changes in one (mathe-matically separated from changes in the other) can be difficult to inter-pret. Even in situations where the connection is not as strong, it is not clear that one really can separate the effect of key demographic characteristics (like age, education, income, etc.) from the attitudes to which they are related. For example, one can estimate the separate effects of party identification and ideology. One can then estimate the expected change in the dependent variable related to the change in each independent variable. One could assess the change in expected value of the dependent variable of moving from very conservative to very liberal – holding all other variables constant (including party identification). However, in practice, a change from very conservative to very liberal has a high probability of being associated with a change in party identification as well. Separating these effects may become difficult.

This difficulty in interpretation stems from the non-experimental nature of the data. Because the researcher does not control the application of the treatments (in non-experimental models, these are the various independent variables), one may face closely correlated variables or variables that one cannot change in practice. For example, one may assess the connection of party identification and the salience of terrorism to a respondent. With the non-experimental approach, the treatment (party identification) is observed rather than applied to the research subject. In practice, one cannot simply declare people to be of one party or another. This severely limits our ability to make causal inferences from these sorts of data. One cannot interpret the results of these sorts of non-experimental treatments (where the experimenter does not control the application or distribution of the treatment) to the classical experimental model. The resulting non-experimental data must be interpreted as correlative and one must take great care to account for endogeneity and other threats to inference.

A Multivariate Attitudinal Model of Water Policy Support

To illustrate the traditional attitudinal approach to assessing policy support, we present the results of a survey that included a question battery about support for various policies intended to ensure water quality and accessibility. Knowledge Networks (now GfK) administered the survey on behalf of the Institute of Science, Technology and Public Policy at Texas A&M University.[3]

---

[3] The nationwide survey was conducted in 2013, and the total number of respondents was 2,625. The full survey instrument is available from the authors on request.

We take from this survey a series of questions about support for water policies. Water policies have become an important policy area with the current drought in California and recent droughts in many areas in the United States (Christian-Smith and Fleick 2012). The importance of this policy area has led to previous investigations into the public opinion related to water policy (Clay et al. 2007; Menegeki et al. 2007; Stoutenborough and Vedlitz 2014). Prior research into public support for various water policy options has focused on the attitudinal approach of measurement (e.g., Stoutenborough and Vedlitz 2014). We will use this illustration of the attitudinal measures of support for water policies to illustrate the strengths and weaknesses of the approach and as a basis for comparison to the experimental approach described later.

We will start our demonstration with an analysis of raw support scores for three specific water policies. The three water policies were to: (1) build infrastructure (dams, reservoirs, pipelines) to support water demands during a drought, (2) require mandatory water conservation, and (3) give tax incentives for the installation of water saving equipment. For each policy, respondents were allowed to indicate 'strongly support', 'support', 'unsure', 'oppose', or 'strongly oppose'. A modest number of respondents to each question refused to answer. Table 18.1 provides the distribution of responses across each option for each policy option.

It is immediately apparent how much consensus there is across these dissimilar policy options. There is more strong support for tax incentives than the other two policy options (and a corresponding reduction

Table 18.1: *Descriptive results of attitudes toward water policy options (in percentages)*

	Strongly Oppose	Oppose	Unsure	Support	Strongly Support	Refused
Invest in Infrastructure	1	5	34	44	13	3
Mandatory Conservation	4	13	38	32	9	4
Tax Incentives	2	4	25	48	18	4

N = 2,624

in strong opposition). For the most part, the distributions of the support scores are similar across the policies with support being the modal response for tax incentives and infrastructure. There is less support for mandatory conservation measures, with only modest increases in opposition and 'unsure' becoming the modal response.

This descriptive representation of the support for various policy options provides modest information for policy makers and public managers. There seems to be some level of support for action that bridges different policy instruments. The choice of instruments may matter, however, with public support for mandatory conservation measures being softer (including more 'unsure' responses). The difference in opposition to tax incentives and infrastructure investment is only in the single digits.

Of course, surveys can reveal more about the nature of the support for these policy types than the raw support scores. One can investigate the various correlates of this support using multivariate models. To illustrate this option for investigating policy support, we regressed various demographic factors (gender, age, income), political ideological factors (party identification), and general policy attitudes (general support for government action to address water availability) on the support for these three policy options.[4] Table 18.2 presents the results of an ordered logit analysis of these models.

There is more information here about the dynamics of support for each of the policies and how some members of the community are more (or less) supportive of each policy. The support for each policy becomes more differentiable than it looked in the raw results. Consider the case of party identification. The baseline category for each model is self-identified independents. Republicans are more supportive than independents of infrastructure investment, while Democrats are not statistically differentiable from independents (using the common 0.05 level of statistical significance). This relationship flips for mandatory conservation and tax incentives. In each of those two cases, the Democrats are more supportive of the policy while the Republicans are statistically

---

[4] This chapter focuses on the strength and limitations of the various methods of evaluating policy support. For this reason, we will not go into great detail in the justification of the particular independent variables or the substantive implications of the findings for water policy and public opinion. These models should be considered illustrative of the various approaches.

Table 18.2: *Multivariate analysis of support for water policy options (P-statistics are in parentheses based on robust standard errors.)*

	Infrastructure Investment	Mandatory Conservation	Tax Incentives
Democrat	0.11 (0.237)	0.31 (< 0.001)***	0.30 (0.001)**
Republican	0.34(< 0.001)***	0.02 (0.862)	0.21 (0.025)*
Education Level	−0.01 (0.857)	0.01 (−0.828)	0.24(< 0.001)***
Gender (Female)	−0.06 (0.439)	0.18 (0.015)*	0.06 (0.402)
Income Level	0.02 (0.058)	−0.004 (0.962)	0.02 (0.034)*
Age	0.02 (< 0.001)***	0.01 (< 0.001)***	0.01(0.001)**
General Interest in Government Action	0.12 (< 0.001)***	0.26 (< 0.001)***	0.17(< 0.001)***
N	2,624	2,624	2,624
Wald Test	137.73 (7 df)	361.07 (7 df)	243.86 (7 df)

$* = p < 0.05$, $** = p < 0.01$, $*** = p < 0.001$

indistinguishable from independents. The policy options obviously have varied appeal to people with different party identifications.

There are some differences across demographic characteristics – but only modest differences. Increasing levels of income (here measured on a 19-point scale – not in dollars) are associated with higher levels of support for infrastructure investment and tax incentives. The differences are modest with a one-category increase in income having only a fraction of the effect of party identification. Similarly, increasing age (in years) has a modest association with increasing support for infrastructure investment and mandatory conservation. In the case of mandatory conservation, it takes a 30-year difference in age to equal the difference between Democrats and independents.

Finally, there is a large and significant association between the belief that 'government should take action in dealing with water issues in your area'[5] and the support for these specific water policies. For each of the policies, this general attitude toward government action to address water needs was strongly associated with support for the specific policies. The size of the effect varied (with mandatory conservation

[5] This was measured on a 0–10 scale from 'no need for government action' to '[there is] a strong role for government to act'.

having the strongest effect), but this factor was significant across each policy option.

The general attitude toward government action to address water issues is a useful place to summarise the limitations of the traditional survey approach to assessing water support. It will surprise few people that this general attitude is related to greater support for specific water policies. It is not clear what a policy maker or water manager can do with such information. Like demographic and ideological characteristics, it is not clear how a policy maker or public manager can change this characteristic if he or she wanted to increase support for a policy. More troubling, this attitude is likely closely related to ideological attitudes. It is not clear that we can attribute causal direction to the relationship given the closely connected nature of these variables. Knowing there is a correlation between party identification and support for the water policies may provide some guidance on the audience that will require persuasion, but it does not provide a mechanism for accomplishing this persuasion.

The fundamental problem with this approach (and why one has to use guarded language like 'is associated with' rather than 'causes') is that the independent variables are not experimental treatments controlled by the investigators. The respondents come to the survey with their party identifications, ages, general attitudes toward policy making, etc. These are not randomly assigned and are often deeply interconnected. As a result, isolating the effect of any particular independent variable is exceedingly difficult.

An Experimental Alternative to Assessing Policy Support

There is an alternative tradition to studying support for public policies coming from environmental economics (Mitchell and Carson 1989), an approach that eventually adopted an experimental approach. This approach seeks to put a monetary value on goods that are not traded on an actual market. Examples of these sorts of goods include water quality and access to public amenities like parks. Since there is no direct trade in the goods, there is no mechanism to establish a price for the amenity. Policy makers may want to put a dollar value on the amenity to assess whether it is defensible to invest in the amenity at the level required to support its continued provision. For example, a policy maker or public manager may want to know whether the million-dollar annual budget for a local park is warranted given the level of support within the community of potential users of the park. While there are methods for assessing the 'use value' of the park (by admissions and fees), these methods are thought to ignore the 'passive use' or 'existence value' of amenities – the values generated for non-users by knowing that the amenity exists, could potentially be used in the future, or that are used in ways that do not generate typical indicators of 'use value' such as admissions (Arrow et al. 1993: 2). The key was to identify the public's 'willingness-to-pay' (WTP for an amenity). The result was a method known as WTP studies or contingent valuation (CV) methods. These methods continue to be popular (Bateman 2002; Competition Commission 2010) – especially in the domain of environmental policy and management (Stigka et al. 2014).

The earliest approach to establishing the WTP was to ask a direct question much like the attitudinal approaches to support reviewed in the previous section (Mitchell and Carson 1989). A survey could simply ask a respondent how much he or she would be willing to pay to ensure continued access to the amenity. The survey expected respondents to provide a dollar amount with as little (potentially leading) material in the question itself.

The direct elicitation of a WTP figure for a respondent was subject to several criticisms (Arrow et al. 1993). It is not clear how respondents come up with their answer to the question. The decision situation is entirely artificial with no actual money exchanging hands. This may allow respondents to dramatically exaggerate their actual WTP. There is no actual commitment in the survey, so people can exaggerate their WTP for policies they support. The result was an unreliable estimate (likely overestimate) of WTP that may not provide much insight into the actual support for the policy (Arrow et al. 1993: 12–13).

An experimental approach emerged to address some of the problems (Arrow et al. 1993: 18–25). Rather than asking respondents for a dollar amount, a referendum approach asks respondents to either support or oppose a specific proposed dollar amount. Respondents are provided a randomly determined dollar amount within some reasonable range. For example, the survey may ask whether the respondent would support an increase of $10 a month to their water bill to pay for a new water treatment technology. Respondents may be provided a random dollar amount between $5 and $15. The result is a system that is robust against strategic overestimate. One cannot declare that you are willing to pay an unrealistic amount to skew the results (like $1,000 more a month on a water bill). This approach does not completely eliminate the possibility that respondents strategically support a proposed price that they would not actually pay. However, the reduction of the choice to support or opposition reduces the potential bias of radically exaggerated, unrealistic dollar amounts proposed to the respondents (Arrow et al. 1993).

The experimental approach also provides an advantage over the traditional attitudinal approaches discussed in the previous section. The randomisation of the treatment (the proposed prices for the referendum) disconnects the treatment from correlation with other variables. This allows one to study the treatment as an experiment and not worry about the correlation between the treatment and other (even unmeasured) correlates. The treatment (the proposed prices) is strongly independent of other variables, allowing for one to make causal inferences where this was difficult with the attitudinal and other non-experimental approaches. Here the treatment is randomised and uncorrelated with the other attributes. Any effect of the random treatment is uncontaminated by correlation with other independent variables.

Furthermore, the referendum approach simulates a realistic experience (an actual referendum). The respondents to surveys are unlikely to ever be asked an open-ended question on a ballot. This renders a traditional WTP/CV open-ended question peculiar. A referendum question, on the other hand, simulates a realistic experience of being asked an 'up or down' question on a referendum ballot. This realism in the decision task should contribute to the external validity of the study results (Arrow et al. 1993: 25). These advantages have led the more recent assessments to similarly prefer experimental approaches to contingent valuation and WTP over direct solicitation of prices (Competition Commission 2010).

The referendum approach is not without its critics. In a study comparing traditional CV approaches to the referendum approach, Carson and colleagues (1998) demonstrate that the more elaborate referendum approaches did not lead to dramatically different results. The exception to the general similarity of the results in their case related to the Exxon Valdez oil spill was that the referendum approach had more respondents choose 'not sure/don't know' for their response. These results may indicate that non-experimental CV results are comparable to experimental referenda approaches, but they fail to demonstrate a dramatic flaw in the referendum design.

A second key limitation of this approach is the specificity of the treatment – a proposed price for the policy. The reduction of policy support to WTP is non-problematic for certain types of policies, particularly policies that call for the direct expenditure of public funds (raised through taxes) to provide a service. This framework fits the canonical examples of parks and environmental amenities. The framework is less well suited for policies that do not have such a direct connection between expenditures and an amenity. A regulatory policy, for example, would be difficult to assess in terms of a WTP. In the regulatory policy, the expenditures would be related to the regulatory personnel and any general economic effect of the regulation. This indirect connection between expenditures and the provision of the amenity renders the mental exercise of a hypothetical WTP even more abstract.

Most fundamentally, the experimental referendum approach does not avoid the problem of being a hypothetical scenario in which there is no credible commitment to exchange resources. Just as with the original WTP approaches, the survey respondent may be willing to exaggerate his or her willingness to accept a specific referendum proposal strategically if he or she supports the policy in general. The referendum approach minimises this bias by reducing the choice set to accept or oppose, but the bias is still present. The result could be an inflated absolute value of the average WTP but may still allow for useful inferences about how the willingness to accept a referendum changes in the value of the proposal.

An Experimental Model of Water Policy Support

To illustrate the experimental approach to evaluate policy support, we implemented a referendum-style WTP experiment in the survey discussed earlier. Respondents were asked to accept or oppose a proposed increase of $1 to $10 a month on their water bill to 'guarantee a secure supply of water in your area'. Respondents only saw a whole dollar value between $1 and $10 with the treatments balanced across each of these 11 options. Which dollar amount each respondent saw was randomised.

We will start with two basic models of the experimental results illustrating the effect of the proposed cost of water sustainability on support for the policy. Each model is a logit regression with robust

Table 18.3: *Raw toward water policy results (P-statistics are in parentheses based on robust standard errors.)*

	Linear Model	Dummy Variable Model
Dollar Increase (linear)	−0.12 (< 0.001)***	
Increase from $1 to $2		−0.17 (0.390)
Increase from $1 to $3		−0.41 (0.037)*
Increase from $1 to $4		−0.41 (0.038)*
Increase from $1 to $5		−0.56 (0.004)**
Increase from $1 to $6		−0.86 (< 0.001)***
Increase from $1 to $7		−0.74 (< 0.001)***
Increase from $1 to $8		−0.99 (< 0.001)***
Increase from $1 to $9		−1.03 (< 0.001)***
Increase from $1 to $10		−1.03 (< 0.001)***
Constant		
n	2,568	2,568
Wald Test	65.14 (1 df)	70.56 (9 df)

* = $p < 0.05$, ** = $p < 0.01$, *** = $p < 0.001$

standard errors since the dependent variable is either support for (the positive outcome) or opposition to the water policy referendum. Table 18.3 presents the results of these basic analyses.

The linear model takes the cost treatment as a linear independent variable increasing from a proposed $1 increase on water bills to $10. As expected, increases in the proposed cost are related to a reduction of support for the referendum. Remember that the prompts were randomised. This means that the various factors we previously saw related to support for water policies (party identification, age, etc.) are not related to the application of the treatment. The result is a strong inference that increases in the proposed cost of water policy cause a reduction in support for the water policy.

Another advantage of the referendum approach is the option to break down the treatment into specific prompts to look for inconsistencies in the trend across the dollar values. An ideal response would increase steadily for each dollar increase proposed with the effect of a $1 increase being identical between $1 and $2 or $9 and $10. To assess the accuracy of the linearity assumption of the first model on Table 18.3, we also present a model where each treatment from $2 to

$10 (with $1 being the baseline) is allowed to have a separate effect. The results of this analysis are in the second column of Table 18.3.

The investigation of the linearity assumption reveals modest variations from the ideal linear trend but, ultimately, that the linear assumption is justified. The dummy variable for the difference between $1 and $2 is not statistically significant. However, all of the other differences are statistically significant at the 0.05 level. There are some points where the linearity seems to break down temporarily. The coefficients suggest that the trend is flat from $3 to $4 and from $9 to $10. There is also a particularly large jump from $5 to $6. However, the Wald test statistics of the two models suggest that there was only a small gain (5.42 on the likelihood value) for the extra eight degrees of freedom. Simulations of the predicted probability suggest that each increase of a dollar in the referendum price reduces the predicted support probability by 2 per cent with a 73 per cent support at $1 and just under a 50 per cent support level (49.2%) at $10.

While this provides concrete information about the predicted levels of support at varying prices of the amenity (water sustainability, for this example), there is more that one can investigate with the experimental WTP model. One can look at whether levels of support vary across specific subpopulations within the community. Specifically, one can investigate whether either the slope (the responsiveness to increases in price) or the intercept (general support that is not responsive to price) of the WTP function changes among different subpopulations. Given the importance of party identification in the earlier models of support for water policies, we illustrate this approach by investigating whether any differences exist between two subpopulations and other respondents in their support for the referendum: Democrats and people who reported high levels of support for government action to address water sustainability. The results are reported in Table 18.4.

The subpopulation analysis always compares members of a specific subpopulation to all other members of the population. In the first subpopulation analysis, we compared Democrats to all other members of the samples. As expected, the linear trend for the dollar increase in the referendum is still significant. The lack of statistical significance of the interaction term indicates that Democrats are no more or less responsive to the increases in the referendum price than non-Democrats. The lack of a party identification effect on the slope of the WTP curve is interesting given the strong effect of party

Table 18.4: *The subpopulation analysis of Democrats in the willingness to pay experiment (P-statistics are in parentheses based on robust standard errors.)*

	Democrat Subpopulation Model	Pro-action Subpopulation Model
Dollar Increase (linear)	–0.12 (< 0.001)***	–0.13 (< 0.001)***
Subpopulation Effect	0.42 (0.034)*	0.69 (< 0.001)***
Interaction of Subpopulation and cost	0.01 (0.760)	0.01 (0.643)
Constant	0.99 (< 0.001)***	0.86 (< 0.001)***
N	2,568	2,568
Wald	91.17 (3 df)	150.32 (3 df)

* = $p < 0.05$, ** = $p < 0.01$, *** = $p < 0.001$

identification in the earlier models. There is an effect on the intercept, however. Democrats are more likely to support the referendum across all levels (though, again, not in a way that alters the slope of the WTP curve). Thus, while Democrats are more supportive of the referendum, they are affected similarly by price increases. To illustrate this point, simulations suggest that at a $1 referendum price, a Democrat is expected to support the referendum with a 79 per cent probability. This compares to the unconditional support of 73 per cent in the full population model. Even at the $10 level, a Democrat is expected to support the referendum at 57 per cent probability, compared to 49 per cent in the full population model.

The analysis of the subpopulation supporting government action to address local water issues (which includes those who responded with a 6 or greater on the 11-point scale, a group that makes up 46% of the sample) finds a similar pattern. Supporters of government action to address water issues are more supportive of the referenda in general, but again their response to increases in the proposed referendum price does not differ from the rest of the population. Interestingly, the differences in baseline level of support (the constant) between supporters and opponents of government action are even greater than the differences based on party identification. Simulations reveal that pro-government action respondents have an expected support probability of 81 per cent for referenda priced at $1. This is greater for the general population (73%) or Democrats (79%). At the $10 referendum, pro-government action respondents have a predicted support probability of 61 per cent (compared to 57% for Democrats and 49% for the full population). This more specific attitude linked to government action in the domain of water policy has a stronger effect than the more general effect of party identification.

One has to interpret the subpopulation analyses with caution. While the experimental treatment (the referendum price) is randomised, the subpopulation indicators are not. Affiliating oneself with a political party is not random. The results provide evidence that Democrats are more supportive of the referenda (and, thereby, action to promote water sustainability), but they respond to changes in referendum prices just as everyone else does. This is evidence that the treatment effect is not conditional on this particular subpopulation, but the general effect is not an experimental one and all normal caveats about non-experimental models apply to that inference. The same is true of the subpopulation who is supportive of government action to address water needs. They respond to the experimental treatment in a way that is not statistically distinguishable from the general population but have more support of the referenda in general.

Discussion and Conclusion

The preceding analyses provide two distinct approaches to studying support for government policies. In the first set of examples, we employed a traditional survey approach to ask for levels of support on a point scale (here an 11-point scale). The approach provides some evidence of similar levels of support across the various policy options – but with the presence of some differences. The more detailed multi-variate analysis revealed some patterns within the support data, suggesting that different groups supported different policies to different degrees. Party identification and support for government action in general were related to levels of support. However, this approach faces substantial challenges when it comes to causal inference. The independent variables (like party identification, support for government action, age, etc.) are not controlled by the researcher and are not randomly distributed in the population. Complex (or even simple) interactions between these factors make it quite difficult to make causal inferences.

The alternative to the traditional survey approach was an experiment based on a willingness-to-pay referendum. Here the researcher is able to randomise the treatment to separate the effect of price differences from the various demographic or ideological factors. The results of the experimental component of the study were clear. People, as expected, supported water policies less as the cost increased. In probability terms, a strong majority (73%) eroded to less than a majority (49%) as the price of the proposed water policy increased from $1 to $10 a month. A non-experimental supplement to this analysis revealed that the stronger support for government action on water sustainability, as well as affiliation with the Democratic Party, are associated with a general increase in support for the referenda. But there were no difference in responsiveness to the experimental treatment for either of these subgroups, when compared to the rest of the population.

Each of these approaches promises different sorts of insights into public support for programs. The attitudinal approach provides for targeted assessments of specific programs. This case of water policies revealed that support was generally similar across three different water policy tools with weaker support for mandatory conservation than tax incentives and infrastructure investment. This approach allowed for a more nuanced analysis of the differences in support across various social groups with modest differences observed across ages and incomes but noticeable differences across partisan identification and support of general government action in the domain.

This case demonstrated the utility of the attitudinal approach, but also highlighted some of the limitations. The direct interpretation of the levels of support is difficult to interpret. It is not clear what strong support means and whether a specific policy is likely to exceed what may be soft support for the policies. The respondents may support conservation requirements – until the specific requirements begin to fall on them personally. Comparative judgments are possible, but the ambiguity of the underlying scales may raise questions about the importance of these differences. More importantly, the independent variables in the multivariate analysis are not controlled or randomised. As a result, it is hard to make any causal inference and a policy maker or public manager may wonder what the use is of information about factors she or he cannot control.

The experimental alternative, in the form of a WTP referendum survey, addresses this need for causal inference. The WTP referendum allows for the randomisation for the treatment (a price on the referendum). Randomisation creates the opportunity for strong causal inferences about the treatment. The limitation is that this opportunity is limited to a specific form of treatment and a limited range of policy options. The approach only works to derive a price. For questions that are not related to price or where price is not the primary issue, the approach will not provide a great deal of insight. Where this evaluative tool fits the question, it provides a strong answer. However, it may not fit in all cases.

Despite these limitations, the experimental approach may provide useful information for public managers across a range of situations. Being able to connect policy proposals to specific prices provides the most specific information available for the political viability of different projects where the costs will fall to the public. This can help in defining the viability of bond elections, increases in fees, etc. in areas ranging from utility services (as studied here) to education, environmental remediation, or parks and recreation.

The experimental approaches also provide a plausible counterpart to the demographic and ideological investigations common in the non-experimental tradition. The ability to assess how the slope and the intercept of the proposed prices vary across subpopulations allows for the identification of groups likely to oppose a policy and whether the opposition is a function of the specific cost (subpopulations with different slope estimates) or likely to be present regardless of price (subpopulations with different intercept estimates). These sorts of assessments open up new possibilities for public managers across a wide range of policy areas.

In the end, the key will be for policy makers and public managers to fit the tool for assessing public support to the situation at hand. There are significant difficulties in learning from attitudinal survey data. However, the method allows for great flexibility in the nature of policies and types of support or opposition. The experimental approach provides stronger inferences, but can only do so within a specific type of question and a specific type of evaluation. Each strategy has its strengths and weaknesses and each – possibly in combination – has an important place in the repertoire of public administrators and policy makers.

References

Arrow, K. J., R. Solow, P. R. Portney, E. E. Leamer, R. Radner, and H. Schulman. 1993. 'Report of the NOAA panel on contingent valuation', *Federal Register* 58: 10 (January 15, 1993), 4601–14.

Bateman, I. J., R. T. Carson, B. Day, W. M. Hanemann, N. Hanley, T. Hett, M. Jones Lee, G. Loomes, S. Mourato, E. Ozdemiroglu, and D. W. Pearce 2002. *Economic Valuation with Stated Preference Techniques: A Manual.* Northampton, MA: Edwin Elgar.

Carson, R. T., W. M. Hanemann, R. J. Kopp, J. A. Krosnick, R. C. Mitchell, S. Presser, P. A. Ruud, V. K. Smith, M. Conway, and K. Martin 1998. 'Referendum design and contingent valuation: the NOAA panels' no-vote recommendation', *The Review of Economics and Statistics* 80(2): 335–8.

Christian-Smith, J., P. H. Gleick, H. Cooley, L. Allen, A. Vandenwarker, and K. A. Berry 2012. *A Twenty-First Century US Water Policy.* New York: Oxford University Press.

Clay, D. E., C. Ren, C. Reese, R. Waskom, J. Bauder, N. Mesner, G. Paige, K. Reddy, M. Neibauer, and R. Mahler 2007. 'Linking public attitudes with perceptions of factors impacting water and attending learning activities', *Journal of Natural Resources and Life Sciences Education* 36: 36–44.

Competition Commission 2010. *Review of Stated Preference and Willingness to Pay Methods.* Retrieved from www.competition-commission.org.uk/our_role/analysis/summary_and_report_combined.pdf. Accessed February 2, 2016.

Menegaki, A. N., N. Hanley, and K. P. Tsagarakis 2007. 'The social acceptability and valuation of recycled water in Crete: a study of consumers' and farmers' attitudes', *Ecological Economics* 62(1): 7–18.

Mitchell, R. C. and R. T. Carson 1989. *Using Surveys to Value Public Goods: The Contingent Valuation Method.* Washington, DC: Resources for the Future.

Pew Research Center 2016. 'January 2016 religion and politics survey', Available at: www.people-press.org/2016/01/22/budget-deficit-slips-as-public-priority/. Accessed 2 February 2016.

Stigka, E. K., J. A. Paravantis, and G. K. Mihalakakou 2014. 'Social acceptance of renewable energy sources: a review of contingent valuation applications', *Renewable and Sustainable Energy Reviews* 32 (April): 100–6.

Stoutenborough, J. W. and A. Vedlitz 2014. 'Public attitudes toward water management and drought in the united states', *Water Resource Management* 28: 697–714.

19 Legislative Oversight of the Bureaucracy: Insights from Formal Modelling and Experimental Testing

SUSUMU SHIKANO, MICHAEL F. STOFFEL,
AND MARKUS TEPE

Introduction

Formal models have become an important and powerful analytical instrument within political science (see Hinich and Munger 1997; Morton 1999), and their clarity and flexibility also allows researchers to describe and analyse complex interactions in the field of public management (see Bendor 1988; Gailmard and Patty 2012 Gehlbach 2013; and Gill 1995 for review). According to Morton, a model is formal 'when a researcher expresses the real-world situation in abstract and symbolic terms in a set of explicitly stated assumptions' (1999: 36). The virtue of formal models is twofold. First, in contrast to theoretical models that dispense with formal description, formal models proceed from stating a set of axioms and then entail the use of logical rules of proof to derive empirical propositions. In this respect, they force researchers to focus on the relevant parts of a theoretical argument or mechanism, discarding irrelevant or marginal aspects. Thereby, they help to formulate and explore clear causal mechanism. Second, they allow researchers to derive predictions about human behaviour in a specific decision situation, sometimes including 'precise quantitative predictions about behaviour' (Palfrey 2006: 916). Depending on the specific type of social interaction that is described by a formal model, social choice and game theory offer analytical tools (e.g., spatial modelling, backward induction, Nash equilibria) to solve such models and to derive predictions of human behaviour. Laboratory experiments serve to test the empirical validity of these predictions. To do so, it is of particular importance that the experimental design fully represents the decision situation described by the formal model without becoming self-affirmative or even trivial.

Analytical precision and the ability to predict come at the expense of some rigorous but sometimes contested assumptions about human behaviour, with many formal models using the assumption sometimes referred to as *homo economicus*. Formal models of bureaucracy assume instrumentally rational and self-interested agents. Thus, the prediction derived from a formal model presumes that the *homo economicus* assumption is true. The natural research design to test the empirical validity of predictions derived from a formal model is the use of laboratory experiments, which are discussed in more detail in Chapter 7. The controlled environment of a laboratory experiment enables researchers to out their model to a test in its stylised form, that is, to alter the model parameter of theoretical interest while keeping all other parameters constant and thereby attributing differences in behaviour to differences in the setting of a model parameter.

Within the field of political economy, there is a long-standing tradition of testing such formal model predictions with experimental methods (see Palfrey 2006 for an overview; Palfrey 2009). This strand of research dates back to Charles Plott, who himself was inspired by Vernon Smith's work in experimental economics (e.g., Plott and Smith 1978; see also Fiorina and Plott 1978). In explicating his approach, Smith (1982) emphasised that experiments allow for a micro-economic system that encompasses a well-specified environment and a set of institutions, which are in accordance with the formal model at stake. At the same time, Smith and others have developed a toolbox to generate such micro-systems in the laboratory setting (e.g., the induced value theory).

Ironically, experimental results obtained from testing formal models often deviate from the predicted solution (e.g., for rates of cooperation that deviate from equilibrium prediction in the prisoners' dilemma; see Cooper et al. (1996) or Kahn and Murnighan (1993), and in the trust game, see, e.g., Johnson and Mislin (2001)). In sum, these experimental findings are no longer considered an artefact, but launched a process of reconsidering the validity of the *homo economicus* assumption. To what extent such deviations can also be observed in laboratory tests of formal models of bureaucracy will be addressed in this chapter using the example of legislative oversight.

The virtues of formal modelling and experimental studies for public management research can be demonstrated using the context of bureaucrat behaviour under different oversight regimes. For this purpose, we follow a hands-on approach to explain the nexus between formal modelling and experimental testing using a modified version of the so-called oversight game. This particular game describes the standard principal-agent problem, which is prominent in public management research. In its simplest form, a principal (e.g., minister) delegates a task to an agent (e.g., civil servant). The latter then fulfils the task on behalf of the former as long as their preferences are in line with each other. However, if preferences diverge or if we allow for slack, the result induced by the agent's behaviour will not be optimal for the principal because monitoring is partial at best.

We proceed as follows. In the next section, we explain how the oversight game is set up as a formal model and how the model is solved in order to obtain predictions about the behaviour of legislators and bureaucrats. Moreover, we show how researchers can extend or modify a model. One reason for modifying an existing model is to determine whether different institutional settings (represented through different versions of the model) induce different behavioural patterns. For example, in the principal–agent interaction of principal and bureaucrat, it may make a difference whether employees are hired (and fired) according to their political leanings after an election (United States) or whether they are hired as a civil servant and cannot be replaced (Germany). The subsequent section demonstrates how the oversight game can be implemented in a laboratory experiment. In the fourth section, we give advice on how human behaviour in the laboratory should be analysed and compared with predicted behaviour. In the concluding section, we discuss further benefits and limitations of formal modelling and experimental testing in public management, setting out an agenda for future research.

Setting Up a Formal Model of Oversight and Deriving Predictions

The relationship between legislators and bureaucrats has been described and analysed using the principal-agent framework. That is, bureaucrats implement laws on behalf of legislators. If both bureaucrats and legislators share common interests, bureaucrats' expertise makes the implementation of laws efficient and effective. However, if their preferences diverge, bureaucrats shirk or even sabotage the legislators' goals (Brehm and Gates 1999). Legislators can take precautions

Table 19.1: *Pay-off structure of the inspection game*

	Control		No Control	
Crime		−c+r		0
	y−f		y	
No crime		−c		0
	0		0	

against such non-compliant behaviour by bureaucrats. One way is by undertaking so-called police patrol oversight in which legislators monitor and, if necessary, punish bureaucrats (McCubbins and Schwartz 1984). Of course, legislators have to bear the costs for monitoring in this vein. As the name 'police patrol oversight' indicates, the situation of legislators and bureaucrats is quite similar to the strategic interaction between policemen and citizens, for whom the inspection game was formulated initially (Rauhut 2009; Tsebelis 1990).

The basic setup of the inspection game is as follows. There are two players, a policeman and a citizen, who interact in the sequential game. Either of them has two actions at his disposal to choose from. First, the citizen decides whether to commit a crime. Second, the policeman decides whether to control the citizen. Neither of them has information about the other player's decision.

Mutual pay-offs of the players are represented in Table 19.1, in which actions of the citizen (policeman) are given in rows (columns). Within each strategy pair (e.g., crime-control), the citizen's utility resulting from the actions is given first (here: $y-f$). If a citizen commits a crime and is not controlled by the policeman, he receives a benefit of $y > 0$. However, if he is controlled, he has to pay a penalty fee of size $f > 0$. For the policeman, controlling is associated with costs $c > 0$, but if he detects a crime, he is rewarded for his service with r. We do not include further agents in our model here (e.g., victims, judges) because we are solely interested in the strategic interaction of policemen and citizens.

There are different concepts by which games in the given form can be solved. In this chapter, we rely on the most prominent of these, the so-called Nash equilibrium, which states that no player in an N-person game has an incentive to unilaterally deviate from his strategy given the strategies of all other players (Nash 1951). Stated differently, there is no other strategy that gives each player a higher expected utility than her current strategy given the current strategies of all other players (though there may be strategies that give the same expected utility). Depending on the specific parameter configuration, different trivial or more interesting equilibria emerge from the setting. We present the rather trivial situations first. Given that costs of patrolling exceed the possible reward, the policeman provides no oversight and the citizen always commits a crime. Likewise, if the benefit from committing a crime exceeds a possible punishment, the citizen again always commits a crime. Yet in the more meaningful situation in which both the fee for the citizen exceeds the benefit from committing a crime (f > y > 0) and the reward for the policeman exceeds the patrolling cost (r > c > 0), there is no Nash equilibrium in pure strategies. A pure strategy is a strategy which completely defines the player's action.

However, we can allow players to assign positive probability to more than one strategy, i.e., to play more than one strategy in expectation. In this case there is an equilibrium by definition (Nash 1951). In our example, the citizen will sometimes (but not always) commit a crime. The according probabilities can be obtained in the following way. In a Nash equilibrium, no player has an incentive to unilaterally deviate from her *optimal strategy given the strategies* of the other players. Thus, one has to find the particular strategy mix of the policeman for which both strategies of the citizen give the same expected utility. Let $\Pr(control) = \beta$, then $EU(crime|\beta) = EU(no\ crime|\beta)$. Inserting the utilities from Table 19.1 gives $(y - f) + (1 - \beta)y = \beta \cdot 0 + (1 - \beta) \cdot 0$. Solving for β gives $\Pr(control) = y/f$. The same procedure applies to the policeman, who has to be made indifferent between controlling and not controlling the citizen. Let $\Pr(crime) = \alpha$, then $\alpha(-c + r) + (1 - \alpha)(-c) = \alpha \cdot 0 + (1 - \alpha) \cdot 0$, which gives $\Pr(crime) = c/r$. To summarise, both players are expected to mix their strategies with a certain probability:

$$\Pr(\text{Control}) = y/f$$
$$\Pr(\text{Crime}) = c/r$$

An interesting implication is that it is not a higher penalty fee, but lower patrolling costs and higher rewards for the officer which lead to a lower crime rate. This result directly follows from the property of mixed Nash equilibria that each player seeks to make their opponent indifferent between using their strategies. That is, given the specific probability of committing a crime, the expected utility of the officer is the same, no matter whether he controls or not.

While the inspection game in the present form captures aspects of the legislator–bureaucrat relation, there are notable differences. The formulation of the inspection game implies that it is clear whether a citizen committed a crime once he is controlled by another authority. In contrast, legislators are not fully informed about the performance of bureaucrats since policy implementation does not always bring out clear outcomes. Thus, legislators have to make their decision whether to punish bureaucrats based on imperfect information.

Formal modelling allows us to extend the original inspection game so that it captures relevant aspects of legislative oversight with imperfect information. First, a bureaucrat decides whether to provide high-quality services (H) with effort, e, or low-quality services ($\neg$H) with no effort, 0. If high-quality services are provided, the legislator receives a policy-rent of size b, otherwise 0. Second, the legislator decides whether to monitor the bureaucrat's behaviour (O) at costs c or not ($\neg$O). The initial stages correspond to the inspection game. However, in case the legislator decides to monitor, the oversight game has further stages affecting players' payoffs. At the third stage, the legislator is informed about the bureaucratic behaviour. However, this information is subject to random noise. That is, information from monitoring is false in some instances with probability π. At the fourth stage, the legislator decides whether to punish the bureaucrat with fee f. The legislator, himself, is subject to public scrutiny in the media and at elections. Depending on the public assessment of the bureaucrat's behaviour, the legislator receives a positive utility (if he punishes (P) a shirking bureaucrat) or a negative utility (if he does not punish a shirking bureaucrat (not P) or if he punishes a compliant bureaucrat) of size s. The entire structure of the game as well as the payoffs are summarised in Figure 19.1.

We set three assumptions in order to rule out trivial or implausible equilibria. First, we require that the punishment fee for the bureaucrat be greater than the effort necessary for providing high-quality service, that is, f > e (effective punishment). Second, we require that voters be sufficiently responsive to the way in which the legislator deals with the bureaucracy. Stated differently, the gains for the legislator from good

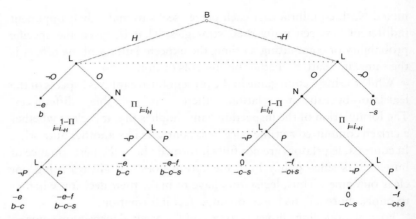

Figure 19.1: Game structure

oversight are sufficiently high in order to outweigh his costs of observation, that is, $2 \pi s > c$ (responsive electorate), whereas π is the probability of getting false information from monitoring, s is the negative utility from not punishing a shirking bureaucrat, and c is the costs of observation. Third, we require that the accuracy of the signal received from observing the bureaucrat's behaviour, $\frac{1}{2} < \pi \leq 1$. That is, the signal is strictly more informative than a random toss (so it is an informative signal). The first two assumptions rule out trivial pure strategy Nash equilibria analogously to the inspection game. The third assumption rules out implausible situations. If the opposite were the case, the signal would still be informative, but the legislator would always assume the opposite of what the signal indicates, which is rather awkward.

The solution to the oversight game depends on the accuracy of the signal, π. The more interesting equilibrium occurs if the value of information contained in the signal surpasses a specific threshold ($\pi > 2/3$). That being the case, the legislator can make his decision about whether to punish the bureaucrat conditional on the signal (punish only if the signal indicates low performance). In this equilibrium both the legislator and the bureaucrat play a mixed strategy. The legislator mixes between observe and punish only given the signal indicates low performance with probability α and does not observe with $(1-\alpha)$. The bureaucrat mixes between providing high quality with probability β and low quality with $(1-\beta)$, where

$$\alpha = e/\{(2\pi - 1)f\}; \tag{1}$$

$$\beta = (2\pi s - c)/\{(1 + \pi)s\}. \tag{2}$$

Even though the particular calculus for obtaining this result is slightly more complex than in the simple inspection game between citizen and policeman, the underlying logic of the mixed strategy Nash equilibrium is the same. For both players, we seek to find the strategy mix of the other player that makes the player under investigation indifferent between playing his strategies. Therefore, the probability with which the legislator observes the bureaucrat depends on the bureaucrat's effort for delivering high service as well as on the size of the punishment.

However, if the signal is too noisy ($\pi < 2/3$), it is a strictly dominant strategy for the legislator to observe and punish no matter what the signal indicates. In turn, the bureaucrat will never provide high-quality service since it does not alter the legislator's behaviour. In the case that $\pi = 2/3$, both equilibria exist. Moreover, if e > f, working does not pay off for the bureaucrat, he delivers low quality ($\neg$ H), and the legislator always observes and punishes. Given that c > 2 π s, observing does not pay off for the legislator and the bureaucrat delivers low quality ($\neg$ H). The equilibria mutually exclude each other (except for strict equalities (3 π s $-$ s)/2 = c, e = f, and c = 2 π s). Thus, there is only one Nash equilibrium at a time (see also Shikano et al forthcoming).

These solutions carry some implications concerning legislator and bureaucrat behaviour. Analogously to the inspection game, bureaucrat behaviour is not affected by the size of a possible punishment (f), but by the monitoring costs and possible rewards for the legislator. This is apparent in Equation (2). The solutions presented earlier also provide some new insights, which could not be obtained in the inspection game. Equation (2) shows a positive relationship between β and π: the more accurate the information is, the more likely the bureaucrat will provide high-quality services. Furthermore, the equilibrium holds only for $\pi > 2/3$. If information is too noisy, one cannot expect the bureaucrat to make an effort to provide high-quality services.

There are good reasons for being sceptical about the predictions of game-theoretic models for legislative–bureaucracy interactions. Even though the concept of mixed strategies is at the heart of formal modelling, its empirical relevance has repeatedly been met with scepticism (Chiappori, Levitt, and Groseclose 2002: 1138). It is not clear whether and how individuals actually come to generate a lottery over their pure strategies in order to make their opponent indifferent. Evidence from laboratory experiments on this issue is rather mixed (e.g., Brown and Rosenthal 1990; McCabe, Mukherji, and Runkle 2000; Ochs 1995; O'Neill 1987). Moreover, the study of Bloomfield (1994) indicates that subjects might use different strategies from the Nash solution to determine their optimal choice. Therefore, we set up an experimental in line with the oversight game and tested our predictions.

Designing an Experimental Setting Corresponding to the Formal Model

In our experimental application, we therefore compare a variety of parameter combinations for the costs of observation c, the punishment fee f, and the accuracy of information π in six different treatments. In the initial four treatments, we combine low and high observation costs (c = 3 or c = 7) with a low and high punishment fee (f = 10 or f = 20). In all of these treatments, we set π = 0.8. In the fifth and sixth treatments we fix observation costs and punishment fee at their higher level, but alter the accuracy of information π. That is, π is set to 0.6 in the fifth treatment and to 0.9 in the sixth treatment. Table 19.2 presents

Table 19.2: *Parameterisation and mixed strategy solutions*

	Low Cost Low Fee	Low Cost High Fee	High Cost Low Fee	High Cost High Fee	Noisy	Accurate
B	10	10	10	10	10	10
e	5	5	5	5	5	5
s	5	5	5	5	5	5
c	3	3	7	7	7	7
f	10	20	10	20	20	20
π	0.8	0.8	0.8	0.8	0.6	0.9
Pr(H)	56	56	11	11	0	21
Pr(O)	83	42	83	42	100	31
N	20	16	20	20	20	20

an overview of the different treatments. It also includes the Nash predictions for the probability that the bureaucrat delivers high-quality services, Pr(H), and the probability that the legislator investigates the bureaucrat's behaviour, Pr(O).

We chose to vary these parameters because it is more feasible to change them in real-world applications than the other parameters. The remaining parameters, in contrast, are tied to specific institutional designs or are inherent to the actors, which is why these are held constant across treatments. More precisely, both bureaucrats and legislator benefits b are set to 10 across treatments. Effort e that the bureaucrat has to invest in order to provide high-quality service is set to 5, as is the popularity penalty or bonus s applying to the legislator for (not) detecting a bureaucrat that provides low quality.

Subjects were given instructions – both written and oral – about the rules and the play of the game before the experiment. In particular, subjects were randomly assigned at the very beginning to play either the role of a legislator or the role of a bureaucrat and then kept their role throughout the entire experiment. Subjects were randomly paired in each round, not receiving any identifying information about their opponent. During each round subjects played the game in the same way as it has been given in the previous section. That is, the bureaucrat decides to deliver a high- or low-quality service and the legislator decides whether to observe the bureaucrat. Given the signal from observation the legislator may punish the bureaucrat. We did not call the players 'legislator' and 'bureaucrat', but used a neutral framing with the labels 'player A' and 'player B' to preclude any confounding connotations. In order to give subjects an opportunity to learn the structure of the game and the consequences of their decisions for their payoff, subjects played three training rounds with no effect on their eventual payoff. The play of the game proceeded according to the game-theoretical model in the previous section. After each round, both players were informed about their own actions, their partner's actions, and the resulting payoffs.

All subjects were informed about their possible earnings, which comprised a €3 show-up fee and the sum of all tokens gained from playing 30 rounds of the oversight game. The exchange rate to convert tokens into Euros was 0.01. The average earning plus show up-fee was €8.71, which is just slightly below the equivalent pay of a student assistant working 45 minutes. An average session took about 45 minutes, including instruction and disbursement. We conducted a total of six sessions, each time inviting 20 subjects. Since four subjects did not attend the session for the low-cost and high-fee treatment, we have 116 subjects in total, half of whom were bureaucrats and legislators, respectively. They may seem to be much lower than those of observational studies (e.g., survey experiments) and problematic in terms of statistical power. However, laboratory experiments have at least two important advantages over observational studies. First, we can easily repeat measures of individual subjects in multiple rounds, which should lead to a more reliable measurement even if these repeated measures are not fully independent from each other.[1] Second, the controlled environment of a laboratory experiment provides rather comfortable conditions to draw causal inferences. Therefore, we need a smaller sample size than observational studies, which need larger samples to compensate for noise. Most subjects were students from the University of Oldenburg, who had been invited via the Online Recruitment System for Economic Experiments (ORSEE) by Greiner (2015). The experiment was implemented in the computer programme z-Tree (Fischbacher 2007) using the between-subjects design. The experimental sessions were conducted at the Oldenburg laboratory for experimental social sciences (OLExS).

Evaluating Experimental Results

The most straightforward way to assess the accuracy of a formal model is to compare its predictions directly to the results obtained from a corresponding experiment. In the example given previously, we can compare the model predictions to the mean rate of high-quality implementation (on side of the bureaucrat) and control (on side of the legislator) for every treatment. However, it assumes that there is no further non-treatment factor for the subjects' behaviour, which is unrealistic even in the controlled laboratory situation. In contrast, one can reasonably assume due to the random assignment of the treatments that the further non-treatment factors affect subjects across treatments in the same way on average. Therefore, we should observe whether the model predictions correspond to the relative differences between treatments in Table 19.3.

---

[1] Further, one can randomly assign different treatments to each subject (crossover experiments). By combining this design with analysis of covariance or multilevel model with subject factors one can improve its inference (Shikano et al. 2012).

Table 19.3: *Aggregate-level results of different cost-fee treatments*

Bureaucrat's probability to provide high-quality service

		Control Cost		
		High (11)		Low (56)
Punishment Fee	High	35	<	50
		≈		≈
	Low	30	<	51

Legislators' probability to observe the bureaucrat's behaviour

		Control Cost		
		High		Low
Punishment Fee	High (42)	43	<	64
		∧		≈
	Low (83)	58	<	70

≈ means no significant difference at $\alpha = 5\%$
Predicted values from the theoretical model are given in parentheses.

We begin with inspecting bureaucrat decision-making. According to the theoretical model, bureaucrats should provide high-quality service more often under the high-cost than under the low-cost treatments, while changes in the punishment fee should have no effect. The empirical results are in line with these predictions. However, it should be mentioned that the mean rate of high-quality implementation was higher than the model prediction for high-cost treatments. There is no clear-cut explanation for this fact. We speculate that some subjects had a higher tendency to cooperate in general, for example, because they were altruistic or tried to conform to social expectations.

In contrast to bureaucrats, legislators deviated from the predictions at first glance. According to the model, legislators should control bureaucrats more frequently in the low than in the high punishment fee treatments, while the control costs should not matter. However, legislators appear to have reacted to their own costs of control. Furthermore, among the low-cost treatments, the punishment fee did not lead to significant differences in legislators' decisions.

Table 19.4: *Aggregate-level results over periods*

Period	Low Cost Low Fee	Low Cost High Fee	High Cost Low Fee	High Cost High Fee	Noisy	Accurate
Pr(H)						
1–10	49	49	34	40	26	53
11–20	48	54	34	38	21	54
21–30	56	48	22	28	28	57
Prediction	56	56	11	11	0	21
Pr(O)						
1–10	62	71	49	44	47	43
11–20	72	56	56	38	53	42
21–30	76	64	68	46	71	36
Prediction	83	42	83	42	100	31
n	20	16	20	20	20	20

The line of argument presented earlier alleges that all decisions are taken independently from one another, are taken in an identical way, and, most important, that subjects comprehend the situation in which they are placed. Thus, the only behavioural differences between individuals should be the ones that arise from the different treatment settings. This assumption is debatable, since individuals adapt their decisions over the course of 30 rounds. Therefore, we also partition our results into different phases of the experiment in Table 19.4: beginning (1–10), middle (11–20), and end (21–30). During the beginning phase, legislators clearly do not behave according to our theoretical model. This result changes for the middle and the ending phases. In both these later phases of the game, we find a statistically significant difference in the legislators' tendency to observe the bureaucrat between the high and low punishment fee treatments, which is in line with the prediction. What is more, the costs of observation do not affect legislator decision-making for the low fee treatments in the ending phase. Thus, subjects in the role of legislators appear to have needed more time than the three initial training rounds to adapt their behaviour to the decision-making situation and to find their optimal strategy. After this adaptation process had come to an end, their behaviour was in line with our theoretical expectations.

Table 19.5: *Aggregate-level results of different information accuracy treatments*

		$\pi = 60\%$		$\pi = 80\%$		$\pi = 90\%$
B's Pr(H)	Forecast	0		11		21
	Results	25	<	35	<	55
L's Pr(O)	Forecast	100		42		31
	Results	57	>	43	≈	40

≈ means no significant difference at $\alpha = 5\%$

We will now turn to the effect of information accuracy (Table 19.5). Our theoretical model predicts that bureaucrats provide high-quality service more often if the information from inspection is more accurate. Our results are in line with this prediction, again with the caveat that bureaucrats provided high-quality service much more frequently than predicted in general. Concerning the legislators, their tendency to observe the bureaucrat's behaviour should decrease as the information becomes more accurate. Even though there is no significant difference between the $\pi = 80\%$ and $\pi = 90\%$ treatment, the relative relationship supports the theoretical model.

Finally, we assess whether differences exist across treatments in the way legislators react to the information they obtain from oversight. From a theoretical point of view, the effect of information accuracy on the decision of the legislator whether or not to punish the bureaucrat stems from his own expected benefit. In particular, under the noisy information treatment ($\pi = 60\%$) he is predicted to punish the bureaucrat irrespective of the information obtained from control. Under the medium ($\pi = 80\%$) and high ($\pi = 90\%$) information treatments, he should punish according to the signal. To test this, we compare the probability of punishment dependent on the information content (Table 19.6). In line with the prediction, legislators punish bureaucrats much more frequently under the low information treatment, even if the signal indicates high-quality service from the bureaucrat (50.7%). In contrast, there is no significant difference among the other treatments as expected (with the exception of the pair of the low-cost and high-fee and high-cost and low-fee treatments).

To summarise, the aggregate-level results largely confirm the predictions from our game-theoretic model. The evidence for bureaucrat

Table 19.6: *Information content and punishment decision*

	Low Cost	Low Cost	High Cost	High Cost		
	Low Fee	High Fee	Low Fee	High Fee	Noisy	Accurate
Punishment in case of information for high quality						
Forecast	0%	0%	0%	0%	100%	0%
Result	13.7%	7.1%	22.2%	17.6%	50.7%	12.7%
Punishment in case of information for low quality						
Forecast	100%	100%	100%	100%	100%	100%
Result	97.8%	94.4%	97.6%	96.1%	95.8%	90.0%

decision-making in this regard is particularly solid, but also legislator decision-making is in line with the theoretical prediction acknowledging some adaption to the situation. Namely, it is not higher punishment fees, but rather lower control costs and higher information accuracy that make bureaucrats provide high-quality services. With regard to legislators, their own costs of control affect their decision-making to a certain degree, but also the size of the punishment and the accuracy of information obtained from oversight. In particular, legislators clearly tend to punish at low levels of information accuracy, irrespective of whether or not the signal from oversight indicates good quality service by the bureaucrat.

Theoretical and Practical Implications

The oversight game has previously been used to describe and analyse the relationships between legislators and the bureaucracy in the principal-agent framework (McCarty and Meirowitz 2007). In this chapter we present and test a modification of the oversight game that focuses on the accuracy of information gained from oversight. Depending on information accuracy, costs of oversight for legislators, and the punishment fee for shirking bureaucrats, the model provides predictions that substantially differ from previous studies, which treat the information from oversight as accurate and without uncertainty. More specifically, information accuracy not only affects the location, but also the nature of the equilibrium in oversight games. Bureaucrats never provide high-quality services if information accuracy is below a certain threshold.

Legislators, on their part, are aware of this fact and strictly control and punish bureaucrats. If information accuracy exceeds this threshold, bureaucrats take a mixed strategy in which the quality of their service increases with the accuracy of information and decreases with the control costs legislators have to bear from oversight.

The experimental results support the model predictions. At the aggregate level bureaucrats and legislators show expected behaviour. Most important, increasing information accuracy makes it more likely that bureaucrats provide high-quality services and legislators waive the control.

Our results carry some relevant implications for policy makers and public managers. In order to increase both effectiveness and efficiency of legislative oversight, they can pursue two strategies. First, they can reduce the costs of oversight, for example, through developing routines. Moreover, legislators can install experts in the corresponding policy field or can appoint former bureaucrats to controlling positions. Second, regardless of other aspects of an oversight situation, legislators can always raise the accuracy of information, thus enabling them to engage themselves in oversight less frequently while having a higher level of compliance at the same time. In this way, legislators not only increase their own payoff, but also the payoff of bureaucrats, since more accurate information makes the decisions of legislators more predictable and reliable for bureaucrats. In fact, policy makers in OECD countries have already invested time and money to establish a broad range of performance-monitoring systems at various levels of bureaucratic activity (OECD 2011). Such monitoring systems might be steps in the right direction if they are capable of improving the level of information accuracy in legislative oversight.

Challenges and Outlook for Public Management Research

Even though the oversight model extended the inspection game, it still remains a very stylised representation of reality. Further extensions can help to provide a more realistic picture of the interaction between legislators and bureaucrats. For example, the model structure with a single legislator and a bureaucrat can be relaxed in different ways. First, a legislator can choose one from multiple bureaucrats to implement a law or provide a public service. In reality, legislators have such a choice among possible bureaucratic agencies. In such a situation, the legislator can utilise another instrument to prevent agency loss: screening bureaucrats a priori. Second, there may be multiple legislators who collectively authorise a bureaucrat to implement a law and jointly monitor the bureaucrat's behaviour. Under such circumstances, a free-rider problem can arise among individual legislators as one can exploit the other by letting the latter monitor the bureaucrats. These extensions correspond to realistic situations where the legislators and bureaucrats interact with each other. Furthermore, beyond relaxing the two-player game structure, we can also extend the delegation chain in the oversight game. In the real political process, coalition partners authorise ministers, who, in turn, delegate law implementation to their bureaucrats. Furthermore, there are delegation chains inside the bureaucratic hierarchy itself.

We elaborated on one extension elsewhere, namely the situation of multiple bureaucrats (Stoffel, Shikano, and Tepe 2015). In that piece, a legislator has to choose among two bureaucrats with different effort levels for high-quality service implementation. The legislator may screen the bureaucrats before making this decision and delegating a task to the chosen bureaucrat. Yet we find that screening never pays for the legislator given that bureaucrats know whether or not they were screened. Consequently, the expected utilities from both subgames with and without screening remain identical. This kind of counterintuitive result is quite difficult to achieve without formal modelling.

In addition to extending formal models to better capture reality, one can also modify the laboratory experiment set-ups. One possibility, which is unfortunately not taken too often, is to extend the pool of subjects beyond students. In our example, we are modelling strategic interactions between legislators and bureaucrats. It is a straightforward idea to use these specific groups of persons as subjects. This, however, does not necessarily improve the external validity of experimental results. Inviting legislators and bureaucrats makes sense only if we expect these specific groups to respond to treatments in a different way than student subjects. Another possibility is to introduce so-called de-neutralised treatments: by using such labels as 'bureaucrats', 'legislators', and 'public service', one induces social desirability, civic responsibilities, or further intrinsic motivations. By comparing results from the setting using neutral labels (player A vs. B) and results from the setting with de-neutralised labels (player legislator vs. bureaucrat) that may induce some intrinsic motivation, one can try to capture the effect of intrinsic motivations in the legislator–bureaucratic relationship.

Experimental research designs just recently began to enter the mainstream of public administration and management research (see Anderson and Edwards 2014; Baekgaard et al. 2015; and Margetts 2011 for review). In this line of research, laboratory experiments exploring formal models of bureaucracy remain rare despite their unique capacity to detect causal relationships. A potential way to overcome the niche existence of formal models of bureaucracy is to locate them in a broader complementary research design agenda in which formalisation is one way to express and explore a theoretical argument. In a recent review of formal models of bureaucracy Gailmard and Patty (2012) point out that over the last decades, there has been a continuous increase of studies using formal models to explore the functioning of bureaucratic institutions. Many of these studies move beyond the classical principal agent setting to explicate the role of cheap talk and signaling (e.g., Crawford and Sobel 1982) or the acquisition of expertise (Huber and McCarty 2004) in bureaucratic hierarchies. In this view, testing the empirical validity of these formal models with the means of a laboratory experiments is just one component of an empirical research agenda. Different research designs have different strength and weaknesses. Laboratory in the field experiments, field experiments, and survey experiments may help to increase external validity of laboratory findings by picking up another aspect of the same theoretical claim, and thereby may contribute additional components of a broader experimental research strategy. Running the inspection game with 'real' bureaucrats using a laboratory in the field setting may help to improve external validity but come at the expense of other methodological (e.g., appropriate monetary incentives, working time regulations) and substantive theoretical issues (influence of factors which are not considered in the formal model such as bureaucratic personality). Yet, if one dispenses with the idea of measuring revealed preferences, a simple one-shot version of the oversight game could also be implemented in a survey which could be sent to a broader audience, including political and bureaucratic practitioners. In such research collaboration, formal modellers could reassure themselves about what should be left outside of the model, while researchers drawing on broader experimental data can make the observed correlations theoretically more plausible (see, for one possible example, Tepe 2016).

References

Anderson, D. M. and B. C. Edwards 2014. 'Unfulfilled promise: laboratory experiments in public administration research', *Public Management Review*, 17(10): 1–25.

Baekgaard, M., C. Baethge, J. Blom-Hansen, C. Dunlop, M. Esteve, M. Jakobsen, B. Kisida, J. Marvelf, A. Moseleyc, S. Serritzlewa, P. Stewarte, M. K. Thomsena, and P. J. Wolf 2015. 'Conducting experiments in public management research: a practical guide', *International Public Management Journal*, 18(2): 323–42.

Bendor J. 1988. 'Formal models of bureaucracy', *British Journal of Political Science*, 18(3): 353–95.

Bloomfield, R. 1994. 'Learning a mixed strategy equilibrium in the laboratory', *Journal of Economic Behaviour and Organization*, 25(3): 411–36.

Brehm, J. and S. Gates 1999. *Working, Shirking and Sabotage: Bureaucratic Response to a Democratic Public*. Ann Arbor: University of Michigan Press.

Brown, J. N. and R. W. Rosenthal 1990. 'Testing the minimax hypothesis: a reexamination of O'Neill's game experiment', *Econometrica*, 58(5): 1065–81.

Chiappori, P. A., S. D. Levitt, and T. Groseclose 2002. 'Testing mixed-strategy equilibria when players are heterogeneous: the case of penalty kicks in soccer', *American Economic Review*, 92(4): 1138–51.

Cooper, R., D. V. DeJong, R. Forsythe, and T. W. Ross 1996. 'Cooperation without reputation: experimental evidence from prisoner's dilemma games', *Games and Economic Behaviour*, 12(2): 187–218.

Crawford V. P. and J. Sobel 1982. 'Strategic information transmission', *Econometrica*, 50(6): 1431–5.

Fiorina, M. P. and C. R. Plott. 1978. 'Committee decisions under majority rule: an experimental study', *American Political Science Review*, 72(2): 575–98.

Fischbacher, U. 2007. 'Z-Tree: 'Zurich toolbox for ready-made economic experiments', *Experimental Economics*, 10(2): 171–8.

Gailmard, S. and J. W. Patty 2012. 'Formal models of bureaucracy', *Annual Review of Political Science*, 15: 353–77.

Gehlbach, S. 2013. *Formal Models of Domestic Politics*. Cambridge: Cambridge University Press.

Gill J. 1995. 'Formal models of legislative/administrative interaction: a survey of the subfield', *Public Administration Review*, 55(1): 99–106.

Greiner, B. 2015. 'Subject pool recruitment procedures: organizing experiments with ORSEE', *Journal of the Economic Science Association*, 1.1: 114–25.

Hinich, M. J. and M. C. Munger 1997. *Analytical Politics*. Cambridge: Cambridge University Press.

Huber J. and N. McCarty 2004. 'Bureaucratic capacity, delegation, and political reform', *American Political Science Review*, 98(3): 481–94.

Johnson, N. and A. Mislin 2011. 'Trust games: a meta-analysis', *Journal of Economic Psychology*, 32: 865–89.

Kahn, L., M. Murnighan, and J. Keith 1993. 'Conjecture, uncertainty, and cooperation in prisoner's dilemma games: some experimental evidence', *Games and Economic Behaviour*, 22(1): 91–117.

Margetts, H. Z. 2011. 'Experiments for public management research', *Public Management Review*, 13(2): 189–208.

McCabe, K., A. Mukherji, and D. Runkle 2000. 'An experimental study of information and mixed-strategy play in the three-person matching-pennies game', *Economic Theory*, 15(2): 421–62.

McCarty, N. and A. Meirowitz 2007. *Political Game Theory: An Introduction*. Cambridge: Cambridge University Press.

McCubbins, M. D. and T. Schwartz 1984. 'Congressional oversight over-looked: police patrols versus re alarms', *American Journal of Political Science*, 28(1): 165–79.

Morton, R. B. 1999. 'Methods and models', in *A Guide to the Empirical Analysis of Formal Models in Political Science*. Cambridge: Cambridge University Press.

Nash, J. 1951. 'Non-cooperative games', *The Annals of Mathematics*, 54(2): 286–95.

Ochs, J. 1995. 'Games with unique, mixed strategy equilibria: an experimental study', *Games and Economic Behaviour*, 10(1): 202–17.

OECD. 2011. *Government at a Glance 2011*. Paris: OECD Press.

O'Neill, B. 1987. 'Nonmetric test of the minimax theory of two-person zerosum games', *Proceedings of the National Academy of Sciences*, 84(7): 2106–9.

Palfrey, T. R. 2006. 'Laboratory experiments', in *Handbook of Political Economy*, B. Weingast and D. Wittman (eds.). Oxford: Oxford University Press: Oxford. pp. 915–36.

Palfrey, T. R. 2009. 'Laboratory experiments in political economy', *Annual Review of Political Science*, 12: 379–88.

Plott, C. R. and V. L. Smith 1978. 'An experimental examination of two exchange institutions', *Review of Economic Studies*, 45(1): 133–53.

Rauhut, H. 2009. 'Higher punishment, less control?' *Rationality and Society*, 21(3): 359–92.

Shikano, S., T. Bräuninger, and M. Stoffel 2012. 'Statistical analysis of experimental data', in *Experimental Political Science: Principles and Practices*, B. Kittel, W. Luhan, and R. Morton (eds.). Palgrave. pp. 163–77.

Shikano, S., M. Stoffel, and M.Tepe Forthcoming, 'Information Accuracy in Legislative Oversight: Theoretical Implications and Experimental Evidence', *Rationality and Society*.

Smith, V. L. 1982. 'Microeconomic systems as an experimental science', *The American Economic Review*, 72(5): 923–55.

Stoffel, M., S. Shikano, and M. Tepe 2015. 'Choosing the right bureaucrat: does screening of bureaucrats pay?' Paper prepared for delivery at the Annual Conference of the European Political Science Association, 2015, Vienna.

Tepe, M. 2016. 'In public servants we trust? A behavioural experiment on public service motivation and trust among students of public administration, business sciences and law', *Public Management Review*, 18(4): 508–38.

Tsebelis, G. 1990. 'Penalty has no impact on crime: a game theoretic analysis', *Rationality and Society*, 2(3): 255–86.

20 Experimental Research for Nonprofit Management: Charitable Giving and Fundraising

MIRAE KIM, DYANA MASON, AND
HUAFANG LI

Significance and Context of the Topic

The nonprofit sector delivers many public goods and services by relying heavily on both charitable giving and government support from grants and contracts. Understanding why and how citizens voluntarily support the provision of public services and goods has broad implications for public managers and policy makers. This chapter introduces some important theories and empirical studies on charitable giving within the context of nonprofit management. In the United States, there has been rapid growth in private philanthropy and government grants and contracts over the past few decades; private philanthropic contributions to nonprofits increased almost 25 percent between 1998 and 2004 (Salamon 2010), while the number of nonprofit organisations has also increased dramatically (Roeger, Blackwood, and Pettijohn 2012). The result is intensified competition among nonprofit organisations for donations and much greater research attention is being paid to how donations are made to nonprofit organisations. Such a trend is not idiosyncratic in the United States, and a great volume of empirical studies have been conducted with the goal of identifying mechanisms of charitable giving.

While charitable giving has been traditionally considered the main source of income for nonprofit organisations, support from government is another significant source. For instance, government grants and service fees paid by the government accounted for about 32 per cent of nonprofit revenue in the United States, whereas private contributions accounted for about 13 per cent of nonprofit revenue (McKeever and Pettijohn 2014). Not including government grants, annual government contract fees in the United States account for upwards of $100 billion of nonprofit revenue (Boris et al. 2010). Some scholars argue that government funding helps nonprofit organisations not only directly, but also indirectly because such funding leverages public trust and confidence in nonprofits as key players in public service delivery (Hansmann 1980; Light 2011; Steinberg 2006; Wise 1990), which results in more donations from private sources. Others, however, contend that public support of nonprofits discourages rather than encourages private giving because it 'crowds out' private giving (Brooks 2000b; Roberts 1984, 1987; Warr 1982, 1983). The rationale for this perspective is that citizens believe organisations that receive public grants already have sufficient support through tax dollars and do not need additional funds. The substantial amount of private donations and government funding makes it important to understand the dynamic relationship between these two means of support.

In this chapter, we briefly review the literature on charitable giving to understand the underlying mechanisms that motivate individual contributions. Despite a growing body of experimental research on altruism and charitable giving, only a limited number of public and nonprofit management studies use experiments. In order to assess the efficacy of experimental methods for better understanding charitable giving to nonprofits, we present three recent studies that use experimental approaches in various contexts: (1) an online survey with a representative US population sample that examines if government funding crowds out private giving in a simulated situation (Kim and Van Ryzin 2014); (2) a laboratory experiment in China that seeks to understand the influence of individual motivations, organisational strategies, and governmental support (Li et al. 2015); and (3) a randomised controlled field experiment in partnership with a US nonprofit organisation that investigates the effect of image motivation on low-income donors (Mason 2015).

We chose these three studies because they cover various experimental approaches in different contexts. Kim and Van Ryzin (2014) used a survey experiment where participants were asked to divide an endowment between two hypothetical nonprofit organisations, one of which varied in how much government funding it had. In the second study, the authors tested the 'money illusion', which argues that people make different decisions in laboratory experiments based on whether they were donating real money or hypothetical 'play' money (Fehr and Tyran 2001; Shafir, Diamond, and Tversky 1997). The third study introduced in this chapter is an experimental study of image motivation conducted in the field with a real organisation and participants (Mason 2015). The description of three different types of experimental studies – online survey, laboratory experiment, and field experiment – allows us to illustrate both advantages and disadvantages of each experimental method that can be employed to enhance our knowledge of public and nonprofit management.

Non-experimental Research on Charitable Giving to Nonprofits

For the past few decades, there has been a significant amount of research focused on the determinants of charitable giving, including how and why individuals donate money to nonprofit organisations. Bekkers and Wiekping (2011) classified the extant research on motivations for charitable giving into eight categories: need and solicitation (i.e., individuals learn about the need and are asked to give), rational consideration of the costs and benefits of giving, inherent altruism of individuals, reputational gains or other psychological benefits, the influence of one's values and the efficacy of one's gifts (i.e., ability to make a difference). In the following literature review, we focus mainly on two primary theoretical approaches to charitable giving: (1) the rational cost-benefit analysis of the decision to give, and (2) reputational gain or other psychological benefits individuals receive from being perceived as altruistic.

Early models of charitable giving, mostly developed by economists, assumed that private and public provision of public goods existed in equilibrium. In other words, the public was assumed to be neutral as to who provides public goods and services they demand, such as education or health care (Warr 1982). Theorists of this perspective (Bernheim 1986; Samuelson 1955) have therefore argued that people would voluntarily give money or time to provide for a public good up to the point that government steps in, at which point government funding 'crowds out' private gifts because the same goods and services can be produced without private gifts. In other words, individual gifts are viewed as substitutes for government funds to provide necessary public goods and services.

However, anecdotal and empirical evidence does not support this theory of neutrality. Studies have shown that individuals contribute far and beyond the amounts expected even when governments provide support for the same public goods and services. Thus, scholars suggest there must be an additional benefit that individuals receive from making donations, because government funding appears to create only an incomplete or partial crowding out of individual giving. Becker (1976, 1978) and Andreoni (1989, 1990) argued that individuals receive some sort of gratification from their gifts, which Andreoni termed a 'warm glow' (1989, 1990). Further, the crowding-out effect has been tested mostly on archival data and has provided only mixed results (Horne, Johnson, and Van Slyke 2005; Hughes, Luksetich, and Rooney 2014; Nikolova 2014; Payne 1998; Simmons and Emanuele 2004; Steinberg 1991).

Other scholars have argued that government funding 'crowds in' or promotes additional support for nonprofit organisations (Brooks 1999, 2000a, 2000b; Diamond 1999; Schiff 1990). This group of scholars contends that when governments provide grants or contracts for key services to high-performing nonprofit organisations, it signals the high quality of programmes to private donors. In a similar vein, some scholars have argued that wealthy and influential philanthropists send a signal to other potential donors that the nonprofit organisation they support is worthy of contributions (Andreoni 2006; Glazer and Konrad 1996). Also, organisational matching, i.e., when private donors match their gifts to government, corporate, or other charitable donations, has been theorised to encourage individual giving (Karlan and List 2007; Karlan, List, and Shafir 2011; Rondeau and List 2008). This line of inquiry assumes that individuals have limited access to the relevant information and limited capacity to judge the quality of nonprofit organisations, so these large 'leadership' gifts or government grants provide signals that help donors assess organisations and decide to give.

Social psychologists have taken a different approach to uncover the underlying mechanisms for charitable giving. Social psychologists 'tend to explain altruism as an outcome of a decision-making process in which the internal characteristics of the actors join with the external environment in a pattern of mutual influence' (Monroe 1994: 881). In other words, alongside rational self-interest, rules and norms of the environment guide donors' giving decisions. Cialdini and Goldstein (2004) suggest that social influence, i.e., the subtle pressure society places on individuals to comply and conform, may influence behaviour, particularly when one is being watched by others. Individuals are concerned about their public image and have a desire to be seen as 'good' by their family, peers, and communities (Ariely, Bracha, and Meier 2009). Individuals who want to be seen as good will also act more pro-socially (Benabou and Tirole 2006). Given this argument, people are more likely to act altruistically since altruism, which in this case is charitable giving, is a value often associated with being 'good'. Similarly, Harbaugh (1998a, 1998b) argues there is a 'taste for prestige' that incentivises donors to contribute and in particular, to make large contributions. That is, providing gifts makes people feel prestigious or signals their wealth and goodness to others.

Scholars have focused extensively on these questions and there has been growing use of both laboratory and field experiments to begin untangling the mechanisms of charitable giving. For example, a widely cited study by Shang and Croson (2007) used an experimental manipulation of social information to discover that individual donations are influenced by information about other people's contributions. However, there have been only a limited number of experimental studies done in the context of nonprofit management, and only a few have found their way into the leading journals in nonprofit scholarship. A review of more than 700 articles published in the *Nonprofit and Voluntary Sector Quarterly* between 2000 and 2014 found only seven articles where the primary research design used an experimental method (Mason 2013). The lack of accessible research in the nonprofit sector that uses experimental methods could be preventing practitioners from using evidence-based approaches to maximise their fundraising and volunteer recruitment efforts (Mason 2013).

Additionally, the existing studies that focus on nonprofit and charitable giving are based primarily on archival data or on independently developed surveys that are used by only a small number of scholars in the field. Archival data and survey results both have well-documented limitations (Grønbjerg 2002; Hall 2001; Mason 2013). A great number of observational studies in the field have relied on the Internal Revenue Service (IRS) Form 990 data, which nonprofit organisations submit annually to the IRS. However, the 990 data have been shown to be rife with errors and limitations (Tinkleman and Neely 2011), and survey data often suffer from measurement issues (for a review, see Hall 2001). Indeed, Grønbjerg and Clerkin (2005: 233) state that 'almost without exception, the existing nonprofit information systems are limited in scope', providing limited data of interest to researchers and practitioners. Additionally, relying on observational data alone makes it difficult to determine causal relationships or eliminate alternative explanations for key findings. According to Nobel Laureate Elinor Ostrom, 'careful experimental research designs frequently help sort out competing hypotheses more effectively than does trying to find the precise combination of variables in the field' (1998: 17).

Experimental studies have started to receive growing attention in public management studies (Perry 2012; Wright and Grant 2010), and incorporating more experimental designs will likely help nonprofit scholars overcome barriers they often face. In the United States, nonprofit organisations cover a wide range of activities and vary greatly in size (Blackwood et al. 2012). Given this diversity, one of the major challenges in nonprofit research is collecting comprehensive data to make reliable comparisons across the fields, types, regions, and sizes of nonprofit organisations. The IRS 990 tax returns used in large-scale, cross-sectional studies (Froelich et al. 2000; Grønbjerg 2002; Lampkin and Boris 2002) are comprehensive[1], but cannot provide much non-financial and programme-related information. More importantly, working with this type of archival data often limits the extent to which researchers can determine the direction of causal relationships. Due to hidden factors that are not easily controlled in non-experimental research, many of the previous studies on charitable giving had to remain ambiguous with respect to the direction of the causal relationship. Yet identifying the cause is the most important aspect of understanding why individuals decide to give.

Ultimately, the use of experimental designs in nonprofit management studies can help both scholars and practitioners better understand the motivations behind individual donations that are critical to the ability of nonprofits to provide public service. By developing a set of randomised, controlled field and laboratory experiments, we can examine alternative theoretical explanations for the inconsistent empirical results of previous studies. In the following sections, we discuss three studies that illustrate the various ways in which experimental designs can be used to inform nonprofit management.

---

[1] All nonprofit organisations with gross receipts of at least $50,000 must file Form 990 or 990 EZ.

The Crowding-Out Effect: A Survey Experiment

In the first study, Kim and Van Ryzin (2014) used an online survey experiment to examine how government grants influence individuals' giving decisions. To probe this question, participants in the experiment were endowed with a hypothetical $100 donation budget and asked to allocate this money between two nonprofit arts organisations. The description of the second organisation, however, was experimentally varied in terms of how much government funding it had. Thus, the first hypothetical organisation served as a point of comparison or meaningful alternative to the second organisation, which contained the experimental variation. Specifically, participants were randomly assigned to one of four variations of the second organisation's funding status: (1) the organisation received no direct government funding; (2) the organisation received direct government funding for 33 per cent of its budget; (3) organisation received direct government funding for 67 per cent of its budget; and (4) the organisation received direct government funding for 33 per cent of its budget specifically from the National Endowment for the Arts (NEA). This last condition was designed to test for a possible 'crowding-in' effect that might flow from a prestigious, merit-based NEA grant (as opposed to more general government funding). In all other respects, the descriptions of the organisations remained the same.

Thus, the varied descriptions of the second organisation served as the experimental treatment and were designed to see how the level and type of government funding influences the amount participants were willing to give. The results (Figure 20.1) were clear: participants in this study gave substantially less when the receipt of government funding was mentioned, i.e., group 1 compared to groups 2 and 3. These results confirmed that the presence of government funding crowds *out* private giving within the described scenario. Nonetheless, the experiment did not find evidence that the size of government funding makes a difference in government grants crowding out private giving. When the average giving made by group 2 (i.e., 33 per cent of budget coming from government support) and group 3 (i.e., 67 per cent of budget coming from government support) were compared, no significant difference was spotted. Finally, this experiment found only limited signalling effect of prestigious government funding; when the NEA grant was mentioned as the type of government funding, the amount of giving increased but only marginally (comparison of group 2 and group 4).

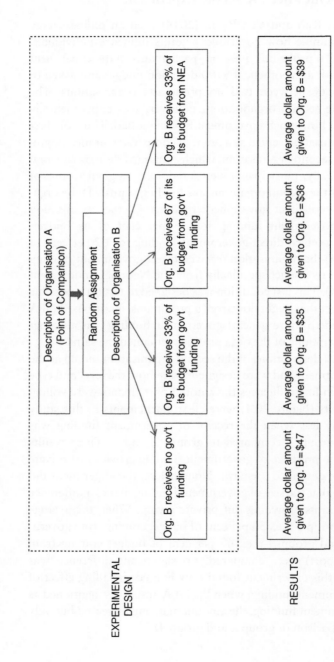

Figure 20.1: Experimental design and results

Matching Grants, Emotions, and Real Money: A Laboratory Experiment

The second experimental study differs from the study just presented because it incorporates real money and organisations into the experiment. It is possible that participants will behave differently in real situations than in hypothetical situations. To address this possibility, the second study used real money in a laboratory experiment to examine the impact of individual-level factors (i.e., whether money was earned, and if an emotional story was told about a charitable cause), organisational-level factors (if a charity provided grants to match donations according to a predetermined match ratio, e.g. 1:1), and governmental-level factors (government support) to nonprofits on individual giving decisions (Li et al. 2015). The experiment was conducted in a university in China, and used student participants who were randomly recruited. As in the first study, participants were randomly assigned to one of four groups where they received either: (1) an emotional story and no matching grants; (2) an emotional story and 1:1 matching grants; (3) no emotional story and no matching grants; or (4) no emotional story and 1:1 matching grants.

During the experiment, first, participants were given 20 RMB (about 3 USD) and asked to donate a portion of that to one of the five nonprofit organisations. Participants were asked to indicate the percentage of their money they were willing to give, which could vary from none to all (100 per cent) of 20 RMB. Participants had five nonprofit organisations described to them, two were described as receiving a high level of government support (China Red Cross Foundation and China Fupin Foundation); one was described as receiving a moderate level of government support (Shenzhen One Foundation); and two were described as receiving a low level of government support (Nandu Foundation and Tencent Foundation).

Next, the experiment asked participants to count the number of zeroes in 15 rows with each row showing '0' or '1' randomly in 15 columns. If participants counted the correct number of zeroes in one row, they were able to earn 1.5 RMB. An incorrect answer meant the participant did not earn the money. This task was given in order to make participants feel like they were earning their money. Researchers then asked participants to donate a portion of their earned money (ranging from 0 RMB to 22.5 RMB) to one of the five organisations.

In the first experimental setting, participants were willing to give on average 25 per cent of 20 RMB (the unearned money that was granted to them) to one of the five nonprofits. When participants were asked to give using the money they had earned through the counting task, the giving rate dropped to 20 per cent. This result supports the 'easy money' hypothesis, that is, donors who use money simply given to them donate more to nonprofits than those who must earn the money through some effortful, work-like task.

When participants read the emotional story before deciding on their donations, the average percentage of giving was 20 per cent, which is somewhat higher than the rate for participants who did not read the emotional story (17 per cent). This finding is significant statistically and confirms the hypothesis that donors moved by emotional stories give more to nonprofit organisations, although the effect was not large.

Contrary to the study's hypothesis about the effect of matching grants, the matching mechanism was not found to increase individual giving. The participants who were incentivised with the matching grant chose to give at a much lower level (12 per cent) than those who did not get the matching option (21 per cent). This suggests that, in the China context where matching grants are rarely used, matching grants may be seen as organisations' financial resources and thus crowd out individual donations.

Lastly, the study found some contrary evidence regarding the hypothesis that government support to nonprofit organisations will crowd out individual giving. In the experiment, only 16 per cent of participants gave to the private foundations that had a low level of governmental support. In contrast, participants gave more to organisations that received a high level of government support – the China Fupin Foundation attracted the highest percentage of donors (39 per cent) and the China Red Cross Foundation had the highest average giving rate (28 per cent). These findings indicate that Chinese donors prefer to give to nonprofit organisations that are supported by government, probably because government support signals the high quality of an organisation. In addition, it should be noted, that both Fupin and the Red Cross are real organisations that have established reputations among the Chinese public.

Image Motivation: A Field Experiment

The third study (Mason 2015) provides an approach that is distinct from the previous two studies. Even though the second study incorporated real money and organisations, the participants were mostly university students, who are not typical donors. Mason's (2015) study is a good example of how the nonprofit literature could benefit from conducting field experiments, which are advantageous because they can establish the external validity of the findings. Mason's (2015) field experiment investigated the effects of image motivation on individuals' intention to participate in a community giving programme. Providing recognition or publicity in exchange for a charitable gift can be driven by image motivation, which is defined as 'the desire to be liked and well regarded by others' (Ariely, Bracha, and Meier 2009: 544).

The experiment was conducted in partnership with a nonprofit organisation in Los Angeles, California, that provides childcare services to low-income families. The sample was drawn from both client households of the organisation and the vendors providing childcare services over the previous 18 months. All potential participants were invited to participate in a Community Giving Programme (CGP) in partnership with local supermarket chains. After signing up, participants could contribute to the organisation by purchasing goods with their regular shopping rewards card. The market then donated a portion of each purchase to the nonprofit – on average approximately $20 per year per participant.

Clients and providers were randomly sorted into one of four different groups – two control groups and two treatment groups. English speakers, or those who spoke other languages besides Spanish, were randomly assigned to: (1) receive a letter written in English asking to participate the CGP (control group) or (2) receive a letter written in English asking to participate in the CGP with a promise to publish the participant's name in an upcoming newsletter (treatment group). To control for the large population of households who spoke Spanish as their first language, Spanish speakers were randomly assigned to (3) receive a letter written in Spanish asking to participate in the CGP (control) or (4) receive a letter written in Spanish asking to participate in the CGP with a promise to publicise their participation (treatment). The experiment was designed this way to examine the differences between Spanish-speaking and English-speaking participants.

The letter included a detailed letter with information on CGP, a card which the participant could fill out, and a postage-paid return envelope. The treatment groups' letters, however, also included information presented at the top of the letter, in bold type, which said, 'Your name can appear in an upcoming newsletter! This is how your name might appear...' followed by a text mock-up of what the newsletter would say: '[Organization] thanks our new Community Contributions Supporters! These individuals have signed up to support [the organization's] programs every time they shop....' This was followed by four actual previous participants, showing '<YOUR NAME HERE>' on the list. Those who received the letter could then visualise the acknowledgement they could expect for participating.

The results showed that participants who were incentivised by the promise of publicity (image motivation) were 1.56 percentage points (6.43 per cent response rate) more likely to respond to the campaign than the control group (4.87 per cent). This treatment effect was also seen in a statistical analysis of the responses, where receiving the treatment letter was statistically significant ($p < 0.05$) to whether they responded than those who received the control letter, controlling for factors like household language, household income, and whether they were a vendor or client. In addition, Spanish speakers who received the Spanish letter responded at much higher rates in both the treatment (9.86 per cent) and control groups (7.43 per cent) than those who received the English letter (5.61 per cent and 4.25 per cent, respectively). Also, service providers were more likely (6.79 per cent) than clients (6.16 per cent) to respond to the campaign that used image motivation.

These results indicate that image motivation can have an effect on whether individuals respond to an invitation to participate in a fundraising programme. Although the response rates were modest, a 1–2 per cent increase in return rate for any organisation in a fundraising appeal can be quite significant for the group's fundraising goals. Surprisingly, Spanish-speaking donors were much more likely than English speakers who received the English letter to respond to a fundraising invitation if the appeal was in their first language. This finding has implications for how nonprofit organisations segment and manage their donor bases, and since it's one of the first findings along this dimension (cross-cultural communication in nonprofit fundraising), it provides an opportunity for much more research.

Table 20.1: Image motivation response rates

	Control Group (no publicity)				Treatment Group (publicity)				Total Response
		N	Percent	[95% Conf. Interval]		N	Percent	[95% Conf. Interval]	
Overall	111	2278	4.87	3.99 5.76	142	2208	6.43	5.41 7.46	253
Clients	70	1364	5.13	3.96 6.30	78	1266	6.16	4.83 7.49	148
Providers	41	914	4.49	3.14 5.83	64	942	6.79	5.18 8.40	105
English Letter	78	1834	4.25	3.33 5.18	100	1782	5.61	4.54 6.68	178
Spanish Letter	33	444	7.43	4.98 9.88	42	426	9.86	7.02 12.70	75

Theoretical and Practical Implications

This chapter has presented three different experimental studies that examine charitable giving and help inform nonprofit management. Previous empirical studies that assess whether government grants crowd out individual giving have been unable to uncover the real cause of the crowding out (or in) because hidden factors are hard to detect in observational data. Consequently, the scholarship on this topic has not reached a consensus, despite a large volume of studies to date. The online survey experiment study by Kim and Van Ryzin (2014) was the first of its kind in the nonprofit management field to experimentally demonstrate evidence of a crowding-out effect. This study provides insights for public managers who must make funding decisions, and for nonprofit managers who must raise funds from both government and private donors.

The laboratory experiment Li and his colleagues (2015) conducted in China show that donors act differently when money is given to them than when money is earned by their real efforts. Their results also show how experimental results can differ in a different giving culture. For instance, they found matching grants, which usually increase giving rates in the United States, crowd out individual giving in China. Thus, the study signals the potential that experimental designs have for comparative studies across different countries where various giving traditions and cultures can be observed.

In the field of charitable giving research, identifying the direction of the causal relationship, that is, what motivates donors to give, is perhaps the most important goal because nonprofit managers need to effectively target their potential donors. Mason's (2015) study is a good example of how experimental designs can reveal the cause of different giving decisions. Experiments are useful here because they allow researchers to vary the conditions in which participants are asked to make their giving decisions. The importance of publicity in philanthropy has been known mostly through anecdotal evidence, but until recently was never empirically demonstrated; Mason (2015) is the first experiment to provide empirical evidence of the non-trivial impact image motivation makes on giving decisions.

Challenges and Suggestions for Future Experimental Research

Despite the contribution these three experimental studies make to the nonprofit literature, they also have limitations. Addressing such limitations can help future studies in nonprofit management implement more rigorous experimental study designs and measure the effect of alternative explanations. The first experimental study (Kim and Van Ryzin 2014) used hypothetical money and organisations, so it is possible that individuals acted differently than they would in a real-life situation. In other words, the disincentive these authors found for individual giving may not work the same way in more real-world contexts. Relatedly, how each participant felt about the size of the $100 donation budget they received to allocate between the two organisations may influence their decision differently in a real situation. For some participants, the $100 budget may seem too small to give much thought to and for others it may seem like too large a gift; this evaluation could interfere with participants' consideration of the presence of government funding. These individual factors are a common limitation of many online survey experiments. Future researchers should consider experimental designs that might overcome such limitations, for example laboratory experiments using real money or field experiments involving real organisations.

In the second study, Li and his colleagues (2015) used an experiment that may address such limitations because its design lets participants donate with real money they earned from completing given tasks. This study showed that participants act differently with earned money versus money that was given to them. This study also incorporated five real nonprofit organisations that are currently operating in China. However, the participants were limited to students in one university, which raises some questions about the generalisability of the findings. Further, the number of participants was relatively small (N = 173) for the number of conditions in the experiment, which decreases the statistical power of the study. This study incorporated four different conditions and five nonprofit organisations to which donors could choose to give; the presence of so many conditions makes it challenging to identify the real cause of observed outcomes. Future studies that use experiments should be careful when deciding how many conditions to vary, given the available sample size, or, if possible, it is recommended to conduct power analysis to support the validity of the results.

The third experiment (Mason 2015) suffered from a similar issue of small sample size. The study generated a relatively low response rate to the community giving programme; the author's attempt to identify the effect of the experimental treatment would have been benefited from a much larger sample size or a higher response rate. In experimental studies, dealing with the issue of small sample size is common because it is not easy to recruit enough participants with the limited budget and time that most researchers and nonprofits have. Further, limited resources make it difficult to observe the effect of an experimental design over a long period of time. Perhaps if there was more understanding in the nonprofit sector of the benefits that experimental studies can offer, more resources would flow into the field so that researchers could conduct experiments with a larger number of participants. By working in partnership with nonprofit organisations, field experiments also provide real-world giving scenarios that may not only benefit research, but could also have implications for the organisation where the experiment is set. It is also worth considering the ways in which experimental research may be administered in similar ways across cultures and countries to determine differences in cultural norms around giving and volunteering. While this chapter focused primarily on the literature and findings in the US context (with the exception of Li et al., which was set in China), there are significant opportunities to engage in experimental research around the world.

Although this chapter focused on theories of altruism and charitable giving, laboratory and field experiments can be helpful in addressing many questions that relate to nonprofit management more generally, or government–nonprofit relationships specifically. For example, what rationales drive some nonprofit organisations to create rainy day funds while others do not? Are donors indeed discouraged by seeing a large amount of overhead costs? Are there ways that government contracts with nonprofit organisations could be better designed and managed? In order to move into this new avenue of research using experiments, the field must first appreciate the potential benefit experimental designs have for answering many questions that other methodological approaches have left unanswered. Doing so could generate more financial and human resources, which are necessary to initiate relatively high-cost experiments either in a laboratory setting or in the field. Online survey experiments can be a cost-efficient option, but only if enough appropriate participants can be recruited. In all cases, the choice of the type of experiment should be based on the specific research questions; identifying the right kind of design is the first step towards successful experimental research.

References

Andreoni, J. 1989. 'Giving with impure altruism: applications to charity and Ricardian equivalence', *The Journal of Political Economy* 97 (6): 1447–58.

Andreoni, J. 1990. 'Impure altruism and donations to public goods: a theory of warm-glow giving', *The Economic Journal* 100 (401): 464–77.

Andreoni, J. 2006. 'Leadership giving in charitable fund-raising', *Journal of Public Economic Theory* 8 (1): 1–22.

Ariely, D., A. Bracha, and S. Meier 2009. 'Doing good or doing well? Image motivation and monetary incentives in behaving prosocially', *American Economic Review* 99 (1): 544–55.

Becker, G. S. 1976. 'Altruism, egoism, and genetic fitness: economics and sociobiology', *Journal of Economic Literature* 14 (3): 817–26.

Becker, G. S. 1978. *The Economic Approach to Human Behavior*. Chicago: University of Chicago Press.

Bekkers, R. and P. Wiepking 2011. 'A literature review of empirical studies of philanthropy: eight mechanisms that drive charitable giving', *Nonprofit and Voluntary Sector Quarterly* 40 (5): 924–73.

Benabou, R. and J. Tirole 2006. 'Incentives and prosocial behavior', *American Economic Review* 96 (5): 1652–78.

Bernheim, B. D. 1986, 'On the voluntary and involuntary provision of public goods', *American Economic Review* 76(4): 789–93.

Blackwood, A., K. Roeger, and S. L. Pettijohn 2012. *The Nonprofit Sector in Brief: Public Charities, Giving and Volunteering*. Washington, DC: Urban Institute.

Boris, E. T., E. de Leon, K. L. Roeger, and M. Nikolova 2010. *Contracts and Grants between Human Services Nonprofits and Governments*. Washington, DC: Urban Institute. www.urban.org/research/publication/con tracts-and-grants-between-human-service-nonprofits-and-governments.

Brooks, A. C. 1999. 'Do public subsidies leverage private philanthropy for the arts? Empirical evidence on symphony orchestras', *Nonprofit and Voluntary Sector Quarterly* 28 (1): 32–45.

Brooks, A. C. 2000a. 'Is there a dark side to government support for nonprofits?' *Public Administration Review* 60 (3): 211–18.

Brooks, A. C. 2000b. 'Public subsidies and charitable giving: crowding out, crowding in, or both?' *Journal of Policy Analysis and Management* 19 (3): 451–64.

Cialdini, R. B. and N. J. Goldstein 2004. 'Social influence: compliance and conformity', *Annual Review of Psychology* 55 (1): 591–621.

Diamond, A. M. 1999. 'Does federal funding "crowd in" private funding of science?' *Contemporary Economic Policy* 17 (4): 423–31.

Fehr, E. and J.-R. Tyran 2001, 'Does money illusion matter?' *American Economic Review* 91 (5): 1239–62.

Ferris, J. M. and El. Graddy 1991. 'Production costs, transaction costs and local government contractor choice', *Economic Inquiry* 29 (3): 541–54.

Frederickson, D. G. and H. G. Frederickson 2006. *Measuring the Performance of the Hollow State*. Washington, DC: Georgetown University Press.

Froelich, K. A., T. W. Knoepfle, and T. H. Pollak 2000, 'Financial measures in nonprofit organization research: comparing IRS 990 return and audited financial statement data', *Nonprofit and Voluntary Sector Quarterly* 29 (2): 232–54.

Glazer, A. and K. A Konrad 1996. 'A signaling explanation for charity', *American Economic Review* 86 (4): 1019–28.

Gneezy, U. and J. A. List 2006. 'Putting behavioral economics to work: testing for gift exchange in labor markets using field experiments', *Econometrica* 74 (5): 1365–84.

Gneezy, U., S. Meier, and P. Rey-Biel 2011. 'When and why incentives (don't) work to modify behavior', *The Journal of Economic Perspectives* 25 (4): 191–209.

Grønbjerg, K. A. 2002. 'Evaluating nonprofit databases', *American Behavioral Scientist* 45 (11): 1741–77.

Grønbjerg, K. A. and R. M. Clerkin 2005. 'Examining the landscape of Indiana's nonprofit sector', *Nonprofit and Voluntary Sector Quarterly* 34 (2): 232–59.

Hall, M. H. 2001. 'Measurement issues in surveys of giving and volunteering and strategies applied in the design of Canada's national survey of giving, volunteering and participating', *Nonprofit and Voluntary Sector Quarterly* 30 (3): 515–26.

Hansmann, H. B. 1980. 'The role of nonprofit enterprise', *The Yale Law Journal* 89 (5): 835–902.

Hansmann, H. B. 1987. 'Economic theories of nonprofit organisations', in *The Non-profit Sector: A Research Handbook*, edited by W. W. Powell. New Haven, CT: Yale University Press, 27–42.

Harbaugh, W. T. 1998a. 'The prestige motive for making charitable transfers', *American Economic Review* 88 (2): 277–82.

Harbaugh, W. T. 1998b. 'What do donations buy? A model of philanthropy based on prestige and warm glow', *Journal of Public Economics* 67 (2): 269–84.

Horne, C. S., J. L. Johnson, and D. M. Van Slyke 2005. 'Do charitable donors know enough – and care enough – about government subsidies to affect private giving to nonprofit organisations?' *Nonprofit and Voluntary Sector Quarterly* 34 (1): 136–49.

Hughes, P., W. Luksetich, and P. Rooney 2014. 'Crowding-out and fundraising efforts', *Nonprofit Management and Leadership* 24 (4): 445–64.

John, P., S. Cotterill, L. Richardson, A. Moseley, G. Stoker, C. Wales, G. Smith, H. Liu, and H. Nomura 2013. *Nudge, Nudge, Think, Think: Experimenting with Ways to Change Civic Behaviour*. London, A&C Black.

Karlan, D. and J. A. List 2007. 'Does price matter in charitable giving? Evidence from a large-scale natural field experiment', *American Economic Review* 97 (5): 1774–93.

Karlan, D., J. A. List and E. Shafir 2011. 'Small matches and charitable giving: evidence from a natural field experiment', *Journal of Public Economics* 95 (5): 344–50.

Kim, M. and G. G. Van Ryzin 2014. 'Impact of government funding on donations to arts organisations: a survey experiment', *Nonprofit and Voluntary Sector Quarterly* 43 (5): 910–25.

Lampkin, L. M. and E. T. Boris. 2002, 'Nonprofit organization data', *American Behavioral Scientist* 45 (11): 1675–1715.

Li, H., J. Liang, Y. Liu, and H. Xu 2015. 'What influences charitable giving? An experimental study', *Working Paper*.

Light, P. C. 2011. *Making Nonprofits Work: A Report on the Tides of Nonprofit Management Reform*. Washington, DC: Brookings Institution Press.

Mason, D. P. 2013. 'Putting charity to the test: a case for field experiments on giving time and money in the nonprofit sector', *Nonprofit and Voluntary Sector Quarterly* 42 (1): 193–202.

Mason, D. P. 2015. 'Recognition and cross-cultural communications as motivators for charitable giving a field experiment', *Nonprofit and Voluntary Sector Quarterly* 45 (1): 192–204.

McKeever, B. S. and S. L. Pettijohn 2014. *The Nonprofit Sector in Brief 2014: Public Charities, Giving and Volunteering*. Washington, DC: The Urban Institute Center on Nonprofits and Philanthropy.

Monroe, K. R. 1994. 'A fat lady in a corset: altruism and social theory', *American Journal of Political Science* 38 (4): 861–93.

Nikolova, M. 2014. 'Government funding of private voluntary organisations: is there a crowding-out effect?' *Nonprofit and Voluntary Sector Quarterly* 44 (3): 487–509.

Ostrom, E. 1998. 'A behavioral approach to the rational choice theory of collective action: presidential address, American Political Science Association, 1997', *American Political Science Review* 92 (1): 1–22.

Payne, A. 1998. 'Does the government crowd-out private donations? New evidence from a sample of non-profit firms', *Journal of Public Economics* 69 (3): 323–45.

Perry, J. L. 2012. 'How can we improve our science to generate more usable knowledge for public professionals?' *Public Administration Review* 72 (4): 479–82.

Roberts, R. D. 1984. 'A positive model of private charity and public transfers', *Journal of Political Economy* 92 (1): 136–48.

Roberts, R. D. 1987. 'Financing public goods', *Journal of Political Economy* 95 (2): 420–37.

Roeger, K. L., A. Blackwood, and S. L. Pettijohn 2012. *The Nonprofit Almanac 2012*. Washington, DC: Urban Institute Press.

Rondeau, D. and J. A. List 2008. 'Matching and challenge gifts to charity: evidence from laboratory and natural field experiments', *Experimental Economics* 11 (3): 253–67.

Saidel, J. R. and S. L. Harlan 1998. 'Contracting and patterns of nonprofit governance', *Nonprofit Management and Leadership* 8 (3): 243–59.

Salamon, L. M. 1999. *America's Nonprofit Sector: A Primer*. New York, Foundation Center.

Salamon, L. M. 2010. 'The changing context of nonprofit leadership and management', in *The Jossey-Bass Handbook of Nonprofit Leadership and Management* (3rd edition), edited by D. O. Renz and Associates, 77–100. San Francisco CA: Jossey-Bass, A Wiley Imprint.

Samuelson, P. A. 1955. 'Diagrammatic exposition of a theory of public expenditure', *The Review of Economics and Statistics* 37 (4): 350–6.

Schiff, J. A. 1990. *Charitable Giving and Government Policy: An Economic Analysis*. Westport, CT: Greenwood Press.

Shafir, E., P. Diamond, and A. Tversky 1997. 'Money illusion', *The Quarterly Journal of Economics* 112 (2): 341–74.

Shang, J. and R. Croson 2007. 'A field experiment in charitable contribution: the impact of social information on the voluntary provision of public goods', *The Economic Journal* 119 (540): 1422–39.

Simmons, W. O. and R. Emanuele 2004. 'Does government spending crowd out donations of time and money?' *Public Finance Review* 32 (5): 498–511.

Smith, S. R. and M. Lipsky 1993. *Nonprofits for Hire: The Welfare State in the Age of Contracting*. Cambridge, MA: Harvard University Press.

Steinberg, R. 1991. 'Does government spending crowd out donations?' *Annals of Public and Cooperative Economics* 62 (4): 591–612.

Steinberg, R. 2006. 'Economic theories of nonprofit organisations', in *The Non-profit Sector: A Research Handbook*, second edition, edited by W. W. Powell and R. Steinberg, 117–39. New Haven, CT: Yale University Press.

Tinkelman, D. and D. G. Neely 2011. 'Some econometric issues in studying nonprofit revenue interactions using NCCS data', *Nonprofit and Voluntary Sector Quarterly* 40 (4): 751–61.

Trivers, R. L. 1971. 'The evolution of reciprocal altruism', *The Quarterly Review of Biology* 46 (4): 35–57.

Van Slyke, D. M. 2007. 'Agents or stewards: using theory to understand the government–nonprofit social service contracting relationship', *Journal of Public Administration Research and Theory* 17 (2): 157–87.

Warr, P. G. 1982. 'Pareto optimal redistribution and private charity', *Journal of Public Economics* 19 (1): 131–8.

Warr, P. G. 1983. 'The private provision of a public good is independent of the distribution of income', *Economics Letters* 13(2–3): 207–11.

Wise, C. R. 1990. 'Public service configurations and public organisations: public organization design in the post-privatization era', *Public Administration Review* 50 (2): 141–55.

Wright, B. E. and A. M. Grant 2010, 'Unanswered questions about public service motivation: designing research to address key issues of emergence and effects', *Public Administration Review* 70 (5): 691–700.

PART IV

Issues and Implications

21 | Replication of Experimental Research: Implications for the Study of Public Management

RICHARD M. WALKER, M. JIN LEE, AND
OLIVER JAMES

Introduction[1]

Replication is increasingly recognised as an important part of the production of knowledge in not only the natural sciences, but also the social sciences (Francis 2012; Freese 2007; Nosek and Lakens 2014; Sargent 1981; Schmidt 2009). This chapter concentrates on replication in the context of public management experiments. There are multiple definitions of replication and many social science journals now have a standard for replication of published work in the sense of requiring authors to make their data, programs, and relevant details available to permit other researchers to reproduce the results that appear in the published paper. The checking of analysis is one important type of replication, and the issue of replicability is important for most kinds of method. Replication of this kind is important; however, less discussed but also important is replication that goes beyond the checking of data and rerunning of code. Replications of experiments can be divided into two categories. *Direct replications* implement the same experimental procedure as previous research, and *conceptual replications* attempt to replicate findings including tests of hypotheses by using different experimental procedures or materials (Schmidt 2009). Direct replication is often taken as the heart of experimental replication. This chapter sets out a set of distinctions discussed by Tsang and Kwan (1999) that unpack different forms of direct replication based on whether researchers use the same or different samples and same or different populations and extends into conceptual replication based on whether researchers use different experimental procedures or materials in their research.

[1] The research is partially funded by General Research Fund Grant of the RGC Grant: Project No.: #9042434, CityU grant #11611516.

Replication has theory-based and practical benefits for the study of public management. This chapter illustrates these benefits using experiments about red tape as an example of their application to a core public management topic. Direct replications in particular can help uncover errors (and even fraud) and can help researchers understand if previous experimental findings have simply emerged by chance (Ioannidis 2005), decreasing false discovery rates. Replications can help generalise findings to contexts or subject populations beyond those where the initial experiment was conducted, helping to address the criticism sometimes made of experiments that their findings can lack generalisability (Cartwright and Hardie 2012). Relatedly, replications of experiments to other contexts can help assess the expectations of theory about how and why findings vary between settings.

Public management is a discipline that, as well as having an interest in theory development and evaluation, addresses real-world problems. As such, it is what Herbert Simon (1996) termed a 'science of design' – that is, a science addressing questions about the best way to design policies, programs, and organisations that can deliver public services (Shangraw and Crow 1989). If the theories examined, tested, and developed to enhance the practice of public management do not have broad applicability, then public management scholars fail to deliver a design science. These aspirations make the context within which studies are conducted a central concern of researchers (Freese 2007; Lewin 1943; Morrell and Lucas 2012). However, in public management research, the replication of prior studies is typically limited to the examination of theories using non-experimental methods in different contexts (which themselves can be compromised by using different measurement and analysis) or the inclusion of similar measures in studies with different primary research questions. Both approaches contribute to the accumulation of sound public management theory and evidence that can assist with appropriate policy and administrative designs. However, we suggest that public management should make much more explicit use of replications of experiments.

Replication in Public Management

Replications are not widely conducted in public management although, on the narrower definition of replication, researchers are making more of their data and code available for others to inspect and use.

A reasonable measure of the amount of replication research going on is the amount of published work that explicitly describes itself as replication. A search for replicat* was conducted in the Web of Science in mid-2015 in the journals *Journal of Public Administration Research and Theory*, *Public Administration*, *Public Administration Review*, and *Public Management Review*. The title and abstract search resulted in only 10 articles carrying the term *replication*, or derivatives thereof. The majority of these studies discussed results that were replicated, or samples or methodologies that can be, or were, replicated. Two studies replicated prior work but were non-experimental. Posner and Schmidt (1994) undertook a literal replication of a prior survey of US federal government executives while Van Ryzin (2006) carried out a replication of one of his prior studies on expectation-disconfirmation theory using survey methods, incorporating extensions of methodology.

Given the limited use of the term *replication* explicitly in articles, and the possibility that replication may have been conducted without it being described as such, we delved deeper into the *Journal of Public Administration Research and Theory* (JPART) by undertaking a Google Scholar search. This search engine examines the full body of text and not just the abstract. This investigation revealed a much wider use of the term *replication*. Studies using the term *replication* fell into five categories. The first group of articles used the word *replication* with no reference to the act of replicating research, of which there were 43. Four studies undertook replication of others' research. In the third group, 10 articles discussed the need to replicate the study conducted in order to establish generalisability. Seventeen articles used replication when discussing methods, for example, noting that they were replicating measures used in prior studies or that data should be archived to permit replication. In the fifth group, 23 articles undertook the replication of prior work, largely focused on observational research studies, and typically replicated part of a study. This brief analysis indicates that the majority of articles that use the term *replication* normally do so from a methodological perspective to validate measures or to test if an aspect of their study findings comported with prior work in the field.

The growth in public management studies employing experimental methods has not been matched by their replication and extension: none of the studies discussed so far replicated previously published experimental studies, although some replications of experiments in JPART have been conducted of experiments by the same research team reported within the same article (e.g., James 2011; Jilke, Van Ryzin, and Van de Walle 2016). Though there are challenges in publishing replications – notably editorial preference for new findings on fresh topics results in replications being discouraged – their publication is increasing in other social science disciplines (e.g., Francis 2012; Nosek and Lakens 2014). The lack of replication of experimental public management research makes it urgent to address this deficit. This need is particularly pressing given the prior dearth of resources for undertaking studies such that findings from experiments have relatively high internal validity so are worthy of checking, the small N problem of samples in some studies leading to research that by chance can produce extreme results not reflecting general tendencies, and the potential for contextual limitations of findings that can limit relevance to specific narrow domains. Experiments also offer a great opportunity for different forms of replication because, as experimentation involves manipulation, which should be specified by the researcher, the procedures of a well-conducted experiment are typically clear for researchers to attempt replication.

Approaches to Replication

Literal, exact replications that are the same in all respects are neither feasible nor realistic; it is impossible to replicate a prior study exactly because time has passed or subjects have changed (Rosenthal 1991). However, most social science researchers accept the principle that some related forms of direct replication are possible. Researchers who have a different view tend instead to adopt an historical, idiographic method that views research findings as the unique outcome of complex interactions between contexts and researchers, making them inherently difficult to replicate. There are considerable benefits from replication of different kinds, and in the remainder of this section we focus on a framework of types of replication developed by Tsang and Kwan (1999) and previously applied to general (rather than exclusively experimental) research in business management.

Tsang and Kwan (1999) set out different kinds of replication study by contrasting the study as using the 'same measurement and analysis' or 'different measurement and/or analysis' and whether the study uses the 'same data set' or 'same population' or 'different population'. This framework results in six different forms of replication, and these are

Table 21.1: *Six types of replication*

	Same Measurement and Analysis	Different Measurement and/or Analysis
Same data set	1) Checking of measures and analysis	2) Reanalysis of data
Different data but same population	3) Exact replication	4) Conceptual extension
Different data from different population	5) Empirical generalisation	6) Generalisation and extension

Source: Adapted from Tsang and Kwan (1999)

laid out in Table 21.1. While Tsang and Kwan's terminology suggests different populations in terms of different participants, for example, different groups of public managers in different service areas or jurisdictions, the ideas also apply analogously to different contexts, for example, the same public managers operating in different institutional settings (such as if they were transferred between different types of organisations).

The first type is defined by using the same measurement and analysis with the same data set; thus, it is replication as 'checking of analysis'. This form is akin to auditing studies, reflected in requiring data sets to be publicly lodged at the review or publication stage. Second, when different measurement or analysis is applied to the same data set, the replication can be seen as a 'reanalysis of data'. This may be performed because new, more sophisticated analytical tools have been developed since the original study was conducted. This approach has benefits in assessing the robustness of findings using alternative analytical methods and thus the validity of evidence about empirical implications of theory.

Third, the same measurement and analysis can be applied to the same population, applying the original research procedures with the aim of reproducing the original results in an exact replication but using a different sample of participants from that population, for example, a different sample of public managers from a given country. This approach has a stronger theory testing focus than the checking of analysis because the validity of the prior study is tested in a new, independent sample. If similar results are obtained, the reproduction of prior evidence further validates the foundations and theoretical conjecture of the original study.

Fourth, a conceptual extension involves procedures different from those of the original study but still aimed at testing the same theory and drawing a sample from the same population. Conceptual extensions seek to test the generalisability of the fundamental causal process or theory across various operationalisations of the experimental procedures, treatments, or measurements. However, a single conceptual extension replication cannot verify prior findings comprehensively because null findings may arise from the alternative procedures, measurements, and analysis. Consequently, a number of conceptual extension replications using similar and dissimilar measurement and analysis may be required to clearly advance knowledge. Conceptual extension replication is commonly practised using non-experimental or quasi-experimental designs; however, the adoption of alternative research designs may not adequately assist in the quest for robust theories supported by evidence, and further experimental studies are often desirable.

Tsang and Kwan (1999) final two replication categories are both replications with different populations but differ in using either the same or different measurement and/or analysis. The fifth kind, empirical generalisations use the same research design, measures, and analysis, and assess if findings will hold up in different populations. Sixth, generalisations and extensions use a different population and do not implement the original measurement and analysis. However, if results differ, it is not always known if these are a result of poor or different design or change of population. Having said this, generalisations and extensions represent an important step in testing the findings of a public management study in one context and applying them to another. Findings from a study with both a different population and context with variation to the research design can help theory strengthening through external validity and different methods.

Perhaps the most straightforward of the six types of replication are checking of data and analysis, reanalysis, and exact replication. However, even these forms can present complexity. Checking of data and analysis requires careful recordkeeping by the initial researchers and the capacity of those conducting the replication to understand and implement what was done and any departures in findings by the replication. Reanalysis requires careful consideration of why different analytical techniques might lead to different results.

A further consideration in replication is whether the replication should be done by the same researchers who did the original study or by an independent research team. An argument in favour of independence is that researchers may have less emotional or other attachment to findings and can be impartial, which makes the research less subjective in terms of dependency on who is carrying it out. An argument against independence is that the involvement of the original researchers can be beneficial for knowing what to do and how to do the replication and interpret its findings. For example, there is considerable tacit knowledge in research that can be difficult to codify and thus replicate independently. However, on balance, given the desirability of research findings not to depend on who conducts the research, a more independent approach to replication is generally preferable, although there is likely to be variation on a case-by-case basis.

Two important questions public management researchers can consider when undertaking replications with extensions are incentives and the nature of the subject pool. Incentives are sometimes paid because they are assumed to enhance performance in the study and reduce variability in the data (Morton and Williams 2010). However, social psychologists argue that financial incentives may affect the results of experiments. Research subjects may partake in research projects because it is interesting or enjoyable, or because they think it serves important purposes, which is sometimes labelled intrinsic motivation. Alternatively, extrinsic motivation from financial incentives suggests that subjects are self-interested and self-serving and thus require a cash payment or some other tangible incentive to ensure they will volunteer for and diligently carry out assigned tasks in research studies (Deci et al. 1999). The presumption in behavioural economics tends to be that such incentives have no negative side effects; in the public management literature on motivation and public service, in contrast, some researchers contend that incentivising extrinsic motivation crowds out intrinsic motivation, which can have a damaging effect on study findings by lowering the performance of the subject (Frey and Jegen 2001). Public managers are often presumed to be intrinsically motivated to serve others and improve society. Arguments on public service motivation suggest that public sector workers are not so much motivated by monetary rewards, but rather by their service ethos and its various manifestations (Vandenabeele et al. 2014). The impact of incentives on research subjects is an important issue for study, especially if extrinsic motivations may crowd out intrinsic motivations and thus lead to results that are different from those in studies that provide incentives.

A number of studies use students as subjects and it is possible to argue that students, particularly MPA students, are managers in waiting and thus good subjects. Indeed, in many universities MPA students are in fact already working professionals. This argument has not been tested, however, and public management scholars who work with experimental research methods could undertake separate replications using both students and managers. Comparison of findings between these different subject groups will help answer chronic concerns in the discipline about practical relevance. Typically, it is expected that studies conducted on practising managers will have more external validity, while those conducted among students will be more difficult to generalise to the real world of public management. This is because public managers – not students – are the objects of the theories and hypotheses being tested. However, MPA and other postgraduate students engaged in courses on public management and policy are likely to at least hold similar values as practising managers, and indeed some of them may even be practising managers (although perhaps with less seniority and professional experience). These issues, like that for incentives, remain to be fully explored in public management research.

Replicating a Study of the Perceptions of Red Tape

There are many ways to replicate, and each approach has different aims and advantages. In this section, we use examples to illustrate two forms of replication from Table 21.1, the empirical generalisation approach and the generalisation and extension approach. These replications are based on Kaufmann and Feeney's (2014) study of red tape perceptions. Kaufmann and Feeney adopt Bozeman's (1993: 283) definition of red tape: 'rules, regulations, and procedures that remain in force and entail a compliance burden for the organisation but have no efficacy for the rules' functional object'. Red tape is a burdensome process and interrupts efficient work; however, it is hard to capture red tape because it is based on personal working style and working purpose, and thus perception. Bozeman (2012) argues that the perception of red tape is not related to the rules and procedures themselves, but is more concerned with their relative effectiveness, or ineffectiveness. Kaufmann and Feeney (2014) extend this logic and argue that it is not only burdensome rules and procedures, but outcome favourability that affect red tape perception. People might feel that rules or procedures are less burdensome when they get a positive outcome, rather than a negative outcome.

Therefore, Kaufmann and Feeney (2014) hypothesised that rule burden and outcome favourability will affect perceived red tape, and develop four types of vignettes to study this. The vignettes describe a student's event around class registration in a university. The student, Robin, needs to register for a mandatory course, and only one class is suitable for Robin's schedule. However, the class is already full, so Robin requests an exception for registration from the class coordinator with a rational reason. Scenario A describes relatively short administrative procedures and a positive outcome, where Robin's request is accepted. Scenario B describes the same short procedure but with a negative outcome, where Robin's request is rejected. Scenario C describes long procedures and a positive outcome, and Scenario D describes long procedures and a negative outcome.

The four vignettes were randomly assigned across a sample of MPA students in a US university. Alongside the vignettes, the survey carried a number of pretest questions on personal character (bureaucratic personality, locus of control, and risk preference) and general red tape perception in everyday life and red tape perception at the university. The dependent variable drew directly on Bozeman's definition with a small addition: 'If red tape is defined as "burdensome administrative rules and procedures that have negative effects on the organization's effectiveness", how would you assess the level of red tape that you encounter *in this story?*' (Kaufmann and Feeney 2014: 183).

The replication of Kaufmann and Feeney (2014) was conducted in Hong Kong with surveys implemented in March, May, and September 2015. We used the same survey questionnaire described in the original study, and invited the same level of students at City University of Hong Kong. The survey was distributed in classes on the masters of arts degree in public policy and management, an equivalent qualification.

Table 21.2 presents the descriptive statistics of participant characteristics for both studies. The original study analysed 81 MPA students in the United States and the replication study analysed 136 MPA students in Hong Kong. The samples were similar in the sense of red tape perception on average from both daily life (USA = 5.74,

Table 21.2: *Descriptive statistics from original study and replication study*

	Original Study	Replication Study
Location	United States	Hong Kong
Language	English	English
Size of sample	81	136
Experimental red tape perception	6.70 (2.44)	6.53 (1.86)
Scenario A	5.19 (2.20)	6.16 (1.68)
Scenario B	6.71 (2.39)	6.58 (1.68)
Scenario C	7.11 (2.68)	6.66 (1.94)
Scenario D	7.86 (1.77)	6.68 (2.14)
Bureaucratic personality	3.56 (0.45) [0.57]	3.35 (0.45) [0.32]
Locus of control	2.36 (0.52) [0.79]	3.22 (0.45) [0.62]
Risk preference	2.57 (0.43) [0.75]	2.41 (0.52) [0.83]
Gender	0.63 (Female = 1)	0.54 (Female = 1)
Age	29.52 (6.24)	26.81 (4.78)
General red tape perception	5.74 (2.15)	5.68 (1.49)

Mean (S.D.) [Cronbach's Alpha]

HK = 5.68) and the vignettes (USA = 6.70, HK = 6.53). Two of the personality measures led to similar mean scores: bureaucratic personality (USA = 3.56, HK = 3.35, though the alphas reported here were low) and risk preference (USA = 2.57, HK = 2.41). However, for the locus of control measure, the mean score in the United States was lower than for Hong Kong (USA = 2.36, HK = 3.22). The Hong Kong sample is also slightly younger than the US sample (HK = 26.81, USA = 29.52).

As shown in Table 21.2 and Figure 21.1, the differences between red tape perceptions in each scenario are clear in the US sample, but are not so distinct in the Hong Kong sample. In the US sample, scenarios show perceptions of red tape continuously increasing from vignette A, B, C, through D. This is important because Scenario C shows a long administrative procedure that is associated with higher red tape than Scenario B. It seems that the long administrative procedure has more impact on perceptions of red tape than the negative outcome. In the Hong Kong sample, the difference between red tape in each scenario is not clear-cut. In particular Scenarios B, C, and D show similar levels of perceived red tape. Notable here was the smaller standard deviation recorded in Hong Kong in

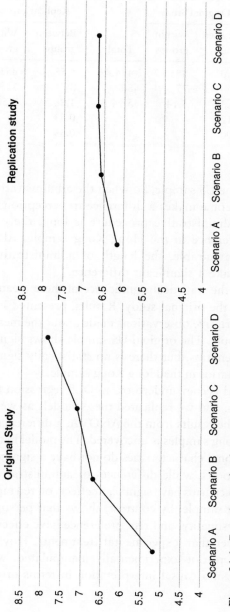

Figure 21.1: Experimental red tape perception from original study and replication study

Table 21.3: *ANOVA analysis of experimental red tape perception across scenarios*

	Original Study			Replication Study		
	Between groups	Within groups	Total	Between groups	Within groups	Total
Sum of squares	79.02	395.87	474.89	5.58	451.58	457.16
Df	3	77	80	3	129	132
Mean square	26.34	5.14	5.94	1.86	3.50	
F	5.12			0.53		
Sig.	0.00			0.66		

comparison to the US sample. So when the administrative procedure is short, the outcome makes a difference to perceptions of red tape, but when the administrative procedure is long, the outcome does not make a difference in the Hong Kong sample. Also, when the outcome is unfavourable, the length of administrative procedure also does not make a significant difference.

We tested for the statistical significance of these mean scores using ANOVAs, as in the original study. Results, presented in Table 21.3, support the descriptive observations made about the means across the Hong Kong sample. The original US sample shows significant difference between scenarios, but there is no statistically significant difference among scenarios in the Hong Kong sample.

Kaufmann and Feeney undertook an OLS regression to predict red tape perceptions, and we replicated these models as well. As may be expected given the results from the ANOVA, a difference between the US and Hong Kong samples is uncovered. The model in the US sample shows that personal characteristics do not have a significant effect on red tape perceptions, while differences of administrative length and outcome in the scenarios have significant effects on red tape perception. The Hong Kong sample, by contrast, shows that personal character, bureaucratic personality, and risk preference have effects on red tape perceptions rather than experimental treatments. However, because these factors were not experimentally manipulated, we would not want to give them a causal interpretation in terms of effects on red tape perceptions.

Table 21.4: *Standardised OLS regression predicting red tape perceptions*

Measures	Original Study		Replication Study	
General red tape	0.26**	(0.12)	0.49***	(0.11)
Bureaucratic personality	−0.19	(0.71)	0.22**	(0.33)
Locus of control	0.04	(0.46)	−0.05	(0.36)
Risk preference	0.06	(0.55)	−0.24**	(0.31)
Age	−0.14	(0.07)	−0.07	(0.03)
Gender	0.06	(0.49)	−0.13	(0.30)
Version B	0.30**	(0.69)	0.13	(0.44)
Version C	0.32**	(0.71)	0.16	(0.40)
Version D	0.46***	(0.59)	0.16	(0.43)
N	81		116	
F	3.74***		6.53***	
R-squared	0.34		0.36	
Adjusted R-squared	0.25		0.30	

*** < 0.001; ** < 0.05; * < 0.01; (std. err.)

Differences between the original study and our replication suggest the findings of the original experiment cannot be generalised across settings. However, these differences may be explained in a number of ways, notably the factors associated with country culture and context, which may have important bearings on studies of administrative procedures and outcome favourability toward red tape perception, together, perhaps, with issues of language. These issues are discussed in more detail in the next section.

When planning the replication, potential differences were anticipated; thus we included an extension. Specifically, we included questions that asked how students in Hong Kong relate to Robin's situation and feel about the positive outcome from Robin's request. Because the original hypothesis is outcome favourability, we reasoned, it might be helpful to test whether students favour the scenario's outcome in a more direct way. Therefore, we extended the replication into a conceptual replication by adding one more dependent variable question in each scenario: 'Do you agree with Ms. Jones's decision?', with Ms. Jones being the name we gave to the class coordinator in the scenario.

Table 21.5: *Agree to Ms. Jones's decision*

	Scenario Type				
	A	B	C	D	Total
Disagree	5	10	9	17	41
	(16.13%)	(34.48%)	(23.68%)	(56.67%)	
Agree	26	19	29	13	87
	(83.87%)	(65.52%)	(76.32%)	(43.33%)	
Total	31	29	38	30	128
	(100%)	(100%)	(100%)	(100%)	

The original study assumes that students will agree with Ms. Jones's decision, so subjects will perceive a positive outcome in Scenarios A and C and that they will disagree with Ms. Jones's decision in Scenarios B and D. However, it turns out not all students agree or disagree with Ms. Jones in our replication study. As shown in Table 21.4, around 50 per cent of students in Scenarios B and D also agree with Ms. Jones's decision to reject Robin's exceptional registration.

Then we can make an alteration based on students' thinking about Ms. Jones's decision. We can separate the students who support acceptance of Robin's exceptional registration, and the students who do not. The first group would fit to the original assumption, so they might feel positive about the outcome in Scenarios A and C, and negative about the outcome in Scenarios B and D. The second group would be reversed on outcome favourability.

Table 21.5 presents the ANOVA analysis for two groups. These results are indicative but need to be interpreted with caution because they could have been affected by allocation to different treatment groups and are not causal, because they are not experimentally manipulated. However, they are suggestive of differences between different groups' treatment effects based on how they viewed the decision. In both groups, the differences of red tape perception between scenarios are not significant. Even though the differences are not significant, the red tape perception shows a pattern like Figure 21.2. The graph in the left side is red tape perception of students who support Robin's exceptional registration, as the original study assumed. Different from the US sample, students' red tape perception is more sensitive to the outcome rather than the length of administrative

Table 21.6: ANOVA analysis of the groups who support/do not support Robin's registration

	Supporting Robin's registration			Not supporting Robin's registration		
	Between groups	Within groups	Total	Between groups	Within groups	Total
Sum of squares	9.77	238.72	293.49	4.70	131.30	136.00
Df	3	76	79	3	41	44
Mean square	3.26	3.733		1.57	3.20	
F	0.87			0.49		
Sig.	0.46			0.69		

procedures. So when the outcome is positive as they expected, even though the administrative procedure is long, students assess lower levels of red tape compared to the shorter procedure with the negative outcome. When students do not support Robin's situation, the length of administrative procedure and outcome favourability show mixed effects.

Based on the results from Table 21.2 to Table 21.6, we find some differences between the US sample and the Hong Kong sample. First of all, their baseline of perception would be general red tape perception from their daily life and university experience. The general red tape perception is slightly higher in the US sample (USA: 5.74, HK: 5.68, Table 21.2). Because the baseline is similar, it is worthwhile to compare the red tape perceptions of the two countries directly.

The average level of red tape perception from the scenarios is also slightly higher in the US sample than in the Hong Kong case (USA: 6.70, HK: 6.53). The red tape perception from Scenario A is higher in the Hong Kong sample (USA: 5.19, HK: 6.16), but in Scenario B, the Hong Kong sample reports lower red tape perception. In the Hong Kong sample, red tape perceptions from Scenarios B (6.58), C (6.66), and D (6.68) are similar, but lower than red tape perception from Scenario B (6.71) in the United States. Red tape perception in Scenarios C (7.11) and D (7.86) in the US sample are of course higher than those in the Hong Kong sample.

The US students perceive less red tape from Scenario A than their general red tape perception from daily life and university

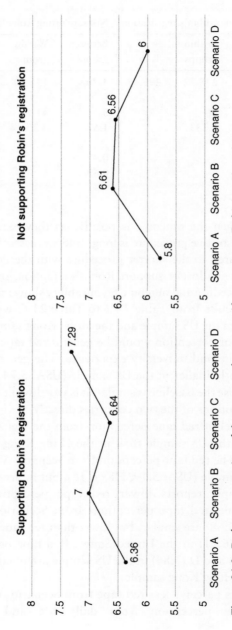

Figure 21.2: Red tape perception of the groups who support/do not support Robin's registration

experience. For US students, Scenario A is seen as a less burdensome administrative procedure than, or having less negative impacts on a university's effectiveness, based on Bozeman (2012)'s definition. Students perceive higher levels of red tape from Scenario B to D than general red tape. On the other side, Hong Kong students perceive that every scenario includes higher levels of red tape than normal life situations.

In both the United States and Hong Kong, the red tape perceptions from the scenarios show the same order, namely A, B, C, and then D, so both the US and Hong Kong students perceive the highest level of red tape in Scenario D. In addition, the standard deviation for Scenario D (1.77) is also smaller than for the other scenarios (A: 2.20, B: 2.39, C: 2.68). However, Hong Kong students have various perceptions about Scenario D. Even though Hong Kong students had the highest level of red tape perception in Scenario D, the differences between other scenarios are very little and standard deviation is the biggest among scenarios (A: 1.68, B: 1.68, C: 1.94, D: 2.14). For both the US and Hong Kong samples, people who perceived higher levels of red tape in their daily life also saw higher levels of red tape from the scenarios (Table 21.4).

Implications for Theory and Practice

The replication described in this chapter is unusual in public management research and the usefulness for understanding the topic of red tape comes in part because the results of the replication do not confirm the prior study's findings using a similar design and materials in a new context. This could suggest that there are weaknesses in the theory assessed by the Kaufmann and Feeney study, or that measurement and analysis could be improved. However, we do not come to this conclusion. Throughout this chapter we have placed emphasis on public management theory as being affected by context and populations of subjects, and as being a design science that integrates this view into practical policies and programmes. In transplanting Kaufmann and Feeney's US-based study to the Far East, a number of issues arise that seem likely to explain, in part, the differences in findings and the theoretical and practical implications of the replication.

Cultural differences occur in a number of ways, including language, the common relationship between universities and students, and a culture associated with collectivism. The sample of subjects is a mixture of Mainland Chinese and Hong Kong students. While Hong Kong is part of greater China, the political and economic systems are very different and there are variations in culture, which may lead the two groups of students to interpret authority in very different ways. In the case of Hong Kong, students read and write English at university. However, their primary reading and speaking language is Cantonese, and their second language is not English, but standard Chinese (≈Mandarin). For the mainland students, their first language is Mandarin and their second English. While students can read the vignettes in English, they might think that the story is not realistic, it is too academic, or it does not reflect their day-to-day understanding of university life. Linguistic factors may also influence the results.

The central rule concept used in the replication may result in different interpretations. Red tape is commonly translated as the Chinese term Fan-Wen-Ru-Jie (繁文縟禮), and it means vexatious rules and process. So Chinese cultured people might already have some sense about red tape, and their perception cannot just come from the English definition provided in the survey question. That might be why the general red tape measure has a stronger effect in the OLS model in the Hong Kong sample (Table 21.4).

It is reasonable to anticipate that the East Asian context of the replication will weaken the relationships identified in the original studies. Hong Kong offers differences in culture, society, and organisation in contrast to the location of the original study (Hofstede Centre 2015). Hong Kong has a mixed culture between traditional Chinese collectivist culture (emphasising group interests, cooperation, and personal relationships) and a more Western, business-oriented culture that is very different to the individual culture of a country such as the United States or Switzerland (which has a culture emphasising individual relationships and direct communication), where a number of the original studies were conducted. Hong Kong forms one of the subcultures of Chinese culture, which uses the written Chinese language. Chinese cultures mainly have two written forms, simplified Chinese and traditional Chinese, but include hundreds of various speaking languages. Hong Kong people use traditional Chinese, which is different from the official type of mainland China, and speak Cantonese. Hong Kong has faced many immigrants and refugees during the twentieth century, including the effects of world wars, and many Asian local wars and ideological or religious conflicts. So many people who live in Hong Kong have multiple layers of identities coming from Chinese-language cultures, local cultures where their ancestors or parents come from (locals in China, Britain, and many of Southeast Asia), and Hong Kong local culture. Variations from the original research findings can therefore be anticipated, allowing us to probe both intercultural variations in the theory and its robustness across cultures.

Last, while public bureaucracy in Hong Kong looks much like that in the West, the literature would suggest that government agencies in Hong Kong are much more hierarchical than those in the West, with a duty-based culture, and are leadership centric (Berman et al. 2010). The consequence for this study is that rules are likely to be more tolerated, particularly red tape, and public organisations held in higher regard. This would suggest that not only might findings be weaker in the replication, but they may even be reversed. However, it is important not to overstate the case for difference. A number of studies also point toward similarities in experience between the East and the West. In relation to the characteristics of management reform, Christensen and colleagues (2012) show how many reforms in China are strongly influenced by the West, and display similar origins and characteristics. A recent study by Van der Wal and Yang (2015) found that administrative values between the East and West display more similarities than differences. These findings of similarities lead to the following proposition: the results of the replications on organisational design will be in the same direction as the original studies, but weakened by Hong Kong's diverse culture.

Challenges and an Agenda for Replication in Public Management

The challenge is readily apparent: there is an urgent need for replications of public management studies that implement experimental designs. When scholars implement replication studies, there are a number of research design options based on varying data sets, population, measurement, and analysis, as recommended by Tsang and Kwan (1999). Replications that draw on empirical generalisations or generalisations and extensions are likely to be very useful for a design science such as public management by showing whether policies and programmes have the same effects across different populations and contexts. Empirical generalisations, as demonstrated for the case of red tape, replicate the original study with a new population and examine the external validity of prior studies. Given the lack of replication studies to date, conducting empirical generalisations will offer a number of important insights to the discipline.

Having laid down this challenge, and one that is technically achievable, there remain some problems to surmount. First and foremost will be dealing with the norms of academic publication. Many have noted the expectations of journal editors for new and innovative research findings that report positive results (see, e.g., Nosek and Lakens 2014). Arjen van Witteloostuijn (2015) has persuasively discussed the normative and institutional pressures within the management and business community, and in doing so shows that across an increasing number of disciplines the unwillingness of scholars to conduct, or perhaps editors to publish, replication studies has led to problems of validity of our knowledge. When replications have been mounted in disciplines, including social psychology and medicine, it has not always been possible to achieve results that reflect the original study, resulting in some controversy and also some progress in knowledge. Given the limited number of experimental replication studies in public management, there is an opportunity to make important strides for theory and to inform policy making by using replications to ensure that our theories and evidence are robust and relevant to particular contexts of interest. We urge others to engage with this agenda.

References

Berman, E. M., Moon, M. J., and Choi, H. S., ed. 2010. *Public Administration in East Asia: Mainland China, Japan, South Korea, Taiwan*. Boca Raton, FL: CRC Press.

Bozeman, B. 1993. 'A theory of government "red tape"', *Journal of Public Administration Research and Theory* 3(3): 273–304.

Bozeman, B. 2012. 'Multidimensional red tape: a theory coda', *International Public Management Journal* 15(3): 245–65.

Cartwright, N. and Hardie, J. 2012. *Evidence-Based Policy: A Practical Guide to Doing It Better*. Oxford: Oxford University Press.

Christensen, T., Dong, Lisheng, P., M., and Walker, R. M. 2012. 'Imitating the West? Evidence on administrative reform from the upper echelons of

Chinese provincial government', *Public Administration Review* 72(6): 798–806.

Deci, E. L., Koestner, R., and Ryan, R. M. 1999. 'A meta-analytic review of experiments examining the effects of extrinsic rewards on intrinsic motivation', *Psychological Bulletin* 125(6): 627.

Francis, G. 2012. 'The psychology of replication and the replication of psychology', *Perspectives on Psychological Sciences* 7(6): 585–94.

Freese, J. 2007. 'Replication standards for quantitative social sciences. Why not sociology?', *Sociological Methods & Research* 36(2): 153–72.

Frey, B. S. Reto, J. and Jengen, R. 2001. 'Motivation crowding theory', *Journal of Economic Surveys* 15(5): 589–611.

Hofstede Centre. 2015. http://geert-hofstede.com/. Accessed March 7, 2016.

Ioannidis, J. P. A. 2005. 'Why most published research findings are false', *PLoS Medicine* 2(8): e124.

James, O. 2011. 'Performance measures and democracy: Information effects on citizens in field and laboratory experiments.' *Journal of Public Administration Research and Theory*, 21(3): 399–418.

Jilke, S., Van Ryzin, G. G., and Van de Walle, S., 2015. 'Responses to decline in marketized public services: an experimental evaluation of choice overload', *Journal of Public Administration Research and Theory* doi: 10.1093/jopart/muv021.

Jilke, S., Van Ryzin, G. G., and Van de Walle, S. 2016. 'Responses to decline in marketized public services: An experimental evaluation of choice overload.', *Journal of Public Administration Research and Theory* 26(3): 421–432.

Kaufmann, W. and Feeney, M. K. 2014. 'Beyond the rules: the effect of outcome favourability on red tape perceptions', *Public Administration* 92(1): 178–91.

Lewin, K. 1943. 'Defining the "field at a given time"', *Psychological Review* 50(2): 292–310.

Morrell, K. and Lucas, J. W. 2012. 'The replication problem and its implications for policy studies', *Critical Policy Studies* 6(2): 182–200.

Morton, R. B. and Williams, K. C. 2010. *Experimental Political Science and the Study of Causality: From Nature to the Lab.* Cambridge: Cambridge University Press.

Nosek, B. A. and Lakens, D. 2014. 'Registered reports: a method to increase the credibility of published results', *Social Psychology* 45(3): 137–41.

Posner, B. Z. and Schmidt, W. H. 1994. 'An updated look at the values and expectations of federal-government executives', *Public Administration Review* 54(1): 20–4.

Rosenthal, R. 1991. 'Replication in behavioral research'. In J. W. Neuliep (Ed.), *Replication Research in the Social Sciences*, 1–30. Newbury Park, CA: Sage.

Sargent, C. L. 1981. 'The repeatability of significance and the significance of repeatability', _European Journal of Parapsychology_ 3(4): 423–43.

Schmidt, S. 2009. 'Shall we really do it again? The powerful concept of replication is neglected in the social sciences', _Review of General Psychology_ 13(2): 90–100.

Shangraw, R. F., Jr. and Crow, M. M. 1989. 'Public administration as a design science', _Public Administration Review_ 49: 153–8.

Simon, H. A. 1996. _Sciences of the Artificial._ 3rd Ed. Cambridge, MA: MIT Press.

Tsang, E. W. K. and Kwan, K.-M. 1999. 'Replication and theory development in organizational science: a critical realist perspective', _Academy of Management Review_ 24(4): 759–80.

Van der Wal, Z. and Yang, L. 2015. 'Confucius meets Weber or "managerialism takes all"? Comparing civil servants' values in China and the Netherlands', _International Public Management Journal_ 18(3): 411–36.

Van Ryzin, G. G. 2006. 'Testing the expectancy disconfirmation model of citizen satisfaction with local government', _Journal of Public Administration Research and Theory_ 16: 599–611.

Van Witteloostuijn, A. 2015. _What Happened to Popperian Falsification? A Manifesto to Create a Healthier Business and Management Scholarship – Towards a Scientific Wikipedia._ The Netherlands: Tilburg University.

Vandenabeele, W., Brewer, G. A., and Ritz, A. 2014. 'Past, present, and future of public service motivation research', _Public Administration_ 92(4): 779–89.

22 The Experimental Turn in Public Management: How Methodological Preferences Drive Substantive Choices

STEVEN VAN DE WALLE

In their search for empirical credibility, public management researchers may look for topics that lend themselves more easily to experimental methods. That in itself is not surprising in a field that has only recently discovered experimental research. This chapter looks at how the use of experimental methods may change the questions asked in the field of public administration and management. Possible consequences are a focus on discrete interventions and marginal changes, rather than on protracted system changes, and a continuing shift away from studying public organisations themselves to a study of the behaviour of individuals within these organisations.

Each change in methods and methodological preferences brings with it a change in what is studied. Sometimes, this is because new methods allow for studying things and phenomena that could not be studied in the past. In other cases, changed methodological preferences themselves change the researcher's focus. An example of the first is the (belated) adoption of multilevel statistics in public management research, which stimulated a shift towards studying 'large-N' multilevel settings. Hence the interest in studying local governments, schools, or hospitals because such settings require using more advanced multilevel designs. Another example is the renewed interest in political and public communication at a time when tools for analysing social media data became widespread. An example of the latter is the quantification of the discipline and the related use of (large) surveys, which has resulted in a shift to individuals (and their attitudes and behaviours) and away from the field's traditional focus on institutions.

In this chapter, I show how methodological preferences may drive substantive research choices. I first discuss different reasons why experiments have become popular in public administration. I then

461

show how the choice of an experimental approach influences what topics or questions are studied, and how they are studied. I end by sketching a number of implications for the future of experimental research in the field of public management and for publication practice.

Substance over Method, or Method over Substance?

The choice of research tools and designs depends on the substance studied in a discipline. For a historian, archival work obviously makes more sense than setting up an experiment, which requires a prospective rather retrospective approach. As a rule, studying a topic is best done using a variety of methods. Methods, however, may come to dominate substance because, as Kinder explains, 'Relying exclusively on one method constricts the range of questions that seem worth pursuing. Which questions are interesting and which are not is seen through the filter of what one is able to do. Methodological preoccupations inevitably and insidiously shape substantive agendas' (2011: 526). Methodological choices and preferences may drive what questions are seen as worth studying. Concerns with either external or internal validity likewise influence the choices that are made in doing research and selecting a topic or cases. Concerns in the discipline with external validity rather than internal validity lead to a focus on ever larger surveys, an increasing concentration on comparative case methods, and a rise in cross-sectional and cross-national research. Single-organisation studies and case studies have lost much of their standing, despite the fact that such studies have brought the discipline some of its seminal theoretical insights (just think about gypsum plants (Gouldner 1964) and forest rangers (Kaufman 1960)). Serious concerns about internal validity coupled with a desire to strengthen the discipline's empirical credibility have now stimulated a move to experimental methods. In line with Kinder, I argue that diversification in the methodological repertoire is essential to understand important questions. Also in line with Kinder (2011) and Kinder and Palfrey (1993), I argue that experiments are a valuable addition to the field of public management.

Why Experiments?

Public management as a field clearly had some catching up to do when it comes to using experiments (and indeed methods in general), especially with other disciplines like political science and economics pecking at its borders (see Chapter 1 for an overview of experiments in public management). In development studies and development economics, the randomised controlled trial (RCT) revolution included many experiments involving public service delivery in the education or health sectors (see Banerjee and Duflo 2012, for examples). Scholarship on decision making in public management has hardly moved to using experiments, while it has in other disciplines. Political scientists and economists increasingly move onto public administration and public management's 'turf' when conducting experiments involving all kinds of public decision making or the delivery of public services and public goods. How can we explain the discipline's belated turn to experiments as a research method? In this section, I distinguish between three potential explanations: fashions and bandwagon effects, the search for credibility, and custom.

Experiments as a Fashion?

In his presidential address to the American Sociological Association in 1975, Lewis Coser talked about a 'method in search of substance', reflecting on editors' decisions to stop accepting papers not using certain – then innovative – quantitative methods. In other words, newness in methods appeared to be seen as a quality criterion. Indeed, for the ambitious researcher, it makes sense to surf the wave of attention for experimental methods: journals and special issues court your copy and publishers want your handbook. Such academic bandwagons are a regular occurrence in most disciplines. Cass Sunstein, in this respect, referred to cascade effects:

Academics, like everyone else, are subject to cascade effects. They start, join and accelerate bandwagons. More particularly, they are subject to the informational signals sent by the acts and statements of others. They participate in creating the very signals to which they respond. Academics, like everyone else, are also susceptible to the reputational pressures imposed by the (perceived) beliefs of others. They respond to these pressures, and by so doing, they help to amplify them. It is for these reasons that fads, fashions, and bandwagon effects can be found in academia. (2001: 1251)

He links this, among other factors, to utility functions, such as entry to the job market or access to journals. The proliferation of special issues and calls for papers with a focus on experimental public administration and public management is a good stimulus for scholars to move into experimental research. Being among the first to use a method that is gaining recognition gives one advantages on the market for jobs, attention, and resources, where novelty and newness are important rhetorical devices.

Cascades may be information-induced. Especially in a field such as public management, where attention to methodology remains, despite many improvements, still relatively limited and with a lot of uncertainty, the work of well-known scholars and topical choices made by leading journals send information signals to the wider community, creating a cascade of experiments. Something like this appears to be happening now in public management research, as several leading journals have published special issues on experiments and a number of well-known scholars have jumped on the experimental research bandwagon. As the review of the published literature in Chapter 2 documents, the number of experiments published in public administration and management journals has grown rapidly in just the past few years.

The Search for Credibility

Public management has for a long time been regarded as merely applied, and has borrowed many of its theories and methods from more established disciplines such as political science, sociology, or economics. The focus on experiments fits within a wider trend in public management research of attempting to be seen as 'academic' rather than as an applied discipline (Gadellaa, Curry, and Van de Walle 2015). Such a transformation means adoption of the tools or at least the artefacts of real scientists. This transformation is helped by the simultaneous move to a more widespread use of field experiments within governments themselves and of RCTs in applied research. The latter trend has also helped the field not just to strengthen the internal validity of its work, but also the face validity of the work done, because experiments are increasingly seen as valid ways of understanding the world of policy making and service delivery.

Empirical credibility is thought to come mainly from quantitative approaches, and from high internal validity. Neighbouring disciplines, such as economics or political science, have had their own credibility movements before. Choice of research methods influences the perceived quality of the research. Quantifying provides studies with an aura of precision. Changing the name of one's institute or department to 'laboratory' imprints an aura of seriousness on what is going on inside – it will certainly convey a message that serious research is going on, rather than something 'soft'. An additional advantage of the experimental approach is that the simplicity of the designs allows for a high transparency of the research, something that is highly valued following a series of scandals in the social sciences (some of which, it has to be said, related to experimental research).

Custom: The Law of the Instrument

Custom is another mechanism that may explain attention to specific methods. Kaplan, in his 1964 classic 'the conduct of inquiry', called this 'the law of the instrument', which states 'that a scientist formulates problems in a way which requires for their solution just those techniques in which he himself is especially skilled' ([1964] 1998: 28). In other words, what the scientist is able to do determines the method used. Methodological myopia is a less complimentary description of this phenomenon. Method preferences are thus not merely led by substantial questions and the suitability of the method to the research at hand.

This mechanism is one that may work for or against a rapid proliferation of experimental research in the discipline. Most scholars trained in public management departments have received very little training in experimental research. Indeed, using experiments was confined to psychologists and a couple of behavioural economists and political scientists. Younger generations are now just starting to grow up with at least some of the basics of experimental design and analysis in their graduate school training. Still, the absence of experimental training in most public management programmes thus leads to a lack of the use of this method. Other disciplines, such as economics, could profit from the presence of marketing scholars to introduce experimental training into doctoral training curricula, thereby preparing future generations of scholars. Also, in development studies, attention to RCTs has grown substantially (Banerjee and Duflo 2012). In public management, there is as yet no 'school' known for experiments.

To make experimental methods flourish, doctoral students need to be acculturated and training priorities revisited.

How Experiments Change What Is Studied

Using experimental methods, just like using any other method, requires redesigning research questions in such a way that they are amenable to experimental testing. This means some questions are more suitable for experimental testing than others. Examples are, for instance, whether incentives work, or whether providing (performance) information alters behaviour. Experimental approaches, in other words, are excellent means to further our knowledge about some parts of the world of public management and administration, but this selectivity in topics may come to the detriment of other parts of the field. McDermott's review, for instance, showed that the bulk of experimental work in political science concerned voting (2005). When researchers, because of the reasons mentioned in the previous section, select their research question based on preference for using experimental methods, methodological preferences may shape what topics are researched. In a critical account of RCTs by recent Economics Nobel laureate Angus Deaton, he describes the process as follows: 'This goes beyond the old story of looking for an object where the light is strong enough to see; rather, we have at least some control over the light but choose to let it fall where it may and then proclaim that whatever it illuminates is what we were looking for all along' (2010: 429).

A more specific point beyond the general tendency of users of experimental methods to focus on certain topics is the observation that experimental methods can, in fact, only deal with very specific interventions. Experimental designs are particularly useful to study certain topics and processes, and have shown their value in particular in situations where discrete interventions take place. For this reason, experimental research pays particular attention to borders, sudden changes, or cut-off points, such as competitive grant allocations, entry exams, major policy changes, or redistricting. Because of their nature, experiments are also very well suited to test effects of specific interventions in evaluation studies, or for testing specific clinical treatments. Specific quasi-experimental designs allow for studying such situations. Think, for instance, about regression discontinuity designs that are used to study the effect of cut-off points, for example in competitions or selection procedures.

Such approaches are obviously not without value, but the real question is: how often do such situations occur in the real world? Interventions in the real world are seldom discrete. A treatment in real life is almost never a discrete event, but always confounded by other factors and proceeded by policy debates and announcements. Researchers relying on natural or quasi-experiments have frequently tried to solve this issue by redefining major interventions as if they were discrete. In this way, a major social change (a power blackout, a change in registration systems, etc.) is redefined as if it were just a simple decontextualised intervention. Such decontextualisation also makes it easier to identify instrumental variables.

Interventions generally interact to generate outcomes (Pawson and Tilley 1997). In the real world, interventions are often part of a wider package; they are complex, and they are not isolated from their environment. Still, this is something that can be tested using experiments, but it requires very large numbers of experiments, with many variations in treatments and contexts. One could then wonder whether experiments, despite their strong internal validity, are still worth the effort. Experiments are good for establishing causal effects, and that makes them highly effective in situations where causal effects are thought to be fairly simple and probably linear. In other words, they are not particularly useful to unravel complex processes or interactive systems. For the field, this may mean a welcome increase in studies on small changes, marginal improvements, and specific discrete interventions, but a marginalisation of studies on system change. Cartwright, in a paper on the use of RCTs, commented that narrowness of scope may be the price to pay for the obvious benefits of experimental research (2007: 11). In a survey among criminologists on why experiments were not used, a desire not to simplify complex social processes was mentioned prominently, alongside skills, practical issues, and ethics (Lum and Yang 2005).

The issue is not necessarily the external validity of the findings, but the external relevance of the stimulus being tested. Deaton gives the argument that in the real policy world, outcomes of a treatment may be different when, for instance, 'everyone is covered by the treatment rather than just a selected group of experimental subjects'. He gives a concrete example: 'Small development projects that help a few villa-gers or a few villages may not attract the attention of corrupt public officials because it is not worth their while to undermine or exploit them, yet they would do so as soon as any attempt were made to scale up' (2010: 448). An experiment on how subjects react to different forms of performance information (see, e.g., James 2010) on public programmes may well depend to a large extent on the prevalence of publicly available performance information or the existence of a tradition of a government that communicates openly about perfor-mance in the society within which the experiment is fielded. It also depends on whether everyone in society consults such information, or just a small group of people. We thus don't know whether the same effect would be found in a different context. A single treatment also tells us very little about behavioural changes beyond the experiment itself. It could be that presenting subjects with cues about responsibility for road maintenance (see, e.g., James et al. 2016; Marvel and Girth 2016) does indeed change attribution of blame, but at the same time, it may also change subjects' perception of road maintenance beyond the duration of the experiment, by making subjects more attentive to the issue and to cues about responsibility.

The main advantage of experiments, as Chapter 4 discusses, is that they allow testing causal claims. The move to experimental methods in the field, then, implies it is moving from one extreme practice – studying many variables with just a few observations, as, for instance, happens in case studies – to another where just one variable is studied. Monocausality may then emerge as a method artefact.

Implications for the Field

The experimental turn in public management research comes with a number of important implications for the field. First, strong internal validity needs to be coupled with stronger realism. This comes with ethical risks. The field also needs to pay closer attention to repeated experiments and dose-response experiments, and move to multi-arm studies in order to move beyond testing the effect of single discrete interventions, and to test entire theories. This will in turn probably entail a move to formal modelling in the discipline. Finally, it is expected that the experimental turn may change aca-demic publishing.

Enhancing Realism to Build Credibility

Researchers' preoccupation with internal validity and with establishing empirical credibility may mean a lack of attention to realism and external validity (Peters, Langbein, and Roberts 2015). Field experiments, discussed in Chapter 5 of this book, and replications (Chapter 21) go some way to addressing this concern. Still, this emphasis on internal validity risks becoming, as Cartwright (2007) described, a 'vanity of rigor', where internal validity takes precedence over external validity. The desire to use discrete interventions in experiments means that complex policy interventions are sometimes reduced to just one of their core elements. Treatments and interventions in experimental public management research are not only generally discrete; often they are also artificially recreated. This can potentially lead to very unnatural and artificial experimental treatments. Common examples are forcing a subject to look up information on a website or to read instructions, practices that are very far from the reality of how a person perceives government action (media, hearsay, and official communication). Indeed, as McDermott points out, 'subjects may behave one way in the relative freedom of an experiment, where there are no countervailing pressures acting on them, but quite another when acting within the constrained organisational or bureaucratic environments in which they work at their political jobs' (2005: 40). Thus, in the real world, interventions may work differently. For experimental research, this means their external validity is probably the highest in settings where control over the experimental stimuli is the lowest.

Settings used in vignette experiments likewise suffer from a lack of realism, because they need to summarise complex situations in a single vignette. Like-for-like comparisons, keeping all confounding factors under control, are incredibly hard to find, and also explain the attraction of conjoint experiments. Let me give an example of a study on a public–private comparison of customer reactions to service failure, where we wanted to compare customers' reactions to service repair efforts in a public and a private setting. It proved almost impossible to identify a service that was more or less comparable across the two domains, making it difficult to derive any hard evidence about the effects of the treatment (Thomassen et al. 2015). Sometimes, treatments may be so obvious or unrealistic that the experiment can no longer be considered blind to the subjects, or subjects lose their interest in the experiment. Using manipulation checks testing for perceived realism during the experiment, then, is no more than a post hoc justification for the researcher.

The challenge to researchers then is this: do you keep experiments as context-free as possible, by testing abstract interventions, or do you try to maximise the experimental realism, thereby introducing contextual and confounding factors that put internal validity at risk? Dickson (2011) contrasts the approaches in economics with highly stylised, abstract experiments to more naturalistic, context-rich approaches in psychology. Field experiments are a special case, because their setting makes it almost impossible to isolate them from their context. It is for this reason – 'the misunderstanding of exogeneity' – that Angus Deaton claims that 'experiments have no special ability to produce more credible knowledge than other methods' (2010: 424).

Increasing realism also means using study participants that resemble those that would normally receive the stimulus. Public management students or paid online workers may react differently to stimuli, just as a study on performance pay in a call centre may tell us little about how subjects in a tax administration would react. Recently, public management scholars have tried to deal with this problem by moving away from student samples and by relying on representative subject pools, or by doing field experiments involving the population that would normally be subjected to such policy change. High internal validity comes at the cost of narrowness of scope (Cartwright 2007: 12). Increasing realism requires realism of the experimental setting and the intervention, but also realism with regard to the subject pool.

The Ethics of Realism

Increasing the realism of experiments means moving the research closer to the real world. This comes with all kinds of risks. Lijphart, in his seminal 1971 paper 'Comparative politics and the comparative method', described experimental methods as 'the most nearly ideal method for scientific explanation' (1971: 684), but added that for practical and ethical reasons they can only rarely be used. Many topics and especially treatments are ethically out of bounds. Some of these may still be studied through case studies, or perhaps one could use perceptual measures and self-reports, but running an experiment would be unacceptable. A notable recent example is the Montana voting information experiment, whereby real voters received information on how candidates are placed on an ideological scale (Willis 2014). In this way, researchers intervene in real-world processes and become political actors. In public management, ethical issues proliferate once the research goes hand in hand with policy experiments and field experiments. But even in laboratory or online experiments, ethical issues exist, for instance, when one decides to present made-up performance information to subjects, thereby potentially changing their attitude towards government when not debriefed after the experiment.

A Need to Repeat, Dose, and Combine

As I have argued in this chapter, experiments are suited to test the effect of discrete interventions. In order to test theories, however, single experiments are insufficient. Multiple discrete intervention studies tell us more than a one-shot study. Experimentalists in our discipline need to build a tradition of repeated experimentation, as Chapter 21 on replication argues. To increase internal and external validity, both the subject pools studied and the phenomena studied need to be expanded. An example of the first would be when political scientists manipulate the many types of information they provide to subjects to measure changes in voting intentions. An example of the second would be where the presentation of information happens in both a private and more social setting, where the influence of peers may play a role in the formation of someone's attitude or judgment.

First, treatments need to be tested in different subject pools, different research settings, and different contexts. For example, we need to know whether an experiment on, for instance, the interpretation of absolute versus relative performance information about hospitals done with MPA students can be replicated with, say, parents and school performance information, or with medical doctors and hospital metrics in a context of budget cuts. Only then will we be able to say anything meaningful about causal mechanisms in a generalised way. A second extension of current experimental work is towards a tradition of dose-response studies, as is common in medical research. One needs to experiment with many different doses to study the effects of a treatment, and thereby not just look at differences in means between two groups, but also at trends, nonlinear effects, thresholds, outliers, and subgroups. Only then can validity be established.

It is only when our experiments are set up in such a way that they test all steps in a causal mechanism, and all aspects of an intervention in a complex set of trials, involving many different subject pools, that they become useful (again, this does not make experiments entirely different from other methods). In other words, the experiment is able to find whether an intervention works, but can only say how and why it works after a series of experiments. Such multi-arm studies are still incredibly rare in the social sciences. This makes doing experiments in public management a more complex and time-consuming way of doing research than it might at first appear, especially when one wants to use experiments to test the effect of real policy interventions in complex environments.

A Move to Formal Modelling

Just like survey research, experiments are especially useful for exploring topics that have already received attention, where theory development has already started, and where exploratory and descriptive research has taken place. Incidentally, unexpected experimental findings may give rise to new theory development. The deductive nature of experiments requires theories that can be turned into testable hypotheses. This means progress in experimental research may lead to more of an emphasis on formal modelling in the discipline, as Chapter 19 discusses. Through formal models, theories can be transformed into theoretical frameworks consisting of short, clear, and testable statements. In political science, much of the experimental work has focused on elections and voting, a subfield in which formal models have become very important (McDermott 2005: 50).

Often, however, experiments tend to be treatment based, rather than theory based. This is especially the case in the RCT tradition where the main function of experiments is to see whether policy interventions work, rather than to test a theory. Not using theory, and just letting the data speak for itself, has limitations. Theories help protect the researcher against confirmation bias, especially when many dependent variables are measured, allowing for selective shopping (an approach that could, however, be tackled using pre-registered analysis plans).

Moving to formal modelling will enable the discipline to test theories, through relying on a successive set of tests, testing elements of that theory, rather than the entire theory. A theory-driven approach will also result in a more focused test of mediation effects to uncover at least part of the mechanisms, thereby overcoming the critique of experiments being mainly suited to testing what works, not how it works.

A Change in Academic Publishing

A final implication of the experimental turn is that it will require a different publication culture. Currently, articles in public management are rather long, and contain extensive literature reviews and theoretical elaboration. Transposed to the current experimental turn, this means experimental articles in the discipline tend to be quite lengthy, with the empirical section taking up just about half or less of the entire article length. Often, articles also tend to consist of just as single experiment, or in rare cases include a replication on a different subject pool (see, e.g., Jilke, Van Ryzin, and Van de Walle 2016).

A publication culture more fitting the experimental tradition would mean that theory is moved to papers designing formal models, and that literature review sections will mainly concentrate on reviewing earlier experimental findings. To properly test theories, there is a need for articles containing a series of experiments, where each experiment tests part of a theory, varies the dose of the experimental manipulation, or replicates the same experiment on different subject pools. In sum, this will result either in a high volume of rather short articles with one or two experiments, or in longer articles presenting a substantial number of experiments simultaneously.

Concluding Thoughts

Experimental methods are generally seen as the gold standard for evidence. They probably are, if one looks at internal validity. But they are not the only method, and they are just a stage in the research process, which starts with mere observation and description (Gerring 2012). Once theories are formulated, they can be tested using experiments. This comes with all kinds of problems, notably external validity. For the field of public management, this means that we may be well on our way to producing credible knowledge about unimportant things. Experiments do respond, however, to the field's need to gain empirical credibility, especially at a time when economists increasingly focus on public services in their research.

An unexpected positive effect of the experimental turn may be a rapprochement of the academic study of public management and the world of practice. This is somewhat ironic, because the move to methods and designs that are ever more rigorous was partly born out of a discontent with the very strong practice orientation of the field and a reaction of scholars concerned with a lack of scientific rigour in the field. Within the discipline, a strong practice orientation was often seen as antithetical to using advanced methods. Experiments, now, have the potential to bridge this gap between top scholars, mainly interested in innovation and credible methods, and practitioners, who have discovered experiments as a useful method to test policies and real-life public management interventions. Still, experimentalists should not over-claim what they find, and methodological preferences never ought to steer the choice of research topics.

References

Banerjee, A. V. and Duflo, E. 2012. *Poor Economics. Barefoot Hedge-Fund Managers, DIY Doctors and the Surprising Truth about Life on Less than $1 a Day*. London: Penguin Books.

Cartwright, N. 2007. 'Are RCTs the gold standard?' *Biosocieties* 2(1): 11–20.

Coser, L. A. 1975. 'Presidential address: two methods in search of a substance', *American Sociological Review* 40(6): 691–700.

Deaton, A. 2010. 'Instruments, randomization, and learning about development', *Journal of Economic Literature* 48(2): 424–55.

Dickson, E. S. 2011. 'Economics vs. psychology experiments: stylization, incentives, and deception', in Druckman, J. N., Green, D. P., Kuklinski, J. H., and Lupia, A. (eds.). *Cambridge Handbook of Experimental Political Science*. Cambridge: Cambridge University Press, pp. 58–70.

Gadellaa, S., Curry, D., and Van de Walle, S. 2015. 'Hoe bestuurskundig is de bestuurskunde? Nederlandse bestuurskundigen vergeleken met hun Europese vakgenoten', *Bestuurskunde* 25(3): 67–79.

Gerring, J. 2012. 'Mere description', *British Journal of Political Science* 42(4): 721–46.

Gouldner, A. 1964. *Patterns of Industrial Bureaucracy*. New York: Free Press.

James, O. 2011. 'Performance measures and democracy: information effects on citizens in field and laboratory experiments', *Journal of Public Administration Research and Theory* 21(3): 399–418.

James, O., Jilke, S., Petersen, C., and Van de Walle, S. 2016. 'Citizens' blame of politicians for public service failure: experimental evidence about blame reduction through delegation and contracting', *Public Administration Review* 76(1): 83–95.

Jilke, S., Van Ryzin, G., and Van de Walle, S. 2016. 'Responses to decline in marketized public services: an experimental evaluation of choice-overload', *Journal of Public Administration Research and Theory* 26(3): 421–32.

Kaplan, A. (1964) 1998. *The Conduct of Inquiry: Methodology for Behavioural Science*. New Brunswick, NJ: Transaction Publishers.

Kaufman, H. 1960. *The Forest Ranger: A Study in Administrative Behavior*. Baltimore, MD: Johns Hopkins University Press.

Kinder, D. R. 2011. 'Campbell's ghost', in Druckman, J. N., Green, D. P., Kuklinski, J. H., and Lupia, A. (eds.). *Cambridge Handbook of Experimental Political Science*. Cambridge: Cambridge University Press, pp. 525–30.

Kinder, D. R. and Palfrey, T. R. 1993. *Experimental Foundations of Political Science*. Ann Arbor: University of Michigan Press.

Lijphart, A. 1971. 'Comparative politics and the comparative method', *American Political Science Review* 65(3): 682–93.

Lum, C. and Yang, S. M. 2005. 'Why do evaluation researchers in crime and justice choose non-experimental methods?' *Journal of Experimental Criminology* 1(2): 191–213.

Marvel, J. and Girth, A. 2016. 'Citizen attributions of blame in third-party governance', *Public Administration Review* 76(1): 96–108.

McDermott, R. (2005). 'Experimental methods in political science', *Annual Review of Political Science* 5: 31–61.

Pawson, R. and Tilley, N. 1997. *Realistic Evaluation*. London: Sage Publications.

Peters, J., Langbein, J., and Roberts, G. 2015. 'Policy evaluation, randomize controlled trials, and external validity: a systematic review', *Ruhr Economic Papers no. 589*. Bochum: Ruhr-Universität Bochum, Department of Economics.

Sunstein, C. R. 2001. Foreword: 'On academic fads and fashions', *Michigan Law Review* 99(6): 1251–64.

Thomassen, J.-P., Leliveld, M., Ahaus, K., and Van de Walle, S. 2015. *Prosocial Compensation after Service Guarantee Violation in For-Profit and Public Settings*. Mimeo.

Willis, D. 2014. 'Professors' research project stirs political outrage in Montana', *New York Times*, retrieved from www.nytimes.com/2014/10/29/upshot/pro fessors-research-project-stirs-political-outrage-in-montana.html.

23 | Changing How Government Works: The Transformative Potential of an Experimental Public Management *

PETER JOHN

Introduction

One of the persistent themes of public management is the tension between stability and innovation (Kelman 2005). Much of the experience of public management is a consequence of the counter-pressures between these two tendencies, with some bureaucracies engaging in reform, others embarking on periods of change only to return to more conventional pathways. Such a tension is unlikely to be resolved, and exploring it will engage researchers for many years to come just as it has done in the past. But recent developments in the social sciences – greater use of randomised controlled trials (RCTs or field trials) and more generalisable findings from behavioural economics (sometimes called nudging) – have the capacity to tip the balance towards reform and innovation. The two interlocking developments of RCTs and the science of behaviour change have the potential to open up public management and to set off cycles of positive feedback based on the appraisal of evidence and using it to design new policies and administrative procedures.

The aim of this chapter is to demonstrate the salience of the diffusion of new practices of acquiring knowledge within bureaucracies and the knock-on effects of their extended use, in particular

* Versions of this paper have been presented at the University of Southampton, C2G2 seminar, 30 October 2013; to the departmental seminar, University of Exeter, 4 December 2013; to the UK Political Studies Association Annual Conference, in Manchester, 14–16 April 2014; and to the workshop 'Causal effects in political science: the promise and pitfalls of experimental methods' held at the Nordic Political Science Association Conference in Gothenburg, 12–15 August 2014. I thank participants at these events for their comments and reactions.

in the way in which politicians and bureaucrats make and implement policies. Behaviourally informed policies tested by randomised evaluations can empower those who are prepared to risk refutations or confirmations of their ideas, and can help create a more knowledge-hungry public bureaucracy. What may be called an experimental public management is committed to continual testing and improvement, and is less concerned with self-justification and the preservation of existing practices. With its focus on understanding individual behaviour, public managers and politicians can take a more citizen-focused approach to public policies as they are encouraged to think outside their own assumptions.

These claims amount to an ideational argument: new practices and intellectual ideas have the power to shape the behaviour of public managers and politicians. With its strong claims for causal inference (Gerber and Green 2012), the randomised research design has become accepted and influential within the academic disciplines of economics, political science, and social policy, which is also linked to the rediscovery of experimental foundations of statistical analysis and the growing interest in natural and quasi experiments (Dunning 2012; see also Chapter 2 in this volume). The same can be said for the influence of behavioural approaches (Thaler and Sunstein 2008), which have spread across disciplines way beyond economics. As a result of these intellectual confluences, there has been a re-engagement of social science with more practical applications of theory, especially since it is not possible to do field trials without some manipulation of the world, and this requires the assistance of policymakers and public managers. Given the influences on the modern policy process from experts, the media, and international organisations, where ideas about behaviour change and the utility of experiments have diffused, it is no surprise that they should be readily taken up by public agencies, especially given how many social scientists are employed by governments. Some even talk of the emergence of the 'psychological state' whereby public managers use these new techniques as a more precise form of social control (Jones et al. 2013).

The more difficult question is how these ideas intersect with the interests of politicians and public managers with pressures to claim credit, to use evidence selectively, and to progress careers, which are classic themes in the study of the utilisation of evidence by policymakers (e.g., Weiss 1972: chapter 6). There is also resistance to using randomised evaluations within bureaucracies. In other words, in spite of the improvements, there is no nirvana on the horizon, as politics intervenes and remains an integral part of policy-making and evaluation.

To make these arguments, this chapter is divided into the following sections. The first is a review of the use of experimental methods in the policy world and the emergence of policy experiments; the second is a chart through the behavioural revolution in the social sciences, the adoption of behavioural public policies by governments and their direct link to randomised evaluations; the third section sets out the practical dimensions of the process just described, using examples and setting out limitations; and then the conclusion seeks to summarise the developments overall and to assess the balance of forces currently in play as well as to draw implications for understandings of public bureaucracies.

Policy Experiments

A policy experiment is a special kind of RCT or field trial carried out by policy-makers, where the public authority carries out the intervention itself by varying the tools of government under its control, and it contrasts with other field experiments done by researchers using their own resources, though these often involve the collaboration of community groups and some kind of partnership with the relevant public authority. Although policy experiments can be done in house with government or agency researchers, they are more often done in collaborations with researchers and academics, either in an official evaluation or in another form of partnership. The main aim is to test the impact of a policy or existing procedure, or to trial a new way of doing business in the public authority. In that sense, they are practical exercises, but can at the same time answer more general questions in social science theory.

There was an initial interest by policy-makers and academics in policy experiments in the 1920s, which declined and then revived again in the 1960s. One famous example in the UK shows the challenges of doing experiments with close collaboration with policy-makers. The Lanarkshire School milk experiment in 1930 tested whether providing free school milk would improve the health of children, reported and criticised by Student (1931). In this experiment,

20,000 children in 67 schools participated, with half not getting free milk. Assignments were done alphabetically, but teachers adjusted them and swapped the allocations, causing the control students to do better. This trial shows the challenges of working with policy-makers, especially at the delivery end, and the difficulty of reconciling standard administrative procedures and discretion to the demands of randomised evaluation. In political science, the 1920s was also the time when field experiments took place, undertaken by Harold F. Gosnell (1926) on stimulating voter registration (see also Gosnell 1927). But attention has faded since that time (except Eldersveld 1956).

The period from the 1930s is that of the supremacy of the clinical trial whereby medicines and procedures are tested out in many trials and meta-analyses, becoming the official standard for almost all medical treatments and procedures, and in effect shaping understandings and uses of the RCT. Researchers have conducted more than 350,000 clinical trials up to 2002, according to one estimate (cited by Bloom 2005: 12), and medicine and medical practice remains at the heart of the systematic reviewing as in the Cochrane reviews. There are about 25,000 trials published each year with the numbers doubling every 10 years (Henegan 2010).

In spite of their advantages, the use of experiments by social scientists and those in government has been surprisingly infrequent. In spite of the interest in the interwar period, experiments were the exception rather than the rule. Other techniques were preferred, such as mass surveys of public opinion, which became cheaper and more efficient to run in the post-1945 period and gave social scientists and government agencies a range of opportunities for answering research questions that were easier than direct interventions. Survey companies carry out the surveys using standardised methods of sampling and interviewing, then simply supply the data. All the researchers or governments had to do was to ensure the costs of the survey were met. As computing improved through larger memory and customised software, it because easier – even routine – to analyse these surveys. The collection of more reliable data by government agencies encouraged observational studies, which involved the use of ordinary least squares and then other related estimators as familiar methods for use by social scientists and governments. Many social scientists – and thence government researchers – followed the methods of economics and quantitative sociology. They used regression and related techniques to try to understand a range of phenomena. Once these methods become embedded, it is easy to see how they were sustained over time, and why other techniques did not find favour. In any case these methods appeared to offer answers to the big questions in social science or evaluation, and it was only later that social scientists came to realise that some of these questions are in fact hard to answer without improved methods. Moreover, surveys became increasingly expensive and suffered from declining response rates.

Gradually the use of experiments has expanded out from medicine. Influential was the work of Campbell on the statistical properties of experiments and quasi-experiments (Campbell and Stanley 1963), who argued for their use in social settings (Campbell 1957). An important period was the expansion of welfare policies in the 1960s and the demands for stronger evaluations (see Greenberg et al. 2003). An early, prominent example can be found in the use of experiments to test for the effect of negative income tax in the United States (Munnell 1987), which originated out of the Office of Economic Opportunity and were done in New Jersey. These suffered from administrative and organisation problems, a familiar experience with policy experiments. Another early example is with housing assistance in the 1970s, which tested for the impact of direct financial aid (see Orr 1999). In the 1980s, there was an expansion of the range of social programmes evaluated with randomised allocation, in particular welfare-to-work policies (Riccio and Bloom 2001), job training (Bloom et al. 1997; Bloom et al. 1993), and reemployment bonuses (Robins and Spiegelman 2001). Another early productive area is crime with evaluations being done to test hot spots policing (Sherman et al. 1995; Sherman and Weisburd 1995; Weisburd and Green 1995) and peer mentoring (Petrosino et al. 2002). Education is another area of expansion, for example experiments testing class size reduction (Word et al. 1989) and education subsides (see Angrist et al. 2002). The growing interest in RCTs caused scholars to call for more social experimentation as a way of life for government agencies (Campbell 1969; Greenberg et al. 2003), though such periodic advances are also met with the realisation of the high likelihood of failure of implementation with RCTs (see Berk et al. 1985).

One further area of expansion has been in the development field, in particular in the evaluation of aid programmes, with centres of activity at research organisations, including Abdul Latif Jameel Poverty Action

Lab and Innovations for Poverty Action. These experiments have been large scale, such as Olken's performance management experiment in Indonesia (Olken 2005; Olken and Wong 2012). RCTs have now become widely established as a method of evaluation by economists in this field (see Duflo et al. 2007) and link to work in political economy (Humphreys and Weinstein 2009). These studies have involved direct collaboration with policy-makers, such as donor government or aid agencies, that deliver the interventions.

The United States has led the field in the use of RCTs, but other countries have experimented with them too. The UK has had a patchy experience, but the employment department has had a long history of using RCTs going back to the 1980s, mainly testing initiatives to encourage employment (see for a review Greenberg and Shroder 2004). There was a gradual increase in the use of RCTs in the 1990s associated with the Labour government's evidence-based policy initiative, and the publication of the official handbook of evaluation, *The Magenta Book* (HM Treasury 2003), which highlighted RCTs. More recent examples include the evaluation of HM Prison Service Enhanced Thinking Skills Programme (McDougall 2009). One area of expansion has been in education, for example the Welsh government's free breakfast initiative (see Moore et al. 2010), and then the work of the Education Endowment Foundation in funding RCTs. Yet, in spite of their concentration in the medical field, the patchy progress and the history of some failures of implementation, it is fair to say that RCTs are more commonly used now by policy-makers.

Behavioural Public Policy

A considerable amount of academic evidence has appeared in recent years about the importance of more citizen-friendly policy design in achieving more effective public outcomes. The claim is that citizens can be motivated to do more positive acts for themselves and society through better 'choice architectures', such as default mechanisms and carefully tailored information signals that encourage them to make better choices. Such ideas have been influential in economics and psychology for many years. They have been popularised by Richard Thaler and Cass Sunstein in their book *Nudge* (Thaler and Sunstein 2008), and have been widely discussed by local authorities and central governments, such as in the UK, the United States, and France.

President Obama appointed Cass Sunstein to head up the Office of Information and Regulatory Affairs. The Obama administration also launched the Social and Behavioral Sciences Team to encourage nudge-like approaches to improve various federal government programmes and procedures. In France, the Centre for Strategic Analysis of the Prime Minister employed a behaviour science expert, Olivier Oullier, as an advisor on behaviour change policies, and in Germany, various behavioural scientists were recently hired to establish a 'Nudge Unit' within the Federal Chancellery.

Of course, the idea that public agencies should seek to influence the behaviour of citizens is as old as government itself. Governments have always modified individual behaviour and specialists have advised government about how to carry out strategies that require behaviour changes on the part of the population, such as driving cars more safely, ceasing smoking, and reducing risky behaviours. But it would also be true to say that such advice was confined to identifying target populations; offering general incentives to behave differently, such as through the tax system; creating deterrents through the criminal justice system; and providing citizens with information so they can act more responsibly.

The main advances in knowledge have taken place during the past 25 years or so, drawing on the work of psychologists, in particular Slovic, Kahneman, and Tverskey (Kahneman et al. 1982). The central idea is that human beings approach problems with a set of pre-set biases, which influence them towards certain kinds of behaviours. They tend not to react to changes in incentives or from the imposition of extra costs in a straightforward way. External agencies can still influence behaviour, but they need to understand the exact nature of these biases so they can design highly human-centred policies that go with the grain of cognitions, which can produce strong results in the form of changed citizen behaviours.

Such ideas have been highly influential (see John and Richardson 2012). In the UK, in 2004 the Cabinet Office's document *Personal Responsibility and Changing Behaviour: The State of Its Knowledge and Its Implications for Public Policy* (Halpern et al. 2004) made the case for using more knowledge about citizen behaviour and for applying theories of interpersonal behaviour to construct better policies that engage citizens with the state. Government interest in the latest thinking was demonstrated by the work that went into the MINDSPACE report, published by the Cabinet Office and the Institute for Government in March 2010 (Dolan et al. 2010). This guide gathered together key insights from behavioural economics and psychology and listed them in its memorable acronym.

In the UK there has been a step-shift in the interest in behavioural public policy, which has built on a pre-existing set of activities, both from long-running programmes of research in specific policy fields, and the previous government assessment of the state of knowledge in the behavioural sciences. The Labour government 1997–2010 developed an interest in the topic, particularly in policy areas of crime and health, and this is indicated by official publications, such as the papers discussed previously. The former head of the Civil Service, Lord O'Donnell, who was an academic economist, also has a passion for work in the field. The coalition government elected in 2010 set up the Behavioural Insights Team as its main institutional innovation in promoting behaviour change, sometimes referred to as 'the nudge unit' or just BIT (see John 2014). The unit 'draws on insights from academic research in behavioural economics and psychology, to apply them to public policy-making'.[1] It aims to find ways to encourage citizens to adopt more pro-social behaviours and to make better choices. It was created in June 2010 as a unit within the Cabinet Office. It comprised at first seven officials, but expanded in size pretty quickly. It took advice from experts, such as Richard Thaler, and set up an academic advisory panel. Now it is owned partly by Nesta (National Endowment for Science, Technology and the Arts) – a body that spends the money from the national lottery – and partly by the government. BIT is a nonprofit organisation and sits outside government.

The unit uses RCTs to test out interventions. To this end, the team published in 2012 *Test, Learn, Adapt: Developing Public Policy with Randomised Controlled Trials*. Written with academics, this is a guide about how to do experiments (Haynes et al. 2012). The team worked with Her Majesty's Revenue & Customs (HMRC) in February 2011 to pioneer different wordings for the reminder of tax returns, which used RCTs. HMRC then carried out a set of RCTs on tax reminders coordinated by Michael Hallsworth (Hallsworth et al. 2014). Many of these findings are summarised in *Fraud, Error and Debt: Behavioural*

---

[1] www.gov.uk/government/organisations/behavioural-insights-team.

Insights Team Paper (Cabinet Office 2012). What this work shows is that the science of behaviour change and the use of RCTs cohere well.

Behaviour Change and Experimental Public Management

In the preceding pages, the empirical elements to the argument have been assembled. The growth of RCTs has been asserted in the world of policy. At the same time a behavioural revolution in social science is afoot with greater focus on individual psychology and a search to find out which interventions can promote better policy outcomes. In this enterprise, the interests of academia and policy are as one: the expertise of academics needs to be harnessed by public agencies while academic research needs government input to test out its claims.

The close academic–policy partnership increases the input of knowledge into the policy process whether it is through the importance of research design or levering findings from academic papers and converting them into behavioural tests. In the past, much research knowledge tended to follow on from or be separate from the policy-making and implementation process, often being commissioned as an add-on or afterwards, which has been the main reason for the lack of influence of ideas and research on the design of public policies (see Weiss 1997, 1998). Behaviour change and RCTs require the integration of the research and policy processes: the implementer and the researcher need to talk to each other as partners, which can encourage the exchange of ideas between them. Policy-makers and public managers need to understand the research techniques for the interventions to work and research is produced in a timely way and with a high level of impact on policy.

The demands of experimentation and behaviour change can privilege those in bureaucracies who are interested in innovation and in using new ideas to change public services. The commitment to the RCTs is very important because it ensures that the policy-maker or public manager is prepared to accept that there is no effect at all as well as the confirmation of the preferred theory. This takes some courage because policy-makers and public managers do not want to attract blame for trying out policies that do not work, even though the RCT route is a way to ensure that the right policies are in the end chosen. Campbell spoke of experimental administrators, 'who have justified the reform on the basis of the importance of the problem, not the certainty of their answer, and are committed to going on to other solutions if the first one tried fails' (1969: 29). As Brewer and Brewer (2011) remind us, the argument for 'reforms as experiments' made by Campbell and others is long entrenched, though maybe only recently being realised.

As the experiences from the 1960s and 1970s indicate, it is rarely the case that public managers put forward policies dispassionately as there is likely to be considerable investment and sunk costs in existing policy choices and long-running administrative procedures. One example of this is the commitment in the developing world to CDR (community-driven reconstruction) that requires public participation in programmes to decide where the money is spent, which is claimed to be a means of improving outcomes. But the findings of Humphreys and colleagues (2012), based on a large RCT in East Congo examining 200 outcomes in treatment and control villages, shows no impact of CDR. But policy-makers find it hard to accept evaluations which show that a particular intervention does not work (see Weiss 1972: 126–7). In some fields, such as medical interventions and tests for new drugs, it is accepted that evidence from RCTs and meta-evaluations should determine whether a programme or treatment is authorised, and these recommendations are routed into the decision-making process, such as the procedures for drug approval used by the National Institute for Clinical Excellence (NICE) in the UK and the Food and Drug Administration (FDA) in the United States. The question is whether there will be a gradual diffusion of these procedures to other policy fields. At the moment, there is still resistance to using the findings from RCTs. For example, in England between 1998 and 2005, the government commissioned an RCT to study the impact of culling of badgers to limit the spread of bovine tuberculosis. The RCT showed that the cull had no effect. But the government did not accept the findings and commissioned an expert panel to review them, a case study reviewed by Dunlop (2013). The letter that accompanied the report of the expert panel says, 'While badgers are clearly a source of cattle TB, careful evaluation of our own and others' data indicates that badger culling can make no meaningful contribution to cattle TB control in Britain.'[2] However, the government's website states, 'In this trial there were

---

[2] http://webarchive.nationalarchives.gov.uk/20110911090544; www.defra.gov .uk/foodfarm/farmanimal/diseases/atoz/tb/isg/report/final_report.pdf

positive and negative changes in the incidence of TB in cattle as a result of badger culling.'

The other factor that may promote change is a challenge to the hierarchy of who makes decisions in bureaucracies, a shift from the policy-maker or public manager to the street-level implementer or delivery agent, who is the person who has the contact with the citizens, and control over the main things that can vary such as letters and linked-to IT systems/online support. Typically, these individuals are lower down the organisation, or work in lower-status delivery organisations, distant from the peak policy-makers and public managers; they are usually charged with delivering innovations so may be more grounded in administrative matters as a result of their engagement with practical questions, developing a perspective on what works from their day-to-day experience rather than from pre-conceptions or the latest fashions. The switch to a digital-era governance (Dunleavy et al. 2006), where the manipulation of the online presence of government becomes central to the delivery of policy and achievement of outcomes (Margetts and Dunleavy 2013), also shifts the focus to delivery questions, and to the professionals who run such operations. And, indeed, it is websites and social media that provide some of the most interesting opportunities for nudges and RCTs.

There is also an effect of these hands-on collaborations on the academic process too. The academic is forced to think through the ideas in ways that are testable and consistent with the objectives of the policy-maker or public manager and are feasible. Such practical questions may have the effect of ensuring the academic focuses on practical, real-world applications of theory and testing, and may encourage a more active approach to understanding the world, seeking to change it rather than just observe it.

So there is the potential to make bureaucracies more dynamic based on the diffusion of knowledge and a more active approach to testing ideas. Much of the success of the Behavioural Insights Team in the UK is based on selecting ideas offered by public managers working in delivery agencies, applying behavioural insights to the initial claim in partnership with academics, using RCTs to test different claims, and then rolling out good practice. A published study illustrates the process. This is about the use of mobile text messages to collect court fines, reported in Haynes and colleagues (2013). The actual experiment is not the concern here: the two RCTs saw an agency responsible for courts administration, Her

Majesty's Tribunals and Courts Service (HMTCS), randomising mobile text messages into a standard message then with varying degrees of personalisation to other four other messages, which had striking effects showing the importance of using names in the response. It became an important study: it was featured in a prominent government publication and was highlighted in the media (Cabinet Office 2012). What is interesting for the argument of this chapter is the extent to which non-standard processes accompanied the implementation of the RCT. The idea emerged bottom up from within the HMCTS, from a senior administrator who knew of the existence of the mobile phone numbers, from his practical experience of working in the agency, and then he did a pilot to use them. The application of behavioural insights came from the interaction with the Behavioural Insights Team whose members designed extra treatment arms to test out different behavioural insights. The innovation and evaluation were already in train: what social science did was to make the intervention more targeted and to offer a precise test of each nudge through the RCT. The two people working on the project within the agency offices in the south-east region were delivery experts and had practical understandings of the data, so the intervention worked well as a result. The other dimension to the trial is how the relationship between the agency and the sponsor ministry, the Ministry of Justice, evolved. Here HMTCS as a low-status agency was not supposed to hug the limelight, but in fact this trial did not involve the ministry, but attracted a lot of publicity about the agency and BIT. Most importantly, it did not involve the research professionals in the ministry, but bureaucrats in the agency, with not a great deal of social science experience, who worked and designed a nudge intervention with some outside help from BIT and academics. This is different to the conventional, officially sponsored or commissioned approach to policy evaluation as it can emerge bottom up in this way.

The second example is more about the use of experiments as forms of empowerment, which might be able to ensure a feedback loop between administrators/politicians and citizens themselves. It comes from a wave of research in political science that has tried to test various interventions on the behaviour of elites, such as on state legislators (e.g., Butler and Brookman 2011). In this research, the aim was to encourage politicians to be more responsive to demands from locally based citizen interest groups (Richardson and John 2012). Here was a trial testing differently worded letters to local representatives in eight

English local authorities. In some ways the effect of the intervention was modest, with only 18 per cent of locally elected politicians replying, but the better-worded letter did get referred on to local bureaucrats. In addition, the citizen groups got a lot out of it, including, they believed, funding for their projects. But it is possible to see the wider applicability of using this model of RCTs and behaviour interventions by civil society groups to improve the responsiveness of political and bureaucratic actors.

Innovation and Public Management

In this review of the development of RCTs and behaviour change policies, it is clear that there has been an increase in the numbers of RCTs, in particular to test whether public agencies can promote positive behaviour changes among citizens. It is not possible to claim that this is a minor phenomenon, even though much research will continue to use existing technologies. Within public agencies, most policy and implementation decisions will be made without the insights of RCTs as other research and sources of knowledge will continue to apply, as well as all the other sources of influences on policy change, and all the political pressures to introduce new policies. However, the examples cited here illustrate that important changes have happened that affect how policy is made and implemented. The question to answer is how significant and wide ranging they are likely to be.

The argument is that the greater use of RCTs is likely to engage public agencies in an iterative search for knowledge rather than retain their attachment to pre-existing procedures, which is because of the sharp tests RCTs entail. The use of ideas about behaviour change is also likely to lead to questioning of existing practices as they may suggest that standard operating procedures, such as letters and reminders, are devoid of behavioural insights. Public managers who use these methods and ideas are likely to be innovators and champions of change within their organisations. Hence there is the possibility of more experimental public administration emerging as experimentation becomes less the rarity and more the norm in bureaucracies, and would be commissioned by politicians and public managers as a matter of course, or just emerge naturally as policies are rolled out, such as through waiting-list or stepped-wedge designs where each region or area is randomly allocated to get the intervention over time. Rather than think about whether to randomise and to apply behavioural insights, the decision might be to do them by default and only stop doing them in special circumstances where there are ethical or other constraints. This review of the use of RCTs, shows some of these changes happening already, albeit modestly. One example from the UK is the department of Business Innovations and Skills (BIS), which is piloting its policies by RCTs, such as growth vouchers for small and medium enterprises. This readiness to use RCTs may be linked to a sea change in thinking about evaluation in popular publications, a belief that scientific methods should be used more often in public policy (e.g., Henderson 2012).

These changes to the external environment about the desirability of using robust evidence may offer inspiration to the advocates of change within bureaucracies. Studies of public administration stress the importance of routines and sunk costs in organisation systems, and there are examples of bureaucracies initially resisting change (Kelman 2005). But innovation can happen best if it is promoted from inside rather than imposed top down. A previous generation of public management writers discussed the role of change agents (Kanter 1983, 1989) and entrepreneurs (Roberts and King 1991). Here resourcing and higher-level support are essential in fostering change, which in this case applies to behaviour change experimenters. This theme of top down versus bottom up appears in more recent account of innovations in public organisations (see Miles 2013).

Recent work stresses the importance of an interactive kind of governance in driving innovation, where feedback loops extend to the wider community as a way of reinvigorating decision-making (Tofling et al. 2012). Here the next generation of nudge experiments could incorporate community-based nudging, such as in transparency experiments. Such activities could play a role in mimicking citizen-led efforts to constrain public managers and politicians and hold them to account. There is both a top-down and bottom-up dimension to behaviour change. What experiments can do is to make the innovators more precise and evidence based. Some writers talk of the importance of the beta system allowing RCTs to happen to try out new ideas. Christiansen and Bunt (2012) write: 'Beta is a powerful idea to apply to public policy-making. It changes expectations of performance and permanence of public services, given the signal of early-stage development and on-going learning. Beta not only welcomes feedback, but proactively encourages challenges and critique from the public, potential users, colleagues, partners, experts and other relevant actors.'

Of course such developments need to be understood as part of the political process understood both narrowly in terms of organisational processes and internal competition for resources, and more widely as the realm of partisan politics in its quest for blame shifting and credit claiming. In such a febrile environment, there is never likely to be a neutral commitment to evidence. Some of the examples discussed here, such as the tests of controls of badgers, illustrate that the use of RCTs must work within a favourable political context and not against powerful interests. Behaviour change policies work too when the outcomes are indisputably desirable ones, such as more people paying court fines. When nudges are applied to more controversial areas, they are less likely to succeed in being commissioned and in shifting policy. But overall, it is a question of balance rather than behaviour change policies altering policy fundamentally. RCTs shine a light into an otherwise murky policy process and sometimes can inspire positive changes. Once the easy and uncontroversial nudges have been rolled out, there is more opportunity for more challenging and controversial ones once politicians and public managers have become more used to them.

References

Angrist, J., Bettinger, E., Bloom, E., King, E. and Kremer, M., 2002. 'Vouchers for private schooling in Colombia: Evidence from a randomized natural experiment', *The American Economic Review* 92(5): 1535–58.

Berk, R. A., R. F. Boruch, D. L. Chambers, P. H. Rossi, and A. D. Witte 1985. 'Social policy experimentation: a position paper', *Evaluation Review* 9: 385–429.

Bloom, H. S. (ed.) 2005. *Learning from Social Experiments*. New York: Russell Sage.

Bloom, H. S., L. L. Orr, S. H. Bell, G. Cave, F. Doolittle, W. Lin, and J. M. Bos 1997. 'The benefits and costs of JTPA Title II-A programs: key findings from the National Job Training Partnership Act study', *Journal of Human Resources* 32: 549–76.

Bloom, H. S., L. Orr, G. Cave, S. Bell, and F. Doolittle 1993. *The National JTPA Study: Title II-A Impacts on Earnings and Employment at 18 Months*. Bethesda, MD: Abt Associates, Inc.

Brewer, G. A. and G. A. Brewer Jr. 2011. 'Parsing public/private differences in work motivation and performance: an experimental study', *Journal of Public Administration Research and Theory* 21: 347–62.

Butler, D. and D. Brockman 2011. 'Do politicians racially discriminate against constituents? A field experiment on state legislators', *American Journal of Political Science* 553: 463–77.

Cabinet Office 2012. *Applying Behavioural Insights to Reduce Fraud, Error and Debt*. London: Cabinet Office.

Campbell, D. T. 1957. 'Factors relevant to the validity of experiments in social settings', *Psychological Bulletin* 4: 297–312.

Campbell, D. T. 1969. 'Reforms as experiments', *American Psychologist* 24: 409–29.

Campbell, D. T., and J. C. Stanley 1963. *Experimental and Quasi-Experimental Designs for Research*. Chicago, IL: Rand McNally.

Christiansen, J. and L. Bunt 2012. *Innovation in Policy: Allowing for Creativity, Social Complexity and Uncertainty in Public Governance*. London: Nesta.

Dolan, P., M. Hallsworth, D. Halpern, D. King, and I. Vlaev 2010. *MINDSPACE: Influencing Behaviour Through Public Policy*. London: Cabinet Office and Institute for Government.

Duflo, E., R. Glennerster, and M. Kremer 2007. 'Using randomization in development economics research: a toolkit', *Handbook of Development Economics* 4: 3895–962.

Dunleavy, P., H. Margetts, S. Bastow, and J. Tinkler 2006. *Digital Era Governance: IT Corporations, the State and E-Government*. Oxford: Oxford University Press.

Dunlop, C. A. 2013. 'Narrating experiments in public policy: explaining impact through boundary work', paper to the Policy and Politics Annual Conference, Bristol.

Dunning, T. 2012. *Natural Experiments in the Social Science: A Design-Based Approach*. Cambridge: Cambridge University Press.

Eldersveld, S. T. 1956. 'Experimental propaganda techniques and voting behaviour', *The American Political Science Review* 50: 154–65.

Fisher, R. A. 1935. *The Design of Experiments*. Edinburgh: Oliver and Boyde.

Gerber, A. S., and D. P. Green 2012. *Field Experiments Design, Analysis and Interpretation*. New York: William Norton.

Gosnell, H. F. 1926. 'An experiment in the stimulation of voting', *The American Political Science Review* 20: 869–74.

Gosnell, H. F. 1927. *Getting-Out-the-Vote: An Experiment in the Stimulation of Voting*. Chicago, IL: Chicago University Press.

Green, D. P. and A. S. Gerber 2003. 'The underprovision of experiments in political science', *The Annals of the American Academy of Political and Social Science* 589: 94–112.

Green, D. P., and A. S. Gerber 2008. *Get Out the Vote: How to Increase Voter Turnout.* 2nd ed. Washington, DC: Brookings Institution Press.

Greenberg, D., D. Linksz, and M. Mandell 2003. *Social Experimentation and Public Policymaking.* Washington, DC: Urban Institute Press.

Greenberg, D. and M. Shroder 2004. *Digest of Social Experiments.* Washington, DC: Urban Institute Press.

Hallsworth, M., J. A. List, and I. Vlaev 2014. 'The Behavioralist as Tax Collector: Using Natural Field Experiments to Enhance Tax Compliance', unpublished paper, http://econpapers.repec.org/paper/nbrnberwo/20007.htm.

Halpern, D., C. Bates, G. Mulgan, and S. Aldridge, with G. Beales and A. Heathfield 2004. *Personal Responsibility and Changing Behaviour: The State of Its Knowledge and Its Implications for Public Policy.* London: Cabinet Office.

Haynes, L. C., D. P. Green, R. Gallagher, P. John, and D. J. Torgerson 2013. 'Collection of delinquent fines: an adaptive randomized trial to assess the effectiveness of alternative text messages', *Journal of Policy Analysis and Management* 32: 718–30.

Haynes, L., O. Service, B. Goldacre, and D. Torgerson 2012. *Test, Learn, Adapt: Developing Public Policy with Randomised Controlled Trials.* London: Cabinet Office.

Henderson, M. 2012. *The Geek Manifesto: Why Science Matters.* London: Bantam Press.

Henegan, C. 2010. 'How many randomized trials are published each year?', http://blogs.trusttheevidence.net/carl-heneghan/how-many-randomized-trials-are-published-each-year.

HM Treasury 2003. *The Magenta Book: Guidance Notes for Policy Evaluation and Analysis.* London: HM Treasury.

Humphreys, M., R. Sanchez de la Sierra, and P. van der Wind 2012. *Social and Economic Impacts of Tuungane. Final Report on the Effects of a Community Driven Reconstruction Program in Eastern Democratic Republic of Congo.* University of Columbia.

Humphreys, M. and J. M. Weinstein 2009. 'Field experiments and the political economy of development', *Annual Review of Political Science* 12: 367–78.

John, P. 2013. 'Policy entrepreneurship in UK central government: the Behavioural Insights Team and the use of randomized trials', *Public Policy and Administration* 29: 257–67.

John, P. and L. Richardson 2012, *Nudging Citizens Toward Localism.* London: British Academy.

Jones, R., J. Pykett, and M. Whitefield 2013. *Changing Behaviours: The Rise of the Psychological State.* Brighton: Edward Elgar.

Kahneman, D., P. Slovic, and A. Tversky 1982. *Judgment Under Uncertainty: Heuristics and Biases.* Cambridge: Cambridge University Press.

Kanter, R. M. 1983. *The Change Masters: Innovations for Productivity in the American Corporation*. New York: Simon and Schuster.

Kanter, R. M. 1989. 'Swimming in newstreams: mastering innovation dilemmas', *California Management Review* 414: 45–69.

Kelman, S. 2005. *Unleashing Change: A Study of Organizational Renewal in Government*. Washington, DC: Brookings Institution Press.

Margetts, H. and P. Dunleavy 2013. 'The second wave of digital-era governance: a quasi-paradigm for government on the Web', *Philosophical Transactions of the Royal Society A* 28: 1–17.

McDougall, C., A. Perry, J. Clarbour, R. Bowles, and G. Worthy 2009. *Evaluation of HM Prison Service Enhanced Thinking Skills Programme*. London: Ministry of Justice Research Series 3/09 www.justice.gov.uk /publications.

Miles, I. 2013. 'Public service innovation: what messages from the collision of innovation studies and services research?' In S. Osborne and L. Brown (eds.), *Handbook of Innovation in Public Services*. Brighton: Edward Elgar.

Munnell, A. H. (ed.) 1987. *Lessons from the Income Maintenance Experiments*. Federal Reserve Bank of Boston Conference Series 30. Boston: Federal Reserve Bank of Boston.

Murphy, S., G. F. Moore, K. T. R. Lynch, R. Clarke, L. Raisanen, C. Desousa, and L. Moore. 2010. 'Free healthy breakfasts in primary schools: a cluster randomised controlled trial of a policy intervention in Wales, UK', *Public Health Nutrition* 142: 219–26.

Nooteboom, B. 2000. *Learning and Innovation in Organizations and Economies*. Oxford: Oxford University Press.

Olken, B. 2005. 'Monitoring corruption: evidence from a field experiment in Indonesia', National Bureau of Economic Research Working Paper Series p. 11753.

Olken, B., J. Onishi, and S. Wong 2012 'Should aid reward performance?' www.nber.org/papers/w17892.

Orr, L. 1999. *Social Experiments Evaluating Public Programs with Experimental Methods*. Thousand Oaks, CA: Sage.

Petrosino, A., C. Turpin Petrosino, and J. Buehler Colophon 2002. *'Scared Straight' and Other Juvenile Awareness Programs for Preventing Juvenile Delinquency*. Campbell Systematic Reviews.

Riccio, J. A. and H. Bloom 2001. *New Directions in Evaluations of American Welfare-to-Work and Employment Initiatives*. New York: Manpower Demonstration Research Corporation.

Richardson, L. and P. John 2012. 'Who listens to the grassroots? A field experiment on informational lobbying in the UK', *British Journal of Politics and International Relations* 144: 595–612.

Roberts, N. C. and P. J. King 1991, 'Policy entrepreneurs: their activity structure and function in the policy process', *Journal of Public Administration Research and Theory* 1: 147–75.

Robins, P. K. and R. G. Spiegelman 2001. *Reemployment Bonuses in the Unemployment Insurance System*. Michigan: W. E. Upjohn Institute for Employment Research.

Sherman, L. W., D. P. Rogan, T. Edwards, R. Whipple, D. Shreve, D. Witcher, W. Trimble, The Street Narcotics Unit, R. Velke, M. Blumberg, A. Beatty, and C. A. Bridgeforth 1995. 'Deterrent effects of police raids on crack houses: a randomized, controlled experiment', *Justice Quarterly* 12: 755–81.

Sherman, L. W. and D. Weisburd 1995. 'General deterrent effects of police patrol in crime hot spots: a randomized, controlled trial', *Justice Quarterly* 12: 635–48.

'Student' 1931, 'The Lanarkshire milk experiment', *Biometrika* 23: 398–406.

Thaler, R. H. and Sunstein, C. R. 2008. *Nudge: Improving Decisions about Health, Wealth, and Happiness*. New Haven, CT: Yale University Press.

Torfing, J. B., G. Peters, J. Pierre, and E. Sørensen 2012. *Interactive Governance: Advancing the Paradigm*. Oxford: Oxford University Press.

Torgerson, D. J. and C. Torgerson 2008. *Designing Randomised Trials in Health, Education and the Social Sciences: An Introduction*. Basingstoke: Palgrave Macmillan.

Weisburd, D. and L. Green 1995. 'Policing drug hot spots: the Jersey City drug market analysis experiment', *Justice Quarterly* 124: 711–35.

Weiss, C. 1972. *Evaluation Research*. New Jersey: Prentice Hall.

Weiss, C. 1997. 'How can theory-based evaluation make greater headway?' *Evaluation Review* 214: 501–24.

Weiss, C. 1998. 'Have we learned anything new about the use of evaluation?' *American Journal of Evaluation* 191: 21–33.

Word, E., J. Johnston, H. P. Bain, J. Boyd-Zaharias, N. Lintz, C. M. Achiles, J. Folger, and C. Breda 1989. *Student/Teacher Achievement Ratio (STAR) Tennessee's K-3 Class Size Study. Final Summary Report 1985–1990*. Retrieved from http://eric.ed.gov/?id=ED320692.

24 Conclusions – Towards an Experimental Public Management

OLIVER JAMES, SEBASTIAN JILKE, AND
GREGG G. VAN RYZIN

The growth in the use of experiments in public management over recent years is reflected in the studies that are set out in this volume. We have framed the discussion in the context of the discipline and the current and potential contribution of experimentation. The substantive contributions are increasingly broad and deep, and span a range of research questions about core topic areas in public management. The discussion shows that the experimental turn is not a 'mere' application of a generic social science approach towards experimentation, or a passing fashion. The fundamental approach to causal inference and core methods of intervention, random allocation, and comparison of outcomes are shared with much contemporary social science experimentation, but their use in public management is distinctive. There is even the prospect, perhaps surprising in the context of conventional methods, that public management should be considered an experimental discipline. However, we draw the conclusion that experiments should have their place as a methodological approach alongside more established quantitative and qualitative methods. An open dialogue about theory, research questions, methods, and evidence is needed across researchers who use experimental methods, but also between researchers using different methods. For this to happen, non-experimentalists will often need to know more about experimental methods, and experimentalists will need to understand and be open to methods and relevant evidence from other approaches.

This concluding chapter sets out how an experimental approach in public management can be taken forward. We return to the themes introduced in Chapter 1 and show how the material discussed in this book suggests ways in which public management can make the best possible use of experimental methods. First, we discuss how best to develop the potential contribution of experimental methods to public management theory and the appropriate relationship with non-experimental methods. Second, we set out how experiments can best help public management to deliver on its ambitions as a design science. Third, we discuss the changes in research institutions and practices needed for an effective experimental approach in public management and offer some guidance on reporting experimental research and their findings.

Experimentation and Public Management Theory

The current experimental turn in public management takes place within a historical context of earlier use of experiments. Part I of this volume describes the recent rise in use of experiments (see Chapters 1 and 2) and provides the historical context in which experimentation was part of the 'classical roots' of public management, especially its efforts to be a design science informing policy and practice (as Ken Meier and Kendall Funk discussed in Chapter 3). However, whilst the early experiments involved interventions by researchers, the contemporary turn uses more sophisticated methods and has been particularly influenced by their use in health sciences, economics, political science, and psychology. Part II discusses the contemporary methods that, as well as involving interventions by researchers, make use of treatment and control groups with random allocation to these groups, and are careful about treatment integrity, control of the experimental environment, and the measurement of outcomes.

The broad range of public management theory being addressed by use of experiments is discussed by chapters in Part III. These chapters show that theory from psychology, political science, and economics has been particularly influential in many topic areas but that the theory assessed by experiments comes from many other sources too. The chapters show the areas where experiments have challenged evidence from observational studies. However, in most topic areas, experiments have also produced much evidence consistent with that from observational studies. Experiments are sometimes criticised for focusing on narrow questions, missing out on 'big' questions, for example, about macro-structures or major issues of importance to public management. Chapter 22 by Steven Van de Walle injects an important note of caution into considering the experimental turn. However, the risks of limiting the scope of what is studied are mitigated by using a variety of methods. It would be difficult to argue that the potential for experimentation is anywhere near exhausted given their relative scarcity in public management to date.

Experiments can make important contributions to addressing big or otherwise important public management research questions. One way that critics of experiments can go wrong is by thinking too much about experiments in the singular. Experiments sit within programmes of research using multiple experiments, for example, to tease out different causal mechanisms in a theory or to explore mediation or moderation of treatment effects. Replication of experiments is an important part of verifying findings, thinking about contextual variation, and extending theory as discussed in Chapter 21 by Richard Walker and co-authors. As that chapter sets out, replication is currently at an early stage in public management, partly because there are still not that many experiments on most topics, and partly because there are several different definitions of replication and accounts of its proper function.

One important part of an agenda for replication in public management is to run experiments designed to be as identical as possible in certain key respects, with the same treatment, setting for the experiment and outcome measures, but changing the subject pool to another sample from the same population of interest. This narrow form of direct replication can be illustrated by the hypothetical experiment concerning the effects of a training programme on public managers that was the example running through the discussion of design and analysis of experiments in Chapter 4. In this case, narrow replication involves the same experimental treatment (the training programme) implemented in the same setting with the same measures of managerial performance, but using different samples from the population of public managers. The findings of multiple experiments can be combined in a meta-analysis of their treatment effects.

Replication requires careful consideration of what that population of interest is, for example, all public managers, or just those in organisational leadership roles or managing particular kinds of public organisations. Taking samples of this kind and having them participate in laboratory experiments where strong control is possible makes it easier to satisfy the requirements for narrow replication than is often the case for field or survey experiments, but in principle all these types of experiment could be used. This form of replication might be done both by the researchers working on the original experiment and separately by other researchers to assess if this variation affects findings.

Moving beyond narrow replication, other forms of replication are sometimes undertaken to see if a finding is robust to changes in the way treatments are implemented, in the experimental setting, or in the measurement of outcomes. Findings may be robust to these changes or there may be good reasons to expect that findings will vary. One way forward to promote replication studies is to encourage collaboration using teams in different countries. However, if several factors are changed at the same time in a new experiment (as may occur in the replication of an experiment in a different country), it can be difficult to identify the particular factors behind any discovered variation in results.

Experiments require the manipulation of causal factors in some way, and this limitation of the method for addressing topics where interventions are difficult to carry out needs to be recognised. However, experiments can address theories about important institutional structures that are difficult to manipulate, such as macro-features of political systems, by implementing treatments that are analogues to these structures. Relatedly, examining causation at the micro-level of individual perceptions, attitudes, or behavior can provide 'micro-foundations' that underpin major institutional effects. This contribution is illustrated by some examples drawn from chapters in Part III of this book. Experiments about representative bureaucracy, as discussed in Chapter 14, show their contribution to the theory of symbolic representation. This theory suggests that where public employees resemble the demographic characteristics of the citizens they serve, more desirable outcomes will result, such as increased trust, perceptions of legitimacy, or satisfaction. These outcomes occur without any specific actions being taken by bureaucrats themselves. For example, citizen-clients will be more likely to cooperate, helping bureaucrats to deliver services, which will be transformed into better service quality. Thus symbolic representation is a distinct causal mechanism through which representation is linked to organisational performance. This theory is conceptualised on the meso-level, and, as Chapter 14 discusses, several studies have produced supportive evidence at the organisational level. However, symbolic representation has clear micro-level implications, stating that when citizens perceive state agents as being like them, they are more likely to have favourable views towards them. These micro-foundations have not been empirically tested, but they constitute implicit assumptions about the theoretical mechanisms of how symbolic representation may work. The experiments conducted by Gregg Van Ryzin, Norma Riccucci, and collaborators assess these specific micro-level implications of representative bureaucracy using a series of experiments and find some support for the theory.

A different example of the contribution of experiments to micro-foundations of theory comes from Chapter 17 on citizens and users' responses to public service failure. The institutional theory of blame avoidance states that if politicians delegate services away from them (e.g., by contracting service delivery to private sector providers), they will receive less blame if things go wrong in the delivery of these services. In an innovative contribution to theory, Hood (2011) calls this an agency-strategy and gives some observational, mostly aggregate-level, case study evidence about blame in the public sector. However, the institutional theory of blame can be considered as having a micro-level empirical implication that citizens will attribute blame away from politicians if they are told that delivery of a failing service is contracted out. Chapter 17 reports experimental work that finds this micro-level assumption of reduced blame is not found for contracting to a private firm for a typical local public service of street maintenance, although delegation within a public organisation does reduce blame of politicians for the same failure. In addition, politicians who explicitly associate themselves with managing the delivery of a service face more blame from citizens if this service fails.

Conducting research that systematically examines a large set of micro-level implications from a theory can feel almost a Sisyphean task, where the work is endless and there is a constant task of building a body of evidence from many seemingly small interventions, measurements, and associated statistical tests on data. But this does not mean that the experimental turn in public management focuses on questions of low relevance, neglecting the big picture. Examining the micro-foundations may be slow in the sense that it needs to collect many pieces of a larger puzzle, but it builds a credible evidence base by assessing 'big theories' through continued testing and refinement. The benefits of experiments for theory are far from limited to the examples of representative bureaucracy and citizens' responses to public services; the contributions in Part III of this book show the breadth of theories being addressed with experiments.

Not all theories are necessarily suitable for direct experimental testing, but thinking about potential experiments to test theory can help highlight which theories have empirical implications about causal relations and which are less suited to addressing questions of this kind. Highly complex systems with huge spill-over effects between subjects and unstable outcomes can be difficult to address using experiments. In some cases, these can be broken down into a series of stages where an agenda for thinking about different treatments and measures becomes clearer. This process of thinking about what treatments to implement requires consideration of the causal properties of different elements of a theory. For example, broad theories of historical path dependencies about sets of public sector reforms at the country level (Pollitt and Bouckaert 2011) express causal relations in a way that is not amendable to direct empirical evaluation. It is useful to have work that takes a broad perspective, especially to describe macro-trends and patterns, but these perspectives are less centrally focused on establishing evidence about causality.

Appropriate use of different types of experiment can ensure that the empirical implications of theory are tested in contexts to which they are intended to apply, addressing concerns that theory should take context seriously. Conventional laboratory experiments, especially by experimental economists, are often implemented in a stylised, context-free environment to increase the level of experimenters' control to boost internal validity (see Chapter 7). The field experiments discussed in Chapter 5 focus especially on taking the domain to which theories should apply into account in how the experiment is conducted. The specific context-dependent nature of some experimental findings can result in low levels of external validity beyond the context in which the particular experiment was conducted. However, if context varies in ways that affect results, then theory and methods need to take this into account and a series of related experiments in different contexts can be developed. The contributions in this book, especially Chapter 15 on coproduction of public services and Chapter 12 on performance information use by citizens, show how using different related experiments can increase the theoretical scope of applying the experimental method.

Experiments can help the development of new theories. Even experiments in the laboratory that might initially seem limited because they do not have an obvious direct application can give important insights into processes that are difficult to see in non-controlled environments.

Findings from such experiments, such as the strong regularities in biases that experimental participants show when undertaking probabilistic reasoning, potentially inform new opportunities for better designing policies and practices (Guala and Mittone 2005). Alternatively, examining the empirical implications of more established theories may lead to unanticipated findings that run counter to prior theoretical expectations, or findings that hold only for specific subgroups. These findings can be used to refine theories or even suggest new ones to be examined in further experiments. Even experiments conducted by governments themselves using randomised controlled trials to evaluate a policy or programme, rather than to test the empirical implications of theories, can stimulate further theoretically oriented research. This research can look more explicitly at theory about how and why different causal mechanisms affect a programme's effectiveness. Chapter 5 on field experiments and Chapter 23 on changing how governments work through experiments discuss how policy experiments and related randomised controlled trials can help inform future theory.

The approach to experimentation suggested by this book does not involve abandoning observational studies, but instead suggests the benefits of using a range of different methods in programmes of research. The use of experiments is not a result of natural science-envy or faddishness, but instead reflects unease with some claims about causal relations generated by non-experimental methods, as discussed in Chapter 4 on the design and analysis of experiments. In some areas of research, notably medical research, a hierarchy of evidence is suggested with evidence from interventions with randomisation at the top, then other kinds of evidence and finally expert opinion. Our view, consistent with an emerging consensus across much of social science, is that experiments, where they can be conducted, produce the strongest evidence about causal relations. However, non-experimental methods remain important. Experiments do not remove the need to undertake description to map phenomena, or to explore and develop theory about causal relations though other methods, including a range of quantitative and qualitative approaches. This kind of multimethod strategy can help develop research agendas that include the design and implementation of experiments to assess causal relations in detail.

The strength of the experimental method for considering causality focuses attention on the desirability of using observational methods that have strong similarities to experiments for this purpose, when experiments are not possible for one reason or another. Natural experiments and quasi-experiments can offer a good opportunity to exploit policy interventions or 'as if' random allocation when these assumptions can be justified for the particular context of the research. For example, the regression discontinuity design uses an assumption of near random allocation to different treatments either side of a cut-off. Discussion of this kind of method benefits from considering them using the benchmark of an experimental randomised intervention as an ideal research design (e.g., see the discussion in Angrist and Pischke 2014).

Experimentation and the Practice of Public Management

Experimental research often requires researchers to work with practitioners to deliver on the potential of the method to assist public management as a design science. Chapter 5 on field experiments sets out how working with policy makers and managers gives researchers access to naturalistic contexts for experimental research. Chapter 23 by Peter John on changing the way governments work discusses how these relationships are developing in many areas and how experiments are delivering mutually beneficial outcomes. To assist this collaboration, experimental methods should figure more highly in the training of public officials. This development is important not only for them to be informed consumers of findings, but also for them to be able to collaborate with researchers in the design and implementation of experiments. When policy makers work with experimentalists to develop and apply experiments, there is likely to be better understanding of the way the intervention needs to be implemented to ensure valid findings, and better understanding of the way findings can inform policy and practice. At the same time, it is also necessary for researchers to maintain some independence in order to be able to challenge the status quo when their research findings suggest this is necessary.

Several of the chapters in this book demonstrate how close collaboration between scholars and practitioners can lead to the implementation of important experiments and the production of usable knowledge. For example, Chapter 9 by Lotte Bøgh Andersen and colleagues discusses leadership reports based on implementing a leadership training intervention in collaboration with local organisations in education, health, and the banking sector. The results from their large-scale leadership training experiment not only have relevance for public management theory, but can also help organisations to select the most effective leadership trainings for their employees. Similarly, Chapter 15 on coproduction of public services by Simon Calmar Andersen and colleagues reports from a series of field experiments that have been implemented within local school districts in Denmark in close collaboration public education bodies. In order to enhance such strategies, public management experimentalists need to actively reach out and seek a closer dialogue with those working in public and nonprofit organisations.

Extending the concept of collaboration, public management can further develop as a design science by running experiments in the laboratory that inform the development of management reforms. These reforms can then be assessed in real contexts using field experiments in a pilot stage prior to full roll-out of the programme. This process has the side effect of increasing the external validity of experiments, not from merely making an experiment resemble the real world but by shaping the real world of public management by incorporating experimental treatments into the practices of government.

Experimentation and the Institutions and Practices of Research

Experimental methods and their research findings are not well integrated into the institutions of public management research. Currently, most students of public management receive very little formal training in experimental methods, but it would not be difficult to remedy this situation through updating of curricula. The structure of conferences and journals seem in some cases not to be fully equipped to deal with the increasing interest in experimental research and the implications of their use. We will discuss three of the most pressing issues in this regard: i) required reporting standards of experiments, ii) preregistration of experimental designs, and iii) ethical issues raised by experiments.

Reporting Experiments and Their Findings

Reporting is important for transparency of research, including to facilitate peer review of publication, and to allow replication of experimental procedures or findings. Clear reporting also enables results, for example about the size of effects, to be incorporated into meta-analysis or other reviews of findings on particular topic areas. After planning and conducting experiments, public management scholars can risk just reporting as if it was an observational study, for example, just as if it was a regression analysis of survey data. This approach can result in the omission of key components of the experimental procedures, such as the method of random allocation, whether subjects were excluded (and why) or not all collected outcome measures (dependent variables) being reported. There is a lack of clarity in reporting standards for public management experiments, and the community needs more guidance about items that should be reported.

In the medical sciences, the Consolidated Standards of Reporting Trials (CONSORT) guidelines have been adopted by major medical journals as reporting requirements for medical trials (e.g., Schulz, Altman, and Moher 2010). Similarly, the *Journal of Experimental Political Science* has published a set of recommended reporting standards for political science research that were compiled by the Experimental Standards Committee of the American Political Science Association on the basis of the CONSORT reporting standards (Gerber et al. 2014). A similar list of reporting requirements has also been published for political science based on CONSORT (Boutron, John, and Torgersen 2010). Such reporting standards cannot cover everything in the process of designing, implementing, and analysing experiments. They rather serve as an orientation and *minimum* reporting guidelines for researchers wishing to communicate their experiments in a more effective manner. Appendix A of this book has a checklist of minimum reporting standards for experimental research within public management derived from CONSORT guidelines and reporting standards within political science. Whether all this material is included in a final publication depends on the purpose of publication across different forms of outlet, but the information should be kept by researchers and could be available publicly from them. The information should also be available to reviewers considering experimental work submitted for publication. This is a prospective agenda for public management and, in the shorter term, even moving towards a more substantial rather than full implementation of these procedures would be desirable. In addition, Appendix A is useful for researchers designing and conducting experiments to help inform the research process.

Preregistration of Experimental Designs

Researchers need to think carefully about their experimental manipulation before implementing the actual experiment. They need to be clear what they want to manipulate, and how they will do so. Thus there is strong need to carefully theorise about intended effects in the design phase of an experiment. This logic is related to the notion of preregistration of experiments. Preregistration means that researchers register the design and intended analysis strategy of an experiment before it is implemented. It can be an effective way to boost the credibility of experimental results, in part because researchers can justify that their findings about effects are indeed confirmatory and not the result of *p-value* fishing. They serve as a statement that all collected outcome variables are reported in the actual experiment, and that no questionable research practices, such as stopping data collecting from the experiment when desired results are achieved, choosing only significant results from a range of outcomes measured, or looking at treatment effects across multiple experimental subgroups until a statistically significant result is discovered, have been employed.

Preregistration is useful for many types of method, not just experiments. However, the distinct design of experiments, where researchers need to carefully choose treatments and make other crucial design decisions before the study's implementation, makes it ideally suited for preregistration. The focus on developing statements of designs before a study is implemented also allows researchers to get feedback on their design before they carry it out. This practice can help improve and avoid errors in design, which are difficult to correct once an experiment has been conducted. Although most public management conferences are not set up to facilitate the presentation and discussion of research proposals, they could introduce formats in which this could happen. In terms of institutions for storing designs, there are a variety of registries across the social sciences such as the open science framework registry, the experiments in politics and governance registry, or the official registry of the American Economic Association, although no such registry has yet been implemented in public management.

Ethical Issues

Public management experimentation raises a wide set of potential ethical issues, which vary across experiments. It is important that experiments raising potential ethical issues are subject to ethical scrutiny, for example, through institutional review boards. There is considerable variety in how such boards interpret their role and the ethical issues raised by experiments; experimental researchers sometimes face challenges in justifying their experiments to boards that are not familiar with the methods. It should be borne in mind that research is one of the most heavily regulated areas of human activity, in contrast to much government and private sector activity that involves major intervention in people's lives with little active regulation of ethical issues. Here we focus on three concerns that have strong relevance for public management research, beyond the obvious ones of avoiding harm, ensuring special treatment for vulnerable groups (e.g., children), and the need for researchers sometimes to maintain the confidentiality of participants. The three issues are non-full disclosure, deception, and voluntary participation.

Non-full disclosure happens whenever the researchers do not fully reveal what the experiment is about in order to avoid influencing participants. For example, we might be interested in testing how the gender of a leader influences how they are seen by subordinates using vignettes of leaders in which only the first name is varied experimentally. We would instruct respondents to rate the leader, but of course not tell them that we are studying gender effects and that the name of the leaders has been experimentally varied (to avoid social desirability bias and other strategic or otherwise distorting behaviours). It is reasonable not to tell participants absolutely everything about the experiment, especially if no harm is caused to them by participation. If instead full disclosure is implemented without a clear boundary, it could broaden out to become an extremely onerous requirement, burdening participants with all kinds of information about the context of research, history of research on the topic, and researchers' broader interests.

Deception is a more active strategy by researchers and more controversial. It includes researchers knowingly giving wrong information. Say the manipulation is something to do with performance information about local schooling, where some citizens receive one type of information and other citizens another type. Does this need to be real information? If the experimenter presents people with incomplete or artificial information, does this need to be revealed to them? What are the long-term effects of deceiving or misleading workers, citizens, or others – even if this is done for legitimate scientific purposes? These issues are significant for the field of public management, especially because of the real-world contexts of much of our research. An important approach to such ethical concerns where misinformation is given is *debriefing*: explaining to participants in experiments, at the end, what the true aims of the experiment were and what aspects of the experimental situation were manipulated. This debriefing can often be more easily achieved in a laboratory or survey experiment than in a field experiment (where participants may be difficult to contact) and particular caution is needed in the latter domain.

In laboratory and survey experiments, people are usually recruited and volunteer to be part of the study. But in field experiments, say involving a randomly assigned nudge-type strategy to encourage recycling, it may be impractical to obtain fully informed consent or voluntary participation. In the case of unobtrusive field experiments, this design is specifically used to ensure participants are not aware that they are in an experiment. In the recycling field experiment example, researchers may simply distribute leaflets with one kind of message to some households, and leaflets with another kind of message to other households, then observe the volume of curbside recycling collected. Several chapters in this volume show the benefits of this kind of experiment, and we strongly advocate applied public management research. Often nudges to improve public services and outcomes are uncontroversial. But it is important to note that there has been concern about some aspects of the nudge approach. Even those largely defending the approach concede that there can be problems when governments experiment on citizens' behaviour without informed consent (Sunstein 2014). However, these issues can in many cases be resolved through considering the ethical principles and legal justifications for experimenting in ways that allow the benefits for policy and management practices to be assessed.

Concluding Remarks

This volume has had several aims: to introduce public management students and scholars to the logic and methods of experimentation, to showcase the emerging body of new experimental work in public management, and to reflect on the potential and limitations of experimentation to contribute to theory and practice. In compiling this volume, we have been impressed and inspired by the work of our colleagues who are using experiments to shed new light on important public management topics. At the same time, we recognise that, both as a discipline and as a design science, public management still has much to learn about experiments. We hope that this volume helps advance our understanding of the method as well as promote more and better experiments on an increasing range of public management topics. The rise of an experimental public management has shown promise, and we are confident that this is just the beginning of a long and productive approach to better understanding public management theory and practice.

References

Angrist, J. D. and Pischke, J. S. 2015. *Mastering 'Metrics: The Path from Cause to Effect*. Princeton, NJ: Princeton University Press.

Boutron, I., John, P., and Torgerson, D. J. 2010. 'Reporting methodological items in randomized experiments in political science', *The Annals of the American Academy of Political and Social Science*, 628(1), pp. 112–31.

Gerber, A., Arceneaux, K., Boudreau, C., Dowling, C., Hillygus, S., Palfrey, T., Biggers, S., and Hendry, D. 2014. 'Reporting guidelines for experimental research: a report from the Experimental Research Section Standards Committee', *Journal of Experimental Political Science*, 1(1), pp. 81–98.

Guala, F. and Mittone, L. 2005. 'Experiments in economics: external validity and the robustness of phenomena', *Journal of Economic Methodology*, 12(4), pp. 495–515.

Hood, C. 2011. *The Blame Game: Spin, Bureaucracy, and Self-Preservation in government*. Princeton, NJ: Princeton University Press.

Pollitt, C. and Bouckaert, G. 2011. *Public Management Reform: A Comparative Analysis – New Public Management, Governance and the Neo-Weberian State*. Oxford: Oxford University Press.

Schulz, K., Altman, D., and Moher, D. 2010. 'CONSORT 2010 statement: updated guidelines for reporting parallel group randomized trials', *The British Medical Journal*, 340:c332.

Sunstein, C. R. 2014. 'The ethics of nudging'. Available at SSRN.

Appendix Recommended Reporting Guidelines for Experiments in Public Management, a Checklist[1]

1. HYPOTHESES AND THEORIES THEY ARE DRAWN FROM
a. SPECIFIC OBJECTIVES AND HYPOTHESES
i. What question was the experiment designed to address?

ii. What specific hypotheses were tested? (e.g., the causal factor estimated, the expected sign and magnitude of expected effects on outcomes, and whether effects are expected to be homogenous or to vary by subgroup.)

2. METHODS
a. SUBJECT RECRUITMENT
i. What was the exact setting and location of data collection? (e.g., a laboratory room at a university, online survey)

ii. Recruitment date(s) (including follow-ups)?

iii. Any eligibility and/or exclusion criteria for subjects?

iv. How (and by whom) were participants recruited and selected? (e.g., recruitment by researchers, survey recruitment firm)

v. Reponses rate (if applicable)?

b. DESIGN
i. Specific experimental design (e.g., factorial, conjoint, within or between subjects)?

c. TREATMENTS
i. Is there a detailed description of treatments? (e.g., provide all materials in main text or an appendix or supporting documents.)

ii. Was a control and/or placebo group used?

iii. Which method of delivery was used (e.g., pen-and-paper, computer, smartphone, face-to-face, telephone)?

---

[1] Based on Boutron, John, and Torgerson (2010); Schulz, Altman, and Moher (2010); Gerber et al. (2014).

d. *RANDOMIZATION*
  i. Method used to generate the randomization sequence?
  ii. Software used to generate the randomization sequence?
  iii. Type of randomization (e.g., blocking, clustered assignment)?
  iv. What was the unit of randomization? (e.g., individual, household, organisation)
  v. Were participants, those administering the manipulations, and those assessing outcomes unaware of condition assignments (i.e., blinding)?
  vi. If blinding was conducted, how was this achieved?
  vii. Was the random allocation process followed correctly? (e.g., substantial imbalances of characteristics across groups can play a part in revealing failures of implementation)

e. *OUTCOMES*
  i. What were all the compiled outcome measures (i.e., dependent variables)?
  ii. Is a full questionnaire applied in the appendix for outcomes measured by a survey (if applicable)?
  iii. How and when were outcome measures collected?

f. *SAMPLE SIZE*
  i. How was the sample size of the experiment determined?
  ii. Have any stopping guidelines been used for the recruitment of subjects?

3. **RESULTS**
  a. *PARTICIPANT FLOW*
    i. Is there a CONSORT participant flow diagram? (This diagram sets out the sampling of experimental participants, the allocation and delivery of treatment, and any attrition; if space precludes a diagram in a published paper, these details should be provided elsewhere.)

  b. *CONFIRMATORY OR EXPLORATORY?*
    i. Does discussion of results state clearly which of the outcome measures and subgroup analyses (if any) were determined prior to the conduct of the experiment and which are the result of exploratory analysis?

c. *STATISTICAL ANALYSIS*
   i. Is there a report of sample means and standard deviations of all experimental conditions for intention-to-treat analysis (the entire collection of subjects, whether or not the treatment was successfully delivered to them) prior to any further analysis?
   ii. Is there any attrition? If yes, is there a discussion of reason(s) and examination of if attrition is related to pretreatment variables?
   iii. Any other missing data?
   iv. Any weighting procedures used?
   v. Is any other statistical analysis of the data explained and justified?

4. **OTHER INFORMATION**
   i. Was the experiment reviewed and approved by an institutional review board/ethics committee?
   ii. Was an experimental protocol registered prior to the conduct of the study? If yes, where can it be accessed?
   iii. If a replication dataset is available, is it available publicly? (e.g., provide a URL)

Index